THE 1996-97
HOCKEY ANNUAL

THE 1996-97 HOCKEY ANNUAL

MURRAY TOWNSEND

Warwick Publishing

Toronto   Los Angeles

© 1996 Warwick Publishing Inc.

Published by Warwick Publishing Inc.
• 24 Mercer Street, Toronto, ON. M5V 1H3
• 1424 Highland Ave., Los Angeles, CA 90027

ISBN: 1 - 895629 - 71 - 3

Front cover photograph: Dan Hamilton, Vantage Point Studios
Design: Kimberley Davison & Diane Farenick

Distributed in the United States and Canada by:

Firefly Books Ltd.
3680 Victoria Park Avenue
Willowdale, ON
M2H 3K1

Printed and bound in Canada by Best Book Manufacturers.

Introduction

For those who didn't read last year's book, I'd like to inform you that I picked Colorado to win the Stanley Cup final in four games over Florida.

I'd like to, but it would be a blatant lie.

I did pick the Panthers to finish second. Second last, that is.

And I think I mentioned something about Philadelphia being in the final, against St. Louis. It could have happened.... Maybe it was just a year early.

Oh well, that's what makes it fun, and, of course, I'm being much too modest not mentioning all the forecasts that were correct.

There are no shortage of predictions again this year in *The Hockey Annual*. But, there are some changes, as we continue to evolve, and hopefully improve.

For example, there are more statistics. Lots more. We even gave them their own section.

For me, every hockey season is more exciting than the last. I can't wait to see what happens, right from day one. This year is a step above the others, with so many changes in the off-season, and especially with the World Cup of Hockey setting the stage.

Just a couple notes about the text in the book, which shows some of my personal preferences.

I rarely mention salary figures. I almost never pay attention to them, because I don't care. It takes away something from the game for me. We're not so naive that we don't know hockey is a business, but that has nothing whatsoever to do with why we watch it.

It's a turnoff to hear players whining about whether they're going to get five million or six million. Look at what it did to baseball. We can't ignore it completely, however, because financial matters are becoming too much of a consideration in how teams conduct their on-ice business, and it's the fans who, once again, pay the price.

Also, I don't like some of the terminology that has come into vogue the last couple years. For example, I don't use the word "grit" to describe a player. The word just rubs me the wrong way. For the record, ninety percent of the players in the league have "grit".

Another term I don't like is when someone is referred to as a "skill player" or that so and so has a lot of "skill." It's a term usually reserved for non-productive Europeans who are good skaters, puckhandlers and passers. Did you ever hear Mario Lemieux referred to as a "skill player"? Of course not, and who determined that skating, puckhandling and passing were the only categories to be included in the "skill" category? What about goal scoring, shooting, hitting, checking, heart and determination?

Once again some acknowledgements are in order: Thanks to those who put up with my summer time constraints and wild mood swings, including daughters Holly and Heather, and lady friend Janis; thanks to all the teams (except Montreal, as usual) which readily supply crucial statistical information; thanks to Steve Dryden and *The Hockey News* who provide me with more opportunity to gather information and learn about the game; thanks to Bob McKenzie who developed the book's concept with Warwick Publishing; special thanks to my father, who gave me the opportunity to follow my goals; thanks to Nick Pitt, Jim Williamson, Kimberly Davison and Diane Farenick at Warwick for their efforts and support; and thanks especially to the readers.

Murray Townsend, August 6, 1996

Contents

EASTERN CONFERENCE

Boston Bruins

It was like one of those beautiful summer days, when the temperature is just right, the sun is shining, clear blue sky...everything is perfect. Then, out of nowhere, comes an ominous dark cloud which hovers directly overhead. And just sits there.

That pretty much sums up the Bruins year.

They had a new arena, a new coach, and renewed hope with some promising off-season moves. They were going for it, and the future looked bright.

That was the excitement before the storm, however. What follows is a review of the Bruins season of horrors, in mostly chronological order.

* Al Iafrate was expected to return from a knee injury and take his place on the blueline, giving the Bruins one of the better defences in the league. He spent about an hour on the ice in training camp before it was clear his knee wasn't up to it. He didn't play a game all season, after getting in just 12 the year before. He ended up suing the Bruins (and winning) because the Bruins said the latest knee problems weren't caused by hockey and that the contract didn't cover it. Iafrate was traded during the summer to San Jose.

* Sandy Moger breaks his jaw in Boston's first exhibition game.

* Adam Oates sprains his knee at the end of October, and doesn't play again until the end of November.

* Marius Czerkawski, upset at his lack of playing time, demands a trade. Assistant GM Mike O'Connell suggested Czercawski and his ilk were "a bunch of babies" and that he would be better served if he worried about "playing hard for a change."

* Blaine Lacher, who arrived on the scene the previous year in semi-spectacular fashion, is a bust as a sophomore. His goals against average of 3.93, at the time ranked him 41st out of 46 qualifying netminders.

* Lacher says he had lost his confidence. The Bruins have lost confidence in him too, as well as backup Craig Billington, so Scott Bailey gets the call from Providence while the Bruins shop for another goalie. Curtis Joseph is the name most often mentioned. Bailey, who was 3-7-2 in Providence, went undefeated in his first five games. He would go 5-1-2 with a 3.26 goals against average before

renewing acquaintances in Providence. Lacher is sent to the minors for a two week conditioning stint.

* Kevin Stevens, with a higher salary than Bourque, Neely or Oates, sits out a game because of his consistently poor play.

* Joe Mullen, with just three goals in 20 games, undergoes neck surgery in early December and doesn't return until late in the season.

* Kaspar benches Neely and Stevens for a game in Toronto. The two never got on the ice as the cameras continuously focused on them. Neely and Stevens were enraged by the embarassment, with Neely even shedding tears over it.

* Czercawksi is traded to Edmonton along with junior defenceman Sean Brown and a 1996 first round draft pick for Bill Ranford.

* The Bruins give up on Kevin Stevens and trade him to Los Angeles for Rick Tocchet.

* The Bruins unveil their third sweater, a pukish yellow color with a bear on it. The jerseys are the laughing stock of the league, and surely embarassing for future hall-of-famers such as Ray Bourque to wear.

* Dave Reid, having a career year, fractures a finger.

* Todd Elik, who had been one of the team's top scorers and was playing on the top line, is inexplicably sent to the minors.

* Cam Neely is out of the lineup with a sore hip, which turns out to be arthritic. He doesn't return and the Bruins don't know if his career is over.

* Lacher is completely out of the picture, and is loaned to Cleveland of the IHL. During the summer, the Bruins advised his contract would be bought out. Boom, just like that, it's all over for him in Boston.

* Elik, who was back from the minors and once again piling up the points as Oates' left winger, breaks his wrist.

* Rick Zombo fractures a foot.

* The Bruins do their customary nose dive in the playoffs, losing to Florida in five games, and losing badly in most of them.

That's the bad news. The good news won't take so long. They had a great stretch run just to make the playoffs, Ranford gave them solid netminding, Rick Tocchet turned out to be everything Stevens was supposed to be, and Oates and Bourque had their usual outstanding seasons.

TEAM PREVIEW

GOAL: Isn't it ironic that when the Bruins finally get a great goaltender, it's one that they could have had all along. In 1988, Ranford was traded to Edmonton along with Geoff Courtnall for Andy Moog. Moog had some good years in Boston, but in the meantime Ranford was establishing himself as one of the premier goalies in the game. He won a Stanley Cup, a Conn Smythe trophy as the playoff MVP, and starred for Team Canada in the Canada Cup.

Last year the Bruins were a .500 team

when Ranford didn't get the decision, and were 21-12-4 when he did. The goaltending stats at the bottom of this section show how much better he was than everyone else.

You have to feel some for Lacher, whose meteoric rise to prominence was matched only by his meteoric nosedive. It didn't come as a complete surprise, however, because there were doubts even toward the end of last year. He's finished in Boston, but it's likely someone somewhere will give him a chance at the minor league level, and perhaps if he does well there, will resurface in the NHL sometime.

The Bruins also bought out Billington's contract, so he's in pretty much the same boat as Lacher. Billington, however, has more proven NHL experience, and someone might grab him as a backup, even if it's later in the year after some injuries.

So, unless the Bruins get someone else it looks like Scott Bailey is going to get the backup job.

Rob Tallas got some playing time in Providence, and even had a win in one game with the Bruins. The Bruins first round draft pick in 1994, Evgeny Ryabchikov, keeps sinking lower and lower. He spent last year in the East Coast League, so look for him this year in a men's industrial league somewhere. But, no team likes the embarassment of a first round flop, so if Ryabchikov can show something, anything, he might get a chance to move up the ladder more quickly than others.

DEFENCE: If the Bruins can find a way to play Bourque 60 minutes a game instead of just 30 or 35, they just might have a decent defence. The ageless wonder just keeps on doing it as he further enhances his credentials as one of the best defencemen to ever play the game. He added another first team all-star berth to his resume last season, and just missed in a close race with Chris Chelios for the Norris Trophy.

The second best defenceman on the Bruins last season came as a surprise. Kyle McLaren was the ninth pick in last year's draft and was expected to return to junior for more seasoning. Defence is a difficult position to learn at the NHL level, but maybe being able to watch Bourque helped him be a steady, dependable rearguard who did not play like the youngest player in the league.

Another surprise was Dean Chynoweth, who was scooped up from the NY Islanders for a fifth round draft pick. Although he couldn't even crack the Islanders lineup every night, the defensive-minded Chynoweth had a spot in Boston's. He gives them some toughness, a commodity in short supply on the Boston defence.

Don Sweeney is hoping to rebound from a sub-standard campaign in which he was hampered by a shoulder injury for most of the season.

The Bruins didn't want anything to do with Iafrate anymore, so he was shipped to San Jose for Jeff Odgers. Rick Zombo was released.

GOALTENDER	GPI	MINS	AVG	W	L	T	EN	SO	GA	SA	SV %
BILL RANFORD	40	2307	2.83	21	12	4	0	1	109	1030	.894
ROBBIE TALLAS	1	60	3.00	1	0	0	0	0	3	29	.897
SCOTT BAILEY	11	571	3.26	5	1	2	0	0	31	264	.883
CRAIG BILLINGTON	27	1380	3.43	10	13	3	2	1	79	594	.867
BLAINE LACHER	12	671	3.93	3	5	2	1	0	44	284	.845
BOS TOTALS	82	4992	3.23	40	31	11	3	2	269	2204	.878

Among the others, Jon Rohlof hasn't distinguished himself, John Gruden hasn't delivered yet, Steve Staois was rescued from the minors in a deal with St. Louis and played the last 12 games of the regular season, and Philip von Steffenelli was the yo-yo man between Boston and Providence.

This is not a very good defensive unit, but it can be adequate. The Bruins don't really need a lot of offence from the blueline because they have Bourque, so defensive play is important.

They lack depth and they lack people with size who can be intimidating physically. Opposing forwards aren't scared of the Boston defence because there's no reason to be. A couple of big bruisers who can scare the daylights out of opponents would help.

Boston ranked first in penalty minutes. That's by the NHL measure, which ranks them from lowest to most. While Boston was easily the lowest at 12.7 minutes per game, it can't be called best. They averaged five minutes a game less than their closest rival, and 14 less than the most. That's a far cry from the Big Bad Bruins of the seventies, and illustrates their lack of aggressiveness.

FORWARD: The future of Cam Neely is at question; Rick Tocchet was an inspiration last year for the Bruins, but is a 32 years-old whose value as a scoring threat has diminished; and Adam Oates is 34 years-old.

That's the good news.

Oates is one of the best playmakers in the history of the game (see chart below) but he has a slight problem because somebody has to shoot it in the net once he passes it to them. There's nobody to take Neely's place, not a sniper among them. Oates had seven four-point games and one five-pointer last season, and would have had another 100 point season if he hadn't missed 12 games with a knee injury. He can make his linemates look

very good, but he can't perform miracles. With 914 career points, Oates should reach 1,000 this season. It would make the job easier with a supporting cast.

ALL TIME ASSISTS PER GAME

1. Wayne Gretzky	1.41
2. Mario Lemieux	1.21
3. Bobby Orr	.98
4. Adam Oates	.91
5. Paul Coffey	.90

Tocchet's okay to play the right side with Oates. His injury problems are always a concern, so a full season is unlikely, however. He still plays the tough, inspirational style he always has but 30 goals would be a good year now for him. Not exactly Neely numbers.

On the left side of Oates a number of players were auditioned. That includes Kevin Stevens, a major league flop with just 10 goals in 41 games. Shawn McEachern seemed better suited to a second scoring line, so it was free agent signee Todd Elik, normally a centre, who proved best at that spot. Oates liked him there, and Elik scored.

Then the odd part. It looked like Kasper, who was a former teammate of Elik's in Los Angeles, didn't like him for some reason, because he kept trying to move him out. Elik got off to a slow start and ended up not dressing for a pile of games. But, when he hooked up with Oates in January he started scoring. These were the team's top scorers in January.

	G	A	PTS
Oates	6	15	21
Elik	5	11	16
Bourque	2	10	12

Then the Bruins called up Tim Sweeney, whose only scoring success had been in the minors, and started putting him on with Oates, instead of Elik. Elik had points in each of his first three games in February, and then, remember this is after being second on the team in January, he's put on waivers and sent to the minors.

Hello? Did we miss something. Look at February's top scorers, noting the big dropoff in scoring by Oates, and lack of it by anyone else.

	G	A	PTS
Oates	3	10	13
McEachern	4	6	10
Bourque	3	7	10

That's not the end of the story, though. Elik came back in March and actually led the team in scoring for the month. That's also when the team went on a roll with a 9-4-1 record for the month in their drive for the playoffs. The top March scorers are as follows:

	G	A	PTS
Elik	4	13	17
Bourque	0	15	15
Oates	5	10	15

Who knows what this season will hold for Elik and the number one line, but if someone produces on a team that has very little scoring, why are they messing around?

Dave Reid, who also plays the left side, is a pretty amazing guy, and he'll be missed after he signed on with Dallas. At age 31, he set a career high in goals with 23 and a career high in points, with 44. For a guy in a checking role on the third line, who kills penalties, and who missed a month with a fractured finger, to be among the top goal scorers on a team is pretty darn good.

Mind you, the top goal scorer, not counting Tocchet who had some of his with Los Angeles, was Neely. He had 26, despite missing 33 games.

The rest of the forwards are nothing if not mediocre. Josef Stumpel is the number two centre, which spells trouble right there. If Oates is out, Stumpel, who has been knocked for his intensity, doesn't inspire much confidence as the number one man in the middle. Donato was on again, off again, at least as a scorer. Steve Heinze was the same.

McEachern did okay as a second line scorer, but he pulls off disappearing acts too, and during the summer disappeared to Ottawa for right winger Trent McCleary and a third round draft pick. Over the last 14 games of the season when the Bruins needed him most, he scored just three points. McEachern also had an odd home-road scoring breakdown, getting almost twice as many points on the road. He was 10-8-18 at home; 14-21-35 on the road. That's kind of curious, considering he's a Massachusetts product and was supposed to be happy to be home.

In fact, that whole Massachusetts thing hasn't worked out. For a while it looked like the Bruins were going to corner the market on players from their home state, as if that were the most important thing a player had to offer. They ended up dumping many of them off. Stevens, of course, was given the boot, while McEachern and Stephen Leach were traded. Ted Donato, Steve Heinze, and Tim Sweeney still remain.

Sandy Moger was another player who seemed to do okay when he was given a chance, but he's basically a spare part for a checking line. Ron Sutter proved to be a decent addition as a checking line centre, and wasn't playing anywhere at the start of last year. He eventually signed on with Phoenix of the IHL and then with Boston late in the year. He became a free agent again at the end of the season.

The Bruins got used to Neely scoring the goals for them. With him not around, or at reduced capacity it looks to be a very lean year in the scoring department. Many of their key players are aging, and of those remaining there is almost nothing to get excited about.

Maybe Cameron Mann, who had a great playoff with Peterborough last year, leading that team to the Memorial Cup, could cause some excitement. He's a character player who could make an immediate impact.

SPECIAL TEAMS: I said last year in *The Hockey Annual* that it would be interesting to see how the Bruins penalty killing would be this year on the larger ice surface of the new arena. The Bruins have been near the top of this category for a long time, and were coming off two first place rankings.

They fell to 20th overall in the league, which gives an indication just how much the old arena helped them.

The power play was mediocre this year after being projected as one of the best in the league. Without Neely there isn't much hope here for this season. They don't have a power play sniper. They do have Oates and Bourque, however, so we shouldn't expect it to be terrible, just mediocre.

Power Play	G	ATT	PCT
Overall	68	363	18.7% (11th NHL)
Home	40	196	20.4% (11th NHL)
Road	28	167	16.8% (T-12th NHL)

7 SHORT HANDED GOALS ALLOWED (T-2nd NHL)

PENALTY KILLINGG	TSH	PCT	
Overall	67	341	80.4% (T-20th NHL)
Home	36	179	79.9% (23rd NHL)
Road	31	162	80.9% (15th NHL)

13 SHORT HANDED GOALS SCORED (T-7th NHL)

PENALTIES	GP	MIN	AVG
BRUINS	82	1039	12.7 (1st NHL)

COACHING AND MANAGEMENT: If they held a vote to guess which was the coach most likely to be fired first this season, Steve Kasper's name would be at the top of more than a few lists. The biggest surprise is that he's lasted this long, but Sinden showed unusual patience through a lot of hard times. Kasper is supposed to be a good communicator with the players, but some of them wondered on frequent occasions what the heck he was doing.

Sometimes you got the feeling that Kasper's main objective was to make sure the players knew who was boss. A good coach doesn't need to bother with tactics to make that point. There were questions about how he used his players, and the players were often the ones asking the questions.

Maybe part of the reason he wasn't fired is that Sinden gets his back up over that sort of thing. He likes to make sure the players and the media know who's running the show.

At any rate, coaches don't last long in Boston, and if the Bruins don't get off to a decent start, Kasper will be gone, and replaced by another ex-Bruin player.

Sinden is supposed to hand the general manager reigns over to Mike O'Connell soon, but he seems to come up with excuses to stay on the job, instead he's content to just pass over more day-to-day responsibilites.

Sinden is the winningest general manager in NHL history. He has 1,038 wins, ahead of Jack Adams, at 913, and Cliff Fletcher, who is at 891.

DRAFT

Round	Sel.	Player		Pos
1	8	Johnathan Aitken	D	Medicine Hat (WHL)
2	45	Henry Kuster	RW	Medicine Hat(WHL)
3	53	Eric Naud	LW	St. Hyacinthe (QMJHL)
3	80	Jason Doyle	RW	Sault Ste. Marie (OHL)
4	100	Trent Whitfield	C	Spokane (WHL)
5	132	Elias Abrahamsson	D	Halifax (QMJHL)
6	155	Chris Lane	D	Spokane (WHL)
7	182	Thomas Brown	D	Sarnia (OHL)
8	208	Bob Prier	RW	St. Lawrence Univ.
9	234	Anders Soderberg	W	Sweden

There are similarities between first round pick Aitken, and last year's surprise success story, Kyle McLaren. Both are big defencemen drafted from the Western Hockey League at around the same draft position - 8th this year, 9th last year, and both picks were the result of the Glen Wesley trade with Hartford.

The Bruins are hoping there is one more similarity - that Aitken can also make the grade and play in the NHL this year. It was magic with McLaren, so perhaps the Bruins have figured out that there's a good reason. Maybe, with Bourque as a role model, a young defenceman is influenced in a positive way. Why not have the young defencemen around to see first-hand how the game is supposed to be played.

PROGNOSIS: This could be the year the Bruins finally don't make the playoffs and finally don't have a winning season. The streak is currently at 29 years.

The Bruins do have some key things in their favor: Bill Ranford, Ray Bourque and Adam Oates. A team with those three at each key position can't sink too low, but even so, Boston came close to not making the playoffs last year.

Sinden seemed to realize that his veterans were getting on in age and they wouldn't have too many more chances. He stocked up on them, and while it didn't work, it's unlikely he would want to revert to a whole rebuilding process. With that understanding, look for the Bruins to go after some more veterans and hope they can make a run to get into the playoffs, where anything can happen.

PREDICTION:

Northeast Division: 3rd

Eastern Conference: 9th

Overall: 18th

Team Rankings 1995/96

		Conference Rank	League Rank
Record	40-31-11	5	8
Home	22-14-5	7	10
Away	18-17-6	3	6
Versus Own Conference	29-20-7	3	5
Versus Other Conference	11-11-4	9	14
Team Plus\Minus	+12	5	8
Goals For	282	2	5
Goals Against	269	10	17

Average Shots For 34.6		1	1
Average Shots Against	26.8	4	5
Overtime	0-3-10	10	23
One Goal Games	15-10	2	3
Times outshooting opponent	65	1	2
Versus Teams Over .500	14-24-4	10	16
Versus Teams Under .500	26-7-7	2	3
First Half Record	18-17-6	6	11
Second Half Record	20-13-5	2	4

Results: Lost in first round to Florida, four to one.

Record: 1-4

Home: 1-1

Away: 0-3

Goals For: 16 (3.2 per game)

Goals Against: 22 (4.4 per game)

Overtime: 0-0

Power play: 25.9%

Penalty Killing: 83.3%

ALL-TIME LEADERS

GOALS

John Bucyk	545
Phil Esposito	459
Rick Middleton	402

ASSISTS

Ray Bourque	970
John Bucyk	794
Bobby Orr	624

POINTS

John Bucyk	1,339
Ray Bourque	1,313
Phil Esposito	1,012

BEST INDIVIDUAL SEASONS

GOALS

Phil Esposito	70/71	76
Phil Esposito	73/74	68
Phil Esposito	71/72	66

ASSISTS

Bobby Orr	70/71	102
Adam Oates	92/93	97
Bobby Orr	73/74	90

POINTS

Phil Esposito	70/71	152
Phil Esposito	73/74	145
Adam Oates	92/93	142

TEAM RECORD

Last 3 years

	GP	W	L	T	Pts	%
1995-96	82	40	31	11	91	.555
1994-95	48	27	18	3	57	.594
1993-94	84	42	29	13	97	.577

Best 3 regular seasons

1929-30	44	38	5	1	77	.875
1969-70	76	57	14	7	121	.791
1938-39	48	36	10	2	74	.771

Worst 3 regular seasons

1924-25	30	6	24	0	12	.200
1961-62	70	15	47	8	38	.271
1960-61	70	15	42	13	43	.307

Most Goals (min. 70 game schedule)

1970-71	399
1973-74	349
1974-75	345

Fewest Goals (min. 70 game schedule)

1955-56	147
1952-53	152
1951-52	162

Most Goals Against (min. 70 game schedule)

1961-62	306
1985-86	288
1984-87	287

Fewest Goals Against (min. 70 game schedule)

1952-53	172
1956-57	174
1951-52	176

STAT SECTION

Team Scoring Stats

	GP	G	A	PTS	+/-	PIM	SH	Power Play			Short Handed		
								G	A	P	G	A	P
ADAM OATES	70	25	67	92	18	18	183	7	24	31	1	2	3
RAY BOURQUE	82	20	62	82	31	58	390	9	29	38	2	0	2
RICK TOCCHET	71	29	31	60	10	181	185	10	10	20	0	0	0
JOZEF STUMPEL	76	18	36	54	8-	14	158	5	15	20	0	0	0
SHAWN MCEACHERN	82	24	29	53	5-	34	238	3	3	6	2	1	3
TED DONATO	82	23	26	49	6	46	152	7	8	15	0	2	2
CAM NEELY	49	26	20	46	3	31	191	7	8	15	0	0	0
TODD ELIK	59	13	33	46	2	40	108	6	10	16	0	0	0
DAVE REID	63	23	21	44	14	4	160	1	0	1	6	1	7
SANDY MOGER	80	15	14	29	9-	65	103	4	1	5	0	0	0
STEVE HEINZE	76	16	12	28	3-	43	129	0	0	0	1	1	1
DON SWEENEY	77	4	24	28	4-	42	142	2	6	8	0	2	2
KYLE MCLAREN	74	5	12	17	16	73	74	0	0	0	0	1	1
TIM SWEENEY	41	8	8	16	4	14	47	1	2	3	0	0	0
JOE MULLEN	37	8	7	15	2-	0	60	4	1	5	0	0	0
RICK ZOMBO	67	4	10	14	7-	53	68	0	0	0	0	1	1
JON ROHLOFF	79	1	12	13	8-	59	106	1	5	6	0	2	2
RON SUTTER	18	5	7	12	10	24	34	0	0	0	1	1	2
DEAN CHYNOWETH	49	2	6	8	5-	128	38	0	0	0	0	0	0
CLAYTON BEDDOES	39	1	6	7	5-	44	18	0	0	0	0	0	0
PHIL VONSTEFENELLI	27	0	4	4	2	16	20	0	0	0	0	0	0
BILL RANFORD	77	0	3	3	0	2	0	0	0	0	0	0	0
ALEXEI KASATONOV	19	1	0	1	1	12	15	0	0	0	0	0	0
ROBBIE TALLAS	1	0	0	0	0	0	0	0	0	0	0	0	0
RYAN HUGHES	3	0	0	0	0	0	2	0	0	0	0	0	0
ANDRE ROY	3	0	0	0	0	0	0	0	0	0	0	0	0
CAMERON STEWART	6	0	0	0	2-	0	2	0	0	0	0	0	0
MARK CORNFORTH	6	0	0	0	4	4	1	0	0	0	0	0	0
DAVIS PAYNE	7	0	0	0	0	7	2	0	0	0	0	0	0
KEVIN SAWYER	8	0	0	0	1-	28	1	0	0	0	0	0	0
SCOTT BAILEY	11	0	0	0	0	0	0	0	0	0	0	0	0
STEVE STAIOS	12	0	0	0	5-	4	4	0	0	0	0	0	0
BLAINE LACHER	12	0	0	0	0	4	0	0	0	0	0	0	0
JOHN GRUDEN	14	0	0	0	3-	4	12	0	0	0	0	0	0
CRAIG BILLINGTON	27	0	0	0	0	2	0	0	0	0	0	0	0
MARC POTVIN	27	0	0	0	2-	12	14	0	0	0	0	0	0

PLAYOFFS

PLAYER	GP	G	A	PTS	+/-	PIM	PP	SH	GW	OT	S
ADAM OATES	5	2	5	7	3-	2	0	1	0	0	13
RAY BOURQUE	5	1	6	7	4-	2	1	0	0	0	28
RICK TOCCHET	5	4	0	4	7-	21	3	0	1	0	20
SANDY MOGER	5	2	2	4	1-	12	1	0	0	0	12
SHAWN MCEACHERN	5	2	1	3	2-	8	0	0	0	0	7
TED DONATO	5	1	2	3	3-	2	1	0	0	0	7
JON ROHLOFF	5	1	2	3	3-	2	1	0	0	0	14
JOZEF STUMPEL	5	1	2	3	2-	0	0	0	0	0	7
STEVE HEINZE	5	1	1	2	1	4	0	1	0	0	20
TODD ELIK	4	0	2	2	1-	16	0	0	0	0	9
DAVE REID	5	0	2	2	3-	2	0	0	0	0	4
DON SWEENEY	5	0	2	2	3-	6	0	0	0	0	12
CAMERON STEWART	5	1	0	1	0	2	0	0	0	0	2
JOHN GRUDEN	3	0	1	1	0	0	0	0	0	0	2
MARC POTVIN	5	0	1	1	2-	18	0	0	0	0	5
CRAIG BILLINGTON	1	0	0	0	0	2	0	0	0	0	0
TIM SWEENEY	1	0	0	0	0	2	0	0	0	0	1
STEVE STAIOS	3	0	0	0	1-	0	0	0	0	0	5
DEAN CHYNOWETH	4	0	0	0	2-	24	0	0	0	0	3
BILL RANFORD	4	0	0	0	0	0	0	0	0	0	0
RON SUTTER	5	0	0	0	2-	8	0	0	0	0	4
KYLE MCLAREN	5	0	0	0	3-	14	0	0	0	0	13

Buffalo Sabres

Give the Sabres credit. Timing the rebuilding with the buildings. Good idea.

Last season was the final one for The Aud. While not on the same scale as the Montreal Forum farewell, or any other major arena for that matter, the goodbye was emotional enough and helped generate ticket sales. Hard not to see a game there for "the last time." Best of all, it helped deflect attention away from a bad hockey team.

Year two of rebuilding is year one of the new building, the Marine Midland Centre. The new arena will be the star for a while, and yes, deflect attention away from a lousy hockey team.

Good planning, and that's not the end of it.

Hockey seasons, and many other things, are judged in the end according to expectations. The Sabre management made it clear before the start of last season that the fans were to have none. Expectations, that is. They didn't, so Buffalo's season on the ice turned out to be pretty good. The fans couldn't be disappointed, so anything they got out of it was a bonus.

As it turned out, the Sabres were still a lousy hockey team, but they were competitive most of the time, they had a good coach, and not all their big stars were traded away.

Hiring a new coach with no previous NHL experience was also good strategy. No expectations, once again. Ted Nolan turned out to be an extremely pleasant surprise.

Pat LaFontaine and Dominik Hasek aren't young players, and therefore could be sacrificed for the right price in a rebuilding program. The Sabres wisely held on to them. Even if the only reason was that they didn't get their price, it gives the fans two of the best players in the game on which to pin at least some hope. And it shows that all the Sabres' moves aren't just about money.

Rebuilding programs are always full of surprises, for a couple of reasons. First, younger teams are usually inconsistent. One week they play great, the next they stink. One week a player is on fire, the next week he's sitting in the press box. Also, because players get ice time they might not get normally, some of them come through unexpectedly, and some disappoint.

Let's take a look at some of the Sabres surprises from last year.

* Randy Burridge - down and out in Beverly Hills, Burridge was coming off a four-goal season for the Kings, and wasn't exactly in high demand. A native of nearby Fort Erie, Ontario, the Sabres gave him one last

shot. He might not have made fans reminisce about Rene Robert, but he came though on this team, finishing second in team goals and points.

* Derek Plante - was he a one year flash in the pan, or was he just suffering from the sophomore jinx? Plante answered that question in his third season, especially in the second half when his 36 points were second only to LaFontaine.

* Brian Holzinger - the former Hobey Baker winner looked like he was going to be a player, an early Calder Trophy candidate. He finished second to Alexei Zhitnik in pre-season scoring and started off the season with four goals in the first nine games. Then the well went dry. He had one goal in his next 35 games, and finally exasperated, the Sabres sent him to Rochester. He was recalled, then sent back down again. Only in his final callup at the end of the season did he start to produce, with five goals over an eight game span. He returned to Rochester for the AHL playoffs, and put up some nice numbers there.

* Jason Dawe - seemed to be rolling along, everything was fine, he was the third top scorer on the team and then, wham, he was sent to the minors. Big time message. Something about playing hard all the time, if he wanted to play all the time in Buffalo. He ended up scoring 25 goals in 67 games, not bad production.

* Matthew Barnaby - 15 goals and 31 points is excellent bonus production from a player with the most penalty minutes in the league, especially when he had just one goal the previous season.

* No Trade - almost from the start of the season, everybody waited for the hammer to drop. LaFontaine and Hasek would give good value to a rebuilding team which was concerned about the value of their contracts. The two of them were rumored to be going every which way, but ended up staying put.

* Ted Nolan - he was no fill-in coach. He was good. The team had their ups and downs and he often vented his frustrations, unable to understand why his team couldn't play well every single night. He pushed them to play their best.

* Play against top teams - the Sabres often played some of their best games against the best teams. That's a curious result, which gives rise to a number of possibilites.

1. The top teams took them lightly, and because the Sabres were a hard working team, were able to surprise.
2. Buffalo's system was geared to beating good teams, because it could shut down their offence.
3. They got up for those games, and didn't for those against the weaker clubs.
4. Dominik Hasek. The best goalie in the game might have been more inspired to play against the best teams in the game.

TEAM PREVIEW

GOAL: Dominik Hasek was the subject of trade rumors last year. While any player is available for the right price, it's awfully difficult to replace the best goaltender in the game.

Hasek once again led the league in save percentage, and once again won more games on his own than any other goalie. Spectacular isn't a good enough word to describe Hasek. Maybe they could honor him by giving out an award for save percentage and naming it after him. Consider the league save percentage leader over the last three years, the same three years Hasek has been a number one goalie.

NHL SAVE PERCENTAGE LEADER:

1995-96	Dominik Hasek	Buf.	.920
1994-95	Dominik Hasek	Buf.	.930
1993-94	Dominik Hasek	Buf.	.930

Hasek has also led the league in goals against average for two of those years.

There isn't a statistic of any kind that doesn't have some flaws, but more and more people are leaning toward save percentage as a better indication of a goalie's value, as opposed to goals against average. It is relatively new, however, and takes time to be generally accepted.

The problem with goals against average is that so much of it is based on how well the team plays. If they don't give up a lot of shots they're not going to give up as many goals. So, a fairer system is save percentage which is based on the number of goals allowed in relation to the number of shots.

It too is flawed in some respects, however. Good defensive teams might not give up as many quality shots, and if they have good defencemen who clear the front of the net and clear rebounds, the goalie won't won't have the same quality chances as another goalie.

Any way you measure it, however, Hasek is the best in the league.

Andrei Trefilov handled the backup duties capably, and the Sabres have a potential great in Martin Biron on the way up. Down on the farm, Steve Shields was spectacular for Rochester in the playoffs and got most of the playing time for them during the regular season.

DEFENCE: This is sort of an odd defence. In the past, Muckler has put together a mix of older defensive types with the younger more offensive threats. That was a good mix which provided stability and a learning influence on the youngsters.

What they have here now is a mix of older offensive types and younger offensive types, with the odd tough guy thrown in to punch people's lights out.

Veterans Charlie Huddy, Craig Muni and Doug Bodger were all dumped off during the season. Doug Houda was eventually waived and sent to Rochester. The team wasn't playing well anyway, they had some value on the market, and the Sabres wanted the younger players to get more playing time. No great loss with any of them, and besides, the Bodger deal was a bonanza, trading a largely

GOALTENDER	GPI	MINS	AVG	W	L	T	EN	SO	GA	SA	SV %
DOMINIK HASEK	59	3417	2.83	22	30	6	5	2	161	2011	.920
STEVE SHIELDS	2	75	3.20	1	0	0	0	0	4	32	.875
ANDREI TREFILOV	22	1094	3.51	8	8	1	2	0	64	660	.903
JOHN BLUE	5	255	3.53	2	2	0	1	0	15	137	.891
MARTIN BIRON	3	119	5.04	0	2	0	0	0	10	64	.844
BUF TOTALS	82	4976	3.16	33	42	7	8	2	262	2912	.910

disappointing veteran offensive player with a big salary, for two prospects, and two draft picks, including a first rounder in 1996. Bodger wasn't even worth the first rounder.

Besides, if the need comes up for one of those veteran defence-first guys they're easy to find and relatively cheap. Muckler has gone out and got them before.

What remains isn't going to make Hasek sleep like a baby the night before each game. It will help to have Richard Smehlik back in the lineup, because just as he looked to be coming into his own, he was injured and missed all of last season.

Garry Galley is an excellent offensive type, the quarterback that Alexei Zhitnik was supposed to be, but he's 33 years old.

Zhitnik was the subject of trade rumors almost all season long. He doesn't play an intense game, doesn't play well defensively, doesn't come to play every night, and will be the subject of more trade rumors. He's young, however, and he has had some good seasons in the past. He's probably doomed in Buffalo, though. He doesn't fit into this team, but he's an attractive commodity for a lot of other teams looking for some offence from their defence.

Darryl Shannon came over from Winnipeg with Michal Grosek for a first rounder, maybe not such a great deal. In Shannon, they just expect a steady NHL defenceman, and that's largely what they got.

Mark Astley, another offensive-minded type, who spent about a fifth of the season in the press box, is in the mix, as is tough guy Bob Boughner, who got his first crack at the NHL last season after being passed around from a couple NHL teams, and making a career for himself in the minors.

Big Mike Wilson gives them some size, and Jay McKee gives them an excellent prospect for the future, which may be now.

That's if McKee isn't jinxed. Kevin Haller, Philippe Boucher, David Cooper, and Shawn Anderson are some of their many first round defence disappointments.

If things start to go too sour for this group, Muckler will probably go out and get a veteran stay-at-home type to settle things down, and keep Hasek from talking about mutiny.

As it stands now, they're weak defensively. With a rebuilding team, however, you want to get a couple young guys into place, and build around them. They have a number of them in Smehlik, Wilson, McKee, and even Zhitnik.

FORWARD: Pat LaFontaine and Donald Audette, when they're not injured, give the Sabres a pretty good one-two scoring punch. Matthew Barnaby, Brad May and Rob Ray just punch a lot.

Three of the top five penalty minute earners in the league last season were Buffalo forwards, as shown in the list below.

TOP 10 PENALTY MINUTES:

MATTHEW BARNABY	Buf	335
Enrico Ciccone	TB-Chi	306
Tie Domi	Tor	297
BRAD MAY	Buf	295
ROB RAY	Buf	287
Todd Ewen	Ana	285
Denis Vial	Ott	276
Dave Karpa	Ana	270
Jeff Daniels	Hfd	254
Chris Simon	Col	250

This should be the year that a couple of the Sabres highly regarded prospects make the team. They are centre Wayne Primeau and left winger Curtis Brown. The Sabres also like right winger Vaclav Veranada, picked up in the Doug Bodger deal with San Jose.

The problem with rebuilding is that you want to get the prospects into the lineup, but you don't want to rush them. Primeau and Brown have been returned to junior twice now, so they should be ready for a shot, but don't expect them to blow the lights out. They could get a little more seasoning in Rochester.

After LaFontaine and Audette, Randy Burridge can score some as evidenced in his comeback season, as can Derek Plante, another comeback player. Jason Dawe could be a breakout player this year, and Brad May is a perennial breakout player, who never has lived up to the power forward sniper role. Oh well, nobody's giving up on him quite yet. Disappointing Holzinger could easily come around this season, and Mike Peca gives them a decent defensive player at centre.

After the three tough guys noted above, among those challenging for work will be also be Michal Grosek, Scott Nichol, and Dane Jackson. Left winger Grosek is one the Sabres are high on. He couldn't stick with Winnipeg, and didn't even score much in the minors, but he's only 20 years old and did okay at the end of last season with Buffalo.

There's not a lot here yet to get too excited about. Maybe some of the younger players will come through and maybe they won't. There's no sure things in there. In the meantime, they can continue to beat up people. That's a talent area where they rank up among the best.

SPECIAL TEAMS: One of the advantages the Sabres have held in the penalty killing department was the small ice surface at the Aud. In 26 years at that arena they ranked first five times, and in the top five in the league 17 of the 26 years. Pretty amazing.

But, the Boston Bruins had very similar type numbers in their little arena at Boston Garden, and this past season in the Fleet Centre and its bigger ice surface, they finished 20th, their worst ranking ever.

The power play should be considerably better with a healthy Audette. He's a sniper who excels with the man-advantage.

POWER PLAY	G	ATT	PCT	
Overall	76	477	15.9%	(T-20th NHL)
Home	41	253	16.2%	(18th NHL)
Road	35	224	15.6%	(18th NHL)

12 SHORT HANDED GOALS ALLOWED (T-14th NHL)

PENALTY KILLING	G	TSH	PCT	
Overall	74	46	83.9%	(6th NHL)
Home	37	239	84.5%	(T-9th NHL)
Road	37	222	83.3%	(5th NHL)

10 SHORT HANDED GOALS SCORED (T-17th NHL)

COACHING AND MANAGEMENT: The best thing about Ted Nolan as coach was that he didn't allow the rebuilding theme to become a convenient excuse for losing. He wanted to win every game, and he wanted every player to want the same thing. As a result, the Sabres performed better than their talent.

There were reports of some friction between Nolan and Muckler, which doesn't mean a heck of a lot, except that Nolan has established himself to some degree now and if he gets fired other teams will be interested.

John Muckler seems to go about his job properly. Not much use having a bunch of overpriced talent around during rebuilding time. So, you keep the talent that's worth it, and go to it. Mind you, Mogilny ended up doing a lot better in Vancouver than expected.

Muckler is loading up on the young players, draft picks, and prospects, and has a long-term plan. He seems committed to it, and not unlike his former cohort in

Edmonton, most of the time he gets good value for the veterans he trades. And he's smart enough to hold on to them, and then get something for them when their value is highest near the trading deadline.

DRAFT

Round	Sel.	Player	Pos	Amateur Team
1	7	Eric Rasmussen	C	Univ. of Minnesota
2	27	Cory Sarich	D	Saskatoon (WHL)
2	33	Darren Van Oene	LW	Brandon (WHL)
3	54	Francois Methot	C	St-Hyacinthe (QMJHL)
4	87	Kurt Walsh	RW	Owen Sound (OHL)
4	106	Mike Martone	D	Peterborough (OHL)
5	115	Alexei Tezikov	D	Russia
6	142	Ryan Davis	RW	Owen Sound (OHL)
6	161	Darren Mortier	C	Sarnia (OHL)
9	222	Scott Buhler	G	Medicine Hat (WHL)

Rasmussen, the first American-born player taken in the draft, was a freshman last year at the University of Minnesota. He's a big, strong, centre who is supposed to like the physical game.

The Sabres have been more successful with later round picks than first round selections. Only first-rounders Brad May (1990), Wayne Primeau (1994) and Martin Biron (1995) played for Buffalo last year,

and of course, only May regularly. Recent first round flops (while with Buffalo) include David Cooper (1992), Philippe Boucher (1991), Kevin Haller (1989), Joel Savage (1988), Shawn Anderson (1986), Calle Johansson (1985), and Mikael Andersson (1984). Many Buffalo first round picks are still playing in the NHL, including Boucher, Haller, Johansson and Andersson, but they're all on other teams. More first round picks playing for other teams include Phil Housley, Dave Andreychuk, Tom Barrasso, Adam Creighton and Pierre Turgeon.

Current Sabres selected 100th or higher by Buffalo

	YEAR	ROUND	PICK
Steve Shields	1991	5	101
Brian Holzinger	1991	6	124
Derek Plante	1989	8	161
Donald Audette	1989	9	183
Mark Astley	1989	10	193

Other prominent high Sabre draft picks playing for other teams:

Randy Cunneyworth	1989	8	167
Don McSween	1983	8	154
Uwe Krupp	1983	11	214
Darcy Wakaluk	1984	7	144
Ken Baumgartner	1985	12	245
Wade Flaherty	1988	9	181
Sean O'Donnell	1991	6	123
Yuri Khymlev	1992	5	108

PROGNOSIS: The Sabres are still a lousy team, but they have some advantages over other lousy teams. Namely, LaFontaine and Hasek. This won't be their season. Not yet in the tough Eastern Conference. But, they have a chance of approaching the .500 mark, which isn't bad. They need their top players to be healthy to even think about that, and they need some of their younger players to come through on the scoresheet.

Other than that, the defence is weak defensively, goaltending is tops as long as Hasek doesn't get hurt, and the rest of the lineup is loaded with ifs. That usually spells trouble. But, they're not supposed to do much in year two of the rebuilding process. Wait for year three, or four, or five. Just wait, and enjoy the new arena.

PREDICTION:

Northeast Division: 5th

Eastern Conference: 11th

Overall: 21st

Team Rankings 1995-96

		Conference Rank	League Rank
Record	33-42-7	11	20
Home	19-17-5	11	17
Away	14-25-2	10	19
Versus Own Conference	24-27-5	10	17
Versus Other Conference	9-15-2	11	21
Team Plus\Minus	-17	10	17
Goals For	247	7	14
Goals Against	262	9	16
Average Shots For	28.4	11	22
Average Shots Against	35.5	13	26
Overtime	2-6-7	12	25
One Goal Games	14-15	10	16
Times outshooting opponent	20	13	25
Versus Teams Over .500	18-25-4	8	13
Versus Teams Under .500	15-17-3	11	22
First Half Record	18-20-3	10	16
Second Half Record	15-22-4	11	20

PLAYOFFS

- Did not make the playoffs

ALL-TIME LEADERS

GOALS

Gil Perreault	512
Rick Martin	382
Dave Andreychuk	348

ASSISTS

Gil Perreault	814
Dave Andreychuk	423
Craig Ramsay	420

POINTS

Gil Perreault	1,326
Dave Andreychuk	771
Rick Martin	695

BEST INDIVIDUAL SEASONS

GOALS

Alexander Mogilny	92-93	76
Danny Gare	79-80	56
Pat LaFontaine	92-93	53

ASSISTS

Pat LaFontaine	92-93	95
Dale Hawerchuk	92-93	80
Dale Hawerchuk	91-92	75

POINTS

Pat LaFontaine	92-93	148
Alexander Mogilny	92-93	127
Gil Perreault	75-76	113

TEAM RECORD

Last 3 years

	GP	W	L	T	Pts	%
1995-96	82	33	42	7	72	.445
1994-95	48	22	19	7	51	.531
1993-94	84	43	32	9	95	.565

Best 3 regular seasons

1974-75	78	49	16	15	113	.724
1979-80	80	47	17	16	110	.688
1975-76	80	46	21	13	105	.656

Worst 3 regular seasons

1971-72	78	16	43	19	51
1986-87	80	28	44	8	64
1991-92	80	31	37	12	74

Most Goals (min. 70 game schedule)

1974-75	354
1975-76	339
1992-93	335

Fewest Goals (min. 70 game schedule)

1971-72	203
1973-74	242
1995-96	247

Most Goals Against (min. 70 game schedule)

1986-87	308
1987-88	305
1991-92	299

Fewest Goals Against (min. 70 game schedule)

1979-80	201
1977-78	215
1993-94	218

STAT SECTION
Team Scoring Stats

	GP	G	A	PTS	+/-	PIM	SH	Power Play			Short Handed		
								G	A	P	G	A	P
PAT LAFONTAINE	76	40	51	91	8-	36	224	15	24	39	3	0	3
RANDY BURRIDGE	74	25	33	58	0	30	154	6	16	22	0	0	0
DEREK PLANTE	76	23	33	56	4-	28	203	4	10	14	0	1	1
GARRY GALLEY	78	10	44	54	2-	81	175	7	28	35	1	2	3
JASON DAWE	67	25	25	50	8-	33	130	8	7	15	1	0	1
BRAD MAY	79	15	29	44	6	295	168	3	5	8	0	0	0
ALEXEI ZHITNIK	80	6	30	36	25-	58	193	5	18	23	0	2	2
MATTHEW BARNABY	73	15	16	31	2-	335	131	0	0	0	0	0	0
MIKE PECA	68	11	20	31	1-	67	109	4	4	8	3	1	4
DONALD AUDETTE	23	12	13	25	0	18	92	8	7	15	0	0	0
BRIAN HOLZINGER	58	10	10	20	21-	37	71	5	2	7	0	1	1
MARK ASTLEY	60	2	18	20	12-	80	80	0	7	7	0	0	0
DARRYL SHANNON	74	4	13	17	15	92	59	0	1	1	0	2	2
BRENT HUGHES	76	5	10	15	9-	148	56	0	0	0	0	0	0
MIKE WILSON	58	4	8	12	13	41	52	1	0	1	0	1	1
MICHAL GROSEK	23	6	4	10	1-	31	34	2	3	5	0	0	0
DANE JACKSON	22	5	4	9	3	41	20	0	1	1	0	0	0
ROB RAY	71	3	6	9	8-	287	21	0	0	0	0	0	0
ROB CONN	28	2	5	7	9-	18	36	0	0	0	0	0	0
SCOTT PEARSON	27	4	0	4	4-	67	26	0	0	0	0	0	0
DIXON WARD	8	2	2	4	1	6	12	0	0	0	0	0	0
DOUG HOUDA	38	1	3	4	3	52	21	0	0	0	0	0	0
JAY MCKEE	1	0	1	1	1	2	2	0	0	0	0	0	0
BOB BOUGHNER	31	0	1	1	3	104	14	0	0	0	0	0	0
DOMINIK HASEK	59	0	1	1	0	6	0	0	0	0	0	0	0
VACLAV VARADA	1	0	0	0	0	0	2	0	0	0	0	0	0
STEVE SHIELDS	2	0	0	0	0	2	0	0	0	0	0	0	0
SCOTT NICHOL	2	0	0	0	0	10	4	0	0	0	0	0	0
WAYNE PRIMEAU	2	0	0	0	0	0	0	0	0	0	0	0	0
BARRIE MOORE	3	0	0	0	0	0	3	0	0	0	0	0	0
MARTIN BIRON	3	0	0	0	0	0	0	0	0	0	0	0	0
CURTIS BROWN	4	0	0	0	0	0	1	0	0	0	0	0	0
JOHN BLUE	5	0	0	0	0	0	0	0	0	0	0	0	0
GRANT JENNINGS	6	0	0	0	1	28	3	0	0	0	0	0	0
ANDREI TREFILOV	22	0	0	0	0	4	0	0	0	0	0	0	0

Florida Panthers

This is a quote out of a popular pre-season publication from last year: "The Panthers will battle for the worst record in the NHL."

Good call.

Okay, so that particular quote was from this publication. Like who knew? The best anyone else would give them was that the playoffs were a longshot possibility.

But, the finals? Nobody anywhere thought they had a rat's chance in hell to get that far. Even if someone thought the Panthers would do well, they couldn't say so for fear of their sanity being questioned.

It was just the Panther's third NHL season. It was the most successful third season in NHL history. The 41 wins they compiled were the most, and since the original expansion in 1967-68, when one of the new teams was guaranteed a trip to the final two, it was the quickest trip to the finals.

FEWEST YEARS TO REACH FINALS
(POST ORIGINAL EXPANSION)

Florida	3
Buffalo	4

Edmonton	4
NY Islanders	8
Vancouver	12
Calgary	14
Colorado	17
Winnipeg	18
New Jersey	21
Washington	22
Anaheim	- (3)
Ottawa	- (4)
Tampa Bay	- (4)
San Jose	- (5)
Hartford	- (17)

The Panthers got off to a good early start during the regular season. Okay, every cat has its day. Then everybody sat back and waited for them to fall off the fence. And they waited. And waited.

Finally, at the 60 game mark it happened. They went on an 0-8-2 run, won a few, and then lost four in a row. There it was - just as we all suspected, they weren't that good. All that rhetoric about how they were so successful during the first three-quarters of the regular season was just hot air.

After all, they had no scorers, a defence

made up of rookies and castoffs, and a rookie coach. A team like that was doomed in the playoffs. *The Hockey News* oddsmaker (guess who that was), after a teleconference with the publication's NHL experts, deemed them 40-1 longshots to win the Stanley Cup.

So, a team with no scorers, a defence made up of rookies and castoffs, and a rookie coach, started out the playoffs. Their first series win over Boston was a surprise, but not a big one. All it did was delay the inevitable.

They had almost no chance against Philadelphia. They won 4-2.

They had less chance against the offensive powerhouse Pittsburgh team. They won 4-2.

They had some chance against Colorado in the final. They lost 4-0. See, there, they weren't that good. Yeah, right.

How in the world did they get so far? Let us count the ways:

* **Pride** - instilled by coach and veteran players

* **Hard Work** - ditto above

* **Heart** - ditto above

* **Stability** - very few trades during the season. The moves they did make were the right ones

* **Coaching**

* **Toughness**

* **Goaltending**

* **Balanced Non-Scoring** - if a player was in a scoring slump, big deal, he wasn't scoring that much anyway. Besides all the players contributed in more ways than their scoring

* **Great penalty killing**

* **Excellent forechecking and excellent backchecking**

* **Dave Lowry** - the scoring machine notched 10 playoff goals, the same total he had during the regular season

* **Lack of Talent** - sounds ridiculous, but because they were aware the other team had more of it, the Panther players knew they had to work harder.

* **Rat Power** - It all started when Scott Mellanby killed a rat in the dressing room, and then went out that night and scored two goals - a rat-trick. That started the phenomenon that ensured the support of the fans. Some rats with parachutes, some with strings attached, some parking lots giving away free rats. Sure it was crazy. While many considered the rat infestation overkill, it was great for the Miami fans, and great for the game. And it made playing in the Miami Arena awfully tough for opposing players.

Those are some of the reasons why they did so well, but it's all hindsight. There were plenty of reasons why they couldn't be so successful. Some of them the same reasons as above. Throw in lack of experience, lack of scoring talent and so on.

Whatever it is, the Panthers did something special.

TEAM PREVIEW

GOAL: There was trouble with Vanbiesbrouck before last season ever began. He was unhappy with his contract situation and his agent asked GM Bryan Murray to look into a trade.

You could understand the Panthers reluctance to hand out the big money for a long-term contract to an aging goalie, especially considering it would probably be a while until the team became competitive.

Anyway, Murray said nobody was interested in Vanbiesbrouck.

Vanbiesbrouck had a good regular season, but not a great one. And then he had a great playoffs, which is what you want most out of a goaltender anyway. His playoff save percentage of .932 was best in the league, and his miniscule goals against average of 2.25, was fifth.

Backup Mark Fitzpatrick has all kinds of problems off the ice, but does the job on the ice, which is all they can ask for.

DEFENCE: The Panthers have the nucleus of an outstanding defence for years to come.

Ed Jovanovski is the key. He was the best rookie in the league last year. He started his season late, however, after breaking a finger in a pre-season fight, but not too late for *The Hockey News* to recognize him as their rookie of the year.

Next up for Jovanovski is the all-star team. Already, newcomers are being compared to him. He does it all - hits hard, is a competitor, contributes on offence, and is a dominating presence on the ice. Best of all, he's going to get better. Look for him among Norris trophy candidates as soon as this year.

Another rookie who has impressed is Rhett Warrener, who won a gold medal for Canada in the World Junior Championships. First year player, Robert Svehla was outstanding offensively, with 57 points. He was too old, however, to be officially considered a rookie, but otherwise would have been in the running for the Calder Trophy. He only had four fewer points than the winner, Ottawa forward, Daniel Alfredsson.

Paul Laus is the enforcer on the blueline, but he can play, too. Jason Woolley is an offensive threat, mostly for the power play. Veteran Terry Carkner provides more toughness, and leadership. Gord Murphy is another veteran who has grown up with the Panthers, as is Geoff Smith. Magnus Svensson is an older Swede who didn't get to play very often.

The Panthers are big on stability, and part of their success is letting the team grow together. That doesn't always work, but in this case it did, and will. Count on the Panther defensive nucleus staying put for many years to come.

FORWARD: If you're hard working, defensive-minded, team-oriented, and have a lot of character, then you have a chance to play for

GOALTENDER	GPI	MINS	AVG	W	L	T	EN	SO	GA	SA	SV %
J. VANBIESBROUCK	57	3178	2.68	26	20	7	2	2	142	1473	.904
MARK FITZPATRICK	34	1786	2.96	15	11	3	2	0	88	810	.891
FLA TOTALS	82	4979	2.82	41	31	10	4	2	234	2287	.898

this team. Others better do something else extremely well if they want to play regularly.

The only goal scorers of note are Ray Sheppard and Scott Mellanby. Sheppard doesn't do a lot of things well, except one - he puts the puck in the net. The Panthers got him for almost nothing from San Jose, exchanging some draft picks.

Mellanby is establishing himself as one of the league's better power forwards. Those type of guys play it tough, and put the puck in the net on the power play.

Rob Niedermayer had his breakout season last year, just when people were starting to wonder if he was a bust. He had 26 goals, twice what he accumulated in his first two seasons. It usually takes three or four years for a young player to come into his own. Niedermayer wasn't behind schedule at all.

Radek Dvorak had a pretty good start to his career, the only rookie of note among the Florida forwards. He was selected 10th in last year's draft, making him one of the few able to step right into the lineup in their draft year.

Johan Garpenlov had a decent season, often playing on the top line. Martin Straka, the other European forward, played on every team in the NHL last season before the Panthers obtained him on waivers from the Islanders. Actually, he just played for three teams, but in a few years be might be able to include the rest of them. He's one of those guys who plays well in spurts, but exasperates the other times. He couldn't play for Ottawa, and he couldn't play for the Islanders, who just didn't want him anymore. That should tell you what you need to know. If the Panthers can get him with the program they truly are miracle workers.

Captain Brian Skrudland may be the catalyst of this team. He leads a group of faceless castoffs and rejects, the guys who just know their value lies within the framework of the team. Many, such as Dave Lowry in the playoffs, have their individual time in the sun, but they know that's not what it's all about. If they don't go out there and work hard every shift, they know they can be replaced. If they don't buy into the team concept, they know they can find themselves with another team, or even the minors. They're hungry and desperate, scratching and biting, and they've already been thrown out of other places where they were no longer wanted. Hey, we might be able to get another rat analogy in here. The Rat Patrol consists of Dave Lowry, Mike Hough, Stu Barnes, Jody Hull, Tom Fitzgerald, and Bill Lindsay.

Down on the farm, the Carolina Monarchs didn't exactly fit into the Panthers mold. They gave up the most goals in the AHL and scored the second most. Brad Smyth led the league in scoring. He had 68 goals in 68 games and a total of 126 points. Mike Casselman also hit triple figures, with 102 points. Brett Harkins and Steve Washburn weren't far away. Certainly, some scorers to choose from there if they need one. Juniors David Nemirovsky and Jason Podollan could also get a chance.

SPECIAL TEAMS: The Panthers did what they could to beef up the power play when they obtained Ray Sheppard. It still remains that they don't have a lot of offensive types, so the responsibility falls on fewer shoulders. That means less room for error. They should remain middle to lower end of the pack.

Penalty killing is a different story, because they're loaded up on quality. They should finish mid to upper level in this area.

POWER PLAY	G	ATT	PCT
Overall	81	468	17.3% (16th NHL)
Home	45	254	17.7% (15th NHL)
Road	36	214	16.8% (T-12th NHL)

12 SHORT HANDED GOALS ALLOWED (T-14th NHL)

PENALTY KILLING	G	TSH	PCT
Overall	63	370	83.0% (T-9th NHL)
Home	27	185	85.4% (6th NHL)
Road	36	185	80.5% (18th NHL)

11 SHORT HANDED GOALS SCORED (T-12th NHL)

COACHING AND MANAGEMENT: So, Doug MacLean wasn't Bryan Murray's puppet afterall. MacLean, who finished second in coach of the year balloting to Scotty Bowman did an amazing job.

Many thought it was a ridiculous move to fire Roger Neilson and hire MacLean, who had 35 games of professional head coaching experience. MacLean had been a long-time NHL assistant, however, so it wasn't as if he didn't know what was going on.

MacLean got the best out of his team, and in the process showed us how smart he is.

Murray's job was just as impressive. He made all the right moves, and seems committed to building this team with character.

DRAFT

Round	Sel.	Player	Pos	
1	20	Marcus Nilsson	W	Sweden
3	60	Chris Allen	D	Kingston (OHL)
3	65	Oleg Kvasha	W	Russia
4	82	Joey Tetarenko	D	Portland (WHL)
5	129	Andrew Long	LW	Guelph (OHL)
6	156	Gaetan Poirier	LW	Merrimack (Univ.)
7	183	Alexandre Couture	D	Victoriaville (QMJHL)
8	209	Denis Kloptnov	G	Russia
9	235	Russell Smith	D	Hull (QMJHL)

Marcus Nilsson was rated much higher by the Panthers than he was selected. In *The Hockey News*, he was ranked 10th. Nilsson is supposed to be a goal scorer who needs work on his skating.

Third round selection, Chris Allen, was ranked much higher than he was taken as well. He's known for his booming shot, and in an extreme rarity for a defenceman, had more goals than assists (21-17-38) for Kingston in the OHL last season. Other parts of his game haven't measured up yet, but if he can improve on those, he's been talked about as the next Al MacInnis.

PROGNOSIS: Bad News. The Panthers aren't going to finals again this year.

Worse news. The playoffs aren't even a certainty.

What they accomplished last year was magical. But, it's a funny thing about teams that get where they do from hard work, as opposed to talent. It doesn't always work as well as it did the previous season.

And it won't get any easier this time around. They won't be taking anybody by surprise anymore, for one thing. For another, they don't have a lot of talent to fall back on.

The team will be hard pressed to remain motivated over the regular season after what they went through in the playoffs. They will feel almost like exhibtion games to them, and they'll be a chore at times.

Was last season a fluke?
Yes, it was.

PREDICTION:
Atlanta Division: 5th
Eastern Conference: 7th
Overall: 12th

Team Rankings 1995-96

	Conference Rank	League Rank
Record	41-31-10	4	8
Home	25-12-4	3	5
Away	16-19-6	9	14
Versus Own Conference	29-22-5	6	8
Versus Other Conference	12-9-5	8	12
Team Plus\Minus	+2	8	14
Goals For	254	6	12
Goals Against	234	3	5
Average Shots For	28.8	9	19
Average Shots Against	27.8	5	7
Overtime	0-3-10	11	24
One Goal Games	14-12	4	9
Times outshooting opponent	40	7	12
Versus Teams Over .500	19-21-5	6	8
Versus Teams Under .500	22-10-5	6	7
First Half Record	27-12-2	3	4
Second Half Record	14-19-8	10	19

Results: Defeated Boston 4-1
Defeated Philadelphia 4-2
Defeated Pittsburgh 4-3

Lost to Colorado 4-0
Record: 12-10
Home: 7-4
Away: 5-6
Goals For: 61 (2.8 per game)
Goals Against: 57 (2.6 per game)
Overtime: 2-1
Power play: 12.8% (12th)
Penalty Killing: 80.6% (11th)

ALL-TIME LEADERS

GOALS
Scott Mellanby	75
Jesse Belanger	49
Stu Barnes	47

ASSISTS
Scott Mellanby	80
Jesse Belanger	68
Gord Murphy	67

POINTS
Scott Mellanby	155
Jesse Belanger	120
Stu Barnes	111

BEST INDIVIDUAL SEASONS

GOALS
Scott Mellanby	1995-96	32
Scott Mellanby	1993-94	30
Rob Niedermayer	1995-96	26

ASSISTS

Robert Svelha	1995-96	49
Scott Mellanby	1995-96	38
Rob Niedermayer	1995-96	35

POINTS

Scott Mellanby	1995-96	70
Rob Niedermayer	1995-96	61
Scott Mellanby	1993-94	60

TEAM RECORD

Last 3 years

	GP	W	L	T	Pts	%
1995-96	82	41	31	10	92	.561
1994-95	48	20	22	6	46	.479
1993-94	84	33	34	17	83	.494

Best 3 regular seasons

1995-96	82	41	31	10	92	.561
1993-94	84	33	34	17	83	.494
1994-95	48	20	22	6	46	.479

Worst 3 regular seasons

1994-95	48	20	22	6	46	.479
1993-94	84	33	34	17	83	.494
1995-96	82	41	31	10	92	.561

Most Goals (min. 70 game schedule)

1995-96	254
1993-94	233

Fewest Goals (min. 70 game schedule)

1993-94	233
1995-96	254

Most Goals Against (min. 70 game schedule)

1995-96	234
1993-94	233

Fewest Goals Against (min. 70 game schedule)

1993-94	233
1995-96	234

STAT SECTION

Team Scoring Stats

	GP	G	A	PTS	+/-	PIM	SH	Power Play			Short Handed		
								G	A	P	G	A	P
SCOTT MELLANBY	79	32	38	70	4	160	225	19	16	35	0	0	0
ROB NIEDERMAYER	82	26	35	61	1	107	155	11	12	23	0	0	0
RAY SHEPPARD	70	37	23	60	19-	16	231	14	9	23	0	0	0
ROBERT SVEHLA	81	8	49	57	3-	94	146	7	27	34	0	2	2
JOHAN GARPENLOV	82	23	28	51	10-	36	130	8	14	22	0	0	0
STU BARNES	72	19	25	44	12-	46	158	8	13	21	0	0	0
MARTIN STRAKA	77	13	30	43	19-	41	98	6	9	14	0	0	0
JODY HULL	78	20	17	37	5	25	120	2	1	3	0	3	3
TOM FITZGERALD	82	13	21	34	3-	75	141	1	1	2	6	0	6
BILL LINDSAY	73	12	22	34	13	57	118	0	0	0	3	3	6
JASON WOOLLEY	52	6	28	34	9-	32	98	3	19	22	0	0	0
GORD MURPHY	70	8	22	30	5	30	125	4	11	15	0	2	2
RADEK DVORAK	77	13	14	27	5	20	126	0	1	1	0	0	0
BRIAN SKRUDLAND	79	7	20	27	6	129	90	0	1	1	1	1	2
DAVE LOWRY	63	10	14	24	2-	36	83	0	5	5	0	0	0
MIKE HOUGH	64	7	16	23	4	37	66	0	0	0	1	0	1
ED JOVANOVSKI	70	10	11	21	3-	137	116	2	3	5	0	0	0
TERRY CARKNER	73	3	10	13	10	80	42	1	2	3	0	0	0
MAGNUS SVENSSON	27	2	9	11	1-	21	58	2	7	9	0	0	0
GEOFF SMITH	31	3	7	10	4-	20	34	2	0	2	0	0	0
PAUL LAUS	78	3	6	9	2-	236	45	0	0	0	0	0	0
GILBERT DIONNE	7	1	3	4	0	0	12	0	0	0	0	0	0
BRETT HARKINS	8	0	3	3	2-	6	4	0	2	2	0	0	0
RHETT WARRENER	28	0	3	3	4	46	19	0	0	0	0	0	0
BRAD SMYTH	7	1	1	2	3-	4	12	1	1	2	0	0	0
DAVID NEMIROVSKY	9	0	2	2	1-	2	6	0	0	0	0	0	0
J. VANBIESBROUCK	57	0	2	2	0	10	0	0	0	0	0	0	0
STEVE WASHBURN	1	0	1	1	1	0	1	0	0	0	0	0	0
BOB KUDELSKI	13	0	1	1	1	0	23	0	0	0	0	0	0
MIKE CASSELMAN	3	0	0	0	1-	0	2	0	0	0	0	0	0
MARK FITZPATRICK	34	0	0	0	0	12	0	0	0	0	0	0	0

PLAYOFFS

PLAYER	GP	G	A	PTS	+/-	PIM	PP	SH	GW	OT	S	PCTG
DAVE LOWRY	22	10	7	17	8	39	4	0	2	1	45	22.2
RAY SHEPPARD	21	8	8	16	4	0	3	0	0	0	47	17.0
STU BARNES	22	6	10	16	10	4	2	0	2	0	57	10.5
BILL LINDSAY	22	5	5	10	6	18	0	1	1	0	33	15.2
SCOTT MELLANBY	22	3	6	9	10-	44	2	0	0	0	57	5.3
ED JOVANOVSKI	22	1	8	9	2	52	0	0	0	0	51	2.0
ROB NIEDERMAYER	22	5	3	8	8-	12	2	0	2	0	48	10.4
TOM FITZGERALD	22	4	4	8	3	34	0	0	2	0	31	12.9
JASON WOOLLEY	13	2	6	8	3	14	1	0	1	0	27	7.4
PAUL LAUS	21	2	6	8	3	62	0	0	0	0	18	11.1
JOHAN GARPENLOV	20	4	2	6	2-	8	0	0	0	0	35	11.4
ROBERT SVEHLA	22	0	6	6	3	32	0	0	0	0	38	.0
MIKE HOUGH	22	4	1	5	5	8	0	0	2	1	38	10.5
JODY HULL	14	3	2	5	4	0	0	0	0	0	18	16.7
MARTIN STRAKA	13	2	2	4	2-	2	0	0	0	0	20	10.0
RADEK DVORAK	16	1	3	4	2	0	0	0	0	0	36	2.8
BRIAN SKRUDLAND	21	1	3	4	6	18	0	0	0	0	27	3.7
GORD MURPHY	14	0	4	4	1	6	0	0	0	0	53	.0
TERRY CARKNER	22	0	4	4	8	10	0	0	0	0	15	.0
RHETT WARRENER	21	0	3	3	3	10	0	0	0	0	14	.0
STEVE WASHBURN	1	0	1	1	0	0	0	0	0	0	0	.0
J. VANBIESBROUCK	22	0	1	1	0	20	0	0	0	0	0	.0
GEOFF SMITH	1	0	0	0	1-	2	0	0	0	0	0	.0
MARK FITZPATRICK	2	0	0	0	0	0	0	0	0	0	0	.0

GOALTENDER	GPI	MINS	AVG	W	L	T	EN	GA	SA	SV %
J. VANBIESBROUCK	22	1332	2.25	12	10	0	1	50	735	.932
MARK FITZPATRICK	2	60	6.00	0	0	0	0	6	30	.800
FLA TOTALS	22	1397	2.45	12	10	0	1	57	766	.926

Hartford Whalers

Last year was really a couple seasons in one for the Whalers.

This is how the Whalers' year unfolded:

RECORD	OVERALL RECORD
Oct. 7 through Oct. 20	
4-0-1	4-0-1
Oct. 21 through Nov. 5	
1-6-0	5-6-1 Holmgren fired
Nov. 7 through Dec. 31	
6-15-4	11-21-5
Jan. 1 through Mar. 18	
19-10-2	30-31-7
Mar. 20 through Apr.14	
4-8-2	34-39-9

For two and a half months at the start of the new year, the team came together. After a terrible start, they made it back to within one game of .500, but then faltered down the stretch, finishing 11 points back of a playoff spot.

Part of the early problem was that Brendan Shanahan injured his wrist on opening night and it bothered him for the first part of the season. Once he got rolling, he became the impact player he was expected to be when Hartford traded for him from St. Louis.

In the second half, the Whalers were one of the most improved teams. The chart below shows the top four.

Team	First Half (%)	Second Half (%)	Impt
Calgary	12-22-7 (.378)	22-15-4 (.585)	.207
Hartford	14-22-5 (.402)	20-17-4 (.537)	.134
San Jose	7-30-4 (.220)	13-25-3 (.354)	.134
Anaheim	15-22-3 (.415)	20-17-4 (.537)	.122

Given the Whalers' financial situation, it's tough to figure out if the second half improvement is good news. Normally it would be, because it shows the team is coming together, and with some potential still unrealized, it would be cause for optimism. But, if the Whalers are going to be guided by financial restraints, it's no news, because the team won't be allowed to continue their growth.

Another side of the coin is that they have a lot of players in their prime. That often means they can expect a couple of career years. Combine that with the second half improvement and they have something.

Ages of key scorers, as of October 1, 1996:

Brendan Shanahan	27
Geoff Sanderson	24
Nelson Emerson	29
Andrew Cassels	29
Andrei Nikolishin	23
Jeff Brown	30
Jeff O'Neill	20
Robert Kron	29

While we're searching for something here, the reality is that the Whalers don't have an identity. Nothing to make them stand out from other teams. Nothing that says, these are the Whalers. Nothing special.

Shanahan was supposed to provide that, but he can only do so much. As well, there's the constant threat of a trade hanging over his head. Everybody denies everything in these circumstances, but the club has worrisome fiscal responsibilities, and he gets paid a lot of money.

When the new ownership came aboard, it looked like there could be a new era beginning in Hartford. They seemed determined to do the right thing in all facets of the team. Now they just seem determined to save some money until they can get out of town. Not that it's their fault, it's just the nature of the beast.

Great intentions and great expectations.

Some other time.

TEAM PREVIEW

GOAL: Sean Burke was the Hartford Whaler's MVP, for the third consecutive season. He played in a career high 66 games and won 28 of them, also a career best. He also tied a team record with 22 consecutive starts.

The last mark is a growing trend in the NHL. Most teams are picking out their number one goalie and sticking with him the majority of the time.

It used to be that hockey people didn't want to play their top goalie too often for fear of tiring him out. That's no longer much of a consideration, either because teams are desperate to win more often, because they want to get their money's worth with what they're paying number one goalies these days, or because it's just not necessary to provide the rest.

In fact, there's more evidence to suggest that goalies stay sharper the more they play. See Grant Fuhr.

The change in philosophy is notable, even in the last five years. Last season, there were six goalies who played 65 or more games, and more who would have if not for injuries. In the 1990-91 season, there were just two. This season, it wouldn't be surprising if more than ten played at least 65 games.

Backup Jason Muzzatti had something to prove when Calgary pushed him aside, allowing the Whalers to pick him up on waivers. He did an outstanding job as a backup, even posting slightly better numbers than Burke.

DEFENCE: Unless you're big, forget about playing on the Hartford Whaler's defence. Consider their top six:

Brian Glynn	6-4, 218
Glen Featherstone	6-4, 209
Gerald Diduck	6-2, 217
Adam Burt	6-2, 207
Glen Wesley	6-1, 197
Jeff Brown	6-1, 204

Add to that, their top defensive prospect, Marek Malik, who is 6-5, 190, and you have one of the biggest defence units in the league.

Big is good, but is not always better. Some teams have a big defence, but don't play like it. Most of these guys are physical types. Most are also stay-at-home defencemen.

The Whalers don't count on Brown staying home too often, that's not his role. He is an offensive quarterback and he does that part of his job well. He struggled in Vancouver, and had problems with management, but in Hartford he had 38 points in 48 games, and filled a hole the team has had for a long time.

Gone this year is elder statesman Brad McCrimmon, who led the team with a plus 15, and provided the veteran leadership on the blueline. He signed on as a free agent with Phoenix.

There's nothing flashy in the above group of defencemen. You won't find them on all-star teams, Team Canada rosters, or contending for any awards. They just do their job, and as a unit that can be pretty good. They must be doing something right, because the Whalers allowed the fewest goals in team history last season.

FORWARD: There's only a few dependable scorers here. Actually, only one when you get right down to it - Brendan Shanahan.

For some reason, the Whalers have a lot of players who are up and down from year to year in the scoring department.

Sanderson had 34 goals last season, after getting 46 and 41 in his previous two full seasons. Cassels was 22 points behind his career high of 85. Emerson had two seasons with point totals in the seventies with St. Louis and Winnipeg, before falling to 58 last year.

The thing about point totals, however, is that if they go down together, they can go up together. That's why putting freshman centre O'Neill on the top line last year was questionable strategy. It was obvious early that he wasn't ready to match his junior scoring totals at the NHL level right away, so by playing him regularly with the best people, he could have been pulling down the scoring of others. In fact, it was reported that one of the reasons Paul Holmgren was fired was that he wasn't playing O'Neill enough.

O'Neill's very likely going to be a star, and it could have happened last year. They had to give it a try. But, using hindsight, maybe it would have been more prudent to let him earn his way by starting him on the third line.

One other thing about youngsters, although it doesn't necessarily fit in this case, they can be intimidated playing with the top players. Instead of playing their own game, they're trying to suit their style to that of their linemates. When they're put out with lesser players they can be the driving force, and through it, gain more confidence.

Andrei Nikolishin started to emerge last

GOALTENDER	GPI	MINS	AVG	W	L	T	EN	SO	GA	SA	SV %
JASON MUZZATTI	22	1013	2.90	4	8	3	3	1	49	551	.911
JEFF REESE	7	275	3.05	2	3	0	0	1	14	170	.918
SEAN BURKE	66	3669	3.11	28	28	6	3	4	190	2034	.907
HFD TOTALS	82	4979	3.12	34	39	9	6	6	259	2761	.906

year in the second half, and was one of the team's top scorers once he got going.

Down the middle, are O'Neill, Cassels, Nikolishin and tough guy Mark Janssens. A possible and likely addition to that group is Hnat Domenichelli. He was 59-89-148 last year for the Kamloops Blazers in the WHL, and has the experience of two Memorial Cup victories, and one World Junior championship.

On the left side are Shanahan, Sanderson, Paul Ranheim, and Sami Kapanen. Kevin Smyth could get a shot there as well.

On right wing are Nelson Emerson; Robert Kron, who tied his career high with 50 points; Steven Rice; veteran leader Kevin Dineen, and enforcer Kelly Chase.

Some hope, but a lot of ifs, and a lot of maybes. Maybe if some players had career years, they'd be okay. Maybe if the youngsters started shooting the lights out, they'd be okay. Maybe if Shanahan is healthy right from the start the team will have a better overall record.

Maybe. But, maybe not.

SPECIAL TEAMS: The Whalers needed a power play quarterback last season, and picked up one of the better ones in Jeff Brown in a trade with Vancouver. Before Brown, the Whalers were near the bottom of the league with a 14.4% (23-160) power play efficiency. After Brown they were good for 20.7% (44-212), a considerable improvement.

There's a good crew of snipers and playmakers up front so that they could improve on 13th overall. Shanahan had 17 power play markers to lead the team, four short of the team record of 21, set by Sanderson in 1992-93.

The penalty killing was poor once again. Only a few teams gave up more goals when down a man, so an improvement there could translate into more wins.

POWER PLAY	G	ATT	PCT	
Overall	67	372	18.0%	(T-13th NHL)
Home	42	207	20.3%	(12th NHL)
Road	25	165	15.2%	(20th NHL)

9 SHORT HANDED GOALS ALLOWED (T-7th NHL)

PENALTY KILLING	G	TSH	PCT	
Overall	83	429	80.7%	(19th NHL)
Home	39	213	81.7%	(16th NHL)
Road	44	216	79.6%	(19th NHL)

8 SHORT HANDED GOALS SCORED (T-21st NHL)

COACHING AND MANAGEMENT: The Whalers say they're committed to staying in Hartford for the next two years, but that the purse strings will be tighter. Does that mean there's going to be a selloff of the high-priced talent? Maybe not right away, and maybe not so obviously, but you have to figure it will be a consideration for every player.

That means they're doomed to failure. It's not that teams can't make do with less money in some cases, but it often fosters a losing attitude.

The Save the Whale campaign didn't work, and owner Peter Karmanos would like to get out of town as quickly as possible and make some real money. They didn't get the money in State aid they were looking for, and it would cost them too much to get out of their lease. They'll be history in two years unless something drastic happens.

Rutherford hasn't distinguished himself as a general manager, but is aware of one of the key ingredients for winning. He wants character players, and he tries to get them. He doesn't seem to have much patience however, despite the fact that it's a trait he talks about. He wants the players to grow into the team and become a cohesive unit. But, they haven't played well enough to allow him that luxury. And in today's NHL, with more freedom of movement, it's a difficult concept to execute anyway.

Paul Holmgren was fired after just 12 games. That was after starting the season at 4-0. The Whalers tied one, then lost five in a row. During the losing slide, however, they were shut out three times.

Rutherford was critical of the team's work ethic, as well as the benching of rookie Jeff O'Neill. It's not difficult to see how the two could be at odds over that one. It becomes a conflict of interest. Rutherford is looking down the road, while Holmgren was looking at the present knowing that he could be fired if the team didn't win right away. They didn't, he was fired.

Holmgren was replaced by 28-year-old Paul Maurice, who didn't perform any miracles. But, he seems to be a student of the game, and understands the important factors in making a team a winner.

Rutherford said that he wasn't interested in trading Shanahan and that people spreading the rumors should at least have the courtesy to call him.

That's an interesting comment, coming from him. I recall trying to call Rutherford about seven times over a week span a while back. He didn't have the courtesy to return the phone calls. I ran up my long distance budget fencing with his secretary, and after figuring it would be easier to get through to the President, never bothered trying anymore. Maybe that's why they didn't call.

DRAFT

Round	Sel.	Player	Pos	
2	34	Trevor Wasyluk	LW	Medicine Hat (WHL)
3	61	Andrei Petrunen	R-LW	Russia
4	88	Craig MacDonald	C	Harvard
4	104	Steve Wasylko	C	Detroit (OHL)
5	116	Mark McMahon	D	Kitchener (OHL)
6	143	Aaron Baker	G	Tri-City (WHL)
7	171	Greg Kuznik	D	Seattle (WHL)
8	197	Kevin Marsh	LW	Calgary (WHL)
9	223	Craig Adams	RW	Harvard
9	231	Ashkat Rakhmatullin	W	Russia

No first round choice for the Whalers again as they continue to live down the trade with Boston for three first rounders. Presumably, Rutherford has learned the value of draft selections in the first round. Last year's gift, Kyle McLaren, ended up playing regularly for the Bruins, while this year they nabbed another in the top ten. The Whalers only have one more to go, which is in next year's talent laden draft.

The Whalers got Wasyluk in the second round. He's considered a player with a lot of talent, who hasn't shown everything yet, and doesn't show everything every game. Hartford thinks he'll be a good one if he motivates himself to play consistently.

PROGNOSIS: With the Whalers playing a much improved game in the second half, they could carry that on, and maybe make the playoffs this year. The problem is that even with the improved play, they still weren't a .500 hockey team. With little expected in the way of added impact players, due to financial restraints, their only hope of getting better is if youngsters Jeff O'Neill and Andrei Nikolishin show tremendous scoring improvement, and some of the other forwards have career years. Rookie scoring from junior sensation Hnat Domenichelli would be a welcome bonus. Most important, as Shanahan goes, the team goes, so having him healthy right from the start will help.

No problem in goal with Burke, and the defence is sound. It could be close, but with the competition in the Eastern Conference they're not quite there.

PREDICTION:

Northeast Division: 4th

Eastern Conference: 10th

Overall: 19th

Team Rankings 1995-96

		Conference Rank	League Rank
Record	34-39-9	10	19
Home	22-15-4	8	10
Away	12-24-5	11	21
Versus Own Conference	19-29-8	11	21
Versus Other Conference	15-10-1	4	6
Team Plus\Minus	-6	9	15
Goals For	237	9	19
Goals Against	259	8	15
Average Shots For	30.4	7	12
Average Shots Against	33.6	11	22
Overtime	2-3-9	8	19
One Goal Games	12-13	11	18
Times outshooting opponent	30	10	20
Versus Teams Over .500	14-28-6	11	17
Versus Teams Under .500	20-11-3	8	12
First Half Record	14-22-5	11	20
Second Half Record	20-17-4	7	12

PLAYOFFS

- Did not make the playoffs

ALL-TIME LEADERS

GOALS

Ron Francis	264
Blaine Stoughton	219
Kevin Dineen	216

ASSISTS

Ron Francis	557
Kevin Dineen	239
Pat Verbeek	211

POINTS

Ron Francis	821
Kevin Dineen	455
Pat Verbeek	403

BEST INDIVIDUAL SEASONS

GOALS

Blaine Stoughton	1979-80	56
Blaine Stoughton	1981-82	52
Geoff Sanderson	1992-93	46

ASSISTS

Ron Francis	1989-90	69
Mike Rogers	1980-81	65
Andrew Cassels	1992-93	65

POINTS

Mike Rogers	1979-80	105
Mike Rogers	1980-81	105
Ron Francis	1989-90	101

TEAM RECORD

Last 3 years

	GP	W	L	T	Pts	%
1995-96	82	34	39	9	77	.470
1994-95	48	19	24	5	43	.448
1993-94	84	26	52	6	58	.371

Best 3 regular seasons

	GP	W	L	T	Pts	%
1986-87	80	43	30	7	93	.600
1989-90	80	38	33	9	85	.531
1985-86	80	40	36	4	84	.525

Worst 3 regular seasons

	GP	W	L	T	Pts	%
1982-83	80	19	54	7	45	.281
1992-93	84	26	52	6	58	.345
1993-94	84	27	48	9	63	.375

Most Goals (min. 70 game schedule)

1985-86	332
1979-89	303
1988-89	299

Fewest Goals (min. 70 game schedule)

1993-94	227
1995-96	237
1990-91	238

Most Goals Against (min. 70 game schedule)

1982-83	403
1980-81	372
1992-93	369

Fewest Goals Against (min. 70 game schedule)

1995-96	259
1987-88	267
1989-90	268

STAT SECTION

Team Scoring Stats

	GP	G	A	PTS	+/-	PIM	SH	Power Play			Short Handed		
								G	A	P	G	A	P
BRENDAN SHANAHAN	74	44	34	78	2	125	280	17	14	31	2	1	3
GEOFF SANDERSON	81	34	31	65	0	40	314	6	15	21	0	0	0
ANDREW CASSELS	81	20	43	63	8	39	135	6	17	23	0	2	2
NELSON EMERSON	81	29	29	58	7-	78	247	12	16	28	2	0	2
JEFF BROWN	76	8	47	55	8	56	177	5	26	31	0	0	0
ANDREI NIKOLISHIN	61	14	37	51	2-	34	83	4	12	16	1	1	2
ROBERT KRON	77	22	28	50	1-	6	203	8	9	17	1	2	3
PAUL RANHEIM	73	10	20	30	2-	14	126	0	2	2	1	2	3
JEFF O'NEILL	65	8	19	27	3-	40	65	1	3	4	0	0	0
GLEN WESLEY	68	8	16	24	9-	88	129	6	9	15	0	0	0
STEVEN RICE	59	10	12	22	4-	47	108	1	3	4	0	0	0
ADAM BURT	78	4	9	13	4-	121	90	0	1	1	0	0	0
GLEN FEATHERSTONE	68	2	10	12	10	138	62	0	0	0	0	0	0
KEVIN DINEEN	46	2	9	11	1-	117	66	0	3	3	0	0	0
GERALD DIDUCK	79	1	9	10	7	88	93	0	0	0	0	1	1
SAMI KAPANEN	35	5	4	9	0	6	46	0	0	0	0	0	0
BRAD MCCRIMMON	58	3	6	9	15	62	39	0	0	0	1	0	1
MARK JANSSENS	81	2	7	9	13-	155	63	0	0	0	0	0	0
SCOTT DANIELS	53	3	4	7	4-	254	43	0	0	0	0	0	0
KELLY CHASE	55	2	4	6	4-	230	19	0	0	0	0	0	0
SEAN BURKE	66	0	6	6	0	16	1	0	0	0	0	0	0
STEVE MARTINS	23	1	3	4	3-	8	27	0	0	0	0	0	0
BRIAN GLYNN	54	0	4	4	5-	44	46	0	3	3	0	0	0
KEVIN SMYTH	21	2	1	3	5-	8	27	1	0	1	0	0	0
JIMMY CARSON	11	1	0	1	1	0	9	0	0	0	0	0	0
ALEXANDER GODYNYUK	3	0	0	0	1-	2	1	0	0	0	0	0	0
JASON MCBAIN	3	0	0	0	1-	0	0	0	0	0	0	0	0
MAREK MALIK	7	0	0	0	3-	4	2	0	0	0	0	0	0
JASON MUZZATTI	22	0	0	0	0	33	0	0	0	0	0	0	0

Montreal Canadiens

There's nothing uneventful about a Montreal Canadiens season. Somebody sneezes in the wrong language, and it's headlines the next day.

This past season was even more eventful than usual.

Event - captain Mike Keane said it wasn't necessary for him to speak French because the team's on-ice business was conducted in English. Well...off with his head. The ridiculous fervor caused among the zealots in the press was typical, and timely because of the approaching referendum vote on separation.

Event - the arrival of the team's savior - Saku Koivu. It was more of a non-event, as the hero couldn't live up to early expectations. The tiny centre scored 20 goals and 25 assists, not an auspicious debut. One season is hardly a good indicator, and where his true talent lies will become evident within the next two years.

Event - the season opener is a disaster. They lose 7-1 to Philadelphia, with Patrick Roy lasting only 22 minutes and allowing five goals. Game two they lost 6-1 in Miami, game three was a 3-1 loss in Tampa Bay, and game four was a home 4-1 defeat by New Jersey. An 0-4 start, outscored 20-4. Then it hit the fan.

Event - D-Day. Fired - coach, Jacques Demers; GM Serge Savard; assistant coach and director of scouting, Andre Boudrias; scout Carol Vadnais. Hired - coach, Mario Tremblay; GM Rejean Houle.

Event - the Aftermath. In the next 14 games, the Canadiens had a record of 12-2.

Event - the Referendum. You don't think that has an impact on hockey? Well, could they still be called the Montreal Canadiens? For those outside of Canada, the vote was no to Quebec separating from Canada.

Event - Brian Savage. Twenty games into the season, he had 17 goals. The second coming? Nothing could stop him. In the next 62 games, he managed just eight goals.

Event - the Game. Probably the most high-lighted game of the season, you know the one. That's when the Canadiens got bombed 11-1 by Detroit, in Montreal. It's the one where Roy lifts his arms in mock appreciation of an easy save. It's the one where Roy was kept in the net for nine goals, and that was just past the halfway mark of the second period. When finally lifted, Roy walked on the bench by Tremblay who was staring him down, and then walked back to team president Ronald Corey, where he told him it was his last game as a Canadien.

Event - the Trade. Patrick Roy and Mike Keane to Colorado for Jocelyn Thibault, Andrei Kovalenko and Martin Rucinsky.

Event - Martin Rucinsky on Fire. It didn't happen right after the trade, but Rucinsky went to town. He had 19 points during one 10-game stretch, but the best way to show Rucinsky's improvement is to break it down by season halves. In the first half his scoring stats were 8-15-23. In the second half, they were 21-31-52.

Event - the Flip. In Denver, the first meeting of Colorado and Montreal since the trade, the Avalanche won 4-2. At the end of the game, Roy flipped the puck to Tremblay, who was walking across the ice.

Event - the last game in the Montreal Forum. The event of the year. The walk down memory lane was an emotional occasion for everyone, even for long-time Hab-haters in Toronto.

Event - the first game in the Molson Centre.

Event - game one of the playoffs. The Canadiens win the game in Madison Square Garden, getting their 12th consecutive playoff overtime win on a goal by Vincent Damphousse.

Event - game two of the playoffs. Montreal wins again, this time 5-3, to take a 2-0 lead in the series, with both victories coming on the road. Plans for another Stanley Cup parade were being intialized.

Event - four games later, Montreal is out of the playoffs.

TEAM PREVIEW

GOAL: Patrick Roy might have been responsible for a Stanley Cup victory in Colorado, but he was likely tapped out in Montreal. After a poor start, however, he was playing well under Tremblay, until, of course, the celebrated incident.

Thibault did an outstanding job for the Canadiens. Just 20 years old, he didn't let the pressure get to him, and was able to post stats that were better than Roy was doing in Montreal.

Mind you, Roy is a playoff goalie extaordinaire, and Thibault is not, yet. That's where he's going to have to prove himself. When and if he does, then he doesn't have to worry about being the next Patrick Roy, somebody else will be trying to be the next Jocelyn Thibault.

Just for the record, during Roy's time in Montreal, he had 13 different backups. Here's the list: Pat Jablonski, Patrick Labrecque, Les Kuntar, Ron Tugnutt, Frederic Chabot, Andre Racicot, Roland Melanson, J.C. Bergeron, Brian Hayward, Randy Exelby, Vincent Riendeau, Doug Soeteart, and Steve Penney.

The Habs have a couple of players who'd like to vie at least for the backup role. Pat Jablonski, tossed around from team to team, deserves it. He played well most of the time when called upon. The problem is that there are kids waiting for their shot.

Patrick Labrecque, Martin Brochu and Jose Theodore are all considered potential goalies for the Canadiens.

DEFENCE: One problem at a time. Two years ago, the Habs' defence was small, meek and mild. Now, they're just meek and mild. And they can't score.

While they're not terrible, they're anything but a Stanley Cup contending defence.

Stephane Quintal and especially Lyle Odelein are just about the only toughness they have. Scoring is almost non-existent.

The Habs had 23 goals from their defencemen. Only New Jersey, with one fewer, had less. The top point-getter, Patrice Brisebois, had just 36 points, one of the lowest for a team's defenceman leader. Even at that, it was his best offensive season.

Vladimir Malakhov, who has a career high of 57 points, had just 28 goals, and was a constant source of disappointment, not to mention trade rumors.

David Wilkie has earned a spot, and perhaps so has Rory Fitzpatrick, who played each of the playoff games. That leaves Peter Popovic to round out the defence corps.

A lot of other youngers were tried during the season: Marko Kiprusoff, tough guy Craig Rivet, and Francois Groleau. Depending on the injury situation, or training camp, they should get another shot.

Brad Brown is just what the team could use, if and when he's ready. The first round pick in 1994, 18th overall, finally signed last year, and played the last half of the season in Fredericton. He's a big, tough, physical defenceman. A perfect fit.

The Habs have tried to find that type of guy, already in the NHL, but so far it hasn't worked out. Robert Dirk was the latest failed experiment.

The team could also use a quarterback. But, something happens to offensive defencemen when they hit Montreal, almost like a jinx, people who have performed well other places - ecent failures, offensively, include Malakhov and Yves Racine.

This is one position that will probably undergo some changes, if not before the start of the season, than not long into it.

FORWARD: There's potential here for the Montreal forwards to be among the best in the league. You wouldn't guess it though by their goal total from last year, 265, which was their lowest since the 1969-70 season.

But, you might if you consider these factors:

1. Last year, they had eight 20-goal scorers. Some teams have a few guys who can score, some have almost none. Nobody had eight.

2. They're young or in their prime, all of them. Not an oldster in the bunch.

GOALTENDER	GPI	MINS	AVG	W	L	T	EN	SO	GA	SA	SV %
JOCELYN THIBAULT	40	2334	2.83	23	13	3	2	3	110	1258	.913
PAT JABLONSKI	23	1264	2.94	5	9	6	4	0	62	676	.908
PATRICK ROY	22	1260	2.95	12	9	1	0	1	62	667	.907
PATRICK LABRECQUE	2	98	4.29	0	1	0	0	0	7	47	.851
JOSE THEODORE	1	9	6.67	0	0	0	0	0	1	2	.500
MTL TOTALS	82	4987	2.98	40	32	10	6	4	248	2656	.907

3. They didn't get much help from the defence. If the Canadiens can get a major offensive threat from the blueline, he's going to make the forwards better scorers.

4. Potential for more still there. It's not a case of what you see is what you get. Saku Koivu and Valeri Bure were just rookies last year. Others, such as Brian Savage and Martin Rucinsky have shown some great stuff, but not yet for an entire season.

5. Can put together three good scoring lines.

Pierre Turgeon, Damphousse, Koivu and Marc Bureau give them strength down the middle. Bureau handles the defensive chores, while Turgeon, Damphousse and Koivu can fight it out for scoring wingers.

Turgeon sometimes goes into mysterious slumps, but he did lead the team in scoring, his third different team. The Islanders and Buffalo were the others. He also scored 17 power play goals, just three short of the team record.

Koivu might be a good candidate for improvement. He came into the season with higher expectations than he could meet. He wasn't the savior as had been prematurely announced, and he wasn't a lock for rookie-of-the-year.

Damphousse had another great season. His 96 points were just one shy of his career high of 97. His only negative is that he usually gets off to a slow start, then burns up the league in the second half. He makes those around him play better, takes care of his own end, plays a determined game, kills penalties, and works the power play. He might be one of the more underated players in the game.

On the right side, they can choose from Mark Recchi, Valeri Bure, Chris Murray and Turner Stevenson.

Recchi, for some reason, was rumored to be traded often last season. Twenty-eight goals were his lowest in his career, but he's a perfect compliment to a scoring centre like Turgeon, and can just as easily move back up to the 40 goal, 100 point plateau. Bure was a pleasant surprise, scoring two more goals than Koivu, who was the more celebrated rookie. Big, tough, Chris Murray is an attempt to compensate for the lack of size from the Montreal forwards. Any scoring they get from him is a bonus. Turner Stevenson is similar to Murray, but the first round pick from 1990 can contribute more in the scoring department.

Left wingers include Martin Rucinsky, Andrei Kovalenko, Brian Savage, Benoit Brunet and Donald Brashear.

If Rucinsky and Kovalenko can continue their scoring exploits from last year, it makes the trade with Colorado look better. Rucinsky, who had 28 goals, almost doubled his previous career goal total of 31, in 168 games. Kovalenko, also with 28, set his career high. One danger for both of them is that players traded during the season often put up better than normal numbers for the remainder of that season, and then return to form the next year. Kovalenko didn't have a great playoff, and is knocked for his inconsistency, so was knocked and rumored to be trade bait. That's a little unfair in his case, because he was far from the only player in the same boat.

Savage was going for the NHL goal record at the start of the season, as noted in the opening, but then came to a standstill. It will be interesting to see if he can gain some consistency. That leaves Donald Brashear, who's claim to fame, besides fighting, is that he was outscored by Detroit goaltender Chris

Osgood. One goal for Osgood, none for Brashear, who played 67 games, the most without a goal.

Among the younger players who will try for a spot are Darcy Tucker, rookie of the year in the AHL with 29-64-93. Craig Conroy, Scott Fraser, Darcy Tucker and Sebastien Bordeleau all had short auditions in Montreal last season, and have done well in the minors. Last year's top pick, Terry Ryan, slumped in the scoring department with Tri-City in the WHL. He went from 50 goals and 110 points, to 32 goals and 69 points, in 11 fewer games.

SPECIAL TEAMS: If the Canadiens had a legitimate power play quarterback there's no reason why their power play couldn't be among the top two or three in the league. They have a lot of guys who can put the puck in the net with the man-advantage, which means the second unit can score as well. Three players - Turgeon, Damphousse and Recchi, hit double figures, with Rucinsky, Koivu, Kovalenko and Bure not far away.

POWER PLAY	G	ATT	PCT	
Overall	77	405	19.0%	(8th NHL)
Home	42	195	21.5%	(7th NHL)
Road	35	210	16.7%	(T-14th NHL)

11 SHORT HANDED GOALS ALLOWED (T-12th NHL)

PENALTY KILLING	G	TSH	PCT	
Overall	68	382	82.2%	(13th NHL)
Home	38	190	80.0%	(22nd NHL)
Road	30	192	84.4%	(4th NHL)

15 SHORT HANDED GOALS SCORED (T-5th NHL)

COACHING AND MANAGEMENT: Who says experience is necessary? Mario Tremblay didn't have any and he did okay as coach. Rejean Houle didn't have any, and he did okay as general manager.

Tremblay brings enthusiasm and just seems to have a certain air about him. Enthusiasm wears thin, though. Just ask Jacques Demers. After a while, it no longer works as a motivating tool.

Houle did pretty well, too. He made some good deals, and did what he had to in a pressure-packed environment where every move is closely scrutinized - and then criticized.

Houle will have to make some changes to bring the team's game up a level, but he's shown he's not shy about pulling the trigger. His evaluations will have to include the contribution available from the farm system, built by Serge Savard, where there is a lot of good potential.

DRAFT

Round	Sel.	Player	Pos	Team
1	18	Matt Higgins	C	Moose Jaw (WHL)
2	44	Mathieu Garon	G	Victoriaville (QMJHL)
3	71	Arron Asham	C	Red Deer (WHL)
4	92	Kim Staal	C	Sweden
4	99	Etienne Drapeau	C	Beauport (QMJHL)
5	127	Daniel Archambault	D	Val d'Or (QMJHL)
6	154	Brett Clark	D	Maine University
7	181	Timo Vertala	W	Finland
8	207	Mattia Baldi	F	Switzerland
9	233	Michel Tremblay	LW	Shawinigan (QMJHL)

Higgins, who was thought to be a top ten pick, slipped through the cracks down to number 18. That's because he not considered a great skater, and while he's fairly big at 6-1, 170, he's not supposed to be very strong. He brings other things to the party, which include hockey sense, strong two-way play and work ethic. Those are the type of players that later, people will wonder why they weren't chosen sooner. More than a few NHLers have done well with similar qualities, and that includes Vincent Damphousse.

PROGNOSIS: The Canadiens are one of the more exciting young teams in the league. The difference between them and some of the other young teams is that Montreal has plenty of talent. And lots of tradition.

Montreal can put out two or three good scoring lines. Their first two, and possibly their first three, rank up there with the best in the league.

A steady summer rumor was that the Canadiens were trying to obtain Brendan Shanahan. That in itself would make them major contenders.

The defence needs some improvement. A quarterback would be nice, and a big bruiser would be good as well.

There are teams that will be more heavily favored than Montreal to win the Stanley Cup. Probably lots of them. But, don't count out the Canadiens. This could be their year.

PREDICTION:

Northeast Division: 2nd

Eastern Conference: 5th

Overall: 9th

Team Rankings 1995-96

		Conference Rank	League Rank
Record	40-32-10	6	9
Home	23-12-6	5	7
Away	17-20-4	7	12
Versus Own Conference	26-23-7	8	12
Versus Other Conference	14-9-3	5	7
Team Plus\Minus	+8	6	11
Goals For	265	5	10
Goals Against	248	6	11
Average Shots For	28.8	10	20
Average Shots Against	32.3	10	20
Overtime	2-3-10	7	17
One Goal Games	12-11	7	12
Times outshooting opponent	30	9	18
Versus Teams Over .500	16-19-6	7	9
Versus Teams Under .500	24-13-4	7	10
First Half Record	19-18-4	7	11
Second Half Record	21-14-6	4	6

Results: Lost to NY Rangers 4-2

Record: 2-4

Home: 0-3

Away: 2-1

Goals For: 17 (2.8 per game)

Goals Against: 19 (3.2 per game)

Overtime: 1-0

Power play: 9.7% (13th)

Penalty Killing: 74.2% (16th)

ALL-TIME LEADERS

GOALS

Maurice Richard	544
Guy Lafleur	518
Jean Beliveau	507

ASSISTS

Guy Lafleur	728
Jean Beliveau	712
Henri Richard	688

POINTS

Guy Lafleur	1,246
Jean Beliveau	1,219
Henri Richard	1,046

BEST INDIVIDUAL SEASONS

GOALS

Steve Shutt	1976-77	60
Guy Lafleur	1977-78	60
Guy Lafleur	1976-77	56
Guy Lafleur	1975-76	56

ASSISTS

Peter Mahovlich	1974-75	82
Guy Lafleur	1976-77	80
Guy Lafleur	1978-79	77

POINTS

Guy Lafleur	1976-77	136
Guy Lafleur	1977-78	132
Guy Lafleur	1978-79	129

TEAM RECORD

Last 3 years

	GP	W	L	T	Pts	%
1995-96	82	40	32	10	90	.549
1994-95	48	18	23	7	43	.448
1993-94	84	48	30	6	102	.607

Best 3 regular seasons

1976-77	80	60	8	12	132	.825
1977-78	80	59	10	11	129	.806
1975-76	80	58	11	11	127	.794

Worst 3 regular seasons

1939-40	48	10	33	5	25	.260
1925-26	36	11	24	1	23	.319
1935-36	48	11	26	11	33	.344

Most Goals (min. 70 game schedule)

1976-77	387
1981-82	360
1977-78	359

Fewest Goals (min. 70 game schedule)

1952-55	155
1949-50	172
1950-51	173

Most Goals Against (min. 70 game schedule)

1983-84	295
1982-83	286
1992-93	280
1985-86	280

Fewest Goals Against (min. 70 game schedule)

1955-56	131
1953-54	141
1952-53	148

STAT SECTION

Team Scoring Stats

	GP	G	A	PTS	+/-	PIM	SH	Power Play			Short Handed		
								G	A	P	G	A	P
PIERRE TURGEON	80	38	58	96	19	44	297	17	18	35	1	1	2
VINCENT DAMPHOUSSE	80	38	56	94	5	158	254	11	24	34	4	1	5
MARK RECCHI	82	28	50	78	20	69	191	11	19	30	2	0	2
MARTIN RUCINSKY	78	29	46	75	18	68	181	9	14	23	2	2	4
ANDREI KOVALENKO	77	28	28	56	20	49	131	6	8	14	0	0	0
SAKU KOIVU	82	20	25	45	7-	40	136	8	6	14	3	1	4
VALERI BURE	77	22	20	42	10	28	143	5	8	13	0	0	0
PATRICE BRISEBOIS	69	9	27	36	10	65	127	3	16	19	0	0	0
BRIAN SAVAGE	75	25	8	33	8-	28	150	4	3	7	0	0	0
VLADIMIR MALAKHOV	61	5	23	28	7	79	122	2	12	14	0	1	1
TURNER STEVENSON	80	9	16	25	2-	167	101	0	2	2	0	0	0
LYLE ODELEIN	79	3	14	17	8	230	74	0	2	2	1	0	1
STEPHANE QUINTAL	68	2	14	16	4-	117	104	0	6	6	1	1	2
BENOIT BRUNET	26	7	8	15	4-	17	48	3	3	6	1	0	1
PETER POPOVIC	76	2	12	14	21	69	59	0	2	2	0	0	0
OLEG PETROV	36	4	7	11	9-	23	44	0	1	1	0	0	0
MARC BUREAU	65	3	7	10	3-	46	43	0	1	1	0	1	1
CHRIS MURRAY	48	3	4	7	5	163	32	0	0	0	0	0	0
DAVID WILKIE	24	1	5	6	10-	10	39	1	2	3	0	0	0
CRAIG RIVET	19	1	4	5	4	54	9	0	0	0	0	0	0
MARKO KIPRUSOFF	24	0	4	4	3-	8	36	0	1	1	0	0	0
DONALD BRASHEAR	67	0	4	4	10-	223	25	0	0	0	0	0	0
ROBERT DIRK	47	1	2	3	8	48	20	0	0	0	0	0	0
SCOTT FRASER	14	2	0	2	1-	4	9	0	0	0	0	0	0
RORY FITZPATRICK	42	0	2	2	7-	18	31	0	1	1	0	0	0
FRANCOIS GROLEAU	2	0	1	1	2	2	1	0	0	0	0	0	0
PAT JABLONSKI	24	0	1	1	0	2	0	0	0	0	0	0	0
MARK LAMB	1	0	0	0	0	0	0	0	0	0	0	0	0
JOSE THEODORE	1	0	0	0	0	0	0	0	0	0	0	0	0
PATRICK LABRECQUE	2	0	0	0	0	2	0	0	0	0	0	0	0
DARCY TUCKER	3	0	0	0	1-	0	1	0	0	0	0	0	0
SEBASTIEN BORDELEAU	4	0	0	0	1-	0	0	0	0	0	0	0	0
CRAIG CONROY	7	0	0	0	4-	2	1	0	0	0	0	0	0
JOCELYN THIBAULT	50	0	0	0	0	2	0	0	0	0	0	0	0

PLAYOFFS

PLAYER	GP	G	A	PTS	+/-	PIM	PP	SH	GW	OT	S
VINCENT DAMPHOUSSE	6	4	4	8	2	0	0	1	2	1	26
MARK RECCHI	6	3	3	6	1	0	3	0	0	0	13
PIERRE TURGEON	6	2	4	6	1	2	0	0	0	0	18
SAKU KOIVU	6	3	1	4	2	8	0	0	0	0	13
PATRICE BRISEBOIS	6	1	2	3	2	6	0	0	0	0	8
DAVID WILKIE	6	1	2	3	1	12	0	0	0	0	11
MARC BUREAU	6	1	1	2	2	4	0	0	0	0	6
LYLE ODELEIN	6	1	1	2	1	6	0	1	0	0	5
RORY FITZPATRICK	6	1	1	2	1-	0	0	0	0	0	5
BENOIT BRUNET	3	0	2	2	1	0	0	0	0	0	10
PETER POPOVIC	6	0	2	2	3	4	0	0	0	0	2
BRIAN SAVAGE	6	0	2	2	2	2	0	0	0	0	9
OLEG PETROV	5	0	1	1	1-	0	0	0	0	0	1
STEPHANE QUINTAL	6	0	1	1	1	6	0	0	0	0	3
TURNER STEVENSON	6	0	1	1	1-	2	0	0	0	0	7
VALERI BURE	6	0	1	1	1-	6	0	0	0	0	19
PAT JABLONSKI	1	0	0	0	0	0	0	0	0	0	0
CHRIS MURRAY	4	0	0	0	0	4	0	0	0	0	1
ANDREI KOVALENKO	6	0	0	0	2-	6	0	0	0	0	9
DONALD BRASHEAR	6	0	0	0	1-	2	0	0	0	0	0
JOCELYN THIBAULT	6	0	0	0	0	0	0	0	0	0	0

GOALTENDER	GPI	MINS	AVG	W	L	T	EN	SO	GA	SA	SV %
PAT JABLONSKI	1	49	1.22	0	0	0	0	0	1	17	.941
JOCELYN THIBAULT	6	311	3.47	2	4	0	0	0	18	188	.904
MTL TOTALS	6	365	3.12	2	4	0	0	0	19	205	.907

New Jersey Devils

Geez, what happened? Stanley Cup winners one year, out of the playoffs the next?

It wasn't the first time that's happened, but it was the first time in 26 years, and the eighth in NHL history, as the following chart shows. The last time it happened before last season, was after Montreal won the Cup in 1969. One of the players on that team was none other than New Jersey coach, Jacques Lemaire.

Out of Playoffs After Winning Stanley Cup

1995	New Jersey
1969	Montreal
1967	Toronto
1945	Toronto
1938	Chicago
1937	Detroit
1922	Toronto St. Pats
1918	Toronto Arenas

It came down to the last game of the season, with the Devils needing to beat Ottawa, at home. They also needed Philadelphia to beat Tampa Bay, which happened, but it never got that far. The lowly Senators scored four goals in the third period and beat the Devils 5-2. Even worse, former Devil, Tom Chorske, let go in the waiver draft, scored twice for Ottawa.

There was no excuse for New Jersey not winning that game, but there are plenty for not making the playoffs. Here's a sampling of some of them, and then add in any other possible excuse you've ever heard.

* Stanley Cup Letdown - teams that win a Stanley Cup, especially the way New Jersey did, have problems the following year getting motivated for regular season games. The Devils were a team that had to win by hard work. They gave it everything they had, and were on an emotional high. After that, nothing games during the regular season are hard to get excited about. If they had of made the playoffs, though, they might have been able to go a long way.

* Obstruction Crackdown - the Devils were probably more responsible than anyone for the crackdown on obstruction fouls. It was percieved to be a major factor in their game plan, and one of the reasons they won the Cup. Hence the obstruction crackdown to open up the game. Hence trouble for the Devils.

* Claude Lemieux Factor - sure, the guy's a pain, but the Stanley Cup follows him around. His win with Colorado was his third different team. Lemieux wasn't very honorable about his contract situation, saying his signature was on a FAX copy and therefore not valid. It was a way to get more money, and while an arbitration hearing ruled in favor of the Devils, the team figured they were better off without someone like that.

* Wrong Lemieux - the Devils did try to compensate for Claude Lemieux's loss, by getting his brother, Jocelyn. He lasted 18 games, earning zero goals and just one assist, before being shipped out to Calgary.

* Poor Attendance - the Devils aren't going to Nashville, for a long time yet. With some stability in place, it still didn't do anything for attendance. Playing in front of sparse crowds affected the players, who could easily cop an attitude: If they don't care, why should we?

* Poor Leadership - lots of leaders on this team, but this was an excuse suggested by Jacques Lemaire. Captain Scott Stevens seemed to be the one he was pointing his finger at, and the two had at least one heated exchange.

* Injuries - another one offered up by Lemaire. Their injury situation was worse than some, but better than many. The timing was bad, however, with the team missing seven regulars at times.

* Jacques Lemaire - as much as he was revered for the Stanley Cup win, his act seemed to wear thin. He was always criticizing players, and a resentment seemed to build up. Nobody was on the same page, at the same time. Near the end of the season Mike Peluso was sent home because of comments he directed at Lemaire in a team meeting.

* Inconsistency - that's according to captain Scott Stevens.

* Assistant Coach Change - maybe Larry Robinson had a lot more to do with the Devils' winning ways than previously thought. He moved on to Los Angeles to take over as coach, and was replaced by Chris Nilan. Robinson, however, didn't help out the Kings, and neither, apparantly, did Nilan, who was replaced in the off-season by Albany coach Robbie Ftorek.

* Competitive Eastern Conference - in the Western Conference, the Devils would have been in fourth place. Their regular season winning percentage of .524 was only slightly worse than in their Stanley Cup year, when it was .542.

* Bad Stretches - they went on an 0-9-3 road streak, which means for the rest of the season they were an excellent 15-6-7 away from home. They also had a goalless streak of 128 minutes and 29 seconds. Most of the players also had major scoring slumps.

* Expectations Too High - after winning the Cup, people expected them to roll over everyone during the regular season. Keeping in mind they weren't a great regular season team during their championship year, they weren't the type of team to dominate during the regular

season. It was a no-win situation for them. When they didn't win as often as expected it was a disappointment, and that had to affect them psychologically, making them press and perhaps feel the extra pressure. The strangest thing was that last season's winning percentage was the third best in franchise history, but it was probably considered one of their worst seasons.

* Marked Team - everybody guns for the Stanley Cup champs, and because everyone had seen them play so often, they could think of ways to beat them.

* No Power Play - see special teams. They did bring some hired guns on board later in the season - Phil Housley and Dave Andreychuk - but it was too little too late.

* Poor Individual Seasons - just go down the roster and pick out almost any player. Scoring was expected from Stephane Richer and Valeri Zelepukin - they didn't get it.

* Crash Line Crashes - the Holik-McKay-Peluso line, so effective during the Stanley Cup run, were anything but.

* Bad Luck - they must have had a lot of it, because they didn't have any of the good kind.

TEAM PREVIEW

GOAL: There wasn't much more Martin Brodeur could do than he did last year. He played in 77 games and accumulated 4,434 minutes, the most ever in one NHL season. He started every game after December 31, and played in every game after October 18.

The Devils allowed the fewest goals in franchise history, and finished second in goals against. Brodeur was fifth in the league in goals against average, third in wins, and second in shutouts.

Since Brodeur is going to play almost every night, the backup goalie isn't all that important. But, it did create some problems for the team.

First off, Chris Terreri was a quality NHL goalie, not getting quantity in ice-time. He was sent to San Jose, to alleviate another problem. They had a quality youngster in Corey Schwab, who deserved to be in the NHL.

With Terreri gone, that opened up a spot on the end of the bench for Schwab.

Then another problem - they had yet another quality prospect ready to make the jump in Mike Dunham, who was outstanding for Albany in the AHL last season. So, they sent Schwab to Tampa Bay for Jeff Reese. Reese, supposedly is some kind of insurance if Brodeur gets hurt.

GOALTENDER	GPI	MINS	AVG	W	L	T	EN	SO	GA	SA	SV %
COREY SCHWAB	10	331	2.18	0	3	0	0	0	12	119	.899
MARTIN BRODEUR	77	4434	2.34	34	30	12	8	6	173	1954	.911
CHRIS TERRERI	4	210	2.57	3	0	0	0	0	9	92	.902
N.J TOTALS	82	4995	2.43	37	33	12	8	6	202	2173	.907

DEFENCE: There was nothing wrong with the New Jersey defence last year. They did the job, allowing the second fewest goals in the league. And they made sure not to score themselves.

When they line up this year, they once again have two of the game's best in Scott Stevens and Scott Niedermayer.

It's hard to say how long Niedermayer will be around, however, because he was the subject of a lot of trade rumors last season. And you get the impression he wouldn't mind leaving. He, and others, feel his offensive talents are being stifled in the Devils defensive scheme.

That's what Tommy Albelin said, too, after he was traded to Calgary last season. With the reigns loosened, Albelin could play more of an offensive style. In 20 games with the Flames he racked up the points. Uh, one assist, to be exact.

Shawn Chambers, Ken Daneyko and youngster Jason Smith all seem assured of spots on the blueline, leaving room for one more regular.

It won't be Phil Housley, who was a free agent after the Devils played rent-a-goalie last season hoping he would give them an offensive spark and help out the power play.

The system is stocked with talent, so Chris McAlpine, Brad Bombadir, offensive-minded Ricard Persson and junior scrapper Sheldon Souray, should all get a chance to show their stuff. Kevin Dean probably has the inside track.

FORWARD: Either the New Jersey forwards can't score, or the New Jersey defensive system doesn't give them the same opportunies as others.

Oddly enough, the much-maligned defensive system may not be as much to blame as we think. The Devils had the seventh most shots per game in the league. That's an odd stat for a strictly defensive outfit. Combined with their excellent defensive play, it gave them one of the highest per game shot margins in the league.

HIGHEST SHOTS PER GAME MARGINS

	Ave. Shots For	Ave. Shots Against	Per Game Difference
Detroit	32.3	24.2	+8.1
Boston	34.6	26.9	+7.7
NEW JERSEY	32.2	26.5	+5.7
Washington	30.1	24.9	+5.2

You can't always equate shots with scoring chances, but it's usually a pretty good indication. Sometimes, a team can get a lot of shots, but they're not getting inside for the good opportunies, taking less dangerous shots from the perimeter.

The next stat either proves the latter point, or it proves that New Jersey forwards were the gang that couldn't shoot straight.

WORST TEAM SHOOTING PERCENTAGES

	Shots	Goals	Shooting Percentage
NEW JERSEY	2,637	215	8.2%
St. Louis	2,548	219	8.6%
Ottawa	2,204	191	8.7%
Dallas	2,472	227	9.2%
Toronto	2,675	247	9.2%

Either way, the Devils need some scoring. That means shooters who can shoot, scorers who can score, or a system which allows them to score.

The team is aging down the middle with Bobby Carpenter and Neal Broten. Petr Sykora had a decent rookie season, and behind them are little fireplug Steve Sullivan, and Sergei Brylin.

Sykora was widely revered last season, and won rookie of the month for December. During that month he scored 10 of his 18 goals, and he was still a healthy scratch for a game. In the team's last 37 games he had just four goals.

Sullivan had more than that in the 16 games he played. Considered too small, he has turned some heads and changed some minds with his fiery play, which seems to pick up the whole team.

Bobby Holik also plays centre, and Brian Rolston is a candidate there as well. Broten will be 37 this year, and Carpenter 33, so their days are numbered. It's unlikely they could manage to trade either one.

Another centre, Denis Pederson, is ready for prime time so they need to find room. He's a defensive-minded player who fits the mold perfectly. He can also probably score more than Broten or Carpenter.

Yet another centre candidate is Brendan Morrison, who was the player of the year for Michigan in the CCHA, with 28-44-72 in just 35 games.

If that isn't enough, Alyn McCauley was the MVP in the OHL. Another player of the year, this one from Hockey East, was Jay Pandolfo, who was with Boston University. He's a left winger.

On the left side is Steve Thomas, who was obtained in the trade for Claude Lemieux. He had a good year, although he didn't score as many goals as he has in the past. He provides leadership and comes to play every game.

Dave Andreychuk plays left or right wing, and earned 28 goals, most with Toronto, but also most on this team. His main value is on the power play, but his sniping days are all but gone. Valeri Zelepukin's scoring has

fallen right off the map, so he'll battle it out with Rolston, Reid Simpson, enforcer Mike Peluso, and Bobby Holik.

The right side features Bill Guerin, who is expected to score more than 23 goals; disappointing Stephane Richer, who is expected to score more than 20 goals; John MacLean, who is expected to score more than 20; and Randy McKay.

There's a lot of scorers on the Devils forward units, especially for a team that doesn't score. Age is certainly not on their side, but they have a pile of prospects who are going to be pushing for playing time soon.

If one or two of the veterans can return to form, it could jump start some of the others, and they might start putting the puck in the net more often.

SPECIAL TEAMS: Good penalty killing, as expected, and poor power play, as expected.

The power play could be better this year, if Andreychuk has something left. They desperately need a power play quarterback and they desperately need the snipers to start sniping.

POWER PLAY	G	ATT	PCT	
Overall	55	368	14.9%	(24th NHL)
Home	30	192	15.6%	(21st NHL)
Road	25	176	14.2%	(22nd NHL)

9 SHORT HANDED GOALS ALLOWED (T-7th NHL)

PENALTY KILLING	G	TSH	PCT	
Overall	49	319	84.6%	(4th NHL)
Home	17	152	88.8%	(2nd NHL)
Road	32	167	80.8%	(16th NHL)

11 SHORT HANDED GOALS SCORED (T-12th NHL)

COACHING AND MANAGEMENT: Jacques Lemaire has his work cut out for him. Not only has his defensive system come under constant criticism, it seems he's constantly criticizing the players. The same respect he was afforded in his Stanley Cup year, isn't guaranteed anymore. He'll have to earn it back.

General Manager Lou Lamoriello did a good job down the stretch, trying to get the players that would put the Devils into the playoffs. He acquired Housley and Andreychuk to provide more offence and beef up the powerplay. Didn't work, but at least he tried. Another strength of his, is to build a strong farm system. New Jersey has had one of the best for years.

DRAFT

Round	Sel.	Player	Pos	
1	10	Lance Ward	D	Red Deer (WHL)
2	38	Wes Mason	LW	Sarnia (OHL)
2	41	Joshua Dewolf	D	Twin Cities (USHL)
2	47	Pierre Dagenais	LW	Moncton (QMJHL)
2	49	Colin White	D	Hull (QMJHL)
3	63	Scott Parker	D	Kelowna (WHL)
4	91	Josef Boumedienne	D	Sweden
4	101	Josh MacNevin	D	Vernon (BCJHL)
5	118	Glenn Crawford	C	Windsor (OHL)
6	145	Sean Ritchlin	RW	Michigan Univ.
7	173	Daryl Andrews	D	Melfort (SJHL)
8	199	Willie Mitchell	D	Melfort (SJHL)
8	205	Jason Bertsch	RW	Spokane (WHL)
9	225	Pasi Petrilainen	D	Finland

If first pick, Lance Ward, doesn't work, they'll have plenty of others that might. They selected nine defencemen in the draft, and 14 overall in the nine rounds. In the second round alone they had four picks.

Ward wasn't projected to go as high as the Devils picked him. *The Hockey News* had him ranked 30th and Central Scouting had him 20th among North American prospects. He's considered a defensive defenceman.

The Devils are a prepared group at draft time, however, and they're backed up by a lot of success. Last year, they nabbed Petr Sykora with the 17th overall pick.

Normally, they like to bring their prospects along slowly, and have them develop within the system. They're one of the more successful teams in the league in that regard.

PROGNOSIS: After a one-year hiatus from the playoffs, the Devils will be back in the thick of things. Too many strange factors last year contributed to their problems. They were still close, however, and they can turn things around.

The Devils had a better record last year against teams with records over .500 than against teams under .500. That indicates a focus problem, among other things. But, it also shows they have the talent.

The Devils aren't likely to burn up the league, because they still don't have much in the scoring department, but from the blueline back to the net they're still one of the better teams in the league. If the scorers can regain their touch, everything else will be okay, and they can regain their status as a contending team.

PREDICTION:

Atlantic Division: 4th

Eastern Conference: 6th

Overall: 8th

Team Rankings 1995-96

		Conference Rank	League Rank
Record	37-33-12	9	12
Home	22-17-2	10	15
Away	15-16-10	5	10
Versus Own Conference	28-20-8	4	6
Versus Other Conference	9-13-4	10	18
Team Plus\Minus	+7	7	13
Goals For	215	12	25
Goals Against	202	1	2
Average Shots For	32.1	4	7
Average Shots Against	26.5	3	4
Overtime	7-0-12	1	1
One Goal Games	14-13	9	14
Times outshooting opponent	61	2	3
Versus Teams Over .500	21-18-6	2	4
Versus Teams Under .500	18-15-6	10	19
First Half Record	18-19-4	9	15
Second Half Record	19-14-8	5	9

PLAYOFFS

- Did not make the playoffs

ALL-TIME LEADERS

John MacLean	332
Kirk Muller	185
Pat Verbeek	170

ASSISTS

Kirk Muller	335
Bruce Driver	328
John MacLean	321

POINTS

John MacLean	665
Kirk Muller	520
Aaron Broten	469

BEST INDIVIDUAL SEASONS

GOALS

Pat Verbeek	1987-88	46
John MacLean	1990-91	45
John MacLean	1988-89	42

ASSISTS

Scott Stevens	1993-94	60
Aaron Broten	1987-88	57
Kirk Muller	1987-88	57

POINTS

Kirk Muller	1987-88	94
John MacLean	1988-89	87
Kirk Muller	1989-90	86

TEAM RECORD

Last 3 years

	GP	W	L	T	Pts	%
1995-96	82	37	33	12	86	.524
1994-95	48	22	18	8	52	.542
1993-94	84	47	25	12	106	.631

Best 3 regular seasons

1993-95	84	47	25	12	106	.631
1994-95	48	22	18	8	52	.542
1995-96	82	37	33	12	86	.524

Worst 3 regular seasons

1975-76	80	12	56	12	36	.225
1983-84	80	17	56	7	41	.256
1974-75	80	15	54	11	41	.256

Most Goals (min. 70 game schedule)

1992-93	308
1993-94	306
1985-86	300

Fewest Goals (min. 70 game schedule)

1974-75	184
1975-76	190
1978-79	210

Most Goals Against (min. 70 game schedule)

1985-86	374
1986-87	368
1981-82	362

Fewest Goals Against (min. 70 game schedule)

1995-96	202
1993-94	220
1991-92	259

STAT SECTION

Team Scoring Stats

	GP	G	A	PTS	+/-	PIM	SH	Power Play			Short Handed		
								G	A	P	G	A	P
PHIL HOUSLEY	81	17	51	68	6-	30	205	6	29	35	0	0	0
STEVE THOMAS	81	26	35	61	2-	98	192	6	11	17	0	0	0
DAVE ANDREYCHUK	76	28	29	57	9-	64	241	14	14	28	2	1	3
BILL GUERIN	80	23	30	53	7	116	216	8	5	13	0	0	0
JOHN MACLEAN	76	20	28	48	3	91	237	3	12	15	3	1	4
PETR SYKORA	63	18	24	42	7	32	128	8	11	19	0	0	0
SCOTT NIEDERMAYER	79	8	25	33	5	46	179	6	10	16	0	3	3
STEPHANE RICHER	73	20	12	32	8-	30	192	3	1	4	4	1	5
BOBBY HOLIK	63	13	17	30	9	58	157	1	3	4	0	0	0
SCOTT STEVENS	82	5	23	28	7	100	174	2	8	10	1	0	1
BRIAN ROLSTON	58	13	11	24	9	8	139	3	4	7	1	0	1
NEAL BROTEN	55	7	16	23	3-	14	73	1	5	6	1	2	3
SHAWN CHAMBERS	64	2	21	23	1	18	112	2	13	15	0	0	0
RANDY MCKAY	76	11	10	21	7	145	97	3	0	3	0	0	0
VALERI ZELEPUKIN	61	6	9	15	10-	107	86	3	2	5	0	0	0
MIKE PELUSO	57	3	8	11	4	146	41	0	0	0	0	0	0
BOB CARPENTER	52	5	5	10	10-	14	63	0	0	0	1	0	1
STEVE SULLIVAN	16	5	4	9	3	8	23	2	2	4	0	0	0
SERGEI BRYLIN	50	4	5	9	2-	26	51	0	0	0	0	0	0
KEN DANEYKO	80	2	4	6	10-	115	67	0	1	1	0	0	0
REID SIMPSON	23	1	5	6	2	79	8	0	0	0	0	0	0
KEVIN DEAN	41	0	6	6	4	28	29	0	2	2	0	0	0
DENIS PEDERSON	10	3	1	4	1-	0	6	1	0	1	0	0	0
SCOTT PELLERIN	6	2	1	3	1	0	9	0	0	0	0	0	0
RICARD PERSSON	12	2	1	3	5	8	41	1	1	2	0	0	0
JASON SMITH	64	2	1	3	5	86	52	0	0	0	0	0	0
MARTIN BRODEUR	77	0	1	1	0	6	1	0	0	0	0	0	0
PATRIK ELIAS	1	0	0	0	1-	0	2	0	0	0	0	0	0
COREY SCHWAB	10	0	0	0	0	31	0	0	0	0	0	0	0

New York Islanders

The days of building within a team's system and waiting for potential to develop are becoming rarer. Rebuilding years haven't been too successful around the NHL in recent years. Teams have shown they can be competitive quicker by trading and signing free agents. That's a much more attractive route for general managers and coaches, who need to show improvement in order to keep their jobs.

The Islanders are doing it the old fashioned way. The young players aren't all from within their own system, but they've got them, and there's a very positive air about this team. The difference between them and some others trying the same thing, such as Los Angeles, is that the Islanders are getting top of the line potential. Potential that has a chance to be very good.

Former GM, Don Maloney, had the right idea. Although he had opportunities for quick fixes, which ultimately would have probably saved his job, he opted for patience. He got fired, anyway.

Maloney made a lot of the deals that are helping return this team to respectability. He was interested in character players, and those who wanted to play for the team. Kirk Muller, for example, has a reputation as a character player, but he didn't want to play for the Islanders, so Maloney sent him home. And depending on how you look at it, he was smart for hiring Mike Milbury as coach. Smart, because Milbury is a good hockey man, and not so smart because Milbury ended up taking his job.

Milbury, because he's so high on attitude and team play, ended up shuffling out many of the players who were highest on themselves. Somewhat along the lines of what Maloney was trying to do. Milbury also excused many of the veterans, and those he got in return, such as Pat Conacher, were the kind he figured would help the team concept.

Just so we get some perspective here, the Islanders were not a good team last season, and weren't even a mediocre team. They were one of the worst in the NHL, and it was the second worst season in team history.

The Islanders used 18 rookies for at least one game last year. That was easily the most in the league.

Most Rookies Used 1995-96
(followed by top two in games played)

NY Islanders	18 (McCabe, Bertuzzi)
Montreal	14 (Koivu, Bure)
Los Angeles	13 (Yachmenev, O'Donnell)
Buffalo	12 (Holzinger, Wilson)
Calgary	12 (Stillman, Ed Ward)
Edmonton	12 (Satan, Smyth)
Pittsburgh	11 (Roche, Dziedzic)
Anaheim	10 (Lambert, Jomphe)
Boston	10 (McLaren, Beddoes)
Dallas	9 (Marshall, Lehtinen)
Washington	9 (Klee, Witt)
Colorado	8 (Yelle, Klemm)
San Jose	8 (Donovan, Ragnarsson)
Toronto	8 (Warriner, Hendrickson)
Vancouver	8 (Walker, Stojanov)
Hartford	7 (O'Neill, Daniels)
NY Rangers	7 (Sundstrom, Langdon)
Winnipeg	7 (Doan, Kilger)
Florida	6 (Dvorak, Jovanovski)
Ottawa	6 (Alfredsson, McCleary)
New Jersey	6 (Sykora, Sullivan)
St. Louis	6 (Johnson, Roberts)
Tampa Bay	6 (Gavey, Bannister)
Chicago	4 (Daze, Moreau)
Detroit	4 (Dandenault, Pushor)
Philadelphia	2 (Brimanis, Dupre)

The Islanders led in rookie regulars, as well, with Todd Bertuzzi, Niklas Andersson, Bryan McCabe, Darby Hendrickson, Dan Plante and Eric Fichaud. Under the normal course of events, the sophomore jinx not withstanding, you'd expect these players to get better with age and experience.

Their top three scorers are young, as well. Zigmund Palffy, is just 24, Travis Green 25, and Marty McInnis 25. Almost all of the defencemen are kids.

This isn't a make-or-break year for the Islanders, especially because of the young defence, but they should start to show something soon. And within a couple years, they could be extremely good.

It could be a very exciting time for Islanders fans, or it could all end up a bust. Time will tell.

TEAM PREVIEW

GOAL: Three young goalies is better than one. But, only one can be number one, and it looks like it will be Eric Fichaud. He was projected as the goaltender of the future, but may have made the grade a little sooner than expected.

Both Tommy Soderstrom and Tommy Salo had excellent minor league statistics, but so far the two Tommys haven't made an impression at the NHL level.

Soderstrom will probably get the backup role, with Salo biding his time.

Fichaud is a keeper. Obtained from Toronto, in a steal, for Benoit Hogue, and a third and fifth round draft pick, he could turn into one of the outstanding goaltenders in the game.

The problem that could affect Fichaud, something Salo has learned, is that goaltenders are largely a reflection of the team. With Denver in 1994-95 Salo won the IHL's MVP award with a league leading 2.60 goals against average. Jamie McLelland, who had been struggling with the Islanders that year, traded places with Salo before the playoffs and ended up posting a league leading 2.15 playoff GAA. Lesson learned: good team makes a good goalie.

The same thing is going to happen on the Islanders. Once they become a better defensive team, their goalies are going to look better. As it was, Fichaud earned the number one spot because he was better than the others. He's still going to get bombed some nights, but it's part of the on-the-job training.

DEFENCE: This is one of the most exciting defences in the league. They're young, mobile, and almost all can add to the offence. A few are also tough physical specimans.

They may not be the best, however, and for sure they're not the best defensively. But, what potential. That's the exciting part.

Figuring out which will be the starting six is a tough chore. Let's examine the candidates.

Bryan Berard, Age 19, 6-1, 190
(2nd overall pick in 1995)

He has a good chance to be this year's rookie of the year. The Islanders made a deal with Ottawa, in which the number one and number two picks from last season switched teams. Berard was number one, Wade Redden number two. Neither signed last year, so they also have the benefit of an extra year of junior.

Berard was 31-58-89 for Detroit in the OHL last year, in 56 games. He also starred for the U.S. World Junior team. He has a good shot at being the next great offensive defenceman in the NHL.

Kenny Jonsson, Age 21, 6-3, 195
(12th overall pick in 1993)

Another offensive threat, who can play the power play and hold his own defensively. He came over to the Islanders along with Darby Hendrickson and Sean Haggerty from Toronto for Wendel Clark, DJ Smith and Mathieu Schneider. Many observers figure he's going to be an excellent defenceman.

Brian McCabe, Age 21, 6-1, 200
(40th overall pick in 1993)

The only Islander to play every game last season, he also plays an offensive style. Last year, he spent more time learning the defensive side of his duties, but once he gets that under wraps, he could break out offensively. In his best junior season, he was 22-62-84 for Spokane in the WHL. McCabe has the added dimension of physical play. His 156 penalty minutes were second on the team.

Scott Lachance, Age 23, 6-1, 197
(4th overall pick in 1991)

The Islanders are waiting for him to develop into an offensive threat, but he's been hampered by injuries the last couple seasons. He has enough experience now that this could be his year.

Darius Kasparaitis, Age 23, 5-11, 195
(5th overall pick in 1992)

Considered by some to be the dirtiest player in the league, he's afraid of no one,

GOALTENDER	GPI	MINS	AVG	W	L	T	EN	SO	GA	SA	SV %
ERIC FICHAUD	24	1234	3.31	7	12	2	2	1	68	659	.897
JAMIE MCLENNAN	13	636	3.68	3	9	1	1	0	39	342	.886
TOMMY SODERSTROM	51	2590	3.87	11	22	6	0	2	167	1370	.878
TOMMY SALO	10	523	4.02	1	7	1	3	0	35	250	.860
NYI TOTALS	82	4993	3.79	22	50	10	6	3	315	2627	.880

and hits everything he can. He too, however, has been beset with injury problems.

Brent Severyn, Age 30, 6-2, 210
(never drafted)

Resident tough guy led the team with 180 penalty minutes in just 65 games. He spent a lot of years in the minors before getting the call with the expansion Florida Panthers. He's been a regular the last couple of seasons, and is someone who will stick up for his teammates if there's any trouble.

Dennis Vaske, Age 28, 6-2, 210
(38th overall pick in 1986)

A stay-at-home type, he played the first 19 games last year, before being checked from behind by Eric Lacroix. He suffered a severe concussion, and the symptoms, including blurred vision, kept him out of the lineup for the remainder of the season.

Rich Pilon, Age 28, 6-0, 202
(143rd overall pick in 1986)

Yet another Islander defenceman who has missed extensive time with injuries. He's a defensive defenceman who plays it tough.

Chris Luongo, Age 29, 6-0, 199
(92nd overall pick in 1985)

Last year was the first season of his career that he did not spend time in the minors.

Jason Holland, Age 20, 6-2, 190
(38th overall pick in 1994)

Holland may be ready for prime time, but the problem is finding room for him. He's yet another offensive threat, 24-44-57 for Kamloops in the WHL, in 63 games. The goal total is high for a defenceman, and illustrates the big shot he's supposed to have. He might have to start the season in the minors.

The young guys are mostly offensive dynamos, while the older candidates are more of the defensive type. With the injury history of many of the above, it could mean lots of playing time all round, but otherwise it gives Milbury the luxury of spotting the younger players and mixing them in with the veterans.

The top five on the list are all very young. If they play together, the Islanders may learn they need the veterans out there for a steadying influence, depending on the opposing team on a particular night.

If the kids somehow all came together and played their offensive style, they should be a lot of fun to watch. Training camp should be good too, as they fight it out for jobs.

If they don't mesh this year, it's probably not long until they do.

FORWARD: The Islanders would have been in trouble last season if Zigmund Palffy hadn't emerged as a big-time scorer. He went from 10 goals in 33 games in 1994-95 to 43 last season, and from 17 points to 87. Both rather remarkable improvements, and timely since they had very little other offence.

Palffy was in contract negotiations over the summer, going for the customary gigantic raise after getting paid for doing almost nothing the previous two seasons. That prompted an amusing response from Milbury when asked when the club would sign him: "When Ziggy stops being a piggy."

Travis Green was another candidate for the league's most improved player. The NHL doesn't have an award for that, but they should. A smart sponsor should jump on board because it's one that would be discussed throughout the year. Best, the players would be emerging stars, so interest in them would be high. And, it would be a legitimate award, unlike some now that get little attention.

Green went from five goals and 12 points in 42 games, to 25 and 70.

The same optimism that's on board for the defence, is not there for the forwards. They're extremely weak, and have few scorers after Palffy and Green.

Centre is their weakest position. After Green, is Alexander Semak, whose whole NHL career has revolved around one good season, when he had 70 points for New Jersey. Darby Hendrickson plays centre as well, as does free agent signee and defensive specialist, Dave McLlwain.

Right wing is pretty solid, with Palffy and Bertuzzi leading the way. Bertuzzi is in his second full season in the NHL. He should continue to show improvement towards becoming an excellent power forward. His point totals should be better this year.

Dan Plante, was another rookie on the right side. He plays a more defensive game. Mick Vukota is the roughnik. Sean Haggerty, obtained in the Toronto deal, is an excellent junior scorer who could make the grade.

On the left side is Marty McInnis; Niklas Andersson, coming off a decent NHL debut, which included an eight-game point streak to begin his career; Derek King, who just can't pot them like he used to; free agents Mike Donnelly and Brent Hughes; and a couple other possibles, including Ken Belanger, Pat Conacher and Jason Dueling.

Pat Flatley had his contract bought out, and Brett Lindros retired after suffering too many concussions.

As good as the defence is, the forward situation isn't. No scoring is a problem. No centremen is a problem. Too much dependance on talent that has shown for just one season, is also a problem. In other words, there is a problem here.

SPECIAL TEAMS: The power play was surprisingly good for a weak team and should remain that way, with about five defencemen who can be quarterback. The performance of Palffy and Green is the key.

The two also happen to line up as first forwards on the penalty killing unit. Considering the Islanders were one of the worst in the league when short-handed, some of the defensive forwards signed by the Islanders, such as McLlwain or Hughes, should take over that role.

POWER PLAY	G	ATT	PCT	
Overall	70	372	18.8%	(10th NHL)
Home	33	180	18.3%	(14th NHL)
Road	37	192	19.3%	(T-3rd NHL.)

15 SHORT HANDED GOALS ALLOWED (22nd NHL)

PENALTY KILLING	G	TSH	PCT	
Overall	90	414	78.3%	(24th NHL)
Home	38	187	79.7%	(T-24th NHL)
Road	52	227	77.1%	(24th NHL)

8 SHORT HANDED GOALS SCORED (T-21st NHL)

COACHING AND MANAGEMENT: Milbury is a tough, demanding coach, and a tough, demanding general manager. He's well respected, and seems to have made a lot of right moves for this team.

He wasn't able to coax much out of them last year, and he's going to need a lot of patience this year, as well. Maybe even a sense of humor.

DRAFT

Round	Sel.	Player	Pos	
1	3	Jean-Pierre Dumont	W	Val-d'Or (QMJHL)
2	29	Dan Lacouture	LW	Boston University
3	56	Zdeno Chara	D	Slovakia
4	83	Tyrone Garner	G	Oshawa (OHL)
5	109	Andrew Berenzweig	D	Michigan Univ.
5	128	Petr Sachl	C	Czech Republic
6	138	Todd Miller	C	Sarnia (OHL)
7	165	Joe Prestifilippo	G	Hotchkiss (US HS)
8	192	Evgeny Korolev	D	Peterborough (OHL)
9	218	Mike Muzechka	D	Calgary (WHL)

Milbury had a chance to get Alexandre Volchov with the third overall pick, but passed, largely because Volchov is a head case, and the Islanders don't need the aggravation.

Dumont is a speedy winger who will probably return to junior next year. Last year, he was considered one of the most improved prospects. That indicates a good work ethic, and even more potential. He was 48-57-105 in the Quebec league last season.

PROGNOSIS: Because the Islanders had so many injuries last year, they could be a better team based on health alone.

Milbury is building this team into a contender, he hopes, but there are too many holes right now. The defence should be exciting, but it probably can't be very good for a year or two. At forward, there just isn't enough scoring.

The Islanders are on their way, but not this year. The Eastern Conference is too competitive. Improvement is what they can hope for, and that is almost a certainty.

PREDICTION:

Atlantic Division: 7th

Eastern Conference: 12th

Overall: 23rd

Team Rankings 1995-96

		Conference Rank	League Rank
Record	22-50-10	12	24
Home	14-21-6	12	24
Away	8-29-4	13	25
Versus Own Conference	14-34-8	12	24
Versus Other Conference	8-16-2	12	23
Team Plus\Minus	-66	12	24
Goals For	229	11	22
Goals Against	315	13	25
Average Shots For	28.1	12	23
Average Shots Against	32.0	9	18
Overtime	2-5-10	9	22
One Goal Games	6-11	12	24
Times outshooting opponent	25	12	23
Versus Teams Over .500	8-35-7	12	24
Versus Teams Under .500	14-15-3	12	23
First Half Record	11-22-8	12	24
Second Half Record	11-28-2	12	25

PLAYOFFS

   - Did not make the playoffs

ALL-TIME LEADERS

GOALS

Mike Bossy	573
Bryan Trottier	500
Denis Potvin	310

ASSISTS

Bryan Trottier	853
Denis Potvin	742
Mike Bossy	553

POINTS

Bryan Trottier	1,153
Mike Bossy	1,126
Denis Potvin	1,052

BEST INDIVIDUAL SEASONS

GOALS

Mike Bossy	1978-79	69
Mike Bossy	1980-81	68
Mike Bossy	1981-82	64

ASSISTS

Bryan Trottier	1978-79	87
Mike Bossy	1981-82	83
Bryan Trottier	1981-82	79

POINTS

Mike Bossy	1981-82	147
Bryan Trottier	1978-79	134
Pierre Turgeon	1992-93	132

TEAM RECORD

Last 3 years

	GP	W	L	T	Pts	%
1995-96	82	22	50	10	54	.329
1994-95	48	15	28	5	35	.365
1993-94	84	36	36	12	87	.518

Best 3 regular seasons

1981-82	80	54	16	10	118	.738
1978-79	80	51	15	14	116	.725
1977-78	80	48	17	5	111	.694

Worst 3 regular seasons

1972-73	78	12	60	6	30	.192
1995-96	82	22	50	10	54	.329
1973-74	78	19	41	18	56	.359

Most Goals (min. 70 game schedule)

1981-82	385
1978-79	358
1983-84	357

Fewest Goals (min. 70 game schedule)

1972-73	170
1973-74	185
1990-91	223

Most Goals Against (min. 70 game schedule)

1972-73	347
1988-89	325
1995-96	315

Fewest Goals Against (min. 70 game schedule)

1975-76	190
1976-77	193
1977-78	210

STAT SECTION

Team Scoring Stats

	GP	G	A	PTS	+/-	PIM	SH	Power Play			Short Handed		
								G	A	P	G	A	P
ZIGMUND PALFFY	81	43	44	87	17-	56	257	17	22	39	1	1	2
TRAVIS GREEN	69	25	45	70	20-	42	186	14	20	34	1	0	1
MARTY MCINNIS	74	12	34	46	11-	39	167	2	13	15	0	1	1
TODD BERTUZZI	76	18	21	39	14-	83	127	4	3	7	0	0	0
ALEXANDER SEMAK	69	20	14	34	4-	68	128	6	4	10	0	0	0
DEREK KING	61	12	20	32	10-	23	154	5	1	6	1	0	1
KENNY JONSSON	66	4	26	30	7	32	130	3	11	14	0	1	1
NIKLAS ANDERSSON	47	14	12	26	3-	12	89	3	1	4	2	0	2
BRYAN MCCABE	82	7	16	23	24-	156	130	3	8	11	0	1	1
PATRICK FLATLEY	56	8	9	17	24-	21	89	0	3	3	0	0	0
DARBY HENDRICKSON	62	7	10	17	8-	80	73	0	1	1	0	0	0
SCOTT LACHANCE	55	3	10	13	19-	54	81	1	5	6	0	0	0
CHRIS LUONGO	74	3	7	10	23-	55	46	1	1	2	0	0	0
PAT CONACHER	55	6	3	9	13-	18	45	0	0	0	1	0	1
BRENT SEVERYN	65	1	8	9	3	180	40	0	0	0	0	0	0
DAN PLANTE	73	5	3	8	22-	50	103	0	0	0	2	1	3
DARIUS KASPARAITIS	46	1	7	8	12-	93	34	0	0	0	0	1	1
ANDREY VASILYEV	10	2	5	7	4	2	12	0	0	0	0	0	0
DENNIS VASKE	19	1	6	7	13-	21	19	1	5	6	0	0	0
BOB BEERS	13	0	5	5	2-	10	9	0	3	3	0	0	0
DEREK ARMSTRONG	19	1	3	4	6-	14	23	0	1	1	0	0	0
MILAN TICHY	8	0	4	4	3	8	6	0	0	0	0	0	0
BRAD DALGARNO	18	1	2	3	2-	14	11	0	1	1	0	0	0
BRETT LINDROS	18	1	2	3	6-	47	10	0	0	0	0	0	0
RICHARD PILON	27	0	3	3	9-	72	7	0	0	0	0	0	0
MICK VUKOTA	32	1	1	2	3-	106	11	0	0	0	0	0	0
CRAIG DARBY	10	0	2	2	1-	0	1	0	0	0	0	0	0
CHRIS TAYLOR	11	0	1	1	1	2	4	0	0	0	0	0	0
MICAH AIVAZOFF	12	0	1	1	6-	6	8	0	1	1	0	0	0
JARRETT DEULING	14	0	1	1	1-	11	11	0	0	0	0	0	0
ERIC FICHAUD	24	0	1	1	0	0	0	0	0	0	0	0	0
GRIGORI PANTELEEV	4	0	0	0	3-	0	1	0	0	0	0	0	0
JASON WIDMER	4	0	0	0	0	7	1	0	0	0	0	0	0
MICHAEL MACWILLIAM	6	0	0	0	1-	14	4	0	0	0	0	0	0
KEN BELANGER	7	0	0	0	2-	27	0	0	0	0	0	0	0
BOB HALKIDIS	8	0	0	0	4-	37	2	0	0	0	0	0	0
TOMMY SALO	10	0	0	0	0	0	0	0	0	0	0	0	0
JAMIE MCLENNAN	13	0	0	0	0	2	0	0	0	0	0	0	0
TOMMY SODERSTROM	51	0	0	0	0	7	0	0	0	0	0	0	0

New York Rangers

The Rangers have to win the Stanley Cup this year, or next year at the latest. If they don't, their players will soon end up using their hockey sticks as canes.

These guys are old...or else they're experienced. Or to put it another way, the glass is either three-quarters empty, or one-quarter full.

Almost all the key players on the team have seen their best days. Is what they have left enough?

That's just one question. There are plenty more.

* Now that the Rangers have Wayne Gretzky, Mark Messier, Jari Kurri (maybe), Marty McSorley, Jeff Beukeboom, Adam Graves, and Kevin Lowe (maybe), all from the Edmonton Oilers glory days, can they also get Paul Coffey, Glenn Anderson, Grant Fuhr, and Charlie Huddy?

* Why are ex-Oilers so important for teams?

* How many ex-Oilers did the Avalance have on their team?

* What happens if Messier gets injured? Last year, in the eight games he missed, the Rangers were 1-7-1. That included the final five games of the regular season.

* Can Luc Robitaille ever regain his scoring touch? And can Alexei Kovalev ever get one? Can the Rangers trade either one? Kovalev, for sure, if they want to. Robitaille, not likely.

* How much will the Rangers miss Pat Verbeek, who signed with Phoenix as a free agent?

* How come the Rangers didn't give Glenn Healy a chance to play net during the playoffs? He's played well for them in the past, better than Richter on more than one occasion, and Richter wasn't any playoff hero this year, anyway.

* Who is going to benefit most from Gretzky being on the Rangers? Robitaille? Graves? Kovalev? Who is Gretzky going to play with?

* Will Colin Campbell be the first coach fired this season? Sometimes the older players take a while to get up to speed, and sometimes, especially when there are so many "winners" on the team, they save their best for the playoffs.

* How does a team have a 24-game home unbeaten streak (18-0-6) and go 4-10-3 the rest of the time?

* Is (place name of almost any Ranger here) too old?

* Can (place name of almost any Ranger here) play injury-free this season?

* Does the fact that the Rangers faded badly in the second half have anything to do with age? They were third overall in the first half, 15th overall in the second.

* Considering how the Penguins scored almost at will against the Rangers in the playoffs, how are they going to improve defensively? Was it the forwards' fault? The defencemen? The goalie?

* Is it really such a big deal that the Rangers are so old? After all, it seems more and more teams, such as St. Louis, have abandoned youth for experience.

* Are the Ferraro twins - Chris and Peter - (Chris had 99 points for Binghamton in the AHL; Peter had 101) ever going to get a chance to play regularly for the Rangers? Is there room? Are any young players ever going to get another chance?

* What happens if the Rangers don't have a great season? What do they do next?

TEAM PREVIEW

GOAL: No problems here, with one of the better goaltending tandems in the league. Richter, of course, is the clear number one, but Healy plays well enough to earn more playing time.

The problem for Healy is compounded with projected star, Dan Cloutier, waiting in the wings. The first round draft pick from 1994 is tabbed as a can't-miss NHL goalie.

Healy has a reputation of a good playoff goaltender, although the Rangers wouldn't even let him in the game last year, so maybe sometime down the stretch if a team has an injury to their number one man, Healy might become a valuable commodity, and fetch something worthwhile in a trade.

DEFENCE: Brian Leetch is like a kid in this group, and he's 28-years-old. Check out the ages of the other expected regulars, as of October 1 of this year:

Kevin Lowe - 37

Ulf Samuelsson - 32

Doug Lidster - 35

Bruce Driver - 34

Marty McSorley - 33

Jeff Beukeboom - 31

Alexander Karpovtsev - 26

Youngster, Jeff Beukeboom was an unrestricted free agent last season, and the Rangers were smart in re-signing him. It was announced, at one time, that he was signing with St. Louis.

Beukeboom is a valuable defenceman, whose value became greater when his services were put on the open market. It wasn't certain the Rangers would go after him considering they had Marty McSorley, but he's been such a great defence partner for Leetch over the years. Beukeboom is one of the biggest, toughest defencemen in the league. And on this team, he's just a kid.

Leetch, of course, is one of the premier defencemen in the game; McSorley one of the toughest; Samuelsson one of the best defensively, as well as one of the dirtiest.

Driver is the other offensive source from the blueline, leaving Lidster and Karpovtsev. Lowe was still a free agent at press time, but he did say at one time he would be interested in returning as a player-coach.

The Rangers have the size on defence that they wanted, they have experience, they have toughness. The only thing missing is youthful exuberence.

FORWARD: How about a line of Gretzky, between Messier and Kurri. That would be fairly interesting, don't you think?

Kurri was still a free agent at press time, and Messier plays more centre these days. But, Messier probably wouldn't mind moving over, and Kurri is far more likely to sign, knowing what's in store.

It's almost the last chance for these guys. They have to win it all now, or in a year at the latest.

One of the problems for Gretzky and Messier will be finding a sniper to score. Pat Verbeek was the man last year, scoring 41 goals. Messier had 47, but the next top scoring winger was Alexei Kovalev, with 24. And Luc Robitaille was next with 23.

This team is chock full of underachievers and enigmatic types. Kovalev has been a pre-season all-star for the last three years. Armed with an abundance of talent, and projected as a 50-goal scorer, his high in

goals is 24. He's a selfish player, a celebrated diver, inconsistent (one-third of his points came in the team's first 17 games), and he just doesn't get it. But, the Rangers are probably too scared to trade him, just in case he develops into the kind of player he looks like he could be.

Robitaille was another underachiever last year. Twenty-three goals is a ridiculous total for someone who hadn't had fewer than 44 in any full NHL season. Even in the 48 game labor-shortened season he had 23 goals.

Sergio Momesso falls into the enigmatic group. He comes to play only once in a while, and with him, you have to wait until the playoffs to see if he'd like to play his best. He's been doing the same thing for so long, there's no chance of a change. That makes it hardly worth the trouble.

Adam Graves has been a big-time scorer, netting 52 for the Rangers in 1993-94. He has injury problems, so if he can remain healthy, he should be able to improve on 22 goals. In the playoffs, he had seven goals in just 10 games.

The idea, you'd have to guess, is that Gretzky can bring out, or bring back the sniper ability in some of the players, by setting them up.

The rough stuff will be taken care of by Darren Langdon and Shane Churla; Bill Berg will be the agitator, something he can be quite good at; Sergei Nemchinov is the third or fourth line centre; Niklas Sundstrom is a

GOALTENDER	GPI	MINS	AVG	W	L	T	EN	SO	GA	SA	SV %
JAMIE RAM	1	27	.00	0	0	0	0	0	0	9	1.000
MIKE RICHTER	41	2396	2.68	24	13	3	3	3	107	1221	.912
GLENN HEALY	44	2564	2.90	17	14	11	3	2	124	1237	.900
NYR TOTALS	82	4995	2.85	41	27	14	6	5	237	2473	.904

two-way centre or winger, who had a good rookie season concentrating on defence.

The success of the Ranger forwards will depend on how the lines are set up - i.e. who Gretzky plays with, who Messier plays with. It also depends on some of the snipers sniping, how well defensively they play, and whether or not age plays a factor.

Gretzky's all-time scoring marks are easy to figure out. He's first in everything. But, Messier is right up there as well. Here's where he sits on the all-time lists.

Goals: 539
Rank: 16th
Next in Line: Stan Mikita is 15th with 541 goals
Passed last year: Glenn Anderson, Lanny McDonald, Jean Beliveau, Gil Perreault, Bryan Trottier and Frank Mahovlich.

Assists: 929
Rank: 6th
Next: Ray Bourque is 5th with 970, Paul Coffey has 1038, and Marcel Dionne is third with 1,040. Howe is second at 1,049 behind Wayne Gretzky
Passed last year: Bryan Trottier and Stan Mikita.

Points: 1,468
Rank: 5th
Next: Phil Esposito is fourth with 1,590
Has Passed this year: Bryan Trottier and Stan Mikita.

SPECIAL TEAMS: The Rangers are going to miss Pat Verbeek's sniper ability on the power play. His 17 goals won't be easy to replace. Graves could be the man to do it, however. In 1993-94, he had 20 power play goals. Messier is going to score, of course, and so should Robitaille. The added bonus is that Gretzky is going to be passing to them.

On the point is perhaps the premier quarterback in the game, in Brian Leetch, and Bruce Driver can handle the secondary point role just fine.

The Rangers have the potential to shoot the lights out with the man-advantage.

That was offset last year, however, by mediocre penalty killing. Mediocre penalty killing is made worse when a team spends a lot of time killing penalties. Last year, the Rangers were shorthanded 495 times, the most of any team. That was a hefty 179 more shorthanded situations than New Jersey. The 89 goals the Rangers surrendered on the power play were only three fewer than San Jose, which led the league with 93.

The solution there seems quite simple - don't take so many penalties.

POWER PLAY	G	ATT	PCT	
Overall	85	429	19.8%	(5th NHL)
Home	50	208	24.0%	(4th NHL)
Road	35	221	15.8%	(17th NHL)

11 SHORT HANDED GOALS ALLOWED (T-12th NHL)

PENALTY KILLING	G	TSH	PCT	
Overal	89	495	82.0%	(14th NHL)
Home	44	239	81.6%	(17th NHL)
Road	45	256	82.4%	(8th NHL)

6 SHORT HANDED GOALS SCORED (T-24th NHL)

COACHING AND MANAGEMENT: Neil Smith is one of the best general managers in the game. He has a sense of humor, a sense of style, and a sense of doing whatever it takes to win. He's not afraid to try things, and most of the time he's right. He has enough confidence in his own abilities that he doesn't feel threatened, for example, by hiring Mike Keenan, which got them the Stanley Cup.

He has an added advantage of having lots of money on his side.

Sometimes the deals may not look so good when they're made, but there's rhyme and reason for them, and he has a developed concept that chemistry and character are key ingredients for success.

He also has another philosophy that he's noted. He thinks that each season is an entity in its own. In other words, you try to win in the season you're playing, not two years away.

Those kind of general managers are usually the most successful, and while they may have their lean years, they're not reduced to rebuilding jobs which ultimately turn into constant rebuilding. In other words, he's a winner.

Colin Campbell has lasted longer than some expected. He can be verbally explosive at times, which is a good thing when he can shake players into better performances. Best of all, he has Mark Messier on his side, and we all know what happens to coaches if Messier doesn't like them.

DRAFT

Round	Sel.	Player	Pos	Amateur Team
1	22	Jeff Brown	D	Sarnia (OHL)
2	48	Daniel Goneau	LW	Granby (QMJHL)
3	76	Dmitri Subbotin	W	Russia
5	131	Colin Pepperall	LW	Niagara Falls (OHL)
6	158	Olia Sanderg	D	Sweden
7	185	Jeff Dessner	D	Taft (US HS)
8	211	Ryan McKie	D	London (OHL)
9	236	Ronnie Sundin	D	Sweden

Jeff Brown isn't anything like the Jeff Brown currently in the NHL. The Rangers first rounder is more of a defensive defenceman who plays an all round game, and uses a lot of hockey sense.

A lot of top Ranger draft picks were playing in the NHL last season. Only four of them - Leetch, Kovalev, Peter Ferraro and Niklas Sundstrom - played with the Rangers. But, only two from the last 13 years didn't play in the NHL last season - Chris Kontos and Michael Stewart, both of whom are still active.

1981 - James Patrick

1982 - Chris Kontos

1983 - Dave Gagner

1984 - Terry Carkner

1985 - Ulf Dahlen

1986 - Brian Leetch

1987 - Jayson More

1988 - Troy Mallette

1989 - Steven Rice

1990 - Michael Stewart

1991 - Alexei Kovalev

1992 - Peter Ferraro

1993 - Niklas Sundstrom

PROGNOSIS: With the signing of Gretzky, there's a sense of urgency now with this team. The Grandpas not only want to win it for themselves, they feel a sense of responsibility to help Gretzky win one final time.

There's no problem with that type of thinking, but it doesn't always work. For one thing, other teams have players thinking the same way. For another, the talent has to be there. And for another, the talent can't be too old.

The Rangers will win, no problem with

that. But, they need to win in the playoffs. That's where it counts, and there's no assurance of that.

PREDICTION:

Atlantic Division: 3rd

Eastern Conference: 4th

Overall: 6th

Team Rankings 1995-96

		Conference Rank	League Rank
Record	41-27-14	3	5
Home	22-10-9	4	6
Away	19-17-5	2	5
Versus Own Conference	27-19-10	5	7
Versus Other Conference	14-18-4	2	4
Team Plus\Minus	+39	3	6
Goals For	272	4	9
Goals Against	237	5	7
Average Shots For	32.5	2	3
Average Shots Against	30.1	7	12
Overtime	2-1-14	4	10
One Goal Games	9-4	1	2
Times outshooting opponent	43	5	8
Versus Teams Over .500	18-17-9	3	5
Versus Teams Under .500	23-10-5	5	6
First Half Record	25-10-6	2	3
Second Half Record	16-17-8	9	15

Results: Defeated Montreal 4-2

   Lost to Pittsburgh 4-1

Record: 5-6

Home: 1-4

Away: 4-2

Goals For: 34 (3.1 per game)

Goals Against: 38 (3.5 per game)

Overtime: 0-1

Power play: 21.8% (3rd)

Penalty Killing: 86.0% (3rd)

ALL-TIME LEADERS

GOALS

Rod Gilbert	406
Jean Ratelle	336
Andy Bathgate	272

ASSISTS

Rod Gilbert	615
Jean Ratelle	481
Andy Bathgate	457

POINTS

Rod Gilbert	1,021
Jean Ratelle	817
Andy Bathgate	729

BEST INDIVIDUAL SEASONS

GOALS

Adam Graves	1993-94	52
Vic Hadfield	1971-72	50
Mike Gartner	1990-91	49

ASSISTS

Brian Leetch	1991-92	80
Sergei Zubov	1993-94	77
Brian Leetch	1990-91	72

POINTS

Jean Ratelle	1971-72	109
Mark Messier	1991-92	107
Vic Hadfield	1971-72	106

TEAM RECORD

Last 3 years

	GP	W	L	T	Pts	%
1995-96	82	41	27	14	96	.585
1994-95	48	22	23	3	47	.490
1993-94	84	52	24	8	112	.667

Best 3 regular seasons

1970-71	78	49	18	11	109	.699
1971-72	78	48	17	13	109	.699
1993-94	84	52	24	8	112	.667
1939-40	48	27	11	10	64	.667

Worst 3 regular seasons

1943-44	50	6	39	5	17	.170
1942-43	50	11	31	8	30	.300
1944-45	50	11	29	10	32	.320

Most Goals (min. 70 game schedule)

1991-92	321
1974-75	319
1971-72	317

Fewest Goals (min. 70 game schedule)

1954-55	150
1952-53	152
1953-54	161

Most Goals Against (min. 70 game schedule)

1984-85	345
1975-76	333
1986-87	323

Fewest Goals Against (min. 70 game schedule)

1970-71	177
1953-54	182
1967-68	183

STAT SECTION

Team Scoring Stats

	GP	G	A	PTS	+/-	PIM	SH	Power Play			Short Handed		
								G	A	P	G	A	P
MARK MESSIER	74	47	52	99	29	122	241	14	23	37	1	3	4
BRIAN LEETCH	82	15	70	85	12	30	276	7	37	44	0	0	0
PAT VERBEEK	69	41	41	82	29	129	252	17	16	33	0	0	0
LUC ROBITAILLE	77	23	46	69	13	80	223	11	15	26	0	0	0
ALEXEI KOVALEV	81	24	34	58	5	98	206	8	10	18	1	0	1
ADAM GRAVES	82	22	36	58	18	100	266	9	14	23	1	1	2
JARI KURRI	71	18	27	45	16-	39	158	5	9	14	1	2	3
BRUCE DRIVER	66	3	34	37	2	42	140	3	19	22	0	0	0
MARTY MCSORLEY	68	10	23	33	20-	169	130	1	8	9	1	2	3
SERGEI NEMCHINOV	78	17	15	32	9	38	118	0	1	1	0	0	0
SERGIO MOMESSO	73	11	12	23	13-	142	126	6	4	10	0	0	0
NIKLAS SUNDSTROM	82	9	12	21	2	14	90	1	0	1	1	0	1
ULF SAMUELSSON	74	1	18	19	9	122	66	0	3	3	0	0	0
A. KARPOVTSEV	40	2	16	18	12	26	71	1	7	8	0	0	0
DOUG LIDSTER	59	5	9	14	11	50	73	0	2	2	0	2	2
JEFF BEUKEBOOM	82	3	11	14	19	220	65	0	0	0	0	0	0
DARREN LANGDON	64	7	4	11	2	175	29	0	0	0	0	0	0
SHANE CHURLA	55	4	6	10	8-	231	32	0	1	1	0	0	0
KEVIN LOWE	53	1	5	6	20	76	30	0	0	0	0	1	1
BILL BERG	41	3	2	5	6-	41	60	0	0	0	1	0	1
KEN GERNANDER	10	2	3	5	3-	4	10	2	1	3	0	0	0
DAN LACROIX	25	2	2	4	1-	30	14	0	0	0	0	0	0
CHRIS FERRARO	2	1	0	1	3-	0	4	1	0	1	0	0	0
BARRY RICHTER	4	0	1	1	2	0	3	0	0	0	0	0	0
PETER FERRARO	5	0	1	1	5-	0	6	0	1	1	0	0	0
MIKE RICHTER	41	0	1	1	0	4	0	0	0	0	0	0	0
GLENN HEALY	44	0	1	1	0	8	0	0	0	0	0	0	0
JAMIE RAM	1	0	0	0	0	0	0	0	0	0	0	0	0

PLAYOFFS

PLAYER	GP	G	A	PTS	+/-	PIM	PP	SH	GW	OT	S
MARK MESSIER	11	4	7	11	10-	16	2	0	1	0	41
PAT VERBEEK	11	3	6	9	8-	12	1	0	0	0	38
ADAM GRAVES	10	7	1	8	9-	4	6	0	2	0	43
JARI KURRI	11	3	5	8	2-	2	0	1	1	0	31
NIKLAS SUNDSTROM	11	4	3	7	1	4	1	0	0	0	27
ALEXEI KOVALEV	11	3	4	7	0	14	0	0	1	0	31
BRIAN LEETCH	11	1	6	7	11-	4	1	0	0	0	34
BRUCE DRIVER	11	0	7	7	1	4	0	0	0	0	23
LUC ROBITAILLE	11	1	5	6	1	8	0	0	0	0	36
ULF SAMUELSSON	11	1	5	6	1-	16	0	0	0	0	6
SERGIO MOMESSO	11	3	1	4	0	14	0	0	0	0	12
SHANE CHURLA	11	2	2	4	2-	14	0	0	0	0	10
KEVIN LOWE	10	0	4	4	5	4	0	0	0	0	7
JEFF BEUKEBOOM	11	0	3	3	1-	6	0	0	0	0	12
DOUG LIDSTER	7	1	0	1	4-	6	1	0	0	0	5
BILL BERG	10	1	0	1	1-	0	0	0	0	0	8
A. KARPOVTSEV	6	0	1	1	2-	4	0	0	0	0	5
SERGEI NEMCHINOV	6	0	1	1	2	2	0	0	0	0	5
DARREN LANGDON	2	0	0	0	0	0	0	0	0	0	0
MARTY MCSORLEY	4	0	0	0	1-	0	0	0	0	0	3
KEN GERNANDER	6	0	0	0	0	0	0	0	0	0	1
MIKE RICHTER	11	0	0	0	0	0	0	0	0	0	0

GOALTENDER	GPI	MINS	AVG	W	L	T	EN	SO	GA	SA	SV %
MIKE RICHTER	11	661	3.27	5	6	0	2	3	6	308	.883
NYR TOTALS	11	665	3.43	5	6	0	2	3	8	310	.877

Ottawa Senators

Everybody's always cutting up the Senators. Mostly, because they deserve it, as one of the worst teams in NHL history. But, there must be some good news somewhere, and we aim to find it.

Good News: The Senators spent some time in first place in the Northeast Division last year. Perhaps suffering from delusions, GM at the time, Randy Sexton, patted himself on the back and said in the media that he was the only one who thought the team could challenge for a playoff spot.
Bad News: It was only eight games into the season, the record was only 5-3, and they went 13-56-5 the rest of the way to finish last, just where everybody but Sexton thought they would.

Good News: The Senators fired Rick Bowness and hired Dave Allison to "give the team a spark," according to Sexton.
Bad News: The team went 2-22-1 in their next 25 games, when the flame was extinguished on Allison's job.

Good News: General manager Randy Sexton was fired.
Bad News: There is no bad news.

Good News: The Senators hired Pierre Gauthier, considered an up-and-coming talent, as their new general manager.
Bad News: See next year's standings.

Good News: Alexei Yashin said he would never play for the Senators...again.
Bad News: He was lying...again.

Good News: Alexei Yashin finally got his contract squabbles settled.
Bad News: If he gets 20 goals, he'll probably want to renegotiate.

Good News: Steve Duchesne was added to the team to quarterback the power play.
Bad News: What power play?

Good News: Daniel Alfredsson won the Calder Trophy as the best rookie.
Bad News: It was one of the worst years since the sixties for rookies.

Good News: The Senators won the lottery and picked Chris Phillips first overall.
Bad News: It's bad news if you're Chris Phillips.

Good News: Randy Cunneyworth, a 35-year-old, played his heart out and was third on the team in scoring, and second in goals.

Bad News: A 35-year-old journeyman, defensive forward, is third on the team in scoring.

Good News: Alexandre Daigle hits the 41-goal mark.

Bad News: That's his career total, in three years in Ottawa.

Good News: The Senators get a new arena.

Bad News: Not all that many people have seen it yet.

Good News: Damian Rhodes, picked up from Toronto, had two shutouts in a row.

Bad News: That tied him for the franchise lead in shutouts.

Good News: Damian Rhodes played great in net for the Senators.

Bad News: His teammates thought so too, because they spent a lot of time watching him play. The team scored two or less goals in 23 of his 35 starts.

Good News: Prospect Pavol Demitra led the AHL in scoring for part of last season.

Bad News: That's where he plays his best.

Good News: For Steve Yzerman, anyway, when a rumored trade of him to Ottawa didn't go through.

Bad News: Ottawa kids still don't have a player whose name they would be proud to wear on a jersey.

Good News: The Senators allowed just over 100 fewer goals than in any of their previous two full NHL seasons.

Bad News: Nothing bad about that. They still only ranked 21st in that category, but it's an improvement.

Good News: The Senators outshot their opponents 28 times.

Bad News: Their record in those games was 6-20-2.

Good News: The Ottawa winning percentage was the best in their history.

Bad News: It was still the worst in the NHL.

TEAM PREVIEW

GOAL: A pretty good piece of work by the Ottawa scouting department to trade for Damian Rhodes. Stuck in Toronto as Felix Potvin's backup, he was spectacular in net for the Senators. The team goals against average before Rhodes arrived was 4.08. His GAA was 1.31 better, and for the year it knocked off half a goal per game for the team. Pretty impressive.

That didn't translate to a heck of a lot of wins, because his teammates couldn't put the puck in the net, but he still came through and did his job well.

The Senators signed free agent Ron Tugnutt as backup. He's got experience, having played with half the teams in the league. He's only insurance, anyway, because Rhodes is expected to play all the time.

Don Beaupre had a pretty good run as the Ottawa goaltender, or as good as can be expected for an Ottawa goalie, but he may have been running out of gas. A goal a game difference between him and Rhodes is the evidence, along with a birth certificate that said 34-years-old. When he got to Toronto to take Rhodes' place as Potvin's backup, he played poorly.

It's not unusual for traded players to play

above their heads in their first season with a new team, when they were traded during the year. Rhodes may find his second season in Ottawa much more trying than his first.

DEFENCE:

Wade Redden - big, solid, two-way character player.

Chris Phillips - big, solid, two-way character player.

Steve Duchesne - power play quarterback.

Stanislav Neckar - solid, dependable, defensive player.

It's a pretty good nucleus. You can add some spare parts into the mix, such as Frank Musil, Sean Hill, Janne Laukkanen, and whatever else they can come up with. But, it's the top four who are they key.

They first have to make sure Redden and Phillips are ready to play in the NHL. And now Neckar has suddenly become a pain.

He wanted his contract renegotiated. He and his agent, Rich Winter, are pulling a Yashin, claiming they had a verbal agreement with Randy Sexton to have the contract renegotiated under certain circumstances, which they say were met. Whatever. Sexton denies any deal was made.

All this kind of activity does is hurt the team. Smart general managers are taking a stand, and getting rid of troublemakers, knowing they do nothing for the unity, focus and cohesiveness a team needs to become successful.

It would be nice if a team one day sued a holdout for non performance of a contract. That would be real fun. Or refuse to let an overpaid player on the ice until he renegotiated his contract for a lesser amount.

Neckar moves down the totem pole anyway. The only reason he became an item in the first place was because there was such little talent on the team. That's changing. It wouldn't take a lot for Redden and/or Phillips to become the best defencemen the team has ever had.

This is a defence group that isn't likely to excel this year, but with a couple good additions after the top four, it could within a couple years.

FORWARD: When an 82-year-old defensive forward is second on the team in scoring, it says everything you need to know about their scoring power.

Don't blame Randy Cunneyworth, who's actually 35. He played his heart out and had a great year.

Alfredsson took home the Calder Trophy with 61 points. No team leading scorer had so few points. Yashin was second with 39 points. No team runner-up top scorer had so few points.

GOALTENDER	GPI	MINS	AVG	W	L	T	EN	SO	GA	SA	SV %
DAMIAN RHODES	36	2123	2.77	10	22	4	1	2	98	1041	.906
DON BEAUPRE	33	1770	3.73	6	23	0	9	1	110	892	.877
MIKE BALES	20	1040	4.15	2	14	1	1	0	72	560	.871
OTT TOTALS	82	4953	3.53	18	59	5	11	3	291	2504	.884

Alfredsson, in fact, was the only 20-goal scorer, on a team that scored the fewest goals in the league.

There's not a sure thing on the whole team. Yashin is as close as it gets, but sometime during the year he'll say he'll never play another game with Ottawa.

The Senators did pick up Shawn McEachern, who comes over from Boston after an unimpressive season of 24 goals. They didn't want him anymore, and pity the Senators for not knowing, or caring, why.

The team is still waiting for Radek Bonk and they're still waiting for Alexandre Daigle. Both have been failures, but both still have a chance to redeem themselves.

The problem with them is showing consistency, or more in Daigle's case, showing anything at all. Last year, for example, Bonk had nine points in the team's first 10 games. He had just 26 in the next 66. Every time one or the other has a good game, everybody jumps on the bandwagon and says, there it is, it's time.

The two aren't finished yet. And the Senators aren't giving up on them yet. This year, it's make or break for Daigle. Bonk has shown some improvement, however, and if he continues to do so, the team isn't getting rid of him.

Pavol Demitra is another youngster who can play, when he feels like it. He may not feel like it, though, with his agent, Rich Winter, suggesting in yet another bargaining ploy, that the restricted free agent may play in Europe. Demitra brings offence only, scoring big in the minors (81 points in 48 games last year for PEI) and doing a decent job with the Senators last year, scoring 17 points in 31 games. That pro-rates to 45 points over 82 games, which, only on the Senators, looks pretty good. He's iffy though, and certainly not worth a high price tag. His attitude, work ethic, and defensive play have all come into question.

The Senators move their players around a lot by position, especially the younger players, but down the middle there is Yashin, Bonk, Daigle and defensive centre, Ted Drury.

That's not a bad group if they play up to their potential. That's not a bad group if they play up to their potential. That's not a bad group if they play up to their potential...(this is a recording, please do not adjust your book). On the wings are Cunneyworth, McEachern, Troy Malette, Alfredsson, Demitra, Pat Elynuik, free agent signee Denny Lambert, and who knows what else.

Actually, "what else" is the worst forward unit in the league.

SPECIAL TEAMS: The good news is there's nowhere to go but up. That's the bad news, too. And, of course, they could stay the same. That seems like a more likely course. They're not any better than they were, yet.

POWER PLAY	G	ATT	PCT	
Overall	53	430	12.3%	(26th NHL)
Home	29	216	13.4%	(26th NHL)
Road	24	214	11.2%	(26th NHL)

14 SHORT HANDED GOALS ALLOWED (21st NHL)

PENALTY KILLING	G	TSH	PCT	
Overall	83	375	77.9%	(25th NHL)
Home	38	199	80.9%	(T-19th NHL)
Road	45	176	74.4%	(26th NHL)

6 SHORT HANDED GOALS SCORED (T-24th NHL)

COACHING AND MANAGEMENT: Okay, let's start all over again, and hope we get it right this time. Gone is GM Randy Sexton, and coaches Rick Bowness and his replacement, Dave Allison.

In, is Pierre Gauthier as GM, and Jacques

Martin as coach. The only thing we know for sure is that they can't do any worse than their predecessors. That's a good start.

There's no point delving into Sexton's reign as GM. It was brutal. The one thing he deserves credit for, depending on who's giving the credit, is for not buckling under to Yashin and his contract demands. Not a great legacy, however. There is absolutely no chance that he will be hired as a general manager again in the NHL.

DRAFT

Round	Sel.	Player	Pos	
1	1	Chris Phillips	D	Prince Albert (WHL)
4	81	Antti-Jussi Niemi	D	Finland
6	136	Andreas Dackell	RW	Sweden
6	153	Francois Hardy	D	Val d'Or (QMJHL)
8	212	Erich Goldmann	D	Germany
9	216	Ivan Ciernik	W	Slovakia
9	239	Sami Salo	D	Finland

The Senators had some good offers for their first pick. Considering the state of their team, and the record of their previous early draftees, they might have been wise to accept one.

In Phillips, though, they may have finally got the real thing. He's a two-way player who gives the Senators size on the blueline (6-2, 200), character, and leadership. The last two qualities are not in huge supply on the Senators.

For the rest of his picks, GM Gauthier speculated on the European market, and overall, picked defencemen with five of their seven selections. They're weak at every position, however, and since they didn't get their second pick until the fourth round, it doesn't much matter.

PROGNOSIS: This team is terrible. Same as they've always been. Their only hope is that new GM Gauthier can put them on the right track. It's not going to happen overnight however, if it ever does happen.

So far, they've got little going for them. Maybe decent goaltending, but that's it. They are developing a decent defence, but that's going to take a while.

Here's what they should do, which is just what they've been waiting to find out:

1. Dump Yashin

He's a selfish player who doesn't care anything about the team. And there's just no dealing with him and his agent, Mark Gandler. For a team looking for character and leadership, he doesn't fit the mold. They're better off without him.

Yashin has talent, no questioning that, but what a dog. There is demand for his type, a team that has enough character that it won't matter, and can just keep him for his scoring. He'd bring some decent players, too. He would score lots on a good team. On Ottawa, he's not worth the trouble.

2. Dump Daigle

He's a constant reminder of the failed Sexton regime, and is synonymous with losing. He doesn't have a lot of market value right now, however, so make the trade a conditional one. Get a player, and draft picks based on Daigle's production. Maybe all he needs is a change of scenery. He probably needs more than that, but you never know.

3. Put Redden and Phillips into the lineup right away

Some might think it would hurt these players to put them out on the ice for a team that's going to get hammered. Maybe not. Maybe it's like it used to be in the Quebec junior league. The goaltenders got so many shots they got that much better. These guys will get lots of action, and through it should improve. It will be of paramount importance, however, to keep their attitudes up.

4. Build with character

That's how teams like Florida are able to do so well, so soon. They have leaders, character, leaders, hard workers, and leaders. You have some of that on Ottawa, but not enough to fill a fourth line on Florida. If you get rid of the whiners, floaters, and selfish players, it makes everybody else that much better.

PREDICTION:

Northeast Division: Last

Eastern Conference: Last

Overall: Last

Team Rankings 1995-96

		Conference Rank	League Rank
Record	18-59-5	13	26
Home	8-28-5	13	26
Away	10-31-0	12	24
Versus Own Conference	10-43-3	13	26
Versus Other Conference	8-16-2	12	24
Team Plus\Minus	-70	13	25
Goals For	191	13	26
Goals Against	291	12	21
Average Shots For	26.8	13	25
Average Shots Against	30.5	8	15
Overtime	0-3-5	13	26
One Goal Games	4-15	13	26

Times outshooting opponent	28	11	21
Versus Teams Over .500	8-35-2	13	26
Versus Teams Under .500	10-24-3	13	25
First Half Record	8-32-1	13	26
Second Half Record	10-27-4	13	26

PLAYOFFS

- Did not make playoffs.

ALL-TIME LEADERS

GOALS

Alexei Yashin	66
Bob Kudelski	47
Sylvain Turgeon	47

ASSISTS

Alexei Yashin	96
Norm MacIver	73
Alexandre Daigle	64

POINTS

Alexei Yashin	162
Alexandre Daigle	105
Norm MacIver	97

BEST INDIVIDUAL SEASONS

GOALS

Alexei Yashin	1993-94	30
Daniel Alfredsson	1995-96	26
Sylvain Turgeon	1992-93	25

ASSISTS

Alexei Yashin	1993-94	49
Norm MacIver	1992-93	46
Daniel Alfredsson	1995-96	35

POINTS

Alexei Yashin	1993-94	79
Norm MacIver	1992-93	63
Daniel Alfredsson	1995-96	61

TEAM RECORD

Last 3 years

	GP	W	L	T	Pts	%
1995-96	82	18	59	5	41	.250
1994-95	48	9	34	5	23	.240
1993-94	84	14	61	9	37	.220

Best 3 regular seasons

1995-96	82	18	59	5	41	.250
1994-95	48	9	34	5	23	.240
1993-94	84	14	61	9	37	.220

Worst 3 regular seasons

1992-93	84	10	70	4	24	.143
1993-94	84	14	61	9	37	.220
1994-95	48	9	34	5	23	.240

Most Goals (min. 70 game schedule)

1992-93	202
1993-94	201
1995-96	191

Fewest Goals (min. 70 game schedule)

1995-96	191
1993-94	201
1992-93	202

Most Goals Against (min. 70 game schedule)

1993-94	397
1992-93	394
1995-96	291

Fewest Goals Against (min. 70 game schedule)

1995-96	291
1992-93	394
1993-94	397

STAT SECTION

Team Scoring Stats

	GP	G	A	PTS	+/-	PIM	SH	Power Play			Short Handed		
								G	A	P	G	A	P
DANIEL ALFREDSSON	82	26	35	61	18	28	212	8	18	26	2	0	2
ALEXEI YASHIN	46	15	24	39	15-	28	143	8	7	15	0	0	0
RANDY CUNNEYWORTH	81	17	19	36	31-	130	142	4	4	8	0	0	0
STEVE DUCHESNE	62	12	24	36	23-	42	163	7	19	26	0	0	0
RADEK BONK	76	16	19	35	5-	36	161	5	7	12	0	0	0
TOM CHORSKE	72	15	14	29	9-	21	118	0	1	1	2	0	2
SEAN HILL	80	7	14	21	26-	94	157	2	2	4	0	2	2
PAVOL DEMITRA	31	7	10	17	3-	6	66	2	4	6	0	0	0
ALEXANDRE DAIGLE	50	5	12	17	30-	24	77	1	5	6	0	0	0
TED DRURY	42	9	7	16	19-	54	80	1	2	3	0	0	0
ANTTI TORMANEN	50	7	8	15	15-	28	68	0	0	0	0	1	1
TRENT MCCLEARY	75	4	10	14	15-	68	58	0	0	0	1	1	2
ROB GAUDREAU	52	8	5	13	19-	15	76	1	3	4	1	0	1
STANISLAV NECKAR	82	3	9	12	16-	54	57	1	0	1	0	1	1
DAVID ARCHIBALD	44	6	4	10	14-	18	56	0	2	2	0	0	0
MICHEL PICARD	17	2	6	8	1-	10	21	0	2	2	0	0	0
LANCE PITLICK	28	1	6	7	8-	20	13	0	0	0	0	0	0
TROY MALLETTE	64	2	3	5	7-	171	51	0	0	0	0	0	0
DENNIS VIAL	64	1	4	5	13-	276	33	0	0	0	0	0	0
FRANK MUSIL	65	1	3	4	10-	85	37	0	0	0	0	0	0
JANNE LAUKKANEN	23	1	2	3	1-	14	35	1	0	1	0	0	0
PAT ELYNUIK	29	1	2	3	2	16	27	0	0	0	0	0	0
JEAN-YVES ROY	4	1	1	2	3	2	6	0	0	0	0	0	0
PHIL BOURQUE	13	1	1	2	3-	14	12	0	0	0	0	0	0
CHRIS DAHLQUIST	24	1	1	2	7-	14	13	0	0	0	0	0	0
SCOTT LEVINS	27	0	2	2	3-	80	6	0	0	0	0	0	0
DAMIAN RHODES	47	0	2	2	0	4	0	0	0	0	0	0	0
PATRICK TRAVERSE	5	0	0	0	1-	2	2	0	0	0	0	0	0
JOE CIRELLA	6	0	0	0	3-	4	3	0	0	0	0	0	0
DANIEL LAPERRIERE	6	0	0	0	2	4	12	0	0	0	0	0	0
MIKE BALES	20	0	0	0	0	2	0	0	0	0	0	0	0

Philadelphia Flyers

The Flyers are close. Very close. This could be the year they bring the Stanley Cup back to Philadelphia. Last season, it was a case of could have, should have, would have. It was a case of being stopped by the rodent-powered Florida Panthers.

Let's take a look at what they do have, and what they don't have.

What They Have:

*   Impact Player - guess who?

*   Toughness - six players with over 100 penalty minutes, Shawn Antoski leading the way with 204.

*   Big Defence - the six regulars, and their sizes: Kjell Samuelsson 6-6, 235; Chris Therien 6-4, 230; Karl Dykuis 6-3, 195; Kevin Haller 6-2, 183; Eric Desjardins 6-1, 200; Petr Svoboda 6-1, 185.

*   Good Defence - Philadelphia allowed the fourth fewest goals in the league, and the third fewest shots per game.

*   Good Defence without giving up good offence - the Flyers scored the fourth most goals in the league.

*   Goaltending - Ron Hextall is coming off his best regular season in the NHL.

*   Coaching - Terry Murray, who was able to get the good defence without giving up the good offence.

*   Good General Manager - Bobby Clarke has been able to get quality players during the season to strengthen the weaknesses. Last year, he picked up Dale Hawerchuk, Dan Quinn, John Druce, Bob Corkum and Kerry Huffman. More to the point, the players traded for all seem to get with the program.

*   Special Special Teams - sixth on the power play, second in penalty killing.

*   Hunger - last year's second round loss to the upstart Panthers will have them all the more eager to get back into the playoffs and prove it was a fluke. Along with the hunger goes better focus and team unity.

*   Flyers Mystique - the Flyers are one of those teams that have an aura about them. It's not on the same level, of course, as the Montreal Canadiens, but

when a player puts on the Philly uniform, they know it's something a little more special than the norm.

* Ability to win on the road: the Flyers were first in the conference and third in the league.

* Experience - lots of players are in their prime or approaching it. They have just the right measure of experienced players coming down from their prime, whose contributions aren't affected so much by age. Dale Hawerchuk, for example, isn't expected to be the number one centre, and Joel Otto just keeps doing what he's been doing.

* A Second Line - deemed a problem earlier last year, the Flyers went out and got some scoring for a second line. It takes some of the pressure of Lindros and makes them more effective overall.

What They Don't Have:

* Size and Toughness on the Wing - Brendan Shanahan would be a perfect fit. He would be on a lot of teams, of course, but he could be the difference between a Cup and no Cup in Philadelphia. They did add some toughness in the off-season with the signing of free agent Scott Daniels, who had 254 penalty minutes for Hartford last year.

* Potential - what you see is what you get on the Flyers. They don't have much in the way of rookie hopefuls or players waiting for breakout seasons. They were the only team in the league last season that didn't get a goal from a rookie.

* Hope if Lindros is out of the lineup - the Flyers were 42-19-12 when he was in the lineup, and 3-5-1 when he wasn't.

* Consistency - the Flyers didn't have it all the time during the regular season, but it's no big deal. Not many teams do. It's the playoffs that count.

* Powerplay quarterback - they don't have a 70 or 80 point defenceman to run the power play, but it obviously isn't hurting them when they're among the best in the league with the man-advantage. Prospect Janne Niinimaa is an offensive defenceman and he'll be given a chance to make the team this year, and perhaps fill that role eventually.

* Mobile Defence - when the defencemen are big, often you're giving something else up, which is generally mobility and quickness in the puckhandling department. The Flyers showed they were suspectible to strong forechecking in their playoff series against Florida last year.

* The Old Spectrum - a lot of teams have shown a tendency lately not to play well in their new arenas in their first seasons. It takes a while for it to feel like home.

* Claude Lemieux - teams tire of Lemieux eventually, and feel they can get along just fine without him. But, the guy's a Stanley Cup magnet. He won it last year in Colorado, the year before in New Jersey, and previously with Montreal. He will probably be available at the trading deadline, which is when the Flyers should grab him for their Stanley Cup run.

TEAM PREVIEW

GOAL: Ron Hextall is the Rodney Dangerfield of NHL goalies. He doesn't get much respect, and the knock against him is that he can't take the Flyers to the Stanley Cup.

At least he proved he wasn't washed up, when he knocked close to a full goal off his best career goals against average. Before posting a 2.17 GAA last year, his previous best was 2.89 for Philadelphia the season before.

Hextall was tied with Chris Osgood for the league lead in goals against average, and was fifth in save percentage. He certainly didn't choke in the playoffs, either, with a 2.13 GAA.

Garth Snow proved a capable backup, and plays the same style of game as Hextall. Both are aggressive, and neither is very hospitable to guests in front of the net or in the crease.

Ironically, the man Snow beat out for the backup role, Dominic Roussel, who was traded to Winnipeg, was re-signed by Philadelphia as a free agent during the summer.

Hextall will be motivated again this year. The fiery competitor wants the Stanley Cup and aims to get it this season.

DEFENCE: The Flyers have one of the better defences in the league. Their only draftee is Therien; all the rest were obtained from other organizations where they were considered underachievers. They fit together nicely.

As noted above, they have good size, and are good defensively. Not a lot of offence, but not much is needed. Desjardins handled the open power play point spot and responded with a career high in points.

With the big six of Desjardins, Svoboda, Therien, Dykhuis, Haller and Kjell Samuelsson, there's not much room for anyone else. Kerry Huffman was obtained last year and was a credible fill-in, but he was also a free agent after the season.

Others who got playing time last year were Darren Rumble, Aris Brimanis and Jason Bowen. Bowen is a former first-rounder, who at 6-4, 220, would fit the Flyers' defence mode.

But, they might also like a little more puck handling mobility, and are hoping to get it from Finn Janne Niiniman. The second round draft selection in 1993, an offensive defenceman, will be given a shot to make the team.

FORWARD: It doesn't get a whole lot better than the Flyers forward situation. It starts with Lindros, of course, but the team has built enough around him that even without him they're a good group.

Not that they'd want to try it.

The Legion of Doom didn't see all that much action last year because Renberg was injured for 31 games. With the addition of

GOALTENDER	GPI	MINS	AVG	W	L	T	EN	SO	GA	SA	SV %
RON HEXTALL	53	3102	2.17	31	13	7	2	4	112	1292	.913
GARTH SNOW	26	1437	2.88	12	8	4	3	0	69	648	.894
DOMINIC ROUSSEL	9	456	2.89	2	3	2	0	1	22	178	.876
PHI TOTALS	82	5009	2.49	45	24	13	5	5	208	2123	.902

Hawerchuk, his absence wasn't as noticable.

Down the middle, the Flyers have Lindros, Joel Otto, Rob Brind'Amour, Dale Hawerchuk, and Bob Corkum. The latter three also play the wing, and end up at different places depending on the line shuttling.

The Flyer organization has a history of getting more out of player than what they were giving at their previous stop. Hawerchuk, Pat Falloon, and Dan Quinn all fit into that category last season.

On the left side is 51-goal man John LeClair, Quinn or Brind'Amour, Shjon Podein, tough guy Shawn Antoski, and one of the right wingers.

The right side is patrolled by Renberg, Hawerchuk, Pat Falloon, Trent Klatt, Rob DiMaio, and new addition roughnik Scott Daniels.

Lots of depth, good defence, some decent secondary scoring, and a couple enforcers. A power forward for the second line would be nice. That's about it.

SPECIAL TEAMS: The Flyers have great special teams players. On the power play, LeClair, Lindros, Brind'Amour, Desjardins and a third forward, make them one of the best in the league. LeClair is one of the best snipers in the game, Lindros is Lindros, and the rest just do their jobs. The low ranking for the road power play is curious, however, but probably nothing to worry about. It did create some heavily weighted home point totals for players. If they could bring the road power play percentage even up to just average it would make a big difference.

Penalty killing was outstanding as well last year, especially with a host of two-way forwards who can all do the job.

POWER PLAY	G	ATT	PCT
Overall	82	417	19.7% (T-6th NHL)
Home	51	212	24.1% (T-2nd NHL)
Road	31	205	15.1% (21st NHL)

7 SHORT HANDED GOALS ALLOWED (T-2nd NHL)

PENALTY KILLING	G	TSH	PCT
Overall	62	437	85.8% (2nd NHL)
Home	28	210	86.7% (4th NHL)
Road	34	227	85.0% (3rd NHL)

12 SHORT HANDED GOALS SCORED (T-9th NHL)

COACHING AND MANAGEMENT: Clarke is one of the best general managers in the business. He might be the best at recognizing what a team needs and then going and getting it. As long as he's running the show in Philadelphia they should always have a competitive team.

He probably figures right now that the Flyers are a player or two away from winning the Stanley Cup. Whatever they need, he'll find.

Terry Murray is getting the same rap as his brother Brian had when he was a coach - great during regular season, but can't win in the playoffs. Figure on Clarke giving him one more kick at the can. He did an excellent job of making this team outstanding both on offence and defence, with a system that works both ways. What the problem is in the playoffs isn't known, but he'd be wise to spend a lot of time trying to figure it out.

DRAFT

Round	Sel.	Player	Pos	
1	15	Dainius Zubrus	RW	Caledon (MTJHL)
3	65	Chester Gallant	RW	Niagara Falls (OHL)

5	124	Per-Ragnar Bergqvist	G	Sweden
5	133	Jesse Boulerice	D	Detroit (OHL)
7	187	Roman Malov	LW	Russia
8	213	Jeff Milleker	C	Moose Jaw (WHL)

Zubrus is considered a high risk pick. There are no problems with his talent level, except for consistency. And he's not considered much of a team player, opting instead to try and do it all himself. He only played at the tier II level of junior hockey in Canada last season, so will need time to develop. If and when he makes it to the NHL, however, he could turn out to be a flashy offensive scoring machine.

PROGNOSIS: The Flyers can win the Stanley Cup. They have more than enough ingredients. The only problem is, to win it, you need some luck. Talent is better than luck, of course, but just having the talent doesn't guarantee victory.

Clarke knows the Flyers are close, so he won't waste the opportunity. If they're found lacking anywhere during the season, he'll fix it in time for the playoffs.

When they get to the playoffs, they'll need leadership, unity and focus. If they get it, they're the Stanley Cup champions.

PREDICTION:

Atlantic Division: 1st

Eastern Conference: 1st

Overall: 2nd

Team Rankings 1995-96

		Conference Rank	League Rank
Record	45-24-13	1	3
Home	27-9-5	2	3
Away	18-15-8	1	3
Versus Own Conference	30-19-7	2	3
Versus Other Conference	15-5-6	1	2
Team Plus\Minus	+54	1	4
Goals For	282	2	4
Goals Against	202	3	4
Average Shots For	0.8	6	11
Average Shots Against	25.8	2	3
Overtime	4-3-13	5	11
One Goal Games	11-10	6	11
Times outshooting opponent	54	3	4
Versus Teams Over .500	19-19-6	4	6
Versus Teams Under .500	26-5-7	1	2
First Half Record	23-11-7	4	5
Second Half Record	22-13-6	1	3

Results: Defeated Tampa Bay 4-2

Lost to Florida 4-2

Record: 6-6

Home: 3-3

Away: 3-3

Goals For: 37 (3.1/game)

Goals Against: 28 (2.3/game)

Overtime: 1-3

Power play: 21.1% (5th)

Penalty Killing: 88.9% (2nd)

ALL-TIME LEADERS

GOALS

Bill Barber	420
Brian Propp	369
Tim Kerr	363

ASSISTS

Bobby Clarke	852
Brian Propp	480
Bill Barber	463

POINTS

Bobby Clarke	1,210
Bill Barber	883
Brian Propp	849

BEST INDIVIDUAL SEASONS

GOALS

Reg Leach	1975-76	61
Tim Kerr	1986-87	58
Tim Kerr	1985-86	58

ASSISTS

Bobby Clarke	1975-76	89
Bobby Clarke	1974-75	89
Mark Recchi	1992-93	70

POINTS

Mark Recchi	1992-93	123
Bobby Clarke	1975-76	119
Bobby Clarke	1974-75	116

TEAM RECORD

Last 3 years

	GP	W	L	T	Pts	%
1995-96	82	45	24	13	103	.628
1994-95	48	28	16	4	60	.625
1993-94	84	35	39	10	80	.476

Best 3 regular seasons

1975-76	80	51	13	16	118	.738
1979-80	80	48	12	20	116	.725
1973-74	76	51	18	11	113	.718

Worst 3 regular seasons

1969-70	76	17	35	24	58	.382
1968-69	76	20	35	21	61	.401
1971-72	78	26	38	14	66	.423

Most Goals (min. 70 game schedule)

1983-84	350
1984-85	348
1975-76	348

Fewest Goals (min. 70 game schedule)

1967-68	173
1968-69	174
1969-70	197

Most Goals Against (min. 70 game schedule)

1992-93	319
1993-94	314
1981-82	313

Fewest Goals Against (min. 70 game schedule)

1973-74	164
1967-68	179
1974-75	181

STAT SECTION

Team Scoring Stats

	GP	G	A	PTS	+/-	PIM	SH	Power Play			Short Handed		
								G	A	P	G	A	P
ERIC LINDROS	73	47	68	115	26	163	294	15	24	39	0	1	1
JOHN LECLAIR	82	51	46	97	21	64	270	19	18	37	0	0	0
ROD BRIND'AMOUR	82	26	61	87	20	110	213	4	22	26	4	2	6
DALE HAWERCHUK	82	17	44	61	15	26	180	6	18	24	0	1	1
PAT FALLOON	71	25	26	51	14	10	170	9	10	19	0	0	0
ERIC DESJARDINS	80	7	40	47	19	45	184	5	25	30	0	2	2
DAN QUINN	63	13	32	45	6-	46	109	7	11	18	0	0	0
MIKAEL RENBERG	51	23	20	43	8	45	198	9	8	17	0	0	0
JOEL OTTO	67	12	29	41	11	115	91	6	8	14	1	2	3
JOHN DRUCE	77	13	16	29	20-	27	128	0	4	4	0	1	1
PETR SVOBODA	73	1	28	29	28	105	91	0	13	13	0	0	0
SHJON PODEIN	79	15	10	25	25	89	115	0	1	1	4	1	5
CHRIS THERIEN	82	6	17	23	16	89	123	3	1	4	0	0	0
ROB DIMAIO	59	6	15	21	0	58	49	1	0	1	1	1	2
KARL DYKHUIS	82	5	15	20	12	101	104	1	7	8	0	0	0
BOB CORKUM	76	9	10	19	3	34	126	0	0	0	0	1	1
TRENT KLATT	71	7	12	19	2	44	101	0	3	3	0	1	1
KERRY HUFFMAN	47	5	12	17	18-	69	91	3	9	12	0	0	0
KEVIN HALLER	69	5	9	14	18	92	89	0	2	2	2	0	2
KJELL SAMUELSSON	5	3	11	14	20	81	62	0	0	0	0	0	0
PATRIK JUHLIN	14	3	3	6	4	17	14	1	0	1	0	0	0
SHAWN ANTOSKI	64	1	3	4	4-	204	34	0	0	0	0	0	0
RUSS ROMANIUK	17	3	0	3	2-	17	13	1	0	1	0	0	0
JIM MONTGOMERY	5	1	2	3	1	9	4	0	0	0	0	0	0
YANICK DUPRE	12	2	0	2	0	8	10	0	0	0	0	0	0
PHILIP CROWE	16	1	1	2	0	28	6	0	0	0	0	0	0
ARIS BRIMANIS	17	0	2	2	1-	12	11	0	0	0	0	0	0
DAN KORDIC	9	1	0	1	1	31	2	0	0	0	0	0	0
RON HEXTALL	53	0	1	1	0	28	1	0	0	0	0	0	0
JASON BOWEN	2	0	0	0	0	2	2	0	0	0	0	0	0
DARREN RUMBLE	5	0	0	0	0	4	7	0	0	0	0	0	0
GARTH SNOW	26	0	0	0	0	18	0	0	0	0	0	0	0

PLAYOFFS

PLAYER	GP	G	A	PTS	+/-	PIM	PP	SH	GW	OT	S
ERIC LINDROS	12	6	6	12	1-	43	3	0	2	0	46
JOHN LECLAIR	11	6	5	11	3	6	4	0	1	0	25
MIKAEL RENBERG	11	3	6	9	1	14	1	0	0	0	22
DALE HAWERCHUK	12	3	6	9	0	12	1	0	0	0	48
JOEL OTTO	12	3	4	7	4	11	1	0	1	0	12
ROD BRIND'AMOUR	12	2	5	7	2-	6	1	0	0	0	34
ERIC DESJARDINS	12	0	6	6	5-	2	0	0	0	0	26
PETR SVOBODA	12	0	6	6	6	22	0	0	0	0	17
TRENT KLATT	12	4	1	5	1	0	0	0	0	0	16
PAT FALLOON	12	3	2	5	2-	2	2	0	0	0	37
DAN QUINN	12	1	4	5	3-	6	1	0	0	0	19
KARL DYKHUIS	12	2	2	4	6	22	1	0	0	0	18
BOB CORKUM	12	1	2	3	1-	6	0	0	0	0	11
SHJON PODEIN	12	1	2	3	2	50	0	0	1	0	19
SHAWN ANTOSKI	7	1	1	2	3	28	0	0	1	0	3
JOHN DRUCE	2	0	2	2	1	2	0	0	0	0	8
KJELL SAMUELSSON	12	1	0	1	0	24	0	0	0	0	7
KEVIN HALLER	6	0	1	1	0	8	0	0	0	0	6
RUSS ROMANIUK	1	0	0	0	1-	0	0	0	0	0	1
GARTH SNOW	1	0	0	0	0	0	0	0	0	0	0
JIM MONTGOMERY	1	0	0	0	1-	0	0	0	0	0	0
ROB DIMAIO	3	0	0	0	1-	0	0	0	0	0	1
KERRY HUFFMAN	6	0	0	0	0	2	0	0	0	0	8
RON HEXTALL	12	0	0	0	0	6	0	0	0	0	0
CHRIS THERIEN	12	0	0	0	5-	18	0	0	0	0	17

Pittsburgh Penguins

The Penguins were strictly offence last year. Shoot the lights out, bang down the door, have a party, and let someone else clean up after.

The Penguins scored the second most goals in team history, and compiled the second best record. That's all the more impressive when you consider GM Craig Patrick's outstanding job of tearing this team apart and building it back up prior to last season.

Consider some of the scoring feats.

* 60-goal scorers. Mario Lemieux with 69 goals, and Jaromir Jagr with 62 meant that they were only the second team in NHL history to have two 60-goal scorers. Wayne Gretzky and Jari Kurri were the others when they notched 73 and 71, respectively in 1984-85.

* Top Two Scorers. Not only did Lemieux and Jagr finish one-two in scoring, but Ron Francis only missed by one point for tying for third.

* 100-Point Scorers. Lemieux (161), Jagr (149) and Francis (119) were members of that club, while Petr Nedved missed by just one. Tomas Sandstrom might have

reached that plateau as well, if he didn't miss 24 games with injuries.

* Top-Scoring Right Winger. Jagr's 149 points broke the NHL record for a right winger, surpassing Mike Bossy's record of 147 which he set for the New York Islanders in 1981-82. Jagr also broke the record for assists, with his 87 bettering the 83 Bossy had in 1981-82.

All great stuff, but it didn't get them a Stanley Cup. Mind you, Francis was injured for the playoffs and that could have made a big difference.

Trends change fairly quickly in the NHL. Whatever works is the latest trend. Two years ago it was defence, before that offence. There's a rich recent history of offensive teams winning the Stanley Cup. Edmonton did it four times, and Pittsburgh themselves did it twice.

Ideally, you'd like to have a great offensive team that plays great defence. Those teams are rare. Only one recently stands out, and that was last year's Detroit Red Wings. And look where it didn't get them.

What exactly do you get from a strict offensive team, and what don't you get. Some advantages and disadvantages:

Advantages:

* Are more likely to overwhelm a weaker team than could a good defensive team.

* Entertaining for the fans, and entertaining for the players.

* It's easier for an offensive team to start playing defence, if they have to, than it is for a defensive team to suddenly start scoring goals.

* The numbers show the style wins - during the regular season.

Disadvantages:

* It's more likely for a team to suffer a scoring slump, than it is for another team to suffer a defensive slump.

* Teams can devise a way to shut down scoring; it's a lot more difficult to shut down defence and hard work. See Florida Panthers.

* Offensive star players aren't usually of the tougher variety, so they can be intimidated physically.

* It's more difficult to replace an injured scoring star, than it is a third line checking winger.

* If ice conditions aren't perfect, for example during the playoffs in the high humidity in Miami, it can hamper their game, making puck handling and passing more difficult, and slowing down the speedsters.

* Puts too much pressure on defence and goalies. Last year, only Los Angeles and Buffalo gave up more shots per game.

TEAM PREVIEW

GOAL: The Penguins allowed the third most shots in the league, which meant both Ken Wregget and Tom Barrasso were busy. The two were also busy vying for the number one goaltender job.

Pittsburgh is a rare team in today's NHL because it has two number one goalies. That has its good points and bad points.

The good is obvious, because if one is out with an injury, the other can step right in. Barrasso is frequently out of action for the Penguins.

The bad is that it's not much fun for the participants, both of whom figure they deserve the job. That's especially true in Wregget's case, because it appears that Barrasso is favored. Not by the fans, who like Wregget better, but at times it appears as if it doesn't matter what he does, Barrasso gets the advantage.

Barrasso gets paid about five times as much as Wregget, and has a more impressive history, which includes two Stanley Cup victories, a Vezina trophy, a first team all-star selection and a Calder trophy. The individual awards noted above all came in 1984, however. What he has become known for over the years, is being one of the better puckhandlers, difficult to deal with in the media, and injury prone.

Wregget's legacy is stepping in and playing great, only to be pushed aside when Barrasso is healthy again. The two, in goals against average, are compared below. While GAA often isn't a good comparison from team to team because of different team styles of play, it can be done with two goalies on the same club. Wregget joined Pittsburgh during the 1991-92 season, but we'll start the comparison from when he was with the team from the start of the season.

	BARRASSO		WREGGET	
	GAA	W-L-T	GAA	W-L-T
1992-93	3.01	43-14-5	3.42	13-7-2
Playoffs	2.91	7-5	Did Not Play	
1993-94	3.36	22-15-5	3.37	21-12-7
Playoffs	2.87	2-4	Did Not Play	
1994-95	3.84	0-1-1	3.21	25-9-2
Playoffs	6.00	0-1	3.00	5-6
1995-96	3.43	29-16-2	3.24	20-13-2
Playoffs	2.89	4-5	2.30	7-2

4-year Totals:

	BARRASSO		WREGGET	
Regular Season	3.25	94-46-13	3.30	79-41-13
Playoffs	3.01	6-10	2.62	12-8

The numbers show very similar records during the regular season, and a clear edge to Wregget in the playoffs. Wregget, who didn't get a chance to play during two of his playoff seasons with Pittsburgh, has shown throughout his career that he's a money goalie. Before the Penguins, he put up good playoff numbers for a lousy team in Toronto, including a league leading GAA of 2.29 one season, and for a medicocre team in Philadelphia where he posted a 2.24 GAA.

Wregget doesn't complain about the lack of respect he gets from the Penguins, but the numbers show he has good reason to.

DEFENCE: These guys have their work cut out for them. While the forwards are up getting all the glory, the defence stand alone on the blueline - and often in their own end. The demands on them are as high as any in the league.

What they want from this group is toughness - mental and physical.

In other words, to be successful they have to do their jobs much better than other teams. Their rewards are good plus-minuses; but the price is a lot of bad nights when the opponents embarrass them.

Nothing was more embarassing than the night last season when Pittsburgh was defeated 10-8 at home by the San Jose Sharks. That was the most goals in any game last season, and only three away from the all-time record. The Penguins were also involved in the second highest scoring game, a 9-6 win over Boston. And there was a 7-6 win, a 6-6 tie, an 8-5 win, and lots more of the same.

With all the offence generated by the forwards, there's not much need for more from the defence. That's probably why they traded the inconsistent Sergei Zubov to Dallas for Kevin Hatcher.

The funny thing about Zubov, though, is that he was a plus 28, best among the

GOALTENDER	GPI	MINS	AVG	W	L	T	EN	SO	GA	SA	SV %
KEN WREGGET	37	2132	3.24	20	13	2	4	3	115	1205	.905
TOM BARRASSO	49	2799	3.43	29	16	2	5	2	160	1626	.902
PIT TOTALS	82	4948	3.44	49	29	4	9	5	284	2840	.900

defencemen and third on the team. That statistic doesn't tell us anything about his defensive play, but it does tell us that his offensive style wasn't hurting the team over the long run. Statistically, at least.

Zubov's 66 points, however, can be replaced by Hatcher. He's had two seasons of more than 70 points. Plus, he gives the added dimension of size, and is a better defensive player. Hatcher, though, has his detractors as well. Consistency and using his size are two things he's accused of lacking.

Last year, Chris Tamer and Francois Leroux were the two defencemen who used their size to the best advantage. Those are the type of players Pittsburgh wants and needs. Check out the sizes of the contenders:

Kevin Hatcher	6-4, 225
Francoix Leroux	6-6, 234
Neil Wilkinson	6-3, 190
Chris Tamer	6-2, 212
Chris Joseph	6-2, 210
Dmitri Mironov	6-3, 215
Corey Foster	6-3, 214

Big enough? Maybe the biggest in the league. Ian Moran and J.J. Daigneault, both of whom are under six-feet are also vying for spots.

The Penguins should have a tough, physical presence on defence, but there's only so much they can do. If the team really wants these guys to stand out, they ought to send the forwards back to help out once in a while.

FORWARD: There wasn't much more the Pittsburgh forwards could have done last year. Unless, you count playing a little defence.

You start with two of the best players in the game - Lemieux and Jagr. Then you add another of the best players in the game, Ron Francis. Then you add a 99-point scorer in Petr Nedved, and a veteran winger, Sandstrom, who was on pace for almost a 100 points.

So much for the scoring, so what else do you do?

Okay, if you have two scoring lines, you need A: physical players to surround them. B: Good defensive players. C: some young potential because many of the forwards are getting on in age.

Two of the above are combined in one. Youngsters on board, and their sizes are: Joe Dziedzic 6-3, 227; Glen Murray 6-2, 219; Dave Roche 6-4, 227; Bryan Smolinski 6-1, 202; Alex Stojanov 6-4, 215; Chris Wells 6-6, 223; Rusty Fitzgerald 6-1, 190. A smaller Richard Park also had a lot of playing time last year. He, along with Dziedzic, Roche, Stojanov, Wells and Fitzgerald, were all rookies last season.

Except for Smolinski, and sometimes Murray, none in the above group showed any offence of note. But, most were rookies, so they need a little time.

The team signed free agent Kevin Todd, considered a good defensive centre, in the off-season. He was with Los Angeles last season and scored 16-27-43. Ed Patterson is another defensive-type.

The Penguins also signed Dan Quinn, who returns to Pittsburg after playing for half the teams in the league. Since last in Pittsburgh in 1989-90, here are the teams he has played for each year:

1989-90	Pittsburg, Vancouver
1990-91	Vancouver, St. Lois
1991-92	Philadelphia
1992-93	Minnesota
1993-94	Bern (Switzerland), Ottawa

1994-95	Zug (Switzerland), Los Angeles
1995-96	Ottawa, Philadelphia

If you're good at math, you'll notice that there are far too many names to fit into one lineup. That gives the Penguins some depth, which they felt was lacking last year, and should make competition for jobs in training camp a spirited affair.

SPECIAL TEAMS: The Penguins got off to an amazing start last year, with the power play operating at a record rate. While they still finished first, it did slow down considerably, and in the playoffs it wasn't there at all. Not a problem, though. There's little chance they can finish much lower than first this season, as long as Lemieux is playing.

The penalty-killing strategy is fairly simple - try to score themselves. Lemieux led the league with eight shorthanded markers, and tied for the league lead with nine shorthanded points.

POWER PLAY	G	ATT	PCT	
Overall	109	420	26.0%	(1st NHL)
Home	57	206	27.7%	(1st NHL)
Road	52	214	24.3%	(1st NHL)

12 SHORT HANDED GOALS ALLOWED (T-14th NHL)

PENALTY KILLING	G	TSH	PCT	
Overall	78	467	83.3%	(8th NHL)
Home	36	240	85.0%	(7th NHL)
Road	42	227	81.5%	(11th NHL)

18 SHORT HANDED GOALS SCORED (T-2nd NHL)

COACHING AND MANAGEMENT: A remarkable job by GM Craig Patrick, tearing this team down to help out the financial picture, keeping the best components, and masterminding the shortest and most effective rebuilding job in NHL history. Not only did he make them Stanley Cup contenders, but he's ensuring they remain that way for a while.

Coach Ed Johnston has been around, but he's had a serious lack of success in the playoffs. Before last year, he had just one series win in six. Mostly, all he has to do is put the players out there and let them play. Might be good enough, too.

DRAFT

Round	Sel.	Player	Pos	
1	23	Craig Hillier	G	Ottawa (OHL)
2	28	Paval Skrbek	D	Czech Republic
3	72	Boyd Kane	LW	Regina (WHL)
3	77	Boris Protsenko	RW	Calgary (WHL)
4	105	Michal Rozsival	D	Czech Republic
6	150	Peter Bergman	C	Kamloops (WHL)
6	186	Eric Meloche	RW	Cornwall (COJHL)
9	238	Timo Seikkula	C	Finland

Hillier was the top rated goaltender in the draft, and the first one taken. Although not considered a franchise-type goalie, he was the best of a weaker than normal group, and addresses a long-time need to strengthen the depth at this position for the Penguins.

PROGNOSIS: The question isn't so much what the Penguins need to be better during the regular season, but what they need to be better during the playoffs. Those concerns are being addressed.

They've toughened up the defence with

the addition of Kevin Hatcher, without giving up offence, and they've added a good defensive centre in Kevin Todd.

So, they're one of the best scoring teams, they can count on their veteran goaltenders, and now they're trying to accumulate the meanest, biggest, toughest defence in the league.

All they need to do now is tidy up the supporting cast for the forwards, if they determine it necessary during the regular season; get some more production out of the youngsters; and hope Lemieux can stay healthy enough to play as often as last year.

The Penguins are once again legitimate contenders for the Stanley Cup.

PREDICTION:

Northeast Division: 1st

Eastern Conference: 2nd

Overall: 4th

Team Rankings 1995-96

		Conference Rank	League Rank
Record	49-29-4	2	4
Home	32-9-0	1	2
Away	17-20-4	7	12
Versus Own Conference	34-19-3	1	3
Versus Other Conference	15-10-1	3	5
Team Plus\Minus	+47	2	5
Goals For	362	1	1
Goals Against	284	11	20
Average Shots For	32.2	3	5
Average Shots Overtime	3-2-4	3	8
One Goal Games	16-12	3	5

Times outshooting			
opponent	32	8	17
Versus Teams Over .500	21-17-2	1	3
Versus Teams Under .500	28-12-2	4	5
First Half Record	27-11-3	1	2
Second Half Record	22-18-1	6	11

Results: defeated Washington 4-2
defeated NY Rangers 4-1
lost to Florida 4-3

Record: 11-7

Home: 5-5

Away: 6-2

Goals For: 57 (3.2/game)

Goals Against: 52 (2.9/game)

Overtime: 1-0

Power play: 16.0% (9th)

Penalty Killing: 85.4% (4th)

ALL-TIME LEADERS

GOALS

Mario Lemieux	563
Jean Pronovost	316
Rick Kehoe	312

ASSISTS

Mario Lemieux	795
Syl Apps	349
Paul Coffey	332

POINTS

Mario Lemieux	1,372
Rick Kehoe	636
Jean Pronovost	603

BEST INDIVIDUAL SEASONS

GOALS

Mario Lemieux	1988-89	85
Mario Lemieux	1987-88	70
Mario Lemieux	1992-93	69
Mario Lemieux	1995-96	69

ASSISTS

Mario Lemieux	1988-89	114
Mario Lemieux	1987-88	98
Mario Lemieux	1985-86	93

POINTS

Mario Lemieux	1988-89	199
Mario Lemieux	1987-88	168
Mario Lemieux	1995-96	161

TEAM RECORD

Last 3 years

	GP	W	L	T	Pts	%
1995-96	82	49	29	4	102	.622
1994-95	48	29	16	3	61	.635
1993-94	84	56	21	7	119	.708

Best 3 regular seasons

1993-94	84	56	21	7	119	.708
1994-95	48	29	16	3	61	.635
1995-96	82	49	29	4	102	.622

Worst 3 regular seasons

1983-84	80	16	58	6	38	.238
1982-83	80	18	53	9	45	.281
1984-85	80	24	51	5	53	.331

Most Goals (min. 70 game schedule)

1992-93	367
1995-96	362
1988-89	347

Fewest Goals (min. 70 game schedule)

1969-70	182
1968-69	189
1967-68	195

Most Goals Against (min. 70 game schedule)

1982-83	394
1983-84	390
1984-85	385

Fewest Goals Against (min. 70 game schedule)

1967-68	216
1969-70	238
1970-71	240

STAT SECTION

Team Scoring Stats

	GP	G	A	PTS	+/-	PIM	SH	Power Play			Short Handed		
								G	A	P	G	A	P
MARIO LEMIEUX	70	69	92	161	10	54	338	31	48	79	8	1	9
JAROMIR JAGR	82	62	87	149	31	96	403	20	31	51	0	0	0
RON FRANCIS	77	27	92	119	25	56	158	12	42	54	1	1	2
PETR NEDVED	80	45	54	99	37	68	204	8	12	20	1	2	3
TOMAS SANDSTROM	58	35	35	70	4	69	187	17	13	30	1	3	4
SERGEI ZUBOV	64	11	55	66	28	22	141	3	29	32	2	2	4
BRYAN SMOLINSKI	81	24	40	64	6	69	229	8	10	18	2	0	2
KEVIN MILLER	81	28	25	53	4-	45	179	3	10	13	2	3	5
DMITRI MIRONOV	72	3	31	34	19	88	86	1	6	7	0	2	2
GLEN MURRAY	69	14	15	29	4	57	100	0	0	0	0	0	0
CHRIS JOSEPH	70	5	14	19	6	71	94	0	3	3	0	1	1
NEIL WILKINSON	62	3	14	17	12	120	59	0	0	0	1	0	1
DAVE ROCHE	71	7	7	14	5-	130	65	0	0	0	0	0	0
CHRIS TAMER	70	4	10	14	20	153	75	0	1	1	0	1	1
J.J. DAIGNEAULT	57	4	7	11	6-	53	61	2	6	8	0	0	0
FRANCOIS LEROUX	66	2	9	11	2	161	43	0	0	0	0	0	0
JOE DZIEDZIC	69	5	5	10	5-	68	44	0	0	0	0	0	0
RICHARD PARK	56	4	6	10	3	36	62	0	0	0	1	1	2
DAVE MCLLWAIN	19	2	5	7	5-	6	20	0	1	1	0	0	0
BRAD LAUER	21	4	1	5	5-	6	29	1	0	1	0	0	0
COREY FOSTER	11	2	2	4	2-	2	8	1	1	2	0	0	0
CHRIS WELLS	54	2	2	4	6-	59	25	0	0	0	1	0	1
RUSTY FITZGERALD	21	1	2	3	7	12	15	0	0	0	0	0	0
TOM BARRASSO	49	0	3	3	0	18	0	0	0	0	0	0	0
IAN MORAN	51	1	1	2	1-	47	44	0	0	0	0	0	0
ALEK STOJANOV	68	1	1	2	13-	130	20	0	0	0	0	0	0
ED PATTERSON	35	0	2	2	5-	38	17	0	0	0	0	1	1
KEN WREGGET	37	0	2	2	0	8	0	0	0	0	0	0	0
DRAKE BEREHOWSKY	1	0	0	0	1	0	0	0	0	0	0	0	0
GREG ANDRUSAK	2	0	0	0	1-	0	1	0	0	0	0	0	0
STEFAN BERGKVIST	2	0	0	0	0	2	4	0	0	0	0	0	0
JEFF CHRISTIAN	3	0	0	0	0	2	0	0	0	0	0	0	0
LEN BARRIE	5	0	0	0	1-	18	5	0	0	0	0	0	0
PETER ALLEN	8	0	0	0	2	8	2	0	0	0	0	0	0

PLAYOFFS

PLAYER	GP	G	A	PTS	+/-	PIM	PP	SH	GW	OT	S
MARIO LEMIEUX	18	11	16	27	3	33	3	1	2	0	78
JAROMIR JAGR	18	11	12	23	7	18	5	1	1	0	74
PETR NEDVED	18	10	10	20	3	16	4	0	2	1	54
SERGEI ZUBOV	18	1	14	15	9	26	1	0	0	0	53
J.J. DAIGNEAULT	17	1	9	10	4	36	1	0	1	0	30
BRYAN SMOLINSKI	18	5	4	9	4-	10	0	0	1	0	46
RON FRANCIS	11	3	6	9	3	4	2	0	1	0	23
DAVE ROCHE	16	2	7	9	1	26	0	0	0	0	18
GLEN MURRAY	18	2	6	8	2	10	0	0	1	0	21
CHRIS TAMER	18	0	7	7	0	24	0	0	0	0	23
TOMAS SANDSTROM	18	4	2	6	6-	30	0	0	1	0	44
KEVIN MILLER	18	3	2	5	6-	8	0	0	0	0	36
JOE DZIEDZIC	16	1	2	3	1	19	0	0	0	0	6
BRAD LAUER	12	1	1	2	0	4	0	0	0	0	8
FRANCOIS LEROUX	18	1	1	2	2	20	0	0	1	0	8
CHRIS JOSEPH	15	1	0	1	1	8	0	0	0	0	15
KEN WREGGET	9	0	1	1	0	0	0	0	0	0	0
NEIL WILKINSON	15	0	1	1	2-	14	0	0	0	0	20
DMITRI MIRONOV	15	0	1	1	6-	10	0	0	0	0	10
RICHARD PARK	1	0	0	0	0	0	0	0	0	0	0
COREY FOSTER	3	0	0	0	2-	4	0	0	0	0	4
STEFAN BERGKVIST	4	0	0	0	1-	2	0	0	0	0	0
DAVE MCLLWAIN	6	0	0	0	0	0	0	0	0	0	3
ALEK STOJANOV	9	0	0	0	0	19	0	0	0	0	1
TOM BARRASSO	10	0	0	0	0	8	0	0	0	0	0

GOALTENDER	GPI	MINS	AVG	W	L	T	EN	SO	GA	SA	SV %
KEN WREGGET	9	599	2.30	7	2	0	1	0	23	328	.930
TOM BARRASSO	10	558	2.80	4	5	0	2	1	26	337	.923
PIT TOTALS	18	1159	2.69	11	7	0	3	1	52	668	.922

Tampa Bay Lightning

At the start of last year, if someone had asked you which team would be better, Tampa Bay or the defending Stanley Cup champion New Jersey Devils, it wouldn't take you long to answer.

Remarkably, the Lightning not only grabbed the last playoff spot ahead of the Devils, but they were one point behind Washington, two behind Montreal, three behind Boston, and four behind Florida and fourth place in the Eastern Conference.

Not bad for a fourth year team, and if it weren't for the exploits of the Panthers, they'd be getting a lot more attention for it.

So, how did they manage to do it - make the playoffs so soon? There's is a different tale than that of their even newer expansion cousins in south Florida. Here are some of the reasons for their success this past season.

* Emerging young players - Roman Hamrlik, Chris Gratton, Aaron Gavey, and Jason Wiemer were all drafted by the Lightning, all in the first round except for Gavey, and all have progressed, at varying levels. Hamrlik has emerged already, and ranks among the better defencemen in the league; Gratton is moving steadily up the ladder and could

break out this season; Gavey already has shown value as a third or fourth line centre; and Wiemer, while he hasn't shown much yet, is still hanging in there and could breakout this season.

* Contributing older players - the trick is to have some of these guys, but not too many. And not at the expense of younger players who need playing time. John Cullen, Brian Bellows, Brian Bradley, Petr Klima, David Shaw, Michel Petit, and John Tucker were all over 30 years old last season. Tucker didn't contribute much, but the others all did, more or less at various times in the season. You'd probably prefer your veterans to be "character" players so they could contribute on more than one level, and there were some in that group.

* Hot streak - it can be the difference between making the playoffs and not making them. It should be understood that most every team has their hot streaks and their cold streaks, but the Lightning had two hot stretches that made their season. In mid-November, Tampa Bay was floundering around at 5-10-4, and already being written off. Then

they won five in a row and went on a 9-2-1 tear. When it was over, they were over .500. The Lightning stayed very close to the .500 level until mid-February when they again won five in a row, and again put together a great string of 10-1-1. What a hot streak does for a young team is give them confidence. It tells them they're good enough if they play the right way, and in their case, instead of one good stretch, they had two.

* Goaltending - see Daren Puppa

* Coaching - see Terry Crisp

* Butt-Kicking - twice last season Tampa Bay lost by identical 10-0 scores. You have to work hard to get something positive out of that, but it may have accomplished something. It became a constant reminder, with a little voice inside their head that said, "This is what happens if you don't work hard."

* Stability - the jury is still out on this concept because arguments can be made for both sides. Sometimes a big pile of changes works for a team, and sometimes it doesn't. In this case, we can say few changes were good changes. Trader Phil is no longer a suitable moniker for the Lightning General Manager. The curious thing is that early in the season when the team was struggling, CEO Steve Oto said that the team needed to change its chemistry, and suggested numerous changes were on the way.

* Play against good teams - against teams with records over .500, the Lightning were 18-19-8, which even though it's a losing record, is extremely good. It's one thing to beat the dregs, but winning against the top teams is the key. Not just because it means those teams that could be ahead of them in the standings don't get the points, but because it shows they can play well in the important games. Lousy records against those teams and they could have forgotten about making the playoffs. In the second half of the season, when it would make or break them, they were 11-9-4 against teams over .500.

* Power Play - the Lightning had the fourth best power play percentage in the league, which is pretty remarkable in itself. The difference for them, however, is that it was the power play that got them into the playoffs. In a good-news-bad-news scenario the reason for that was because they were weak at even strength. A team plus-minus of -25 put them 20th overall in the league. They scored the highest percentage of their goals on the power play, as shown below.

Team	Power Play Goals	Total Goals	Percentage on Power Play
Tampa Bay	83	238	34.9%
St. Louis	74	219	33.8%
Toronto	83	247	33.6%
Florida	81	254	31.9%
NY Islanders	70	229	30.6%

The power play numbers contributed to their rise to prominence, but they're also worrisome. Depending too much on the power play to score goals means they're not playing well at even strength. Power plays can shut down, or teams can be careful not to draw penalties against them, or lots of different things. The bottom line is you'd much rather be scoring more at even strength. The Lightning showed how erratic a power play can be in the playoffs when they scored just three times in 35 chances.

TEAM PREVIEW

GOAL: Daren Puppa was rumored to be on the trading block early last year. Whichever teams were close to getting him probably now have bruises on their legs from kicking themselves.

It was a great year for goalies, yet Puppa still made it as a finalist in the Vezina Trophy voting, and won *The Hockey News* award for best goaltender. His goals against average was the lowest of his career and lower than his previous season for the fourth consecutive year. His save percentage was second best in the league, behind only Dominik Hasek.

Puppa's shortcoming is that he has yet to establish himself with a great playoff performance. Many of the teams he's been on didn't even make the playoffs and none have ever gone past the first round. Only twice was he the goalie of choice in a playoff year for his team, and this past season he wasn't able to carry the load because of lower back problems.

His fill-in for the playoffs was Jeff Reese, obtained from Hartford two months into the season for future considerations. Reese is a career backup, who never got the chance to be the number one man. He will, however, get a chance to be the backup in New Jersey, which is where he was traded during the summer, for Corey Schwab, who was their backup.

J.C. Bergeron was supposed to fill the backup role, but he was dispatched to the farm club in Atlanta where he shared time with Derek Wilkinson and Tyler Moss. Wilkinson and Moss are projected as two good goaltenders of the future, but need time to develop.

If the Lightning find themselves out of the playoff picture around the trading deadline, look for them to deal Puppa if he's healthy and having a good year. That way they can get good value in a trade, and they can also start to give their young goalies more playing time.

DEFENCE: Roman Hamrlik was the first choice overall in the 1992 draft. If people questioned the wisdom of that selection in his first few years in the league, they don't anymore. He has become one of the premier defencemen in the league, and perhaps the best young defensive talent. With a lot of the game's best defencemen getting on in years, all-star status is staring him in the face. A Norris Trophy might be asking a little much, but not a top three finish.

Hamrlik's talents are most evident on the power play where he picked up 42 of his 65

GOALTENDER	GPI	MINS	AVG	W	L	T	EN	SO	GA	SA	SV %
DAREN PUPPA	57	3189	2.46	29	16	9	2	5	131	1605	.918
JEFF REESE	19	994	3.26	7	7	1	2	0	54	464	.884
J.C. BERGERON	12	595	4.24	2	6	2	2	0	42	250	.832
DEREK WILKINSON	4	200	4.50	0	3	0	0	0	15	105	.857
T.B TOTALS	82	4993	2.98	38	32	12	6	5	248	2430	.898

points. Only Brian Leetch had more power play points among defenceman and only eight other players at any position had more. He's the cornerstone of the defence corps, and the only star.

The Lightning had little depth at this position last year, but they added some help over the summer. The prize was Craig Wolanin, fresh off his Stanley Cup triumph, obtained from Colorado for future considerations. Jay Wells, a 37-year-old veteran will also help out.

Also on the blueline is Bill Houlder, a free agent signee a year ago, who is an offensive type who has never really blown the doors off at the NHL with his point totals. He specializes in being a secondary man on the power play point. Seventeen of his 28 points came with the man-advantage.

As well, there is Cory Cross, who provides the size at 6-5, 219; Igor Ulanov, who has played with four NHL teams in the last two years; and veterans David Shaw and unrestricted free agent Michel Petit, who will probably sign with the Lightning if they still want him.

Challenging for jobs will be Chris LiPuma, Drew Bannister, and junior Mike McBain.

This is a position already improved from last year, but expect more changes before they're all set.

FORWARD: The Lightning are strong with youth down the middle - Chris Gratton, Aaron Gavey, and likely rookie Daymond Langkow. Add to that the veterans, in Brian Bradley, the only team scoring leader they've ever had, and successful veteran free agent signee John Cullen.

Gratton looks like he's going to be a major league sniper. He has improved steadily each year and this could be his breakout season. A spot on the top line, even if it's at wing, would help facilitate that. It's time for Langkow to play, as well. The successful junior scorer could make a big splash for the Lightning.

Among the veterans up front for the Lightning are Brian Bellows, who accepts his role, whether it be fourth line winger, or power play sniper. At times during the season he was playing like a kid again, and contributing with his stick and his heart. His 12 power play goals were second only to Alexander Selivanov, who had 13.

Selivanov also led the team in goals, with 31, and has been a big bonus for Tampa Bay, especially considering he was obtained from Philadelphia for only a fourth round draft pick. Now, he's likely to be found on the right side of the number one line. He also led the team in traffic tickets, garnering five in a month before his license was thankfully taken away. Three tickets were for speeding, one was for going too slow, and another was for going through a gas station to avoid a red light.

A number of Lightning players have the green light to play either right or left wing. Sometimes found on the right side besides Selivanov, are Bellows, Ysebeart, Klima, and Poeschek.

On the left wing, besides some of the aforementioned, are Shawn Burr, Rob Zamuner, Jason Wiemer, and Patrick Poulin.

Zamuner is a defensive specialist, and was being touted around the league as a possible Selke trophy candidate for best defensive forward. He did not, however, make the final three in the voting.

Poulin is an enigmatic, they-love-me-they-love-me-not type of player who looked like he was going to be a star earlier in his career, and might still be - in the International League.

Jason Wiemer, Tampa Bay's number one

pick, eighth overall, in the 1994 draft, has had his problems, but might very soon break out. What he needs to do is show improvement every year, which he has done so far - but very, very slowly. One of these days he's going to pop a couple in, and keep on popping.

Wiemer might have been better served by joining Canada's National Junior team when they invited him. The Lightning, though, asked for assurance that he would play. And when they didn't get it, Weimer didn't go. What kind of nonsense is that? Do the Lightning guarantee playing time for everybody that tries out with them? For anyone? Of course not, yet that's what they wanted. By being so silly, it was Wiemer who was hurt by it. Tampa could have easily done without him for a couple weeks.

The Lightning have a bunch of mid-range scoring threats, none to score 50 goals. They will hope some of their highly touted young players, such as Gratton, Wiemer, Langkow or Selivanov will continue to score more, and hopefully for them, score lots more. The veterans on this team at forward make solid contributions, but they're all expendable. They fill in the blanks while the team waits for the kids to fill the nets.

SPECIAL TEAMS: Pretty amazing this fourth place power play finish, considering they were among the league worst in their first three years. They did, however, stink during the playoffs.

Not to be overlooked is that their penalty killing also ranked very high, at fifth.

Both of those rankings mask their inefficiency at even strength, which could become a problem if either of these units run in trouble this year.

Hamrlik is highly responsible for the power play proficiency, and Zamuner is the key for the successful penalty killing.

POWER PLAY	G	ATT	PCT	
Overall	83	400	20.8%	(4th NHL)
Home	50	213	23.5%	(5th NHL)
Road	33	187	17.6%	(9th NHL)

13 SHORT HANDED GOALS ALLOWED (T-19th NHL)

PENALTY KILLING	G	TSH	PCT	
Overall	68	439	84.5%	(5th NHL)
Home	35	217	83.9%	(12th NHL)
Road	33	222	85.1%	(2nd NHL)

6 SHORT HANDED GOALS SCORED (T-24th NHL)

COACHING AND MANAGEMENT: Expansion team coaches don't last long, and nowadays coaches don't last long anywhere. That's why the fact that Crisp has been the only Tampa Bay coach, with Esposito as GM, has been so surprising. He's also the longest serving coach in the league, and holds the record for most games coached for an expansion team from its beginning, as noted below.

Most Games Coaching an Expansion Team From its Inception:

Terry Crisp	Tampa Bay	298
Rick Bowness	Ottawa	235
Bernie Geoffrion	Atlanta	208

Still, there were Crisp firing rumors in abundance early in the year, and it was also rumored that Esposito was trying to drive him out so he could give the job to assistant coach Wayne Cashman.

Crisp, who finished third in the Jack Adams Trophy award voting for coach of the year, signed a three-year contract during the summer, despite being rumored as a candidate for the Toronto opening.

Esposito is also the only general manager the team has ever had. He seems to make the right moves, with good draft choices and patience. His dealings with the press leave something to be desired, however.

And one other curious thing. Early in the year, when the team was struggling, he had a meeting with CEO Steve Oto and other top management. They reportedly went through all facets of the team to see how they could turn it around.

Wouldn't that be awfully embarassing for Esposito? A bunch of guys who know little to nothing about hockey trying to figure out with him what to do next? Can you imagine Mike Keenan in the same predicament? Can you imagine any team upper management putting their top man in such an embarassing situation?

DRAFT

Round	Sel.	Player	Pos	
1	16	Mario Larocque	D	Hull (QMJHL)
3	69	Curtis Tipler	RW	Regina (WHL)
5	125	Jason Robinson	D	Niagara Falls (OHL)
6	152	Nikolai Ignatov	D	Russia
6	157	Xavier Delisle	C	Granby (QMJHL)
7	179	Pavel Kubina	D	Czech Republic

Larocque is tall at 6-2, but he's a lightweight at 165 pounds. Better than the other way around, though, because you can put on weight. He'll need to do that as he progresses with his junior career. Skating is seen as his strength.

All four of the Lightning's previous four first round picks - Hamrlik, Gratton, Wiemer and Langkow - are expected to be in their lineup this season. Larocque is a couple years away.

PROGNOSIS: The Lightning are a decent team, but not a great one by any means. The one season rise to prominence may in fact be a mirage, and they could falter this year. Or it could be an omen for things to come.

The defence has improved and goaltending is great, but the even strength situation is worrisome.

It appears the Lightning plan is to be good for a lot of years, not just one or two. They want a solid foundation of young players with which to grow, and they certainly have that. They want to keep to the plan, and so far so good. The Lightning are one of those up in the air teams - difficult to predict. They're not a contender yet, so a one season drop is probably more likely than a move up to the next level.

They should probably remain around the .500 level and still be fighting it out for a playoff spot on the last day of the season.

PREDICTION:

Atlantic Division: 6th

Eastern Conference: 8th

Overall: 16th

Team Rankings 1995-96

		Conference Rank	League Rank
Record	38-32-12	8	11
Home	22-14-5	6	9
Away	16-18-7	6	11
Versus Own Conference	25-23-8	9	13
Versus Other Conference	13-9-4	6	9
Team Plus\Minus	-25	11	20
Goals For	238	8	18
Goals Against	248	6	11
Average Shots For	31.0	5	10

Average

Shots Against	29.6	6	10
Overtime	3-3-12	6	13
One Goal Games	12-11	7	12
Times outshooting opponent	43	6	9
Versus Teams Over .500	18-19-8	5	7
Versus Teams Under .500	20-13-4	9	13
First Half Record	17-17-7	8	12
Second Half Record	21-15-5	4	7

Results: Lost 4-2 to Philadelphia

Record: 2-4

Home: 1-2

Away: 1-2

Goals For: 13 (2.2 per game)

Goals Against: 26 (4.3 per game)

Overtime: 2-0

Power play: 8.6% (14th)

Penalty Killing: 76.7% (15th)

ALL-TIME LEADERS

GOALS

Brian Bradley	102
Petr Klima	63
John Tucker	49

ASSISTS

Brian Bradley	167
Roman Hamrlik	93
John Tucker	82

POINTS

Brian Bradley	269
Petr Klima	133
Roman Hamrlik	130

BEST INDIVIDUAL SEASONS

GOALS

Brian Bradley	1992-93	43
Alexander Selivanov	1995-96	31
Petr Klima	1993-94	28

ASSISTS

Brian Bradley	1995-96	56
Roman Hamrlik	1995-96	49
Brian Bradley	1992-93	44

POINTS

Brian Bradley	1992-93	86
Brian Bradley	1995-96	79
Roman Hamrlik	1995-96	65

TEAM RECORD

Last 3 years

	GP	W	L	T	Pts	%
1995-96	82	38	32	12	88	.543
1994-95	48	17	28	3	37	.385
1993-94	84	30	43	11	71	.423

Best 3 regular seasons

1995-96	82	38	32	12	88	.543
1993-94	84	30	43	11	71	.423
1994-95	48	17	28	3	37	.385

Worst 3 regular seasons

1992-93	84	23	54	7	53	.315
1994-95	48	17	28	3	37	.385
1993-94	84	30	43	11	71	.423

Most Goals (min. 70 game schedule)

1992-93	245
1995-96	238
1993-94	224

Fewest Goals (min. 70 game schedule)

1993-94	224
1995-96	238
1992-93	245

Most Goals Against (min. 70 game schedule)

1992-93	332
1993-94	251
1995-96	248

Fewest Goals Against (min. 70 game schedule)

1995-96	248
1993-94	251
1992-93	332

STAT SECTION

Team Scoring Stats

	GP	G	A	PTS	+/-	PIM	SH	Power Play			Short Handed		
								G	A	P	G	A	P
BRIAN BRADLEY	75	23	56	79	11-	77	189	9	32	41	0	0	0
ROMAN HAMRLIK	82	16	49	65	24-	103	281	12	30	42	0	1	1
ALEXANDER SELIVANOV	79	31	21	52	3	93	215	13	5	18	0	0	0
PETR KLIMA	67	22	30	52	25-	68	164	8	20	28	0	0	0
JOHN CULLEN	76	16	34	50	1	65	152	8	12	20	0	0	0
BRIAN BELLOWS	79	23	26	49	14-	39	190	13	14	27	0	0	0
CHRIS GRATTON	82	17	21	38	13-	105	183	7	7	14	0	0	0
ROB ZAMUNER	72	15	20	35	11	62	152	0	2	2	3	1	4
PAUL YSEBAERT	55	16	15	31	19-	16	135	4	6	10	1	0	1
SHAWN BURR	81	13	15	28	4	119	122	1	0	1	0	0	0
BILL HOULDER	61	5	23	28	1	22	90	3	14	17	0	0	0
MIKAEL ANDERSSON	64	8	11	19	0	2	104	0	0	0	0	0	0
JASON WIEMER	66	9	9	18	9-	81	89	4	3	7	0	0	0
PATRICK POULIN	46	7	9	16	7	16	51	1	0	1	0	0	0
CORY CROSS	75	2	14	16	4	66	57	0	0	0	0	0	0
AARON GAVEY	73	8	4	12	6-	56	65	1	2	3	1	0	1
MICHEL PETIT	54	4	8	12	11-	135	68	0	5	5	0	0	0
IGOR ULANOV	64	3	9	12	11	116	37	0	0	0	0	0	0
DAVID SHAW	66	1	11	12	5	64	90	0	1	1	0	0	0
JOHN TUCKER	63	3	7	10	8-	18	53	0	0	0	0	1	1
RUDY POESCHEK	57	1	3	4	2-	88	36	0	0	0	0	0	0
ADRIEN PLAVSIC	7	1	2	3	5	6	4	0	0	0	0	0	0
DAYMOND LANGKOW	4	0	1	1	1-	0	4	0	0	0	0	0	0
DREW BANNISTER	13	0	1	1	1-	4	10	0	0	0	0	0	0
DAREN PUPPA	57	0	1	1	0	4	0	0	0	0	0	0	0
JEFF TOMS	1	0	0	0	0	0	1	0	0	0	0	0	0
DEREK WILKINSON	4	0	0	0	0	2	0	0	0	0	0	0	0
ALAN EGELAND	5	0	0	0	0	2	1	0	0	0	0	0	0
J.C. BERGERON	12	0	0	0	0	0	0	0	0	0	0	0	0
CHRIS LIPUMA	21	0	0	0	7-	13	8	0	0	0	0	0	0
JEFF REESE	26	0	0	0	0	0	0	0	0	0	0	0	0

PLAYOFFS

PLAYER	GP	G	A	PTS	+/-	PIM	PP	SH	GW	OT	S
JOHN CULLEN	5	3	3	6	4	0	0	1	0	0	6
ROB ZAMUNER	6	2	3	5	1-	10	0	1	0	0	10
ALEXANDER SELIVANOV	6	2	2	4	2	6	0	0	1	1	22
BRIAN BRADLEY	5	0	3	3	5-	6	0	0	0	0	7
PETR KLIMA	4	2	0	2	0	14	2	0	0	0	9
BRIAN BELLOWS	6	2	0	2	2-	4	0	0	1	1	19
MIKAEL ANDERSSON	6	1	1	2	0	0	0	0	0	0	4
SHAWN BURR	6	0	2	2	0	8	0	0	0	0	5
CHRIS GRATTON	6	0	2	2	3-	27	0	0	0	0	4
JASON WIEMER	6	1	0	1	3-	28	1	0	0	0	11
ROMAN HAMRLIK	5	0	1	1	1-	4	0	0	0	0	10
BILL HOULDER	6	0	1	1	0	4	0	0	0	0	8
DAVID SHAW	6	0	1	1	4-	4	0	0	0	0	9
JOHN TUCKER	2	0	0	0	1-	2	0	0	0	0	0
PATRICK POULIN	2	0	0	0	0	0	0	0	0	0	0
RUDY POESCHEK	3	0	0	0	0	12	0	0	0	0	2
DAREN PUPPA	4	0	0	0	0	0	0	0	0	0	0
JEFF REESE	5	0	0	0	0	0	0	0	0	0	0
PAUL YSEBAERT	5	0	0	0	6-	0	0	0	0	0	4
IGOR ULANOV	5	0	0	0	1-	15	0	0	0	0	2
MICHEL PETIT	6	0	0	0	3-	20	0	0	0	0	7
CORY CROSS	6	0	0	0	4-	22	0	0	0	0	6
AARON GAVEY	6	0	0	0	3-	4	0	0	0	0	5

Washington Capitals

The Washington Capitals should consider changing their nickname to the Browns. As in Charlie Brown.

Every year it's the same thing. The team is running, running, running hard to kick the football, and just when it looks like they're going to get there, someone lifts the ball and the Capitals fall flat on their backs.

Let's take the last 14 years, which happen to be the 14 years that Washington has made the playoffs. In 13 of those seasons the Capitals had winning regular season records, three of them with over 100 points, seven of them with at least 90 points. Only once did they make it past the second round of the playoffs, and guess which of those seasons it was? The one year in which they had a losing record.

Seven times in the last 14 years they got knocked out in the first round, and they were the favored team (higher regular season standing) in five of them. In their six first round wins they were the underdog team in three of them.

General manager David Poile was upset at the Washington media for focusing on the negative. Maybe it's because there's good reason.

They have not made it to the Stanley Cup finals in any of their 22 years.

Every other team, with the exception of recent expansion entries and the Phoenix Coyotes, has made it to the finals at least once. The Coyotes failed to make it in 17 years in Winnipeg.

It's more than the fact they lose when they should win, it's that they blow it when they almost have it won. Last year, they won the first two games of their first round series, on the road in Pittsburgh. Then they lost four straight. The year before they held a 3-1 series edge against Pittsburgh, and blew that one too. In 1992 they blew another 3-1 lead to Pittsburgh, and in 1987 they lost to the Islanders after the same 3-1 lead. We won't even bring up the fact that they've lost six playoff overtime games in a row.

What's the deal? Of course, we're comparing different Washington teams, ones that have turned over many different players and a number of coaches. The only constant through the 14 years is Poile. And what's he done wrong? He puts a winning team out there year after year.

If the Capitals were a golfer, say Greg Norman, you'd call them chokers - can't win the big ones. If they were a person (picture Charlie Brown) they'd be known as losers. If they were the Boston Red Sox, they could blame it on a curse, or Bill Buckner.

Maybe it is Poile's fault, just for the sake of argument. Maybe he builds teams that can only succeed in the regular season. That's a difficult concept to swallow however, because the team is often defensive-oriented, which is supposed to be better for the playoffs, and they have had lots of character-type players over the years - the Scott Stevens and the Dale Hunters.

Perhaps it's Poile's choice of coaches. There have been only three - and two of them were brothers, Bryan and Terry Murray. Bryan received much of the blame earlier in Washington, and then after being replaced by his brother, went to Detroit and did the same thing there - winning during the regular season and then falling flat on their faces in the playoffs. Terry has done okay in Philadelphia, taking them to the conference championship his first season, and then faltering some last year when the Flyers were beat out by Florida in the Conference semi-finals. Schoenfeld took New Jersey to the conference championships before he arrived in Washington.

There is one other thing, and while it's purely subjective, it's also noticable. Many of their top scorers over the timespan have been of the "soft" variety. Certainly not Dale Hunter, but lots of others are known for their offence and lack of defence. Players like Mike Gartner, Bengt Gustafsson, Dave Christian, Mike Ridley, Bobby Carpenter (although he took a defensive role later with New Jersey) and Joe Juneau to name some, aren't your prototypical playoff leaders in the Mark Messier, Doug Gilmour mold. Lots of speed and finesse among the above names, but not the scrappy, win-at-all-cost the-team-is-everything types who can take over a series and win it on their own. Maybe a lot of teams can say the same thing, but if Mark Messier were playing for the Caps they wouldn't have gone 22 years without

WASHINGTON RECORD SINCE 1982-83

Season	Record	Points	Overall Standing	Playoff Result
1995-96	39-32-11	89	11	Lost in 1st round
1994-95	22-18-8	52	9	Lost in 1st round
1993-94	39-35-10	88	12	Lost in 2nd round
1992-93	43-34-7	93	10	Lost in 1st round
1991-92	45-27-8	98	2	Lost in 1st round
1990-91	37-36-7	81	9	Lost in 2nd round
1989-90	36-38-6	78	13	Lost in Conference Champ.
1988-89	41-29-10	92	3	Lost in 1st round
1987-88	38-33-9	85	7	Lost in 2nd round
1986-87	38-32-10	86	7	Lost in 1st round
1985-86	50-23-7	107	3	Lost in 2nd round
1984-85	46-25-9	101	3	Lost in 1st round
1983-84	48-27-5	101	5	Lost in 2nd round
1982-83	39-25-16	94	8	Lost in 1st round

reaching the finals. He wouldn't have allowed it.

Now that we've laid some blame around, here's one final thought. Until the last two seasons, everybody played within their own division first in the playoffs, and the Patrick division was one of the toughest. Despite their excellent overall standing, Washington only finished first once in that division. Even the three years they had over 100 points, they still finished second. They were up against powerhouses, who at varying times were the New York Islanders, Pittsburgh, Philadelphia, the New York Rangers, and New Jersey.

Yeah, okay, so get over it, forget the excuses and kick the ball.

TEAM PREVIEW

GOAL: Looks like Jim Carey is getting a label. The same one his team has had for over a decade - plays great in the regular season, falters in the playoffs. Last year's Vezina Trophy winner finished third in goals against average, second in wins, third in games played and first in shutouts.

In the playoffs he was brutal for the second year in a row. After playing 71 games during the regular season he had to suffer the humiliation of giving way to Olaf Kolzig. And Olie the Goalie came through with a 1.94 goals against average, in stark contrast to Carey's 6.19 GAA.

Where does that leave the Caps goaltending situation? There's no point in not playing Carey because he's an excellent goalie - during the regular season. And there's no point not playing Kolzig because he's good too, and probably deserves more playing time with his playoff performance.

That playing time could be with another team, however, because Kolzig has made himself excellent trade bait.

If there's no trade, Carey will get the bulk of the work again, with Kolzig likely getting more playing time.

So the playoffs will come around again and the Caps will have put together a decent regular season as usual. And there in the nets to play the first game, probably against Pittsburgh, will be Carey. The first sign of failure and everyone will be going, "Here we go again."

But, the reputation he's earned is also easy to rid. He just has to play better in the playoffs. Even once.

Getting back to the regular season, one of Carey's phenomenal accomplishments is his shutout total. Last season he had nine, and together with the four he earned in just 28 games as a rookie, he already holds the Capitals' career shutout mark. The most any other active goalie had in his first two seasons is seven, by Tom Barrasso.

DEFENCE: The Washington blueline corps is the best in the league. It has offense skill, defensive skill, size, speed, strength, experience, youth, talent, and depth.

Did we leave anything out?

They're so talented and so deep a bunch of them even played forward at different times during the season to help out a less talented and deep group. If something happened to any one of them, such as an

GOALTENDER	GPI	MINS	AVG	W	L	T	EN	SO	GA	SA	SV %
JIM CAREY	71	4069	2.26	35	24	9	4	9	153	1631	.906
OLAF KOLZIG	18	897	3.08	4	8	2	1	0	46	406	.887
WSH TOTALS	82	4990	2.45	39	32	11	5	9	204	2042	.900

injury or trade, the team wouldn't suffer because they've got replacements chomping at the bit. You could divide them in two and the second team would be better than many in the NHL.

Enough gushing. The top 12 are Phil Housley, Mark Tinordi, Sylvain Cote, Sergei Gonchar, Calle Johansson, Joe Reekie, Brendan Witt, Nolan Baumgartner, Ken Klee, Eric Charron, Steve Poapst and Stewart Malgunas.

Okay, not enough gushing. At least in terms of depth.

Need a defenceman for the power play? Take your pick from four or five.

Need some trade bait? Go fishing.

It was surprising that the Capitals didn't trade last year some of their excess talent on the blueline for people who can score, but injury problems all season played a hand in that. They should do it this year because they desperately need more scoring from the forwards.

A team doesn't want to have a defence that's too young and inexperienced, but they have three young prizes to go with their veterans: Nolan Baumgartner, Brendan Witt and Sergei Gonchar. Those are the three building blocks, with the mix filled in around them. Outstanding.

Housley was a big free agent signing, because no matter how few scorers there are up front, he's going to make the power play much better. He will probably outscore most of the forwards as well.

FORWARD: It's quite obvious, and has been for some time, that Washington needs somebody other than Peter Bondra to put the puck in the net. As it was, they didn't have anybody with half as many as his 52, and only two players who scored a third as many as him. The remarkable thing about that is

that he missed 15 games, six to an early season holdout, and nine to injury.

Consider how dominant Bondra was for Washington, keeping in mind the 15 games he missed:

Highest Percentage of Team Goals:

	Team	Goals	Team Goals	%
PETER BONDRA	WSH	52	234	22.2
Paul Kariya	Ana	50	234	21.4
Alexander Mogilny	Van	55	278	19.7
Brett Hull	StL	43	219	19.6
Theoren Fleury	Cgy	46	241	19.1
Mario Lemieux	Pit	69	362	19.1

If you take Bondra's goals per game pace and multiply by 15 games, his percentage of team goals would be considerably higher at 27.4%.

This is not a one-year thing, either. The previous year Bondra again scored the highest percentage of his team's goals in the league, checking in at 25%.

As impressive as Bondra's numbers are, it's not a particularly good thing. Teams with one goal scorer are easy to stop come playoff time.

So, who else on this team is going to score goals? They have a couple good setup men in Michal Pivonka and Joe Juneau, but they're not goal scorers. Steve Konowalchuk was second with a measly 23, and can probably improve on that, and then there is Keith Jones (18) and Pat Peake (17), who broke his heel in the playoffs after having fractured the thyroid cartilage (whatever that is) around his larynx, after recovering from a bout of mononucleosis the previous season, after recovering from assorted other injuries before that.

Among the other younger players,

Andrew Brunette, who scored 162 points four years ago with Owen Sound, to lead the OHL, played every playoff game and showed some promise; first round selection Jason Allison has been a huge disappointment, scoring zero goals in 19 games with Washington; Jeff Nelson managed to better Allison with zero goals in 33 games; and assorted others that scored lots in Portland in the AHL, but are unproven at the NHL level. Top draft pick Alexandre Volchov might get a chance to play, considering he's a scorer, which, if we haven't mentioned it before, is something they need.

The answer isn't on the Washington roster, so GM David Poile is going to have to make a trade. He really seems to like the players developed within their own system, and that's worked for him to some degree, but they need a goal scorer, a power winger in the mold of a Keith Tkachuk, or Owen Nolan, or Brendan Shanahan. Thirty or forty goals from someone other than Bondra would help out considerably and allow Juneau and Pivonka someone else to pass to.

Juneau's good trade bait, because he's a playmaker with useful power play setup skills and that's a commodity some teams can use. There are some goal scorers out there that won't cost too much. The trend seems to be to pass some of the aging veterans around the league, for contract reasons or whatever. Players such as Ray Sheppard, Dave Andreychuk, Steve Thomas, Wendel Clark, Claude Lemieux, have made the rounds and can get you 30 goals or more for a season or two.

This lack of goal scoring help has gone on for a couple years now. It's time to do something about it.

SPECIAL TEAMS: Considering how gifted Bondra is as a goal-scorer, for some reason he didn't score much on the power play. Only 11 of his 52 goals came with the man-advantage. Pat Peake was only three behind him with eight power play markers, and he only scored 17 in total.

That's not saying something negative about Bondra, because you'd rather have a guy scoring goals at even strength. He had 37 of those, second in the league behind Jagr's 41. Bondra even had four shorthanded markers.

Bondra's not really a hang-around-the-net-and-put-in-the-garbage type of scorer, so maybe they ought to get one of those guys, such as those in the list above, or even Dino Ciccarelli, who is available from Detroit, and used to play with the Capitals. That way, as they did last season at times, they wouldn't have to put a defenceman up there.

Housley is going to make the power play better, much better, but he still needs somebody to pass the puck to.

POWER PLAY	G	ATT	PCT
Overall	63	403	15.6% (22nd NHL)
Home	31	196	15.8% (20th NHL)
Road	32	207	15.5% (19th NHL)

7 SHORT HANDED GOALS ALLOWED (T-2nd NHL)

PENALTY KILLING	G	TSH	PCT
Overall	67	385	82.6% (T-11th NHL)
Home	34	188	81.9% (T-14th NHL)
Road	33	197	83.2% (6th NHL)

12 SHORT HANDED GOALS SCORED (T-9th NHL)

COACHING AND MANAGEMENT: David Poile is one of the best general managers in the league. You can see it in the deals he pulls off, in the number of players he drafts who play for the team, and in their regular season record.

He is also patient, perhaps to a fault. He is not the type to drop the blockbuster deal very often, preferring to wait for the talent they have to mature. But, they've had the same problem for a while now, lack of a goal scorer other than Bondra, and he still hasn't done anything about it.

It's almost a certainty he will this time, though.

This will be Jim Schoenfeld's fourth year behind the Washington bench, which in NHL years is similar to a player going 12 years with the same team. He hasn't had a losing season yet with the Caps so his job doesn't appear to be in jeopardy. He hates losing and isn't afraid to try things to shake his team up. And the nice thing about coaching Washington, when they go into a slump, like all teams do, you don't have to worry about the GM panicking and firing you. He will give you time to work it out.

DRAFT:

1995 DRAFT SELECTIONS

Round	Sel.	Player	Pos	Team
1	4	Alexander Volchkov	C	Barrie (OHL)
1	17	Jaroslav Svejkovsky	RW	Tri-City (WHL)
2	43	Jan Bulis	C	Barrie (OHL)
3	58	Sergei Zimakov	D	Russia
3	70	Jonathan Sim	C	Sarnia (OHL)
3	74	Dave Weninger	G	Michigan Tech
4	85	Justin Davis	RW	Kingston (OHL)
5	126	Matthew Lahey	LW	Peterborough (OHL)
6	153	Andrew VanBrugen	RW	Northern Michigan Univ.
7	180	Michael Anderson	RW	Minnesota Univ.
8	206	Oleg Orekhovsky	D	Russia
9	232	Chad Cavanagh	LW	London (OHL)

Volchov might have gone a player earlier in the draft if not for his attitude. Nobody is disputing his offensive talent, but nobody is singing praises about his character. Arrogant, self-centred, and a prima donna are the common descriptions. Even his junior team in Barrie doesn't want him back.

What might be best is for the Capitals to keep him on their roster to start the season. If he comes through and plays well, so be it, they can live with the attitude. If he doesn't, it should knock him down a peg or two. Then they can send him back to junior with his tail between his legs and he might see the world a little differently.

The Caps' other first round pick, Svejkovsky, is described as a pure scorer, but one who doesn't bring anything else to the party. That might just be okay on the Caps who already are strong on defence, and won't need the Czech to check, but just to score.

PROGNOSIS: The Caps are going to be there, just like always. From the blueline back, they're the best team in the league. They have to figure out a way to get over the playoff hump, however, and this year, much like the previous 22 seasons, could be the one that gets them there.

The lack of goal scoring has reached the ridiculous stage, so that is one area in which they're going to have to improve. If they do, watch out. Rather, when they do.

As well as Washington played last year, they did it with an incredible amount of injuries. If they can keep healthy that alone should make a big difference. Two or three goal scorers and they have a legitimate chance at the Stanley Cup.

PREDICTION:

Atlantic Division: 2nd

Eastern Conference: 3rd

Overall: 5th

Team Rankings 1994/95

		Conference Rank	League Rank
Record	39-32-11	7	10
Home	21-15-5	9	13
Away	18-17-6	4	7
Versus Own Conference	26-23-7	7	11
Versus Other Conference	13-9-4	6	9
Team Plus\Minus	+34	4	7
Goals For	234	10	20
Goals Against	204	2	3
Average Shots For	30.1	8	15
Average Shots Against	24.9	1	2
Overtime	4-1-11	2	4
One Goal Games	16-14	5	10
Times outshooting opponent	53	4	5
Versus Teams Over .500	16-24-5	9	15
Versus Teams Under .500	23-8-6	3	4
First Half Record	20-17-4	5	9
Second Half Record	19-15-7	7	12

Results: Lost in first round to Pittsburgh

Record: 2-4

Home: 0-3

Away: 2-1

Goals For: 17 (2.8 per game)

Goals Against: 21 (3.5 per game)

Overtime: 0-1

Power play: 18.4% (?th)

Penalty Killing: 83.3% (?th)

ALL-TIME LEADERS

GOALS

Mike Gartner	397
Mike Ridley	218
Bengt Gustafsson	196

ASSISTS

Mike Gartner	392
Michal Pivonka	390
Bengt Gustafsson	359

POINTS

Mike Gartner	789
Michal Pivonka	556
Bengt Gustafsson	555

BEST INDIVIDUAL SEASONS

GOALS

Dennis Maruk	1981-82	60
Bob Carpenter	1984-85	53
Peter Bondra	1995-96	52

ASSISTS

Dennis Maruk	1981-82	76
Michal Pivonka	1995-96	65
Scott Stevens	1988-89	61

POINTS

Dennis Maruk	1981-82	136
Mike Gartner	1984-85	102
Dennis Maruk	1980-81	97

TEAM RECORD

Last 3 years

	GP	W	L	T	Pts	%
1995-96	82	39	32	11	89	.543
1994-95	48	22	18	8	52	.542
1993-94	84	39	35	10	88	.524

Best 3 regular seasons

1985-86	80	50	23	7	107	.669
1983-84	80	48	27	5	101	.631
1984-85	80	46	25	9	101	.631

Worst 3 regular seasons

1974-75	80	8	67	5	21	.131
1975-76	80	11	59	10	32	.200
1977-78	80	17	49	14	48	.333

Most Goals (min. 70 game schedule)

1991-92	330
1992-93	325
1984-85	322

Fewest Goals (min. 70 game schedule)

1974-75	181
1977-78	195
1976-77	221

Most Goals Against (min. 70 game schedule)

1974-75	446
1975-76	394
1981-82	338

Fewest Goals Against (min. 70 game schedule)

1995-96	204
1983-84	226
1984-85	240

STAT SECTION

Team Scoring Stats

	GP	G	A	PTS	+/-	PIM	SH	Power Play			Short Handed		
								G	A	P	G	A	P
MICHAL PIVONKA	73	16	65	81	18	36	168	6	18	24	2	2	4
PETER BONDRA	67	52	28	80	18	40	322	11	10	21	4	1	5
JOE JUNEAU	80	14	50	64	3-	30	176	7	21	28	2	0	2
TODD KRYGIER	76	15	33	48	1-	82	181	3	4	7	1	3	4
STEVE KONOWALCHUK	70	23	22	45	13	92	197	7	6	13	1	2	3
KEITH JONES	68	18	23	41	8	103	155	5	9	14	0	0	0
SERGEI GONCHAR	78	15	26	41	25	60	139	4	10	14	0	0	0
SYLVAIN COTE	81	5	33	38	5	40	212	3	12	15	0	2	2
DALE HUNTER	82	13	24	37	5	112	128	4	8	12	0	0	0
PAT PEAKE	62	17	19	36	7	46	129	8	6	4	0	0	0
CALLE JOHANSSON	78	10	25	35	13	50	182	4	11	15	0	2	2
KELLY MILLER	74	7	13	20	7	30	93	0	1	1	2	1	3
STEFAN USTORF	48	7	10	17	8	14	39	0	0	0	0	2	2
MARK TINORDI	71	3	10	13	26	113	82	2	3	5	0	0	0
CRAIG BERUBE	50	2	10	12	1	151	28	1	1	2	0	0	0
KEN KLEE	66	8	3	11	1-	60	76	0	0	0	1	0	1
MIKE EAGLES	70	4	7	11	1-	75	70	0	0	0	0	2	2
JOE REEKIE	78	3	7	10	7	149	52	0	0	0	0	0	0
JEFF NELSON	33	0	7	7	3	16	21	0	0	0	0	0	0
ANDREW BRUNETTE	11	3	3	6	5	0	16	0	0	0	0	0	0
JIM JOHNSON	66	2	4	6	3-	34	49	0	0	0	0	0	0
BRENDAN WITT	48	2	3	5	4-	85	44	0	0	0	0	0	0
MARTIN GENDRON	20	2	1	3	5-	8	22	0	1	1	0	0	0
KEVIN KAMINSKI	54	1	2	3	1-	164	17	0	0	0	0	0	0
JASON ALLISON	19	0	3	3	3-	2	18	0	1	1	0	0	0
STEVE POAPST	3	1	0	1	1-	0	2	0	0	0	0	0	0
ERIC CHARRON	18	0	1	1	3-	22	13	0	0	0	0	0	0
STEWART MALGUNAS	30	0	1	1	10-	32	13	0	0	0	0	0	0
JIM CAREY	71	0	1	1	0	6	0	0	0	0	0	0	0
NOLAN BAUMGARTNER	1	0	0	0	1-	0	0	0	0	0	0	0	0
RICHARD ZEDNIK	1	0	0	0	0	0	0	0	0	0	0	0	0
OLAF KOLZIG	18	0	0	0	0	2	0	0	0	0	0	0	0

PLAYOFFS

PLAYER	GP	G	A	PTS	+/-	PIM	PP	SH	GW	OT	S
JOE JUNEAU	5	0	7	7	4-	6	0	0	0	0	20
SERGEI GONCHAR	6	2	4	6	1-	4	1	0	0	0	29
DALE HUNTER	6	1	5	6	4	24	0	0	0	0	14
PETER BONDRA	6	3	2	5	0	8	2	0	1	0	36
MICHAL PIVONKA	6	3	2	5	1	18	1	0	0	0	17
ANDREW BRUNETTE	6	1	3	4	5-	0	0	0	0	0	7
PAT PEAKE	5	2	1	3	4-	12	2	0	0	0	9
SYLVAIN COTE	6	2	0	2	3-	12	1	0	0	0	25
TODD KRYGIER	6	2	0	2	3-	12	0	0	1	0	15
MIKE EAGLES	6	1	1	2	1	2	0	0	0	0	12
STEVE KONOWALCHUK	2	0	2	2	1	0	0	0	0	0	1
KELLY MILLER	6	0	1	1	1-	4	0	0	0	0	11
KEN KLEE	1	0	0	0	0	0	0	0	0	0	2
NOLAN BAUMGARTNER	1	0	0	0	1-	10	0	0	0	0	0
CRAIG BERUBE	2	0	0	0	1-	19	0	0	0	0	3
KEITH JONES	2	0	0	0	1-	7	0	0	0	0	3
KEVIN KAMINSKI	3	0	0	0	0	16	0	0	0	0	1
JEFF NELSON	3	0	0	0	0	4	0	0	0	0	2
JIM CAREY	3	0	0	0	0	0	0	0	0	0	0
OLAF KOLZIG	5	0	0	0	0	4	0	0	0	0	0
STEFAN USTORF	5	0	0	0	1-	0	0	0	0	0	9
JIM JOHNSON	6	0	0	0	2-	6	0	0	0	0	15
MARK TINORDI	6	0	0	0	2-	16	0	0	0	0	9
ERIC CHARRON	6	0	0	0	1	8	0	0	0	0	2
STEVE POAPST	6	0	0	0	0	0	0	0	0	6	

WESTERN CONFERENCE

Anaheim Mighty Ducks

Almost since the day they were hatched the Ducks held public tutoring sessions so everyone would understand the virtues of patience. So calming and soothing, and oh, so high road. We know how it's done, folks.

If you don't mind waiting just a bit, we promise you our prized potential will develop and make it worth your while. In the meantime, you all can, uh, be entertained by the misadventures of our accident-prone mascot, Wild Wing.

Under those terms, if someone comes along and tries to make a deal for both of the team's last two number one draft picks, you hang up the phone. You call them bad names. You laugh in their face.

You don't wait for an offer you can't refuse.

Oh well, those textbook plans for building a successful hockey team are overrated anyway. So, the Ducks pulled the trigger on a blockbuster that sent two of the league's most touted youngsters, Oleg Tverdovsky and Chad Kilger, to Winnipeg for Teemu Selanne.

Good deal? Yes, said many, but in Winnipeg's favor.

Not so fast. This could also turn out to be a great deal for Anaheim. One that pays dividends immediately, and in the future. Selanne was only 25 years old, had already

led the league in goals, with 76 as a rookie, and was on his way to his second season of over 100 points, in just his second year of playing a full schedule.

Anaheim gets a proven star, if not superstar, for two that may or may not be stars one day. A sure thing for two maybes. And one of the maybes wasn't going to be the next Bobby Orr, as some had predicted for Tverdovsky.

It was abundantly clear that Paul Kariya could not be expected to score every goal for Anaheim, although he was giving it a try. He needed someone else to play, too.

Selanne's contribution to the Ducks was immediate and profound. Consider some before-and-after stats since Selanne played his first game with Anaheim on February 10.

	Before Selanne	After Selanne
Record	18-30-5	17-9-3
Home Record	12-14-2	10-1-2
Road Record	7-16-3	6-8-1
Power Play	11.0%	20.0%

The addition of Selanne helped the Ducks get into the playoff race. That's not such an overrated thing these days because anything can and does happen in the post-season (see

Florida Panthers). Enough of that getting spoiled with early success crap. If you have a chance, go for it.

They almost made it, too. They finished tied in points with Winnipeg but lost the final playoff spot because the Jets had more wins. Anaheim played great down the stretch, and in fact, were one of the top teams in the league over the last month and a half of the season.

Best Records Since March 1

	W	L	T	Pts
Detroit	16	2	3	35
Philadelphia	14	6	1	29
Boston	13	5	3	29
ANAHEIM	12	4	3	27

The stretch run wasn't all Selanne. The turnaround was dramatic and no coincidence, but others played key roles as well, notably Guy Hebert in net, and of course, Kariya.

Selanne set a couple team records in only 28 games, including a 15-game point streak. Kariya set or tied 19 records. Obviously, team records at this stage of the franchise aren't such a big deal, but a second-year player on a third-year team who scores 50 goals and 108 points is cause for celebration.

Most impressive is that the Ducks had two scorers in the top 10, and two 100-plus point scorers. Only Colorado and Pittsburgh accomplished that last season.

Anaheim fans took an instant liking to the change in team format and if nothing else, learned a valuable lesson: A Duck in the hand is worth two in the bush.

TEAM PREVIEW

GOAL: Guy Hebert had his ups and downs last season, and even had to worry about his starting job, but in the final analysis he was number one and deserved to be there. Hebert started the last 17 games of the season and compiled a 12-3-2 mark. There were other factors at work over that stretch, including Selanne's presence, but three shutouts indicate Hebert was a big part of the surge. He also finished an impressive fourth in league save percentage.

Hebert toils in relative anonymity, but he's been the number one man since the Ducks claimed him from St. Louis in the expansion draft. Goalies earn their reputations in the playoffs, so once Anaheim makes them, you'll be hearing a lot more of Hebert. He was also selected to replace John Vanbiesbrouck for Team USA for the World Cup team.

Mikhail Shtalenkov is the backup and there seems little reason to search for another. When he got his chance to play, it wasn't just to spell Hebert, coach Ron Wilson would let him go for a week or two at a time. On three separate occasions he started four games in a row.

That strategy by Wilson suggests a number of things: He was telling his goalies that if they play well they can keep on playing, he was trying to shake up Hebert, or he felt the number one job was for the taking. Hebert's play late in the season should solidify his number one position, but when he hits a dry spell Wilson won't hesitate to go with Shtalenkov.

Down on the farm, in Baltimore, Mike O'Neill, a career minor-leaguer, played 74 of 80 games for the Bandits after being signed as a free agent. Nice, but what's the point? On your developing team, one guy, who isn't likely to ever leave the minors unless someone gets hurt, gets all the playing time? While 21-year-old backup Byron Penstock napped on the end of the bench, the Ducks went and obtained Mike Torchia from Washington, and then didn't play him much either.

The Ducks might like to have a hotshot young goalie in the system on his way up, but for the time being it's not a problem area.

DEFENCE: The Ducks have one thing in abundance at this position: lots of NHL fifth, sixth, and seventh defencemen. It's quite possible that none of them would be regulars on some of the better teams, such as Detroit.

The news isn't all bad, though, because it seems to work for them.

Bobby Dollas probably spends the most time on the ice among Ducks defencemen. Besides playing all 82 games, he killed penalties, lined up on the power play sometimes, and was on the ice in crucial situations. Although he's not a big point-getter, and shouldn't be, he led all defencemen on the team with 30 points, and contributes as a goal scorer. He had eight this past season, seven in the labor-shortened previous year, and nine in the Ducks inaugural campaign. He isn't going to intimidate many people physically, despite his size (6-2, 212), and has never even had as many as 70 penalty minutes in a season. The American Hockey League's most valuable player in 1993, the 31-year-old also usually ends up on the plus side of the plus-minus ledger. In his three years with

Anaheim he is a plus 26, tops on the team, and not bad at all for an expansion club. In his last five professional seasons, he is a plus 121.

Tverdovsky was supposed to fill the offensive defenceman role eventually, and seemed to be coming around before the Selanne deal, but now the Ducks will have to make other arrangements. They had, in fact, made attempts to get help in that area when they obtained Jason York and Milos Holan late the previous year. Holan, of course, was beset by leukemia, and after a bone marrow transplant, was recovering in the off-season. York played 79 games, so he contributed, but not much offensively.

Instead, the Ducks played rent-an-offensive defenceman, picking up Fredrik Olausson from Edmonton off the waiver wire. Olausson, once one of the top offensive defencemen in the league, had fallen so low the Oilers gave him up for nothing. If the Oilers can get something for somebody, they will. Still, Olausson was a decent addition, scoring 18 points in his 36 games with the Ducks, and was good on the power play. He's a walking injury list, however, so while he may stick around, he can't be depended on for much. Not that it matters, guys like him are cheap and easy to find if you need a quick fix for the power play. In fact, the Ducks did it the previous season when they rented Tom Kurvers. And before that, they had Bill Houlder for a season.

David Karpa is another of many Ducks who came cheap and has proven useful. He

GOALTENDER	GPI	MINS	AVG	W	L	T	EN	SO	GA	SA	SV %
GUY HEBERT	59	3326	2.83	28	23	5	3	4	157	1820	.914
M. SHTALENKOV	30	1637	3.12	7	16	3	2	0	85	814	.896
ANA TOTALS	82	4982	2.97	35	39	8	5	4	247	2639	.906

provides the muscle, the heart and the fists, as evidenced by 270 penalty minutes.

Randy Ladouceur, who is 36 years old, watched much of the late-season playoff drive from the press box, and is an unrestricted free agent, so his return is unlikely.

Among the other contenders are Darren Van Impe, who had 58 points in 63 games at Baltimore, Jason Marshall, Oleg Mikulchik, Nicholai Tsulygin and Pavel Trnka. Mike Crowley was a big-time college scorer for Minnesota with 63 points in 42 games, so perhaps he could make the grade eventually as an offensive contributor. None are projected as future NHL stars, although with the lack of depth on the Anaheim blueline, almost everybody gets a chance to show their stuff. That should include draft pick Ruslan Salei, in part because of his age, 21, and the fact that he acclimatized himself to North American hockey last season with Las Vegas in the IHL.

FORWARD: The Ducks have something special here, and we're not talking about the ill-fated Special K line. Kariya, Kilger, and Krygier were outstanding together during the pre-season and early regular season. Kilger, in fact was eighth in the league in pre-season scoring, with 10 points (4-6-10) in just eight exhibition games. During the regular season for Anaheim, he was just 5-7-12, in 45 games. Krygier, who never was a high scorer anyway, eventually found his playing time diminished, battled some with Wilson over it, and then was dispatched back to Washington for minor league goalie Mike Torchia.

Then along came Selanne. Now there's Kariya and Selanne, and whatever else is left over. Fill in the blanks, advisedly with checkers. Check the heck out of everybody and then let Selanne and Kariya do the scoring. Life could be worse.

It's not all that unusual for a team to have two 100-point scorers because often they can feed off each other for points. Most teams, with two such players, often find themselves very high in the standings.

Selanne and Kariya played together for much of their time together, but Wilson wasn't reluctant to break them up and try to balance the scoring. As well, the two aren't going to contend for any defensive forward awards.

Who do you put between them when they're on the same line? Since they don't need the centre to score, ideally a good defensive type who will stay out of their way, would be ideal. Maybe he could dig the puck out of the corners, be a good passer, be the first man back, or head off anybody that wanted to test Kariya and Selanne physically.

Anatoli Semenov played between the two sometimes, but he's a 34-year-old free agent and it's unlikely the Ducks will go out of their way to sign him. Steve Rucchin played between them as well, and may be the best choice among those currently on the Ducks.

The Ducks are weak at centre, and there's little chance moves won't be made before opening night.

Also at centre is J.F. Jomphe, one of many free agent signees on Anaheim. After being called up in early February, he played every game. Shaun Van Allen, who has scored exactly eight goals in each of the last three seasons with Anaheim can play centre or wing, as can yo-yo man David Sacco, who's up and down from the NHL to the minors all the time.

If they don't manage to get a quality centre, look for Kariya to move back there.

After Selanne and Kariya, the wing is unimpressive, but not uninteresting. Roman Oksuita was acquired from Vancouver for Mike Sillinger, and is a regular Houdini. With Vancouver, he scored 10 goals in one 10-

game stretch, and then disappeared for the other 46 games, scoring just six goals. He also had seven goals in 14 games for Anaheim, but part-time players aren't a particularly valuable commodity which is why he was traded three times in two years. He does have some value on the power play.

Joe Sacco is another interesting story. He has a habit of snoozing through the first half of the season and turning it on late.

Valeri Karpov is one player from whom bigger things are expected. That wouldn't be difficult because he's shown very little so far. Actually, his thing is that he looks like he could score. Looks aren't everything, but maybe this is his breakout year.

Garry Valk is a good defensive winger who fits the program, and for the rough stuff the Ducks have Ken Baumgartner, and free agent signee, Warren Rychel. Ironically, the two were together on the Maple Leafs a couple seasons back.

Under the category of whatever happened to... put in the names of Steven King and John Lilley. Both were projected Ducks, but King ran into injury problems, and despite scoring 40 goals in Baltimore, pretty much stayed in Baltimore. He signed with Philadelphia during the summer. Lilley, another free agent, fell so far out of favor, he was loaned to the IHL, and was called up for just one game.

Alex Hicks was probably the biggest surprise of the many free agent signings. Undrafted out of Division III college hockey, after a couple years in the East Coast and International Leagues, he got a shot in mid November when leading Baltimore in scoring. And wouldn't you know it, he played every single one of the remaining games in Anaheim. He didn't tear up the score sheet, but he did score on his first NHL shot, at the age of 26.

Denny Lambert stuck for a while although he failed to score a goal in 33 games, and yet another free agent signee Dwayne Norris led Baltimore with 86 points and had a cup of coffee with Anaheim.

Predicting which of the above will be in the lineup is a difficult task, especially when an Alex Hicks ends up playing almost the entire season with the team, despite no previous notice. Look for more free agent signings.

If it's more scoring the Ducks want, there are three good prospects on the horizon. Johan Davidsson will probably play another year in Sweden before coming to America. Frank Banham led the WHL by a wide margin in goal scoring with 83 goals for Saskatoon, and added 69 assists for 152 points, second best in the league. Mike Leclerc popped in 58 for Brandon, also of the WHL.

SPECIAL TEAMS: Hey, the Ducks are getting better on the power play. After finishing last their first two seasons, they've moved up - to second last.

Actually, there was a lot of improvement after the addition of Selanne. The Ducks scored 28 power play goals in the 28 games Selanne was with them, and 32 goals in the other 54 games. Without Selanne the power play percentage was 11.1%. With Selanne it was 20.3%. Enough improvement for you?

There isn't a quarterback for the power play, unless you count Kariya, who plays the point. That may be better than a defenceman quarterback anyway, and it obviously didn't hurt them because they allowed the fewest shorthanded goals in the league. Before Selanne, some might have suggested the reason for that was because their main concern on the power play was just making sure the other team didn't score. Olausson will play the point also, when he's healthy.

Oksuita showed some promise as a power play sniper, scoring 11 on the season, and six in the 14 games he was with Anaheim. At the same rate he scored in those 14 games, he would have scored 35 goals on the season, which would have been an NHL record.

That's not going to happen because power plays have their ups and downs during a season, and one 14-game stretch isn't a true indication, but Selanne, Oksuita, and a centre up front, along with Kariya and Olausson on the point, is certainly cause for optimism.

POWER PLAY	G	ATT	PCT	
Overall	60	426	14.1%	(25th NHL)
Home	33	221	14.9%	(23rd NHL)
Road	27	205	13.2%	(24th NHL)

5 SHORT HANDED GOALS ALLOWED (1st NHL)

PENALTY KILLING	G	TSH	PCT	
Overall	81	423	80.9%	(17th NHL)
Home	32	201	84.1%	(11th NHL)
Road	49	222	77.9%	(23rd NHL)

10 SHORT HANDED GOALS SCORED (T-17th NHL)

COACHING AND MANAGEMENT: General Manager Jack Ferreira seems to be some kind of free agent signing genius. They're a new team and they need to stock their farm team, but because of the lack of depth on the big team a lot of them get a chance to play, and many have made the most of it. Douris, Hicks, Jomphe, Van Allen, and a pile of other Baltimore regulars who got the call for varying amounts of games, all were signed as free agents. That of course, will probably change once the Ducks have enough of their own draftees to develop, but it's a nice stopgap measure, and one that's paid dividends for the young club.

Ron Wilson might have been close to losing his coaching job last year, but the excellent stretch run gave him a reprieve.

Three years is a long time for a coach in the NHL these days, and three years with an expansion team is even more impressive. Wilson has his run-ins with players, notably Todd Krygier, who lost, and Tverdovsky, who later claimed there was no communication between him and Wilson, and that the team played "stupid hockey." Even Kilger wondered what was going on, suggesting Wilson doesn't have anything to do with some players.

David McNab, who was Director of Player Personnel, was promoted to Assistant General Manager after Pierre Gauthier left to take over the mess in Ottawa. That puts him one step closer to his goal of being an NHL general manager, which is where he will probably be some day.

PLAYOFFS

- Did not make playoffs

DRAFT

1995 DRAFT SELECTIONS

Round	Sel.	Player	Pos	Team
1	9	Ruslan Salei	D	Las Vegas (IHL)
2	35	Matt Cullen	C	St. Cloud St.
5	117	Brendan Buckley	D	Boston College
6	149	Blaine Russell	G	Prince Albert (WHL)
7	172	Timo Ahmoja	D	Finland
8	198	Kevin Kellett	D	Prince Albert (WHL)
9	224	Tobias Johansson	R-LW	Sweden

Ruslan Salei is a 21-year-old from Belarus, who came over to North America last year and played for Las Vegas in the

International League. It's rare for a player to be drafted at his late age, especially at the number nine slot, but he slipped through the draft and only caught attention last year.

Probably the best thing about him is that he might be able to play in the NHL right away, and the Ducks sorely need defencemen. That's one reason why they drafted four of them.

PROGNOSIS: There's no doubt that the Ducks are a better team than before they acquired Selanne. But the strong finish last season may have been a mirage.

Can a team win with two great offensive players, a decent goaltender, a mediocre defence and an almost non-existent supporting cast? Come to think of it, maybe they can.

Making the playoffs is certainly not out of the question, and the Ducks could make a splash once they get there, especially with a lot of defence and a couple guys who can score with the best of them.

They're not strong contenders yet, but with the two building blocks they have, it makes the rest of the pieces fit a lot easier.

PREDICTION:

Pacific Division: 4th

Western Conference: 9th

Overall: 17th

Team Rankings 1995/96

		Conference Rank	League Rank
Record	35-39-8	9	19
Home	22-15-4	4	12
Away	3-24-4	10	20
Versus Own Conference	22-30-4	10	20
Versus Other Conference	13-9-4	4	10
Team Plus\Minus	+8	6	11
Goals For	234	11	20
Goals Against	247	5	10
Average Shots For	28.7	11	21
Average Shots Against	32.1	10	19
Overtime	6-2-8	2	2
One Goal Games	13-13	6	15
Times outshooting opponent	30	10	19
Versus Teams Over .500	11-14-5	3	10
Versus Teams Under .500	24-25-3	10	20
First Half Record	15-22-4	9	19
Second Half Record	20-17-4	5	13

ALL-TIME LEADERS

GOALS

Paul Kariya	68
Joe Sacco	42
Bob Corkum	38

ASSISTS

Paul Kariya	79
Shaun Van Allen	63
Todd Krygier	56

POINTS

Paul Kariya	147
Shaun Van Allen	87
Joe Sacco	82

BEST INDIVIDUAL SEASONS

GOALS

Paul Kariya	1995-96	50
Bob Corkum	1993-94	23
Terry Yake	1993-94	21

ASSISTS

Paul Kariya	1995-96	58
Terry Yake	1993-94	31
Bob Corkum	1993-94	28

POINTS

Paul Kariya	1995-96	108
Terry Yake	1993-94	52
Bob Corkum	1993-94	51

TEAM RECORD

Last 3 years

	GP	W	L	T	Pts	%
1995-96	82	35	39	8	78	.476
1994-95	48	16	27	5	37	.385
1993-94	84	33	46	5	71	.423

Best 3 regular seasons

1995-96	82	35	39	8	78	.476
1993-94	84	33	46	5	71	.423
1994-95	48	16	27	5	37	.385

Worst 3 regular seasons

1994-95	48	16	27	5	37	.385
1993-94	84	33	46	5	71	.423
1995-96	82	35	39	8	78	.476

Most Goals (min. 70 game schedule)

1995-96	234
1993-94	229

Fewest Goals (min. 70 game schedule)

1993-94	229
1995-96	234

Most Goals Against (min. 70 game schedule)

1995-96	247
1993-94	251

Fewest Goals Against (min. 70 game schedule)

1993-94	251
1995-96	247

STAT SECTION
Team Scoring Stats

	GP	G	A	PTS	+/-	PIM	SH	Power Play			Short Handed		
								G	A	P	G	A	P
PAUL KARIYA	82	50	58	108	9	20	340	20	21	42	3	3	6
TEEMU SELANNE	79	40	68	108	5	22	267	9	39	48	1	0	1
ROMAN OKSIUTA	70	23	28	51	4	60	119	11	6	17	0	0	0
STEVE RUCCHIN	64	19	25	44	3	12	113	8	11	19	1	0	1
BOBBY DOLLAS	82	8	22	30	9	64	117	0	8	8	1	1	2
JOE SACCO	76	13	14	27	1	40	132	1	1	2	2	1	3
ANATOLI SEMENOV	56	4	22	26	1-	24	79	0	6	6	0	0	0
SHAUN VAN ALLEN	49	8	17	25	13	41	78	0	2	2	0	1	1
GARRY VALK	79	12	12	24	8	125	108	1	2	3	1	0	1
JASON YORK	79	3	21	24	7-	88	106	0	6	6	0	0	0
FREDRIK OLAUSSON	56	2	22	24	7-	38	83	1	15	16	0	0	0
ALEX HICKS	64	10	11	21	11	37	83	0	0	0	0	0	0
DAVE KARPA	72	3	16	19	3-	270	62	0	3	3	1	1	2
PATRIK CARNBACK	34	6	12	18	3	34	54	1	4	5	0	0	0
VALERI KARPOV	37	9	8	17	1-	10	42	0	4	4	0	0	0
PETER DOURIS	31	8	7	15	3-	9	45	2	2	4	0	0	0
DAVID SACCO	23	4	10	14	1	18	26	2	2	4	0	0	0
JEAN-FRANCOIS JOMPHE	31	2	12	14	7	39	46	2	1	3	0	0	0
DENNY LAMBERT	33	0	8	8	2-	55	28	0	0	0	0	0	0
TODD EWEN	53	4	3	7	5-	285	52	0	0	0	0	0	0
KEN BAUMGARTNER	72	2	4	6	5-	193	32	0	0	0	0	0	0
JIM CAMPBELL	16	2	3	5	0	36	25	1	1	2	0	0	0
MILOS HOLAN	16	2	2	4	12-	24	47	0	1	1	0	0	0
RANDY LADOUCEUR	63	1	3	4	5	47	48	0	0	0	0	0	0
DARREN VAN IMPE	16	1	2	3	8	14	13	0	0	0	0	0	0
STEVEN KING	7	2	0	2	1-	15	5	1	0	1	0	0	0
M. SHTALENKOV	30	0	2	2	0	2	0	0	0	0	0	0	0
VIACHESLAV BUTSAYEV	7	1	0	1	4-	0	9	0	0	0	0	0	0
DWAYNE NORRIS	3	0	1	1	0	2	3	0	0	0	0	0	0
JEREMY STEVENSON	3	0	1	1	1	12	1	0	0	0	0	0	0
SEAN PRONGER	7	0	1	1	0	6	3	0	0	0	0	0	0
JASON MARSHALL	24	0	1	1	3	42	9	0	0	0	0	0	0
JOHN LILLEY	1	0	0	0	1-	0	0	0	0	0	0	0	0
DON MCSWEEN	4	0	0	0	0	4	1	0	0	0	0	0	0
OLEG MIKULCHIK	8	0	0	0	2-	4	0	0	0	0	0	0	0
GUY HEBERT	59	0	0	0	0	6	0	0	0	0	0	0	0

Calgary Flames

The season ended early for the Flames who started off with a record of 4-15-5. Just two months in and they had no chance of making the playoffs. Or, so everyone thought.

So, they just started a new season, and did much better in that one. Check out the numbers below, which show both of them.

	Season 1 Oct. & Nov.	Season 2 Rest of Season
Record	4-15-5	30-22-6
Goals for/game	2.25	3.22
Goals against/game	3.63	2.64
Overall Standing	25	15
Power Play %	11.0	22.0
Power Play Rank	25	12 (overall)
Home Record	1-6-2	17-12-3
Road Record	3-9-3	13-10-3
Fleury Points/game	.83	1.31

The return of Gary Roberts on January 10 was a big factor in the resurgence, although they had already started to come around before that. They were on a 10-7-2 run when he rejoined the team.

With Roberts in the lineup the Flames were 19-12-4 on the season. Without him, they were 15-25-7. After November 30, the team was 11-10-2 without Roberts.

The numbers above show some dramatic differences between the two seasons: goals scored increased by more than one per game; goals against decreased by one per game; and the power play doubled its efficiency percentage. Their January record of 7-2-2 was the third best winning percentage in team history for that month.

None of this helped them in the playoffs, however, as they went down to defeat 4-0 to Chicago. That, of course, was without Roberts.

Roberts retired in the off-season, correctly assessing that his health was more important than playing hockey.

Since winning the Stanley Cup in 1989, Calgary has failed to win a playoff series. Six times they were knocked out in the first round, and the other time they failed to make the playoffs.

Of course, just making the playoffs last year was a coup, although playing in the Western Conference was the only way they could have done it. Only three teams in the whole conference had winning records, and they weren't one of them.

Calgary did okay against the Eastern Conference with a 12-11 record, one of five teams in the west with a winning record. Their problem was more within their own conference where they only had a 22-26-8 mark. The team they had the most trouble with was, oddly enough, the Winnipeg Jets. They were 0-4-0 against them, and were also winless against Colorado (0-4-1) and Detroit (0-3-1). Against the East, they were 7-1 against the teams with records under .500, and 5-10 versus over .500 teams.

Overall, they were 7-17-7 against teams over .500, and 27-18-6 versus teams under .500. In other words, they couldn't beat the good teams. Obviously, that's not a good omen for the playoffs, but ironically, against their first round opponent, Chicago, they were undefeated in the regular season with a 2-0-2 record.

TEAM PREVIEW

GOAL: The Flames desperately want Trevor Kidd to be the number one goalie - he of the high draft selection (11th overall in 1990) and future promise. Others, such as Andrei Trefilov and Jason Muzzatti, were pushed out of the way so Kidd could have the job to himself.

Last year, however, Rick Tabaracci, who had played some games in the minors in each of his seven pro seasons, came along, and gave Kidd a run for his money.

Goalies get reputations: this guy is a backup, that guy is a career minor leaguer, this guy is a starter. Whether or not they've earned their reps, they get them, and they're hard to shake.

Tabaracci's was as a backup or third string goalie. He may have moved up a notch, however, with some excellent play last season. But, naturally, when it comes playoff time, the team has to put the number one man in net. Or, more to the point, the man who is supposed to be number one.

Kidd lost the first game, allowing four goals on 20 shots. Then Tabaracci started game two, giving up three goals on 33 shots. Then Kidd got stoned in game three, allowing five goals in just over a period, and it was all Tabaracci after that. Although the Flames went down in four straight, Tabaracci was spectacular at times, and was at his best in game four when Chicago needed two and a half overtimes and 56 shots to win 2-1.

Another thing in Tabaracci's favor, during the regular season, is that the Flames played better when he was in net. Not just in wins and losses, as shown in the stats below, but the team scored more goals when he was between the pipes.

Calgary only scored five or more goals last season once when Kidd started. But, when Tabaracci was between the pipes, they scored at least five goals on ten occasions. Consider the goal support stats below, which show that Calgary scored .7 goals more per game when Tabaracci started, a considerable difference.

	Starts	Goals For	Ave. Goals scored per start
Kidd	44	115	2.6
Tabaracci	37	123	3.3

It's not that unusual for a backup to have a better winning percentage than a starter. A couple of reasons: Since he only starts on occasion, he's pumped each time he gets to play. His teammates, thinking an inferior goalie is between the pipes, might try to play better defensively to protect their net. Another reason is that backups often play against weaker teams.

Those don't fit Tabaracci, however. He just played well, most of the time.

This season, Kidd will still be considered number one, while Tabaracci will be the lowly backup. But, Kidd is prone to playing poorly at times over a stretch, so now at least the Flames won't be scared to stick Tabaracci right in there. If the Flames make the playoffs, however, you can bet Kidd will be in there, for game one at least.

DEFENCE: Somebody has to be average, and the Flame's defence is probably the one. They're solid, not spectacular. They're average in size, they provide average offence, they're about average in age, and they've got average toughness.

James Patrick was probably the team's most consistent defenceman last year. A good comeback season for the 33-year-old.

They've lost Trent Yawney to free agency and St. Louis, but they still have all-round defenceman, Steve Chiasson. Patrick, Chiasson and Zarley Zalapski all provide them with some mid-range offence, but nothing in the vein of Phil Housley, who was traded to New Jersey late last season.

The Flames gave up Housley and Dan Keczmer in exchange for Cale Hulse, Tommy Albelin, and Jocelyn Lemieux, who became a free agent after the season. Not exactly equal value for one of the best offensive defencemen of all-time, but probably the best they could do. Housley was an unrestricted free agent after the season, and had said he wouldn't re-sign with Calgary, so the Flames weren't exactly dealing from strength.

Albelin's story is rather amusing. When first traded to Calgary, he talked about how good it would be to have the reins taken off, after having to endure New Jersey's strict defensive system. Maybe the Devils knew more than Albelin. In 20 games for Calgary he amassed the grand total of one assist.

Jamie Huscroft was able to provide some muscle, perhaps from an unexpected source, considering he's spent most of his career bouncing around from the minors to the NHL. Hulse is also a roughnik, and could use some playing time.

The prize among the young hopefuls is Denis Gauthier, who played for Canada's national junior gold medal winning team last season. He's big, tough, a solid hitter, and he has some offensive talent as well. In other words, he possesses the raw materials every team in the league would love to have.

Todd Simpson, Joel Bouchard, and Jamie Allison have also been hanging around in Saint John, just waiting for an opportunity to play.

FORWARD: The Flames started off last year in rough shape. Out with injuries was Gary Roberts; Joe Nieuwendyk was a holdout; and Robert Reichel went back and signed in Europe with a German team. The three together could be a first line. The Flames got through it somehow, no small thanks to Theoren Fleury. He did everything for the Flames, including firing a team record 353 shots, 139 more than second place German Titov, and more than twice as many as anybody else. The fiery little guy scored 18 goals more than second place Titov, and again, more than twice as many as anybody else.

GOALTENDER	GPI	MINS	AVG	W	L	T	EN	SO	GA	SA	SV %
TREVOR KIDD	47	2570	2.78	15	21	8	2	3	119	1130	.895
RICK TABARACC	43	2391	2.94	19	16	3	2	3	117	1087	.892
CGY TOTALS	82	4984	2.89	34	37	11	4	6	240	2221	.892

That, of course, is good news and bad news. He was the only consistent offensive threat on a team that scored the fewest goals since their first two seasons in the early seventies.

Roberts has retired, so this season looked even bleaker. But, then a little sunshine. Robert Reichel returned to the team after a year in Germany. He's only 25, and is a proven 40-goal scorer, having done it twice, in the two full seasons before the lockout. He replaces Roberts, and then some because he won't miss as many games.

Add Dave Gagner, obtained from Toronto for a third round draft pick, and things are even brighter. Throw in Jarome Igilna, possible rookie of the year candidate, and the Flames are back in business.

Gagner isn't a kid anymore, at 31-years-of-age, but he's not finished either. Don't go by the fact that he was obtained for a third-rounder. That's a product of the mismanagement in Toronto, ironically Cliff Fletcher. Gagner was down some last season in his scoring stats, playing for two weak teams in Dallas and Toronto. He should return to the 30-goal plateau.

Iginla's a gem - a goal scorer who comes to play every night. He was picked up in the Nieuwendyk deal, that looked at the time to be weighted in favor of Dallas. At the World Junior Championships last year he won the scoring championship, was named to the all-star team, and voted best forward. Another vote and he could place first is in the Calder Trophy balloting.

Instead of one good scorer, the Flames can now put together two decent scoring lines. Players, such as Gagner or Fleury, are going to probably move to wing, so there's no use speculating on line combinations. Reichel, Fleury, Gagner, Iginla, Titov, and one other player should be members.

Titov should play on the left side of one of those lines, and maybe Cory Stillman, who scored 16 goals as a rookie last season.

Michael Nylander is supposed to be a big offensive threat, but he's a poster boy for "talented-looking" European players, who don't know how to pronounce "check" and play with little heart. A wastoid, who sits out games, and never quite "gets it." At least last year he got to play in the playoffs, where he proved once again why he sat them out before. In four games he had zero points, and in 13 career playoff games he is goalless. Nylander might fit on some team, somewhere, but on a team that wants to get by with their work ethic, he's a poor fit.

The only other place they could get some decent scoring is from Marty Murray. He was a big-time playmaker in junior, but is small-time in the size department. The 5-9, 170 pounder, almost a giant next to Fleury, had a decent rookie pro season in Saint John, with 25-31-56 in 58 games.

The rest are role players who provide some toughness, tenacity, and checking. Sandy McCarthy, Ronnie Stern and Paul Kruse are all good tough guys to have around because they can do more than fight. Mike Sullivan is famous for his shadowing technique.

A lot of Flames from last year became unrestricted free agents or were released, almost all were role players: Sheldon Kennedy, Corey Millen, Jocelyn Lemieux, Bob Sweeney, and Claude Lapointe became free agents. Dean Evason was released. Some of them are good third and fourth liners but none were crucial to team success.

The Flames may not have the same quality of defensive specialists this year, but they're improved in the scoring department, which was their first priority. The toughness is already there, and they can fill in with defensive types later if they need to.

Calgary has managed to turn this position from a major weakness to a strength in a very short time.

SPECIAL TEAMS: The power play came on big time after a slow start, as shown in the numbers in the opening. Then it fell asleep in the playoffs, going 0-21 versus Chicago. Experienced power play performers, Reichel and Gagner, should help, but they could use a quarterback for the power play to replace Phil Housley, who does the job as well as anyone.

Penalty killing can't get much worse, so expect it to get better.

POWER PLAY	G	ATT	PCT	
Overall	71	386	18.4%	(12th NHL)
Home	37	198	18.7%	(13th NHL)
Road	34	188	18.1%	(8th NHL)

9 SHORT HANDED GOALS ALLOWED (T-7th NHL)

PENALTY KILLING	G	TSH	PCT	
Overall	80	402	80.1%	(22nd NHL)
Home	34	188	81.9%	(T-14th NHL)
Road	46	214	78.5%	(20th NHL)

11 SHORT HANDED GOALS SCORED (T-12th NHL)

COACHING AND MANAGEMENT: When the Flames got off to their poor start, it wasn't the coach who got the boot. It was the GM for a change, namely Doug Risebrough. Flames upper management said the poor season beginning had nothing to do with Doug Risebrough's firing, but not too long before he had received a contract extension.

If Risebrough was to be blamed for the start, then maybe he should also receive credit for their turnaround, since he was the one who put the team together.

In any event, he'll always be remembered most for THE TRADE, the disastrous Doug Gilmour deal with Toronto.

Al Coates took over the general manager role, and Pierre Page saved his own hide when the team improved considerably. If a coach gets blamed for a team's failures, he at least deserves credit for their successes.

The players deserve some too, though, although it may have been Page who gave it to them. The team was already playing better when the mutiny occurred in mid-December. That was the incident in which Page ordered Chiasson, Housley and Evason off the ice for being a minute late for practice. The rest of the players, led by Stern, and including Kidd who had made it to the ice on time but without all his equipment on, opted to join the three. The incident seemed to pull the players together giving them a better focus toward one common goal.

After that, all around the league, coaches were encouraging their players to mutiny, and were throwing guys off the ice left, right, and centre for being 10 seconds late for practice. Not really, of course, but some probably thought about it for a couple seconds.

Give Coates some extra credit, too, for the way the Igilna deal was pulled off. The Flames made sure they finalized it before the world junior championships, where they figured Igilna would make a big splash. He did, and now Igilna is a more valuable property than Nieuwendyk, who didn't exactly set the world on fire in Dallas.

DRAFT

Round	Sel.	Player	Pos	Team
1	13	Derek Morris	D	Regina (WHL)
2	39	Travis Brigley	LW	Lethbridge (WHL)
2	40	Steve Begin	C	Val d'Or (QMJHL)
3	73	Dimitri Vlasenkov	W	Russia

4	89	Toni Lydman	D	Finland
4	94	Christian Lefebvre	D	Granby (QMJHL)
5	122	Josef Straka	C	Czech Republic
8	202	Ryan Wade	RW	Kelowna (WHL)
9	228	Ronald Petrovicky	RW	Prince George (WHL)

This first round pick will be interesting to watch. The Flames are either going to look like geniuses, or idiots. Morris was ranked 85th among North Americans by Central Scouting, but fifth by Calgary. He's small, by NHL defencemen standards, at 5-11, 180. At Regina he was 8-44-52 in 67 games.

The Flames had similar ranking discrepancies in the second round. The 39th overall pick was ranked 98th by CSB, and their 40th pick was ranked 62nd.

PROGNOSIS: The Flames are as tough as any team to predict. Last year, the Flames were a good defensive team that couldn't score goals. They've added a whole line of scorers in Reichel, Gagner and Iginla. As long as the defence holds up, they're in good shape.

They don't have any stars on defence, although they're capable, and goaltending is in good hands.

The Flames are certainly not a championship caliber team, but they're at least a close to .500 team, and good enough to make the playoffs. No guarantees they won't get knocked out in the first round, as usual, but making it to the post-season is good enough for now.

PREDICTION:

Pacific Division: 3rd

Western Conference: 6th

Overall: 13th

Team Rankings 1995-96

		Conference Rank	League Rank
Record	34-37-11	6	15
Home	18-18-5	7	18
Away	16-19-6	6	12
Versus Own Conference	22-26-8	8	18
Versus Other Conference	12-11-3	5	13
Team Plus\Minus	+10	4	9
Goals For	241	9	16
Goals Against	240	3	8
Average Shots For	30.0	8	16
Average Shots Against	27.0	2	6
Overtime	2-3-11	10	16
One Goal Games	11-14	11	22
Times outshooting opponent	48	2	6
Versus Teams Over .500	7-17-7	9	20
Versus Teams Under .500	27-18-6	6	15
First Half Record	12-22-7	12	23
Second Half Record	22-15-4	3	5

Results: Lost to Chicago 4-0

Record: 0-4

Home: 0-2

Away: 0-2

Goals For: 7 (1.8 per game)

Goals Against: 16 (4.0 per game)

Overtime: 0-1

Power play: 0.0% (15th)

Penalty Killing: 81.0% (10th)

ALL-TIME LEADERS

GOALS

Joe Nieuwendyk	314
Gary Roberts	257
Theoren Fleury	278

ASSISTS

Al MacInnis	609
Gary Suter	437
Theoren Fleury	338

POINTS

Al MacInnis	822
Theoren Fleury	616
Joe Nieuwendyk	616

BEST INDIVIDUAL SEASONS

GOALS

Lanny McDonald	1982-83	66
Gary Roberts	1991-92	53
Joe Nieuwendyk	1987-88	51
Joe Mullen	1988-89	51
Joe Nieuwendyk	1988-89	51
Theoren Fleury	1990-91	51

ASSISTS

Kent Nilsson	1980-81	82
Al MacInnis	1990-91	75
Bob MacMillen	1978-79	71

POINTS

Kent Nilsson	1980-81	131
Joe Mullen	1988-89	110
Joe Mullen	1978-79	108

TEAM RECORD

Last 3 years

	GP	W	L	T	Pts	%
1995-96	82	34	37	11	79	.482
1994-95	48	24	17	7	55	.573
1993-94	84	42	29	13	97	.577

Best 3 regular seasons

1988-89	80	54	17	9	117	.731
1987-88	80	48	23	9	105	.656
1990-91	80	46	26	8	100	.625

Worst 3 regular seasons

1972-73	78	25	38	15	65	.416
1991-92	80	31	37	12	74	.463
1981-82	80	29	34	17	75	.469

Most Goals (min. 70 game schedule)

1987-88	397
1984-85	363
1988-89	354
1985-86	354

Fewest Goals (min. 70 game schedule)

1972-73	191
1973-74	214
1995-96	241

Most Goals Against (min. 70 game schedule)

1981-82	345
1982-83	317
1985-86	315

Fewest Goals Against (min. 70 game schedule)

1988-89	226
1974-75	233
1975-76	237

STAT SECTION

Team Scoring Stats

	GP	G	A	PTS	+/-	PIM	SH	Power Play			Short Handed		
								G	A	P	G	A	P
THEOREN FLEURY	80	46	50	96	17	112	353	17	17	34	5	1	6
GERMAN TITOV	82	28	39	67	9	24	214	13	14	27	2	4	6
MICHAEL NYLANDER	73	17	38	55	0	20	163	4	15	19	0	0	0
GARY ROBERTS	35	22	20	42	15	78	84	9	7	16	0	0	0
CORY STILLMAN	74	16	19	35	5-	41	132	4	13	17	1	0	1
JAMES PATRICK	80	3	32	35	3	30	116	1	16	17	0	1	1
STEVE CHIASSON	76	8	25	33	3	62	175	5	11	16	0	1	1
ZARLEY ZALAPSKI	80	12	17	29	11	115	145	5	5	10	0	0	0
MIKE SULLIVAN	81	9	12	21	6-	24	106	0	0	0	1	2	3
COREY MILLEN	44	7	14	21	8	18	73	2	3	5	0	0	0
SANDY MCCARTHY	75	9	7	16	8-	173	98	3	1	4	0	0	0
PAVEL TORGAJEV	41	6	10	16	2	14	50	0	0	0	0	0	0
RONNIE STERN	52	10	5	15	2	111	64	0	1	1	0	0	0
PAUL KRUSE	75	3	12	15	5-	145	83	0	0	0	0	0	0
DEAN EVASON	67	7	7	14	6-	38	68	1	2	3	0	1	1
BOB SWEENEY	72	7	7	14	20-	65	62	0	0	0	1	0	1
TOMMY ALBELIN	73	1	13	14	1	18	121	0	6	6	0	0	0
JOCELYN LEMIEUX	67	5	7	12	19-	45	90	0	0	0	0	0	0
JAMIE HUSCROFT	70	3	9	12	14	162	57	0	0	0	0	0	0
SHELDON KENNEDY	41	3	7	10	3	36	54	0	0	0	0	0	0
CLAUDE LAPOINTE	35	4	5	9	1	20	44	0	0	0	2	0	2
ED WARD	41	3	5	8	2-	44	33	0	0	0	0	0	0
MARTY MURRAY	15	3	3	6	4-	0	22	2	2	4	0	0	0
YVES SARAULT	25	2	1	3	9-	8	26	0	0	0	0	0	0
TRENT YAWNEY	69	0	3	3	1-	88	51	0	1	1	0	0	0
KEVIN DAHL	32	1	1	2	2-	26	17	0	0	0	0	0	0
RICK TABARACCI	43	0	2	2	0	8	0	0	0	0	0	0	0
TREVOR KIDD	47	0	2	2	0	4	0	0	0	0	0	0	0
LADISLAV KOHN	5	1	0	1	1-	2	8	0	0	0	0	0	0
CRAIG FERGUSON	18	1	0	1	9-	6	20	0	0	0	0	0	0
JARROD SKALDE	1	0	0	0	0	0	0	0	0	0	0	0	0
NIKLAS SUNDBLAD	2	0	0	0	0	0	3	0	0	0	0	0	0
TODD HLUSHKO	4	0	0	0	0	6	6	0	0	0	0	0	0
JOEL BOUCHARD	4	0	0	0	0	4	0	0	0	0	0	0	0
VESA VIITAKOSKI	5	0	0	0	1-	2	7	0	0	0	0	0	0
TODD SIMPSON	6	0	0	0	0	32	3	0	0	0	0	0	0
CALE HULSE	11	0	0	0	1	20	9	0	0	0	0	0	0
DAN KECZMER	13	0	0	0	6-	14	13	0	0	0	0	0	0

PLAYOFFS

PLAYER	GP	G	A	PTS	+/-	PIM	PP	SH	GW	OT	S
STEVE CHIASSON	4	2	1	3	0	0	0	0	0	0	20
THEOREN FLEURY	4	2	1	3	1	14	0	0	0	0	28
CORY STILLMAN	2	1	1	2	2-	0	0	0	0	0	5
JAROME IGINLA	2	1	1	2	2	0	0	0	0	0	6
RONNIE STERN	4	0	2	2	2	8	0	0	0	0	7
GERMAN TITOV	4	0	2	2	0	0	0	0	0	0	13
SHELDON KENNEDY	3	1	0	1	2-	2	0	0	0	0	4
DEAN EVASON	3	0	1	1	1-	0	0	0	0	0	3
JAMIE HUSCROFT	4	0	1	1	2-	4	0	0	0	0	4
ZARLEY ZALAPSKI	4	0	1	1	1	10	0	0	0	0	5
KEVIN DAHL	1	0	0	0	0	0	0	0	0	0	0
CALE HULSE	1	0	0	0	2-	0	0	0	0	0	2
PAVEL TORGAJEV	1	0	0	0	0	0	0	0	0	0	1
CLAUDE LAPOINTE	2	0	0	0	2-	0	0	0	0	0	3
BOB SWEENEY	2	0	0	0	1-	0	0	0	0	0	3
TREVOR KIDD	2	0	0	0	0	0	0	0	0	0	0
RICK TABARACCI	3	0	0	0	0	0	0	0	0	0	0
PAUL KRUSE	3	0	0	0	1-	4	0	0	0	0	3
TOMMY ALBELIN	4	0	0	0	2-	0	0	0	0	0	8
JOCELYN LEMIEUX	4	0	0	0	0	0	0	0	0	0	5
JAMES PATRICK	4	0	0	0	3-	2	0	0	0	0	3
TRENT YAWNEY	4	0	0	0	3-	2	0	0	0	0	1
MIKE SULLIVAN	4	0	0	0	1-	0	0	0	0	0	5
SANDY MCCARTHY	4	0	0	0	3-	10	0	0	0	0	4
MICHAEL NYLANDER	4	0	0	0	4-	0	0	0	0	0	9

GOALTENDER	GPI	MINS	AVG	W	L	T	EN	SO	GA	SV%
RICK TABARACCI	3	204	2.06	0	3	0	0	7	84	.917
TREVOR KIDD	2	83	6.51	0	1	0	0	9	40	.775
CGY TOTALS	4	290	3.31	0	4	0	0	16	124	.871

Chicago Blackhawks

There's never anything normal about a Chicago Blackhawk season. Last year was no exception.

Here's a recap of some of the off-ice incidents, on-ice incidents, and on-paper incidents.

* Their leading scorer was a defenceman - Chris Chelios. New Jersey's Phil Housley was the only other defenceman to lead his team in scoring, but he got most of his points in Calgary before being traded.

* Their second leading scorer was also a defenceman - Gary Suter. Actually, he was tied in points with Jeremy Roenick. The Blackhawks have never even had one defenceman lead the team in scoring, never mind two. In NHL history, no team has had defencemen finish one-two in team scoring.

* The Blackhawks were the only team with a winning record, other than Pittsburgh, that gave up more shots than they had themselves. Pittsburgh is understandable because they were offensive dynamos that cared little about their own end. Chicago's is curious because they were decent scorers and excellent defensively.

Only San Jose and Ottawa had fewer than the 27.3 shots the Blackhawks averaged.

* Sometimes the Chicago offence would just go on vacation. Thirteen times they had fewer than 20 shots. That's the most of any team in the league.

* The Jeremy Roenick contract situation was a distraction all year long. There were trade rumors, and talk about how he'd leave at the end of the year when he became a free agent. And he didn't have a particularly good season for the second year in a row. Once considered one of the most talented centres in the league, he was ranked 14th by *The Hockey News* among centres in the pre-season. There's little doubt he was underpaid in relation to other players of his caliber, but when he signed his contract five years ago when it was just fine. The Blackhawks wouldn't renegotiate, which is their right, not to mention the right thing to do. But, J.R. was bitter about it, especially with the contract offer sheet the Blackhawks gave Keith Tkachuk, which the Winnipeg Jets ended up matching.

* More than a third of the way into the season, the Hawks were mired in mediocrity. They had a 12-12-7 record, which included losses at home to San Jose and Ottawa. The rest of the season they had a 28-16-7 mark. They had 20 wins in the first half, and 20 wins in the second half, which indicates a measure of consistency. But, it order to get consistent they needed a stretch of 20-4-4 in mid-season.

* Murray Craven only had 18 goals on the season, but seven of them were game-winners, including one three game span in a row.

* The Hawks were a streaky team at times. Chelios had a 15-game point streak, second longest in the league and the most by a defenceman. Hackett won eight games in a row. The Blackhawks tied for the league lead with a road undefeated streak of eight games, and Jeff Shantz had a 47-game goal-less streak.

* In the playoffs there was the bad potato incident. Ed Belfour and Murray Craven missed a game in their series against Colorado after getting food poisoning in a Denver restaurant, which they figured came from lyonnaise potatoes.

* In another weird playoff incident, Chris Chelios missed game 4 in their series against Colorado with a pulled groin that caused all kinds of speculation. Teams like to keep injuries a secret in the playoffs, and will go to some length not to reveal them. Chelios, who was dressed for the playoff game, didn't show up on the bench, so it was reported he had an equipment problem. No equipment problem lasts for a whole period, however, so ESPN2, which were broadcasting the game, had another story that went over the air. They said Chelios had some kind of personal problem, and that his wife had to go to the dressing room to tell him something, after which Chelios had to leave the arena. The ESPN announcers said that it sounded ominous, and that they couldn't speculate until later just what personal problem Chelios had. Yet another report said he had a hangover.

* Chicago became the first team to average more than 20,000 fans per game during the regular season, and then drew just 17,455 for their opening round playoff game.

* After the season, Joe Murphy was able to become a free agent, when according to the complicated regulations, his salary was under the league average.

TEAM PREVIEW

GOAL: For the first time in recent memory, Ed Belfour had some competition. He's not the type of goalie who needs it, because he's in competition with himself, and even gets angry when he allows goals during the warmup. But, it was good for the Blackhawks, especially when he was injured.

Jeff Hackett, before last season, had the worst winning percentage in the history of the NHL for goalies with over 100 games. A lot of that had to do with playing on lousy New York Islander and San Jose teams. Now, he has only about the second worst winning percentage, after putting together a good run with some outstanding goaltending.

He took a little playing time away from Belfour, but don't expect him to share the number one job. He could, however, be showing off for a potential trade, which would give him more playing time. If not, he's proven himself to be good insurance should Belfour get hurt or need a rest.

DEFENCE: Chris Chelios will turn 35-years-old this season. He might as well be 25, because he has shown no signs of slowing down. He won his third Norris Trophy last season, and was a first-team all star for the third time in the last four years. He's not getting older, he's getting better.

Chelios certainly hasn't been babied by the Blackhawks when it comes to ice-time. Maybe that's what keeps him going. One of these days he's going to slow down and lose a step or two, because that's what happens to old guys. But, there doesn't appear to be any sign that it will happen this year.

Gary Suter is 32 years old, no youngster himself, but he too isn't showing his age, and is invaluable on the power play. Forty-one of his 67 points came with the man-advantage.

The two cornerstones of the defence, and power play pointmen, hog most of the ice-time, but they have some other talent back there as well.

Keith Carney played every game last year, and 52 more than he had played in the NHL in any of his previous seasons. He also led the team with a plus 31.

Eric Weinrich has also settled in as a regular; and will be joined by Steve Smith, when he's healthy; tough guy Enrico Ciccone, when he's not suspended; and Cam Russell, another rugged backliner.

Those hoping for work include Brad Werenka and Ivan Droppa.

Chicago is high on prospect Thomas Gronman, giving up a second round draft pick in 1998 to get him from Colorado. He's a big guy, at 6-3, 200, who played last year in Finland.

The Hawks have size, toughness, offence, and the best defenceman in the league last season. About the only thing they might like is a fountain of youth, and a little more depth.

FORWARD: Jeremy Roenick is a restricted free agent with big contract demands, but Chicago is sure to match any offer. If they do match, they can't trade him for a year. If anything, the Blackhawks will probably trade the unhappy Roenick before they have to match.

They need Roenick because they don't have much at centre without him. Bernie Nicholls and Denis Savard were lost to free agency, but the Hawks did re-sign aging veteran Brent Sutter.

They also picked up free agent, Kevin Miller, a good two-way player, who should fit perfectly with this club. He should be good for 20 goals, which on this team, is almost a goldmine.

One possible centre candidate is Dimitri Nabokov, last year's first round draft pick, 10th overall. He's big, at 6-2, 210, which is what the Hawks would like at centre, but it may be a little too soon for him. They also have Jeff Shantz, who has established himself as a fourth line centre, third line at best; and Steve Dubinsky, who is in a similar position as Shantz.

GOALTENDER	GPI	MINS	AVG	W	L	T	EN	SO	GA	SA	SV %
JIM WAITE	1	31	.00	0	0	0	0	0	0	8	1.000
JEFF HACKETT	35	2000	2.40	18	11	4	2	4	80	948	.916
ED BELFOUR	50	2956	2.74	22	17	10	3	1	135	1373	.902
CHI TOTALS	82	4999	2.64	40	28	14	5	5	220	2334	.906

They've got more problems, with Joe Murphy gone to free agency as well. He didn't exactly have a banner year, with just 22 goals and 51 points, but he was still one of their better forwards, and according to him, a "big-game" player.

At left wing is Eric Daze, who probably should have won the Calder Trophy as rookie of the year over Ottawa's Daniel Alfredsson, and would have won it, if he hadn't had a couple scoring slumps. He still got 30 goals, though, and he's bound to keep on improving.

Murray Craven also patrols over there and there are a couple good prospects coming along. Ethan Moreau didn't have as good a season as the Hawks would have liked in his first pro year, with 21 goals and 41 points in Indianapolis, so he might not quite be ready yet, although he remains a top prospect. He can play centre as well. Eric Lecompte is another another big guy who could make a run at making the Hawks, although his scoring totals weren't that impressive either, with 24 goals for Indianapolis.

Bob Probert is a left winger as well, and he started off very disappointingly for the Hawks. He didn't play as spirited a game as they would have liked, although he came around more later in the season.

The forwards can change wings as needed, but lining up on the right side is Tony Amonte, toughnik Jim Cummins, and Sergei Krivakrasov. The Hawks acquired Ravil Gusmanov from Winnipeg at the trade deadline, and he could get a shot after putting up some good numbers in a short time at Indianapolis.

The Hawks like to be big and intimidating up front. Ideally, they'd like a bunch of 6-3, 215 pounders crushing guys and scoring goals. But, who wouldn't? Size remains a priority for them, however, so the players they acquire, sign, or call up are more likely to be bigger than average.

SPECIAL TEAMS: For the Blackhawks to be ranked 15th on the power play is almost unbelievable. They had the best duo in the league on the point, in Chelios and Suter, and Jeremy Roenick up front. Anybody added to that mix should just be gravy.

It looked, however, as if Chelios and Suter were trying to do everything themselves. Suter tied Roenick with 12 power play goals, and Chelios had seven. Suter's total was the most in the league by a defenceman. With two quarterbacks on the point, they're supposed to move it to the snipers. Maybe they just couldn't find any.

They were first in the league the previous season, so a return to form would probably be in order. Penalty killing was excellent, however, thanks in large to Chelios, but also to some good defensive veteran centremen who might not be around this year.

POWER PLAY	G	ATT	PCT
Overall	63	356	17.7% (15th NHL)
Home	28	175	16.0% (19th NHL)
Road	35	181	19.3% (T-3rd NHL)

7 SHORT HANDED GOALS ALLOWED (T-2nd NHL)

PENALTY KILLING	G	TSH	PCT
Overall	65	447	85.5% (3rd NHL)
Home	26	222	88.3% (3rd NHL)
Road	39	225	82.7% (7th NHL)

COACHING AND MANAGEMENT: If first year coach, Craig Hartsburg, was intimidated by being in the NHL, he didn't show it. Of course, he was a long time player himself.

He didn't hesitate to sit out big-name players, such as Murphy and Craven, and wasn't going to tolerate anything but the best from his players. It took a while for the team concept to come together, but it did after a mediocre start. Hartsburg demands the most from his players, and won't be satisfied until he gets it all.

GM Bob Pulford likes his veterans and he likes them to come cheap. He can be a hard-liner with the pocketbook, but he knows how to put a team together to compete for a playoff spot. He considers each season an entity in its own, which means they're always competitive. The Hawks have never missed the playoffs since he joined them in 1977.

DRAFT

Round	Sel.	Player	Pos	
2	31	Remi Royer	D	St.Hyacinthe (QMJHL)
2	42	Jeff Paul	D	Niagara Falls (OHL)
2	46	Geoff Peters	C	Niagara Falls (OHL)
5	130	Andy Johnson	D	Peterborough (OHL)
7	184	Mike Velinga	D	Guelph (OHL)
8	210	Chris Twerdun	D	Moose Jaw (WHL)
9	236	Alexei Kozyrev	D	Russia

The Hawks did a funny thing at the draft. They traded their first round pick (21st) to San Jose for two second round picks (31st and 42nd). When it came time for the 31st pick, they were able to grab the 10th rated player among North Americans.

Royer is an offensive defenceman with a great shot. His totals were 22-23-45 last year, odd numbers for a rearguard. It's best, however, to get an offensive defenceman with a high goal total, because then you know he's doing it himself, and his points aren't reflective of his teammates. Another plus in Royer's favor is that he had 289 penalty minutes last season.

When a player falls that low after being ranked that high, it means he has a down side. For Royer, it's his defensive play. He will need to improve in that area, but there's a ton of offensive defencemen in the NHL who can't find their own end. If he can keep piling up the goals, he'll be in good shape, and on a team that has little depth on defence, he could fast-track his way to the NHL.

PROGNOSIS: The Hawks weren't all that far away last season. They lost a playoff game to Colorado in the third overtime, which if they had won would have given them a 3-1 lead in the series.

As usual in Chicago, it's out with the old, and in with the...old. They have to restock key veterans, and got a good start when they signed Miller. They have some good minor league prospects, but they don't know yet if they can play, and Pulford doesn't run any babysitting service.

A return to form of Roenick would be great, but otherwise they could use some more dependable scoring.

They're not likely to set the league on fire, but a big, tough, hard-working team is always a threat in the playoffs. And with Chelios on defence, you can never count them out.

PREDICTION:

Central Division: 4th

Western Conference: 7th

Overall: 14th

Team Rankings 1995-96

		Conference Rank	League Rank
Record	40-28-14	3	6
Home	22-13-6	3	8
Away	18-15-8	3	3
Versus Own Conference	25-19-12	3	9
Versus Other Conference	15-9-2	2	3
Team Plus\Minus	+55	3	3
Goals For	273	5	8
Goals Against	220	2	5
Average Shots For	27.3	12	24
Average Shots Against	28.4	3	8
Overtime	1-4-14	13	22
One Goal Games	6-11	12	23
Times outshooting opponent	39	6	14
Versus Teams Over .500	12-15-2	4	11
Versus Teams Under .500	28-13-12	3	9
First Half Record	20-13-8	3	7
Second Half Record	20-15-6	4	8

Results: Defeated Calgary 4-0
Lost to Colorado 4-2

Record: 6-4

Home: 3-2

Away: 3-2

Goals For: 30 (3.0 per game)

Goals Against: 28 (2.8 per game)

Overtime: 3-2

Power play: 15.2% (11th)

Penalty Killing: 90.6% (1st)

ALL-TIME LEADERS

GOALS

Bobby Hull	604
Stan Mikita	541
Steve Larmer	406

ASSISTS

Stan Mikita	926
Denis Savard	666
Doug Wilson	554

POINTS

Stan Mikita	1,467
Bobby Hull	1,153
Denis Savard	1,021

BEST INDIVIDUAL SEASONS

GOALS

Bobby Hull	1968-69	58
Al Secord	1982-83	54
Bobby Hull	1965-66	54

ASSISTS

Denis Savard	1987-88	87
Denis Savard	1981-82	87
Denis Savard	1982-83	86

POINTS

Denis Savard	1987-88	131
Denis Savard	1982-83	121
Denis Savard	1981-82	119

TEAM RECORD

Last 3 years

	GP	W	L	T	Pts	%
1995-96	82	40	28	14	94	.573
1994-95	48	24	19	5	53	.552
1993-94	84	39	36	9	87	.518

Best 3 regular seasons

	GP	W	L	T	Pts	%
1970-71	78	49	20	6	107	.686
1971-72	78	46	17	5	107	.686
1973-74	78	41	14	23	105	.673

Worst 3 regular seasons

	GP	W	L	T	Pts	%
1927-28	44	7	34	3	17	.193
1953-54	70	12	51	7	31	.221
1928-29	44	7	29	8	22	.250

Most Goals (min. 70 game schedule)

1985-86	351
1982-83	338
1981-82	332

Fewest Goals (min. 70 game schedule)

1953-54	133
1955-56	155
1951-52	158

Most Goals Against (min. 70 game schedule)

1981-82	363
1985-86	349
1988-89	335

Fewest Goals Against (min. 70 game schedule)

1973-74	164
1971-72	166
1963-64	169

STAT SECTION

Team Scoring Stats

	GP	G	A	PTS	+/-	PIM	SH	Power Play			Short Handed		
								G	A	P	G	A	P
CHRIS CHELIOS	81	14	58	72	25	140	219	7	24	31	0	6	6
JEREMY ROENICK	66	32	35	67	9	109	171	12	7	19	4	3	7
GARY SUTER	82	20	47	67	3	80	242	12	29	41	2	3	5
TONY AMONTE	81	31	32	63	10	62	216	5	13	18	4	0	4
BERNIE NICHOLLS	59	19	41	60	11	60	100	6	16	22	0	1	1
ERIC DAZE	80	30	23	53	16	18	167	2	4	6	0	0	0
JOE MURPHY	70	22	29	51	3-	86	212	8	7	15	0	0	0
DENIS SAVARD	69	13	35	48	20	102	110	2	8	10	0	0	0
MURRAY CRAVEN	66	18	29	47	20	36	86	5	1	6	1	1	2
BOB PROBERT	78	19	21	40	15	237	97	1	4	5	0	0	0
BRENT SUTTER	80	13	27	40	14	56	102	0	1	1	0	0	0
JEFF SHANTZ	78	6	14	20	12	24	72	1	0	1	2	1	3
KEITH CARNEY	82	5	14	19	31	94	69	1	0	1	0	1	1
SERGEI KRIVOKRASOV	46	6	10	16	10	32	52	0	0	0	0	0	0
ERIC WEINRICH	77	5	10	15	14	65	76	0	1	1	0	0	0
STEVE SMITH	37	0	9	9	12	71	17	0	2	2	0	0	0
JAMES BLACK	13	3	3	6	1	16	23	0	0	0	0	0	0
BRENT GRIEVE	28	2	4	6	5	28	22	0	0	0	0	0	0
JIM CUMMINS	52	2	4	6	1-	180	34	0	0	0	0	0	0
ENRICO CICCONE	66	2	4	6	1	306	60	0	1	1	0	0	0
STEVE DUBINSKY	43	2	3	5	3	14	33	0	0	0	0	0	0
KIP MILLER	10	1	4	5	1	2	12	0	3	3	0	0	0
CAM RUSSELL	61	2	2	4	8	129	22	0	0	0	0	0	0
ED BELFOUR	50	0	2	2	0	36	0	0	0	0	0	0	0
DANTON COLE	12	1	0	1	0	0	6	0	0	0	0	0	0
ETHAN MOREAU	8	0	1	1	1	4	1	0	0	0	0	0	0
JEFF HACKETT	35	0	1	1	0	8	0	0	0	0	0	0	0
JIM WAITE	1	0	0	0	0	0	0	0	0	0	0	0	0
IVAN DROPPA	7	0	0	0	2	2	1	0	0	0	0	0	0
BRAD WERENKA	9	0	0	0	2-	8	2	0	0	0	0	0	0
MIKE PROKOPEC	9	0	0	0	4-	5	5	0	0	0	0	0	0

PLAYOFFS

PLAYER	GP	G	A	PTS	+/-	PIM	PP	SH	GW	OT	S
JEREMY ROENICK	10	5	7	12	6	2	1	0	1	1	21
BERNIE NICHOLLS	10	2	7	9	3	4	1	0	0	0	11
JOE MURPHY	10	6	2	8	1	33	0	0	2	1	38
ERIC DAZE	10	3	5	8	4	0	0	0	1	0	32
GARY SUTER	10	3	3	6	1	8	2	0	1	0	27
TONY AMONTE	7	2	4	6	2	6	1	0	0	0	14
JEFF SHANTZ	10	2	3	5	2-	6	0	0	0	0	9
MURRAY CRAVEN	9	1	4	5	1-	2	1	0	0	0	17
ERIC WEINRICH	10	1	4	5	2	10	1	0	0	0	13
DENIS SAVARD	10	1	2	3	0	8	0	0	0	0	12
CHRIS CHELIOS	9	0	3	3	2	8	0	0	0	0	28
KEITH CARNEY	10	0	3	3	1-	4	0	0	0	0	11
BRENT SUTTER	10	1	1	2	3-	6	0	0	0	0	18
BOB PROBERT	10	0	2	2	1-	23	0	0	0	0	20
SERGEI KRIVOKRASOV	5	1	0	1	4-	2	0	0	1	1	6
JAMES BLACK	8	1	0	1	1-	2	0	0	0	0	6
ENRICO CICCONE	9	1	0	1	1-	30	0	0	0	0	4
JEFF HACKETT	1	0	0	0	0	0	0	0	0	0	0
CAM RUSSELL	6	0	0	0	1-	2	0	0	0	0	4
STEVE SMITH	6	0	0	0	2-	16	0	0	0	0	3
ED BELFOUR	9	0	0	0	0	4	0	0	0	0	0
JIM CUMMINS	10	0	0	0	1-	2	0	0	0	0	3

GOALTENDER	GPI	MINS	AVG	W	L	T	EN	SO	GA	SA	SV %
ED BELFOUR	9	666	2.07	6	3	0	1	2	3	323	.929
JEFF HACKETT	1	60	5.00	0	1	0	0	0	5	32	.844
CHI TOTALS	10	727	2.31	6	4	0	1	2	8	355	.921

Colorado Avalanche

You can only enjoy a Stanley Cup victory so long. Well, actually, your whole life, but that's only after you've finished playing. The immediate concern is repeating.

We could go on and on, trying to figure out how and why the Avalanche won the Cup, but we've already heard it all before. The bottom line is they were the best.

So, what about this year?

That's the tough part. The emotional high these players were on can't be duplicated in any part by any game during the regular season. Consequently, Stanley Cup winning teams often have poor follow-up seasons. The New Jersey Devils found that out the hard way when they didn't even make the playoffs after their win. Consider what happened to the last five champions.

	Champion	Following Season
1995	New Jersey	Failed to make playoffs
1994	NY Rangers	22-23-3 regular season - lost second round
1993	Montreal	96 points, but knocked out in first round
1992	Pittsburgh	119 points, lost in second round
1991	Pittsburgh	Won Stanley Cup

The trends keep changing, but it seems that usually only the extremely dominant teams repeat as champs. The Avalanche are a great team, but they're not dominant. They do have a number of things in their favor, including youth, depth, Patrick Roy, Marc Crawford, Pierre Lacroix, Joe Sakic and Peter Forsberg. The biggest thing against them is that there are 26 teams. Seeing as how Florida made it to the final last season, there are an awful lot of clubs that can contend.

Getting all the way back and winning again won't be easy, but they have as good a chance as anyone.

A few miscellaneous notes from last season's Stanley Cup victory.

* The Avalanche didn't lose two games in a row during the playoffs.

* In their final 10 seasons in Quebec, the team did not make it past the first round of the playoffs. They played a total of five playoffs series, compared to the four they played just last year in Denver.

* Joe Sakic only missed by one goal tying the all-time playoff record of 19 in one year, held by Reggie Leach for

Philadelphia in 1976, and Jari Kurri for Edmonton in 1985.

* Sakic set an all-time record, with six game-winning goals.

* Claude Lemieux became only the fifth player in NHL history to win the Stanley Cup two years in a row, with two different teams. The list is shown below.

	First Year Team Year		Second Year Team Year	
Claude Lemieux	NJ	1995	Col.	1996
Al Arbour	Chi.	1961	Tor.	1962
Eddie Litzenberger	Chi.	1961	Tor.	1962
Ab McDonald	Mtl.	1960	Chi.	1961
Lionel Conacher	Chi.	1934	Mtl M.	1935

* Claude Lemieux became only the third player in NHL history to win the Stanley Cup with three different teams. He won with Montreal, New Jersey and Colorado.

The others:

3	Larry Hillman	Det; Tor; Mtl
3	Gordon Pettinger	NYR; Det; Bos

* The last time a team was able to win a championship in their first year after moving to a new city was the 1937 Washington Redskins in the NFL.

TEAM PREVIEW

GOAL: It's fair to say two things: Patrick Roy didn't win the Avalanche the Cup on his own; and the Avalanche wouldn't have won the Cup without Roy.

Perhaps the greatest goaltender of all-time, and perhaps the greatest playoff goaltender of all time. His playoff numbers speak for themselves.

Most Playoff Games by a Goalie:

PATRICK ROY	136
Billy Smith	132
Grant Fuhr	121

Most Playoff Minutes Played by a Goalie:

PATRICK ROY	8,418
Billy Smith	7,645
Grant Fuhr	7,071

Most Playoff Wins by a Goaltender:

Billy Smith	88
PATRICK ROY	86
Ken Dryden	80

Last year, before the start of the season the Avalanche had two excellent young goalies vying for the number one job. Always there, though, was the suspicion that neither Jocelyn Thibault or Stephane Fiset could carry the team to the Stanley Cup finals.

Both are gone. Thibault to Montreal in the Roy deal; Fiset during the summer went to Los Angeles along with Colorado's number one 1998 draft choice to Los Angeles for Pierre Lacroix's son, Eric, and the Kings' top draft pick.

That leaves a backup job open. And Roy can't play for too many more years anyway. J.F. Labbe was on the playoff roster, but the team has an outstanding prospect in Marc Denis. If he's not ready, the team will shore up with an easily available veteran.

DEFENCE: Sylvain Lefebvre is one of the best strictly defensive defencemen in the league; Sandis Ozolinsh is one of the best strictly offensive defencemen. Bookends, with some good reading inbetween.

Obtaining Ozolinsh gave the Avalanche the quarterback they were lacking. It came with a high price tag - power forward, Owen Nolan - but obviously it was worth it. Ozolinsh has 56 goals in four seasons, three seasons worth of games, which works out to an average of 19 goals per 82 games. It's one thing for defencemen to pile up the points with assists, but when they contribute with goals it gives them an added dimension.

They might just as well rename the plus-minus trophy the Sylvain Lefebvre trophy. Whether or not the statistic has enough merit to deserve serious consideration, the fact remains Lefebvre almost always does well at it, as shown below:

1995-96	Colorado	+26
1994-95	Quebec	+13
1993-94	Toronto	+33 (best on team)
1992-93	Toronto	+ 8
1991-92	Montreal	+ 9
1990-91	Montreal	-11 (worst on team)
1989-90	Montreal	+18
	Total	**+96**

Curtis Leschyshyn has been even more impressive at that statistic the last two years. He finished first on the Avalanche last

season with a +32; the season before he was second in the league with a +29 in the shortened schedule.

Adam Foote came into his own last year, with no better evidence than the fact he was invited to play for Team Canada in the World Cup after Ray Bourque dropped out.

Uwe Krupp is the other returning regular from last season. Krupp, of course, scored the Stanley Cup winning goal in the third overtime of game four in the final versus Florida.

Character player, Craig Wolanin, was traded to Tampa Bay during the summer for future considerations. Kind of a high price for Wolanin to pay, just for being responsible for one playoff goal. He cried about it, what more do they want?

Of course, that wasn't the reason, but you'd have to think those future considerations must be pretty good for the Avalanche to give up a key defenceman.

Alexei Gusarov, who proved to be much more valuable than expected, was lost to free agency, so it could be they were going to make a concentrated effort to re-sign him.

Jon Klemm and Norwegian Anders Myrvold should battle it out for whatever playing time is left over.

FORWARD: What can you say about Joe Sakic that hasn't already been said. Nothing.

What can you say about Peter Forsberg that hasn't already been said. Nothing.

GOALTENDER	GPI	MINS	AVG	W	L	T	EN	SO	GA	SA	SV %
PATRICK ROY	39	2305	2.68	22	15	1	3	1	103	1130	.909
STEPHANE FISET	37	2107	2.93	22	6	7	3	1	103	1012	.898
JOCELYN THIBAULT	10	558	3.01	3	4	2	0	0	28	222	.874
COL TOTALS	82	4982	2.89	47	25	10	6	2	240	2370	.899

What can you say about Claude Lemieux that hasn't already been said. Nothing. Nothing good, anyway.

The best forward group in the league has everything. Two of the best scorers in the game in Sakic and Forsberg; impressive secondary scoring in Valeri Kamensky and Scott Young; Claude Lemieux, who is, well, Claude Lemieux; great youngsters, who play it tough, in Adam Deadmarsh and Chris Simon; more young talent in Stephane Yelle; a grizzled veteran winner in Mike Keane; Mike Ricci, who saved his best for the playoffs; and now they even have the GM's son, in Eric Lacroix.

To put it another way, they're all set.

Ricci is probably the most enigmatic of the bunch, and the one most likely to improve. He only had six goals during the regular season, but he should be scoring in the 30-goal range, or 20 at the minimum. He's also the most likely to be traded, because teams think if put into the right situation they can get him scoring again.

The Avalanche don't have much room for newcomers, but the team is in a nice situation whereby they can spot some rookies, and let them learn their way onto the team. Landon Wilson, a power forward, is doing just that. He's projected as a future Avalanche player, but by spending more time in the minors he's picking up the nuances of the game that will make him more valuable when he does earn his place.

The Avalanche filled with veteran defensive types last season, such as Troy Murray and Dave Hannan, who became free agents. Those type of guys are good for the youngsters to learn from, but when the kids are better than the teachers, the lessons become less significant. If the need arises, Lacroix will no doubt go out and find some of them, guys in their last few years who are hungry for a championship.

There's nothing that is going to seriously hamper the Colorado forward situation. Even injuries will hurt less than they would other teams, because they've got ready replacements.

It doesn't get any better.

SPECIAL TEAMS: The key to the success of the power play was obtaining Ozolinsh. They've needed a quarterback for a few years, and they got a good one in Ozolinsh. His job is made easier by the number of snipers looking to add to their goal totals.

The five men the Avalanche can put out with the man-advantage is impressive enough, but when you change the forwards for the second unit, they're still better than half the teams in the league.

The only shortcoming of the power play is that they allowed the most shorthanded goals in the league. Part of the reason is that they usually have a forward back on the point. Another is that Ozolinsh is committed to scoring when up a man, and could care less what the other team is up to.

The good thing about allowing so many shorthanded goals might be that it showed them how it's done. While they were last in that category, they were first in most shorthanded goals scored.

Sometimes teams that score a lot shorthanded aren't paying as much attention to their defensive duties, because they're looking for scoring opportunites. But, that obviously wasn't a problem, because their penalty killing percentage was still among the best.

POWER PLAY	G	ATT	PCT
Overall	86	404	21.3% (T-2nd NHL)
Home	44	212	20.8% (10th NHL)
Road	42	192	21.9% (2nd NHL)

22 SHORT HANDED GOALS ALLOWED (26th NHL)

PENALTY KILLING

	G	TSH	PCT	
Overall	71	439	83.8%	(7th NHL)
Home	29	216	86.6%	(5th NHL)
Road	42	223	81.2%	(13th NHL)

21 SHORT HANDED GOALS SCORED (1st NHL)

COACHING AND MANAGEMENT: It's not often that a Stanley Cup winning coach changes teams the following year, but it almost happened with Marc Crawford.

Come to think of it, maybe it's not that rare, Mike Keenan did it just two years ago. Whether or not Crawford really would have bolted is not for sure, but the Toronto Maple Leafs waited an awful long time to sign Mike Murphy, the coach they said they wanted all along. Rhetoric aside, they really wanted Crawford badly, and the team Crawford has always wanted to coach is Toronto. Whatever was happening behind the scenes, it doesn't matter now, because Crawford will be behind the bench once again.

The mastermind of this team's success was GM Pierre Lacroix. Need a power play quarterback? He got Ozolinsh. Need a great goaltender for the playoffs? He got Roy. Need a playoff winner? He got Claude Lemieux. Need a leader with character? How about Mike Keane? Need anything? He'll go get it. Need to be close to your son? He got Eric.

The last one is a little questionable, but the rest is nothing short of the best general managing job in the league last season.

The son thing could cause problems, however. Do players want to be watching what they say in private, knowing it could get back to the big guy upstairs? Are there going to be hard feelings if Lacroix plays when someone else thinks they should? Is Crawford going to be resentful, thinking perhaps there's a spy in the dressing room?

Of course, we don't know if Lacroix would ever say a word to his father about anything, but when his contract negotiations come up, they could probably sell tickets. Lacroix, the father that is, has been bang on with just about everything he's done, so best to give him the benefit of the doubt on this one.

DRAFT

Round	Sel.	Player	Pos	
1	25	Peter Ratchuk	D	Shattuck (US HS)
2	51	Yuri Babenko	C	Russia
3	79	Mark Parrish	LW	St. Cloud State
4	98	Ben Storey	D	Harvard
4	107	Randy Petruck	G	Kamloops (WHL)
5	134	Luke Curtin	LW	Kelowna (WHL)
6	146	Brian Willsie	RW	Guelph (OHL)
6	160	Kai Fischer	G	Germany
7	167	Dan Hinote	RW	Army (NCAA-ind)
7	176	Samuel Pahisson	C	Sweden
7	188	Roman Pylner	C	Czech Rep.
8	214	Matt Scorsune	D	Hotchkiss (US HS)
9	240	Justin Clark	RW	Michigan Univ.

Ratchuk is an offensive defenseman whose strength is skating. He'll be attending Bowling Green University, so he's considered a long-term project. He'll need to work on the physical side of his game. He wasn't projected as a first-rounder, and was ranked 46th by the CSB among North Americans, but the Avalanche have less of a sense of desperation and can afford to wait.

PROGNOSIS: The Avalanche are too good not to have an excellent regular season, even if everyone is gunning for them. There will likely be a backlash after winning the Cup, however, and they could have some slow times. It probably won't bother them that much, either, because they'll always have the playoffs in the back of their mind, where they've already proven to be best.

The Avalanche don't win with any one element, such as some teams that are strictly defence or strictly offence. That means there's less chance of a breakdown.

Everything has to work out perfectly for a team to win the Stanley Cup, and it may not happen this time around. Maybe, a couple overtime games don't go their way, or they have key injuries at a bad time. But, when the playoffs roll around again, the Avalanche are best bets to be favored.

PREDICTION:

Pacific Division: 1st

Western Conference: 2nd

Overall: 3rd

Team Rankings 1995-96

		Conference Rank	League Rank
Record	47-25-10	2	2
Home	24-10-7	2	4
Away	23-15-3	2	2
Versus Own Conference	34-17-5	2	2
Versus Other Conference	13-8-5	3	5
Team Plus\Minus	+71	2	2
Goals For	326	1	2
Goals Against	240	3	8
Average Shots For	32.2	3	6

Average Shots Against	28.9	4	9
Overtime	2-3-10	11	17
One Goal Games	11-9	3	6
Times outshooting opponent	46	3	7
Versus Teams Over .500	12-8-5	2	2
Versus Teams Under .500	35-17-5	2	8
First Half Record	22-13-6	2	6
Second Half Record	25-12-4	2	2

PLAYOFFS

Results: Defeated Vancouver 4-2

Defeated Chicago 4-2

Defeated Detroit 4-2

Defeated Colorado 4-0

Record: 16-6

Home: 8-3

Away: 8-3

Goals For: 80 (3.6 per game)

Goals Against: 51 (2.3 per game)

Overtime: 5-2

Power play: 21.8% (4th)

Penalty Killing: 85.0% (7th)

ALL-TIME LEADERS

GOALS

Michel Goulet   456

Peter Stastny   380

Joe Sakic   286

ASSISTS

Peter Stastny	668
Michel Goulet	489
Joe Sakic	460

POINTS

Peter Stastny	1,048
Michel Goulet	945
Joe Sakic	746

BEST INDIVIDUAL SEASONS

GOALS

Michel Goulet	1982-83	57
Michel Goulet	1983-84	56
Michel Goulet	1984-85	55

ASSISTS

Peter Stastny	1981-82	93
Peter Forsberg	1995-96	86
Peter Stastny	1985-86	81

POINTS

Peter Stastny	1981-82	139
Peter Stastny	1982-83	124
Peter Stastny	1985-86	122

TEAM RECORD

Last 3 years

	GP	W	L	T	Pts	%
1995-96	82	47	25	10	104	.634
1994-95	48	30	13	5	65	.677
1993-94	84	34	42	8	76	.452

Best 3 regular seasons

1994-95	48	30	13	5	65	.677
1995-96	82	47	25	10	104	.634
1992-93	84	47	27	10	104	.619

Worst 3 regular seasons

1989-90	80	12	61	7	31	.194
1990-91	80	16	50	14	46	.288
1991-92	80	20	48	12	52	.325

Most Goals (min. 70 game schedule)

1983-84	360
1981-82	356
1992-93	351

Fewest Goals (min. 70 game schedule)

1990-91	236
1989-90	240
1979-80	248

Most Goals Against (min. 70 game schedule)

1989-90	407
1990-91	354
1981-82	345

Fewest Goals Against (min. 70 game schedule)

1995-96	240
1984-85	275
1986-87	276

STAT SECTION

Team Scoring Stats

	GP	G	A	PTS	+/-	PIM	SH	Power Play			Short Handed		
								G	A	P	G	A	P
JOE SAKIC	82	51	69	120	14	44	339	17	33	50	6	2	8
PETER FORSBERG	82	30	86	116	26	47	217	7	32	39	3	4	7
VALERI KAMENSKY	81	38	47	85	14	85	220	18	13	31	1	1	2
CLAUDE LEMIEUX	79	39	32	71	14	117	315	9	6	15	2	1	3
SCOTT YOUNG	81	21	39	60	2	50	229	7	11	18	0	1	1
SANDIS OZOLINSH	73	14	40	54	2	54	166	8	24	32	1	0	1
ADAM DEADMARSH	78	21	27	48	20	142	151	3	5	8	0	0	0
CHRIS SIMON	64	16	18	34	10	250	105	4	3	7	0	0	0
STEPHANE YELLE	71	13	14	27	15	30	93	0	1	1	2	2	4
MIKE KEANE	73	10	17	27	5-	46	84	0	2	2	2	3	5
CRAIG WOLANIN	75	7	20	27	25	50	73	0	1	1	3	1	4
MIKE RICCI	62	6	21	27	1	52	73	3	7	10	0	0	0
TROY MURRAY	63	7	14	21	15	22	36	0	0	0	0	2	2
ALEXEI GUSAROV	65	5	15	20	29	56	42	0	4	4	0	0	0
CURTIS LESCHYSHYN	77	4	15	19	32	73	76	0	2	2	0	2	2
DAVE HANNAN	61	7	10	17	3	32	41	1	0	1	1	2	3
ADAM FOOTE	73	5	11	16	27	88	49	1	1	2	0	0	0
SYLVAIN LEFEBVRE	75	5	11	16	26	49	115	2	2	4	0	2	2
JON KLEMM	56	3	12	15	12	20	61	0	1	1	1	1	2
RENE CORBET	33	3	6	9	10	33	35	0	0	0	0	0	0
WARREN RYCHEL	52	6	2	8	6	147	45	0	0	0	0	0	0
UWE KRUPP	6	0	3	3	4	4	9	0	2	2	0	0	0
PAUL BROUSSEAU	8	1	1	2	1	2	10	0	0	0	0	0	0
LANDON WILSON	7	1	0	1	3	6	6	0	0	0	0	0	0
JOSEF MARHA	2	0	1	1	1	0	2	0	0	0	0	0	0
ANDERS MYRVOLD	4	0	1	1	2-	6	4	0	1	1	0	0	0
STEPHANE FISET	37	0	1	1	0	2	0	0	0	0	0	0	0
AARON MILLER	5	0	0	0	0	0	2	0	0	0	0	0	0
PATRICK ROY	61	0	0	0	0	10	0	0	0	0	0	0	0

PLAYOFFS

PLAYER	GP	G	A	PTS	+/-	PIM	PP	SH	GW	OT	S
JOE SAKIC	22	18	16	34	10	14	6	0	6	2	98
VALERI KAMENSKY	22	10	12	22	11	28	3	0	2	0	56
PETER FORSBERG	22	10	11	21	10	18	3	0	1	0	50
SANDIS OZOLINSH	22	5	14	19	5	16	2	0	1	1	52
MIKE RICCI	22	6	11	17	1-	18	3	0	1	0	31
ADAM DEADMARSH	22	5	12	17	8	25	1	0	0	0	40
UWE KRUPP	22	4	12	16	5	33	1	0	2	1	38
SCOTT YOUNG	22	3	12	15	6	10	0	0	0	0	61
CLAUDE LEMIEUX	19	5	7	12	5	55	3	0	0	0	81
ALEXEI GUSAROV	21	0	9	9	13	12	0	0	0	0	15
RENE CORBET	8	3	2	5	3	2	1	0	1	0	9
MIKE KEANE	22	3	2	5	1	16	0	0	1	1	22
STEPHANE YELLE	22	1	4	5	2	8	0	1	0	0	24
SYLVAIN LEFEBVRE	22	0	5	5	6	12	0	0	0	0	22
ADAM FOOTE	22	1	3	4	11	36	0	0	0	0	20
JON KLEMM	15	2	1	3	6	0	1	0	0	0	11
CHRIS SIMON	12	1	2	3	2-	11	0	0	0	0	9
CURTIS LESCHYSHYN	17	1	2	3	4	8	0	0	0	0	9
DAVE HANNAN	13	0	2	2	3	2	0	0	0	0	2
CRAIG WOLANIN	7	1	0	1	2	8	0	0	1	0	5
WARREN RYCHEL	12	1	0	1	4	23	0	0	0	0	4
STEPHANE FISET	1	0	0	0	0	0	0	0	0	0	0
TROY MURRAY	8	0	0	0	4-	19	0	0	0	0	6
PATRICK ROY	22	0	0	0	0	0	0	0	0	0	0

GOALTENDER	GPI	MINS	AVG	W	L	T	EN	SO	GA	SA	SV %
STEPHANE FISET	1	1	.00	0	0	0	0	0	0	0	.000
PATRICK ROY	22	1454	2.10	16	6	0	3	5	1	649	.921
COL TOTALS	22	1460	2.10	16	6	0	3	5	1	649	.921

Dallas Stars

The season started off okay for the Stars. Near the end of the first month they had a 5-3-2 record, and occupied first place in the Central Division. They were scoring lots of goals, were undefeated in five games, and were sitting pretty.

That's the good news from the Dallas season. It never got any better than that. Seven winless games later, they were in sixth place. They moved out of there for a couple games after going undefeated in five, but then they lost six in a row, and it was all over.

Gee, do you see a pattern there? You win some and you lose some, which is exactly how the Dallas season went. A streak here, a streak there. If they had more good streaks they would have made the playoffs.

That's a curious thing about hockey teams. If they can play so well over a stretch of a couple weeks, why can't they do it more often. Or when they play so poorly, how are they able to get so good all of a sudden.

This is how the Dallas streaks went:

	Streak
October 19 - October 28	Undefeated in 5
October 30 - November 15	Winless in 7
November 17 - December 3	Undefeated in 5
December 5 - December 15	Lost 6 in a row
December 21 - January 3	Winless in 7
January 7 - January 17	Winless in 7
February 22 - March 6	Undefeated in 7

Those are just the consecutive streaks of at least five games. There were others of four or more that were interupted by a win or loss.

If you take the above list and trade one winless streak for one undefeated streak, the Stars are a considerably better team, and in the playoffs.

The reality is that, with the exception of the worst teams and the very best teams, everyone puts together similar type streaks throughout a season. It's part of the game. The difference is that those that put together more winning streaks than losing streaks are the more successful ones.

The chart below, from last year, shows the number of games in a streak and the number of teams that had at least one in that category.

Undefeated Streaks:

Games	Teams
5	24
6	21
7	15
8	9
9	6

Winless Streaks:

Games	Teams
5	19
6	14
7	9
8	6
9	6

The chart shows that almost every team has winning and losing streak of some length during a season. There are a number of reasons: Sometimes it's a schedule thing, one player just catches fire, injuries could be a factor, or one of many different things. It's a long season and no team is able to play the same all the way through it.

Still, teams tend to over react, as well as the media and fans, when one of these streaks occur. They tend to panic during the winless streaks, and everybody starts speculating about what's wrong with the team. And they tend to think the winning streaks are more reason for celebration than they really are. Of course, the rules change when they reach mammoth proportions, or occur too often, but most of the time they're just part of the game and mean little.

One thing for the trivia drawer:
The Stars pulled off an incredible feat last year, which is worth noting here. Down 5-3 in the last minute of an October 14 home game, Kevin Hatcher scored at 19:11 to make it 5-4. With goalie Andy Moog out of the net, Mike Modano scored at 19:44. Eleven seconds later, with just five seconds remaining in regulation time, Guy Carbonneau took a pass from Mike Kennedy to give Dallas the 6-5 victory.

TEAM PREVIEW

GOAL: This is an area that has been a sore spot with the Stars for years. It's been a long time since they had a number one man so solid, they didn't have to question the position.

They've never seemed to be quite satisfied with Andy Moog and Darcy Wakaluk.

Both were free agents after the season. Moog was re-signed, while Wakaluk went to Phoenix. Moog is insurance. He's 36-years-old, and the Stars wouldn't have signed him if they had found someone they were sure could replace him.

They may have found him, but they can't be sure until he plays in the NHL.

It's not Allan Bester, who was a rent-a-goalie last season when injuries added up. He had found a home in the IHL, but agreed to help out, and in a unique arrangement, got paid $2,500 for every point he earned in Dallas. That was worth $22,500 for 10 games. He started out hot, winning his first three, before falling prey to the weak team in front of him.

The goalie the Stars are most excited about is Roman Turek. He's experienced at 26, so could step right in if signed, and he led the Czech Republic to the gold medal at the world championships.

Manny Fernandez has also been kicking around for a couple seasons. Considered an excellent prospect at one time, he had some problems with the Michigan K-Wings in the IHL, and was unimpressive when called up to Dallas.

Jordan Willis was the 243rd pick in the 1993 draft, and had an outstanding first pro season for Michigan last year, even making his NHL debut when all the injuries hit, and getting in 19 relief minutes. It was long enough to record his first NHL loss, even though he only allowed one goal.

Turek will have the chance to be the number one man, with the Stars desperately hoping he will turn out to be another Dominik Hasek. If not, Moog probably has another season or two left in him.

Or, there's one other option. As if they didn't have enough goaltending, the Stars signed restricted free agent Arturs Irbe to an offer sheet. San Jose was unlikely to match, so Irbe joins the crowd. Although once considered one of the better goalies in the game, he's moved down the list, close to the bottom.

DEFENCE: The Stars were strong enough defensively, so they could afford to get someone who wasn't. Sergei Zubov could get 70 points fairly easily, and help others increase their offensive production at the same time. Mainly, he will help out on the power play, which needs help badly.

The Stars gave up Kevin Hatcher to Pittsburgh for Zubov. Hatcher is the type of player a lot of teams want, although his consistency level isn't always there. He won the award last season for the player most often rumored to be traded.

Defence is the Stars' strength. They have some excellent young defencemen who have developed nicely.

Derian Hatcher didn't have a great season, but he has still earned status as one of the better all-round blueliners in the league.

Richard Matvichuk is another who has come along. He hasn't been the offensive threat once predicted of him, but his defensive play has improved greatly.

Darryl Sydor played for Hitchcock in junior, where he had 105 points one season in Kamloops. He was a steal, coming from the Los Angeles Kings along with a fifth round draft pick, for Shane Churla and Doug Zmolek.

Veterans Craig Ludvig, Grant Ledyard and Mike Lalor give the Stars a solid unit on the blueline.

Often, though, a defence is only as good as the forwards in front of them, and the goalie behind them. Forwards who come back into their own end, and/or a spectacular netminder, will make them all look that much better.

FORWARD: On paper they didn't look like such a bad forward unit. On the ice they were horrendous last year, however, and couldn't score. Everybody that mattered, had an off season, which could mean something positive for this year.

At centre, they have a solid one-two punch, again on paper. Mike Modano can easily climb back up to the 100-point range, and Joe Nieuwendyk isn't nearly as bad as the 14 measly goals and 32 points he scored after being obtained from Calgary for possible rookie-of-the-year Jarome Iginla, and throwaway Corey Millen. Nieuwendyk has a reputation of being a slow starter, so maybe he just never got going.

One or both of those two is going to be

GOALTENDER	GPI	MINS	AVG	W	L	T	EN	SO	GA	SA	SV %
ANDY MOOG	41	2228	2.99	13	19	7	6	1	111	1106	.900
ALLAN BESTER	10	601	3.00	4	5	1	3	0	30	297	.899
JORDAN WILLIS	1	19	3.16	0	1	0	0	0	1	14	.929
DARCY WAKALUK	37	1875	3.39	9	16	5	4	1	106	975	.891
EMMANUEL FERNANDE	5	249	4.58	0	1	1	0	0	19	121	.843
DAL TOTALS	82	4992	3.37	26	42	14	13	2	280	2526	.889

helped out tremendously with the signing of free agent, Pat Verbeek. They pass the puck, he scores, simple as that. He had 41 goals with the Rangers last year, despite missing 13 games. Plus, he plays it tough, and nobody questions his small size.

Todd Harvey is the other top forward on the Stars. He's coming off a horrendous case of the sophomore jinx. He had just nine goals and 29 points. Look for him to have a break-out season.

Thirty-three-year-old Greg Adams was the second top goal scorer, with 22, and the top power play goal scorer, with 11. You know there's something wrong when he's contributing a major part of the offence. He won't have to do that this year.

Benoit Hogue was obtained to add some scoring punch, and had a nice 11-game point streak. The problem with him is that he can have those streaks, and then have a pointless streak for 11 games.

Consistency was a problem with many of the Stars forwards. Rookie Jere Lehtinen, for example, went the whole month of November, and half of December, without getting a single point. In February, he had 16 of them. Another rookie, Grant Marshall, was impressive at times, not so impressive at others. Young players need to develop consistency, so this year will determine whether they can or not.

Bob Bassen was injured for most of last year after being signed as a free agent, so he could return and make a contribution. Down the middle they could have Modano, Nieuwendyk, Bassen, Guy Carbonneau, and maybe Jamie Langenbrunner, who played most of last season in Michigan for the K-Wings.

On the left side are Adams, Hogue, Mike Kennedy, and Brent Gilchrist, who had one of his better offensive seasons. Randy Wood played there last season, but was an unrestricted free agent.

The Stars replaced him when they picked up free agent Dave Reid, an excellent penalty killer, character player, and surprising offensive contributor. He's coming off his best NHL season, earned at the age of 31. He's obviously one of those guys who gets better with age.

On the right side, there is Verbeek, Harvey, Brent Fedyk, Lehtinen, and Marshall.

As with most teams, a lot of the forwards can play different positions. Harvey, for one, came into the league as a centre.

Again, on paper, they don't look bad at all. They have improved scoring, some good defence, some youthful promise, and some veterans with scoring histories.

If just a few of their forwards stage comeback seasons they're going to be a notably better team.

SPECIAL TEAMS: Not only could the power play not score last season, they couldn't stop the other team from scoring. They had the fifth most power play opportunities in the league, scoring 67 times, but they gave up 20 goals when they had the man-advantage. That's just two short of the league record, of which they already have a share. Curiously, the only team to give up more shorthanded goals was Colorado, who tied Dallas's all-time record of 22. The Avalanche, however, compensated with the second best power play in the league.

Special teams are obviously of great concern, which is why the Stars obtained Zubov. It's also why they picked up Reid, who will improve the penalty killing. The improvement should be complete with power play sniper, Pat Verbeek. He had 17 man-advantage goals last season, six more than anybody else on the Stars. Nieuwendyk and Modano are good power play performers when they're with the right people, so special teams are in for a big boost, and should be the most improved in the league.

POWER PLAY	G	ATT	PCT	
Overall	67	443	15.1%	(23rd NHL)
Home	38	226	16.8%	(16th NHL)
Road	29	217	13.4%	(23rd NHL)

20 SHORT HANDED GOALS ALLOWED (T-24th NHL)

PENALTY KILLING	G	TSH	PCT	
Overall	82	418	80.4%	(T-20th NHL)
Home	44	217	79.7%	(T-24th NHL)
Road	38	201	81.1%	(14th NHL)

8 SHORT HANDED GOALS SCORED (T-21st NHL)

COACHING AND MANAGEMENT: General Manager Bob Gainey had to do something, and he did lots. The team wasn't responding to his coaching - he fired himself. The team wasn't scoring - he went and got Joe Nieuwendyk. Players weren't playing well - he sent them to the minors. The team still wasn't scoring - he traded Kevin Hatcher during the summer for offensive dynamo Sergei Zubov. The power play stunk - he got Pat Verbeek. The penalty killing reeked - he got Dave Reid.

He hasn't had a lot go his way, but the moves during the off-season could change things. At least he's pulling out all the stops to try and improve this team.

Ken Hitchcock took over from Gainey as coach, moving up from the Michigan K-Wings in the IHL. He's been very successful, whether it was with the junior Kamloops Blazers, or the K-Wings, or as coach of Canada's national junior team. He's considered a players' coach and figures the secret of good defence is with the offence. That, of course, is in stark contrast to Gainey. Funny thing, though. The Stars didn't play better offensively after Hitchcock

took over, they played better defensively. Overall, their record wasn't any better at all. And, maybe it's just a coincidence, but one thing the Stars have usually had under Gainey was excellent penalty-killing, not surprising considering he and assistant Doug Jarvis were two of the very best. Their ranking, after Hitchcock took over, went from eighth overall down to 20th. The power play didn't improve appreciatively either, rising just one notch from 24th to 23rd.

BEFORE AND AFTER HITCHCOCK

	Before	After
Games	37	45
Record	11-18-8 .405	15-24-6 .400
Goals-for and against	100-144	127-136
Goals for per game	2.7	2.8
Goals against per game	3.9	3.0

The team is much improved now, and if Hitchcock can get some of those coming off down years to rebound, he has a chance to be coach of the year. Starting off with the team in training camp should help as well.

DRAFT

Round	Sel.	Player	Pos	Team
1	5	Richard Jackman	D	Sault Ste. Marie (OHL)
3	70	Jonathan Sim	C	Sarnia (OHL)
4	90	Mike Hurley	RW	Tri-City (WHL)
5	112	Ryan Christie	D	Owen Sound (OHL)
5	113	Evgeny Tysbuk	D	Russia
7	66	Eoin McInerney	G	London (OHL)

| 8 | 194 | Joel Kwiatkowski | D | Prince George (WHL) |
| 9 | 220 | Nick Bootland | LW | Guelph (OHL) |

Bob Gainey likes players with character, and Jackman showed he has it, in an unusual way. Last year, he was invited to the Prospects Game, played at Maple Leaf Gardens, with all the top draft hopefuls in the country. But, his junior team had a couple important games over that span, so putting the team ahead of his personal gain, he declined to play in the Prospects Game.

Jackman is considered a solid two-way defenceman, and led the OHL with a plus 56. The only knock against him is his size. He's tall enough, at 6-2, but depending on who's doing the telling, he's as light as 166 pounds, or as heavy as 175. Either one, he needs to eat his Wheaties, with sugar on them, so he can bulk up some. If his weight is indeed a problem, he seems the type to take care of it.

PROGNOSIS: I'm going out on a limb here, but I think the Stars could be the surprise team of the season. If they get the goaltending they think they're going to get from Turek, comeback seasons from Nieuwendyk and Modano, a breakout year from Harvey, and free agents Verbeek and Reid to stay at the same level they played at last year, they could be going places.

They have one of the better defence corps, with some added offence in Zubov. Scoring is going to go way up. Their special teams are going to be considerably better, and they have a proven winner in coach Hitchcock.

If Hitchcock can take their talent from paper to ice, the Stars will make the playoffs, and maybe even do some damage.

PREDICTION:

Central Divison: 3rd

Western Conference: 5th

Overall: 11th

Team Rankings 1995-96

		Conference Rank	League Rank
Record	26-42-14	11	22
Home	14-18-9	10	21
Away	12-24-5	11	21
Versus Own Conference	21-26-9	9	19
Versus Other Conference	5-16-5	13	26
Team Plus\Minus	-38	10	21
Goals For	227	12	23
Goals Against	280	9	19
Average Shots Fo	30.1	6	13
Average Shots Against	30.8	8	16
Overtime	1-0-14	5	9
One Goal Games	11-9	3	6
Times outshooting opponent	35	9	16
Versus Teams Over .500	3-23-8	13	25
Versus Teams Under .500	23-19-6	8	17
First Half Record	11-20-10	11	22
Second Half Record	15-22-4	10	21

PLAYOFFS

Did not make playoffs

ALL-TIME LEADERS

GOALS

Brian Bellows	342
Dino Ciccarelli	332
Bill Goldsworthy	267

ASSISTS

Neal Broten	586
Brian Bellows	380
Bobby Smith	369

POINTS

Neal Broten	852
Brian Bellows	722
Dino Ciccarelli	651

BEST INDIVIDUAL SEASONS

GOALS

Brian Bellows	1989-90	55
Dino Ciccarelli	1981-82	55
Mike Modano	1993-94	50

ASSISTS

Neal Broten	1985-86	76
Bobby Smith	1981-82	71
Tim Young	1976-77	66

POINTS

Bobby Smith	1981-82	114
Dino Ciccarelli	1981-82	106
Neal Broten	1985-86	105

TEAM RECORD

Last 3 years

	GP	W	L	T	Pts	%
1995-96	82	26	42	14	66	.402
1994-95	48	17	23	8	42	.438
1993-94	84	42	29	13	97	.577

Best 3 regular seasons

1982-83	80	40	24	16	96	.600
1982-82	80	37	23	20	94	.588
1993-94	84	42	29	13	97	.577

Worst 3 regular seasons

1977-78	80	18	53	9	45	.281
1975-76	80	20	53	7	47	.293
1987-88	80	19	48	13	51	.319

Most Goals (min. 70 game schedule)

1981-82	346
1983-84	345
1985-86	327

Fewest Goals (min. 70 game schedule)

1968-69	189
1970-71	191
1967-68	191

Most Goals Against (min. 70 game schedule)

1987-88	349
1983-84	344
1974-75	341

Fewest Goals Against (min. 70 game schedule)

1971-72	191
1970-71	223
1967-68	226

STAT SECTION

Team Scoring Stats

	GP	G	A	PTS	+/-	PIM	SH	Power Play			Short Handed		
								G	A	P	G	A	P
MIKE MODANO	78	36	45	81	12-	63	320	8	21	29	4	1	5
BENOIT HOGUE	78	19	45	64	10	104	155	5	15	20	0	1	1
GREG ADAMS	66	22	21	43	21-	33	140	11	9	20	1	1	2
BRENT GILCHRIST	77	20	22	42	11-	36	164	6	3	9	1	1	2
KEVIN HATCHER	74	15	26	41	24-	58	237	7	15	22	0	0	0
BRENT FEDYK	65	20	14	34	16-	54	113	8	4	12	0	1	1
JOE NIEUWENDYK	52	14	18	32	17-	41	138	8	8	16	0	0	0
DERIAN HATCHER	79	8	23	31	12-	129	125	2	7	9	0	0	0
TODD HARVEY	69	9	20	29	13-	136	101	3	8	11	0	0	0
GRANT MARSHALL	70	9	19	28	0	111	62	0	2	2	0	0	0
JERE LEHTINEN	57	6	22	28	5	16	109	0	5	5	0	0	0
MIKE KENNEDY	61	9	17	26	7-	48	111	4	2	6	0	0	0
GRANT LEDYARD	73	5	19	24	15-	20	123	2	8	10	0	1	1
GUY CARBONNEAU	71	8	15	23	2-	38	54	0	0	0	2	1	3
RICHARD MATVICHUK	73	6	16	22	4	71	81	0	3	3	0	0	0
RANDY WOOD	76	8	13	21	15-	62	159	1	0	1	0	1	1
DARRYL SYDOR	84	3	17	20	12-	75	117	2	8	10	0	0	0
BILL HUARD	51	6	6	12	3	176	34	0	0	0	0	0	0
MIKE DONNELLY	24	2	5	7	2-	10	21	0	1	1	0	0	0
JAMIE LANGENBRUNNER	12	2	2	4	2-	6	15	1	0	1	0	0	0
NIKOLAI BORSCHEVSKY	12	1	3	4	7-	6	22	0	1	1	0	0	0
JIM STORM	10	1	2	3	1-	17	11	0	1	1	0	0	0
MIKE LALOR	63	1	2	3	10-	31	46	0	0	0	0	0	0
CRAIG LUDWIG	65	1	2	3	17-	70	47	0	0	0	0	0	0
ROBERT PETROVICKY	5	1	1	2	1	0	3	1	1	2	0	0	0
BOB BASSEN	13	0	1	1	6-	15	9	0	0	0	0	0	0
MARK LAWRENCE	13	0	1	1	0	17	13	0	0	0	0	0	0
TRAVIS RICHARDS	1	0	0	0	1-	2	0	0	0	0	0	0	0
JORDAN WILLIS	1	0	0	0	0	0	0	0	0	0	0	0	0
PAT MACLEOD	2	0	0	0	0	0	2	0	0	0	0	0	0
ZAC BOYER	2	0	0	0	0	0	3	0	0	0	0	0	0
PATRICK COTE	2	0	0	0	2-	5	0	0	0	0	0	0	0
DAN MAROIS	3	0	0	0	0	2	1	0	0	0	0	0	0
DAN KESA	3	0	0	0	1-	0	0	0	0	0	0	0	0
EMMANUEL FERNANDEZ	5	0	0	0	0	0	0	0	0	0	0	0	0
PAUL CAVALLINI	8	0	0	0	3-	6	5	0	0	0	0	0	0
ALLAN BESTER	10	0	0	0	0	2	0	0	0	0	0	0	0
DARCY WAKALUK	37	0	0	0	0	6	1	0	0	0	0	0	0
ANDY MOOG	41	0	0	0	0	28	0	0	0	0	0	0	0

Detroit Red Wings

Is it live or is it Memorex? Is it a chip, or a cracker? Was it a great season, or was it a lousy playoffs?

Let's start with the regular season, considering it was one of the best in NHL history.

Most Wins in a Season

DETROIT	1995-96	62
Montreal	1976-77	60
Montreal	1977-78	59
Montreal	1975-76	58

Most Points in a Season

Montreal	1976-77	132
DETROIT	1995-96	131
Montreal	1977-78	129
Montreal	1975-76	127

Most Home Wins in a Season

DETROIT	1995-96	36
Philadelphia	1975-76	36
Six teams tied		33

Most Road Wins in a Season

Montreal	1976-77	27
Montreal	1977-78	27
DETROIT	1995-96	26
Boston	1971-72	26
Montreal	1975-76	26
Edmonton	1983-84	26

We could go on for pages on how the Wings dominated last year's regular season. Staggering, most of it. Just check out the team rankings in the statistical section if you want to know more.

All that is great, but when the playoffs start, none of that counts for anything. Oh, maybe an extra home game, but as we saw last year that doesn't mean much anyway.

Detroit was in trouble right from the start. Winnipeg, of all teams, gave them problems, and then St. Louis took them to a seventh game, which was decided in double overtime on a long shot by Steve Yzerman. Then, of course, they were outmatched by Colorado, the eventual Stanley Cup champs.

So, were the other teams that good, or were the Wings that bad? Good question.

They just weren't good enough. A funny thing to say about one of the best regular season teams in NHL history. They were too soft - both physically and mentally.

Winning in the playoffs means

individuals and teams need to take their game to a higher level. Other teams did it. The Wings didn't, or couldn't.

Want some more reasons? The Russian five-man unit stunk, the players got pushed around, they played a perimeter game, and they just didn't pay the price.

All of that means Detroit is the best team not to win the Stanley Cup. In fact, as the list below shows, they've had two of the best four all-time regular season marks, for teams that didn't win the championship.

DETROIT	1995-96	62-13-7	.799
Boston	1970-71	57-14-7	.776
Edmonton	1985-86	56-17-7	.744
DETROIT	1994-95	33-11-4	.729
Philadelphia	1975-76	51-13-16	.738

The Red Wings followed another tradition, which is that finalist losers from the previous year don't win the Stanley Cup or make the finals. In 1983, Edmonton won the Stanley Cup the year after they lost in the finals. Nobody since has made the finals, and of the 12 teams, six lost in the first round or didn't make the playoffs the next year.

* STANLEY CUP FINAL LOSER THE FOLLOWING YEAR (since Conference setup in 1982)

	Final Loser	Next Year
1995	Detroit	Lost Conference Semi-Finals
1994	Vancouver	Lost Conference Semi-Finals
1993	Los Angeles	Missed Playoffs
1992	Chicago	Lost first round
1991	Minnesota	Lost first round
1990	Boston	Lost Conference Finals
1989	Montreal	Lost Division Finals
1988	Boston	Lost Division Finals
1987	Philadelphia	Lost First Round
1986	Calgary	Lost First Round
1985	Philadelphia	Lost First Round
1984	NY Islanders	Lost Division Finals

It's easy to look back and say the Red Wings didn't have what it takes. The problem with that is that we all thought they did - before the playoffs began. Nobody could see anything standing in their way.

One thing they'll have going for them this year is that nobody will be picking them to win the Stanley Cup. With the way predictions have been going for them, it could mean their time has come.

TEAM PREVIEW

GOAL: The thing about posting such a good goals against average with a team such as Detroit, is that it's difficult to tell how much of it belongs to the team. That's not to say Osgood's not good, after all the guy can score goals too, but Mike Vernon, who is probably out of a job this year, was almost the same statistically. Osgood's GAA was 2.17; Vernon's 2.26.

It goes back to that same argument: How good would Osgood be on a team not as good defensively, such as San Jose?

Scotty Bowman showed Vernon some deference to age and experience, starting him for a few games in the playoffs. Clearly, though, Osgood was the number one man, and Bowman's decisions caused some head scratching. Sanity eventually prevailed, however, with Osgood taking over the role exclusively. Probably, too late.

With minor-leaguer Kevin Hodson ready for prime-time, and another Adirondack goalie, Norm Maracle, showing something, there really isn't room anymore for Vernon.

DEFENCE: The Detroit defence will have a slightly different look this season. Mike Ramsey, who had a great career, is retiring. Marc Bergevin was a free agent, and signed with St. Louis, just like everyone else. Viacheslav Fetisov, was another free agent and although unsigned at press time, could be back with the Wings. That is, if St. Louis doesn't want him.

No problem, though. Detroit still have Paul Coffey, Nicklas Lidstrom, and Vladimir Konstantinov. Those are three of the best in the league.

Coffey, of course, is one of the greatest offensive defencemen of all time, and a lock for the Hockey Hall of Fame when his career his over. Last season, he became the first defenceman to reach the 1,000 assist mark, and only the third at any position. Consider a couple of his offensive achievements so far:

Most Goals by a Defenceman - Career

PAUL COFFEY	372
Ray Bourque	343
Denis Potvin	310
Phil Housley	274
Bobby Orr	270

All-Time Assist Leaders

Wayne Gretzky	1,771
Gordie Howe	1,049
Marcel Dionne	1,040
PAUL COFFEY	1,038
Stan Mikita	926

Coffey is 35 years old this year, but as a 34-year-old he combined with Lidstrom to form the highest scoring defence duo on any team, and for the second year in a row. Coffey might be fading a little bit, but it seems the great skaters, such as him and Mike Gartner, for example, last longer.

Most Points	Top Two Defencemen 1995-96	Points
Detroit	Coffey 74, Lidstrom 67	141
Chicago	Chelios 72, Suter 67	139
Boston	Bourque 82, Sweeney 28	110
Buffalo	Galley 54, Zhitnik 36	90

Most Points	Top Two Defensemen 1999-95	(48 games)
Detroit	Coffey 58, Lidstrom 26	84
NY Rangers	Leetch 41, Zubov 36	77
Chicago	Chelios 38, Suter 37	73
Calgary	Housley 43, Zalapski 28	71

GOALTENDER	GPI	MINS	AVG	W	L	T	EN	SO	GA	SA	SV %
KEVIN HODSON	4	163	1.10	2	0	0	0	1	3	67	.955
CHRIS OSGOOD	50	2933	2.17	39	6	5	1	5	106	1190	.911
MIKE VERNON	32	1855	2.26	21	7	2	1	3	70	723	.903
DET TOTALS	82	4961	2.19	62	13	7	2	9	181	1982	.909

Lidstrom is 10 years younger than Coffey, and is carving his own niche as one of the league's most talented blueliners. Both Lidstrom and Coffey finished behind Konstantinov in Norris Trophy and all-star voting. Konstantinov was a second team all-star and finished fourth in Norris voting.

Konstantinov is excellent defensively; is a big-time bodychecker, although not always clean; and contributes offensively. He also led the league in plus-minus, with a plus 60, 11 better than teammate Fedorov.

Konstantinov's rise to prominence was like a rumor. People started looking at his impressive plus-minus, and as the season wore on he got better and better in people's minds.

Many of our impressions of players are based on reputation. The voters don't get to see each player that often. Ray Bourque, Chris Chelios, Brian Leetch, Paul Coffey and Scott Stevens, have all built up prestige over a long time. People know what they're about, so if they do somthing impressive statistically, such as Konstantinov did, then that's weighed into our overall impression of their season.

If Konstantinov's reputation has been built on the plus-minus, then it's bogus. The statistic isn't a true barometer of anything. As a team, Detroit was a plus 91. If Konstantinov was playing for San Jose, which were minus 74, he'd be closer to a minus 60 than a plus 60.

Some people consider the plus-minus a decent statistic if you're comparing it to your own teammates. Sometimes, but much depends on a player's role with the team. The best defensive forwards are going to play against the top scorers, for example. Doing their job well, by reducing the effectiveness of opposing scorers, could still mean a minus in the statistic. In fact, it happened to Bob Gainey, when he was winning the Selke Trophy as the league's best defensive forward in his Montreal playing days.

On the Wings, it would be almost impossible to come close to a minus, but Konstantinov was aided in another way. Coffey and Lidstrom were playing the points on the power play, where, of course, you can't help your plus numbers. That gave Konstantinov more time at even strength, and on this team, just being on the ice a lot was going to pump up the numbers.

Enough of that. Konstantinov may well deserve to be considered among the best in the game. Just if you think so, don't use the plus-minus stat to justify it.

Joining the defence corps this year should be impressive minor-leaguer and Detroit first-rounder from 1993, Anders Erickson. *The Hockey News* selected him as their minor pro prospect of the year.

Bob Rouse, Jamie Pushor, and whichever big bruisers the Wings can come up with, will be joining them.

FORWARD: During the regular season, the Red Wing forwards played almost to perfection. They scored plenty and played great defensively.

They can do it all again, too.

At centre, Sergei Fedorov is one of the best players in the game. He won the Selke Trophy as the best defensive forward, although it's a reputation award, and more than a few were pushing Rob Zamuner of Tampa Bay, who didn't even get a vote.

Speaking of votes, Fedorov finished sixth in all-star voting for centre. He also finished sixth in voting for right wing, and sixth in voting for left wing. If the league had first, second, third, fourth, fifth and sixth all-star teams, he'd hold all three forward positions on the sixth team. Yes, we're being silly, but it's still true.

Steve Yzerman is coming off a comeback season of sorts, almost reaching 100 points, and leading the team in playoff scoring. It could have been, though, that a constantly rumored trade to Ottawa was enough to scare him into playing his best.

Slava Kozlov continues to play well, while Keith Primeau continues to play well sometimes, and confound people other times. Considering what people had hoped he'd accomplish, he is too often disappointing.

Igor Larionov will be back. Despite the fact that he will turn 36 this season, he's coming off his best NHL season, with 73 points.

That takes care of the main scorers, although you could add Ciccarelli in there. One of these days, though, he's going to Tampa, just like he's always rumored. Bowman wants to give the younger guys more playing time, which is difficult to do because Ciccarelli keeps scoring goals, especially on the power play, where he pumped in 13, second most on the team.

Darren McCarty is a tough guy who scores, Stu Grimson is a tough guy who doesn't. No problem there, they don't need Bob Probert.

Veteran forwards who won't go away, and who play well defensively, include Bob Errey and Doug Brown. Kirk Maltby and Kris Draper are two younger players with the same role. Draper, of course, was the recipient of the infamous Claude Lemieux hit from behind in the playoffs, which broke his jaw.

Youngsters who have shown some offensive talent include Greg Johnson. Johnson got a shot to show his scoring talents when Primeau was lost to the club for eight games in November. He went to town during that time, scoring four goals and seven assists over those eight games. He continued afterwards, scoring 20 points over 15 games, half of his total on the year.

Some youngsters who have never really received a shot at playing on a scoring line with Detroit include Martin Lapointe and Mathieu Dandenault. On a team like the Wings, there are only so many spots available, and they'll have to bide their time, or wait for a break.

SPECIAL TEAMS: The best in the league. Consider the following chart which gives the net special teams numbers, substracting power play goals against from power play goals scored.

	PP Goals For	PP Goals Against	Net
Detroit	97	44	+53
Pittsburgh	109	78	+31
Philadelphia	82	62	+20
Florida	81	63	+18

With the exception of Pittsburgh, those numbers are twice as good as anybody else, and with the exception of Philadelphia and Florida, three times as good as any other team.

The penalty killing was most impressive at home, where they allowed only 14 power play goals in 41 games. Even on the road, where they allowed 30, they were still first.

There's no good reason why the Wings won't be the best special teams team again this year. During the regular season, anyway.

POWER PLAY	G	ATT	PCT
Overall	97	455	21.3% (T-2nd NHL)
Home	51	212	24.1% (T-2nd NHL)
Road	46	243	18.9% (5th NHL)

9 SHORT HANDED GOALS ALLOWED (T-7th NHL)

PENALTY KILLING	G	TSH	PCT	
Overall	44	375	88.3%	(1st NHL)
Home	14	169	91.7%	(1st NHL)
Road	30	206	85.4%	(1st NHL)

17 SHORT HANDED GOALS SCORED (4th NHL)

COACHING AND MANAGEMENT: Scotty Bowman has coached more games in the NHL than anyone else. He's also won more Stanley Cups. Although he said last season that it would be his last, his last will probably only be when he wins the Cup again. Nobody wants to retire on a down note, especially when they're so close.

He's also the Director of Player Personnel - no GM apparently on this team - so he'll be doing his best to get what they lack. He thought they already had it, as did everyone else, when they won more games than any other team in NHL history. He'll likely try to get some big, defensive defencemen, and maybe try to get forwards who are a little more physical.

If it is his last kick at the can, he'll pull out all the stops to make sure this time around there's nothing missing.

DRAFT

Round	Sel.	Player	Pos	
1	26	Jesse Wallin	D	Red Deer (WHL)
2	52	Aren Millcr	G	Spokane (WHL)
4	108	Johan Forsander	W	Sweden
5	135	Michal Podolka	G	Sault Ste. Marie (OHL)
6	144	Magnus Nilsson	W	Sweden
6	162	Alexandre Jacques	C	Shawinigan (QMJHL)
7	189	Colin Beardsmore	C	North Bay (OHL)
8	215	Craig Stahl	RW	Tri-City (WHL)
9	241	Evgenly Afanaslev	LW	Detroit (Midget)

Jesse Wallin is a good skating, defensive type defenceman who can contribute offensively. He's not very physical, but he has shown some leadership abilities.

He says he would like to be a Kevin Lowe type of defenceman.

PROGNOSIS: If Detroit had it all last year and didn't win, how are they going to win this year?

They'll make some minor adjustments, or maybe even a major trade, but the bottom line is still that they can't lose. They're too good.

They're strong at every position, with depth, and some of the best talent in the league.

It's just those darn playoffs, where it counts for real. Will they finally be able to get over the hump and win it all? That's the million dollar question.

PREDICTION:

Central Division: 1st

Western Conference: 1st

Overall: 1st

Team Rankings 1995-96

		Conference Rank	League Rank
Record	62-13-7	1	1
Home	36-3-2	1	1
Away	26-10-5	1	1
Versus Own Conference	43-6-7	1	1

Versus Other

Conference	19-7-0	1	1
Team Plus\Minus	+91	1	1
Goals For	325	2	3
Goals Against	181	1	1
Average Shots For	32.2	24	
Average Shots Against	24.1	1	1
Overtime	3-1-7	3	5
One Goal Games	16-7	1	1
Times outshooting opponent	65	1	1
Versus Teams Over .500	21-6-1	1	1
Versus Teams Under .500	41-7-6	1	1
First Half Record	29-9-3	1	1
Second Half Record	33-4-4	1	1

PLAYOFFS

Results: Defeated Winnipeg 4-2
Defeated St. Louis 4-3
Lost to Colorado 4-2

Record: 10-9

Home: 6-4

Away: 4-5

Goals For: 58 (3.1 per game)

Goals Against: 46 (2.4 per game)

Overtime: 1-2

Power play: 17.9% (8th)

Penalty Killing: 85.4 (5th)

ALL-TIME LEADERS

GOALS

Gordie Howe	786
Steve Yzerman	517
Alex Delvecchio	456

ASSISTS

Gordie Howe	1,023
Alex Delvecchio	825
Steve Yzerman	738

POINTS

Gordie Howe	1,809
Alex Delvecchio	1,281
Steve Yzerman	1,255

BEST INDIVIDUAL SEASONS

GOALS

Steve Yzerman	1988-89	65
Steve Yzerman	1989-90	62
Steve Yzerman	1992-93	58

ASSISTS

Steve Yzerman	1988-89	90
Steve Yzerman	1992-93	79
Marcel Dionne	1974-75	74

POINTS

Steve Yzerman	1988-89	155
Steve Yzerman	1992-93	137
Steve Yzerman	1989-90	127

TEAM RECORD

Last 3 years

	GP	W	L	T	Pts	%
1995-96	82	62	13	7	131	.799
1994-95	48	33	11	4	70	.729
1993-94	84	46	30	8	100	.595

Best 3 regular seasons

1995-96	82	62	13	7	131	.799
1994-95	48	33	11	4	70	.729
1950-51	70	44	13	13	101	.721

Worst 3 regular seasons

1985-86	80	17	57	6	40	.250
1976-77	80	16	55	9	41	.256
1926-77	44	12	28	4	28	.318

Most Goals (min. 70 game schedule)

1992-83	369
1993-94	356
1995-96	325

Fewest Goals (min. 70 game schedule)

1958-59	167
1957-58	176
1976-77	183

Most Goals Against (min. 70 game schedule)

1985-86	415
1984-85	357
1981-82	351

Fewest Goals Against (min. 70 game schedule)

1953-54	132
1952-53	133
1951-52	133

STAT SECTION

Team Scoring Stats

	GP	G	A	PTS	+/-	PIM	SH	Power Play			Short Handed		
								G	A	P	G	A	P
SERGEI FEDOROV	78	39	68	107	49	48	306	11	26	37	3	2	5
STEVE YZERMAN	80	36	59	95	29	64	220	16	22	38	2	5	7
PAUL COFFEY	76	14	60	74	19	90	234	3	30	33	1	0	1
VYACHESLAV KOZLOV	82	36	37	73	33	70	237	9	11	20	0	0	0
IGOR LARIONOV	73	22	51	73	31	34	113	10	16	26	1	2	3
NICKLAS LIDSTROM	81	17	50	67	29	20	211	8	29	37	1	4	5
KEITH PRIMEAU	74	27	25	52	19	168	150	6	9	15	2	2	4
DINO CICCARELLI	64	22	21	43	14	99	107	13	7	20	0	0	0
VIACHESLAV FETISOV	69	7	35	42	37	96	127	1	12	13	1	1	2
GREG JOHNSON	60	18	22	40	6	30	87	5	9	14	0	1	1
VLAD. KONSTANTINOV	81	14	20	34	60	139	168	3	5	8	1	0	1
BOB ERREY	71	11	21	32	30	66	85	2	1	3	2	1	3
DARREN MCCARTY	63	15	14	29	14	158	102	8	2	10	0	0	0
DOUG BROWN	62	12	15	27	11	4	115	0	2	2	1	2	3
TIM TAYLOR	72	11	14	25	11	39	81	1	0	1	1	0	1
KRIS DRAPER	52	7	9	16	2	32	51	0	0	0	1	2	3
MATHIEU DANDENAULT	34	5	7	12	6	6	32	1	0	1	0	0	0
MARC BERGEVIN	70	1	9	10	7	33	26	0	0	0	0	1	1
MARTIN LAPOINTE	58	6	3	9	0	93	76	1	0	1	0	0	0
KIRK MALTBY	55	3	6	9	16-	67	55	0	2	2	0	0	0
MIKE RAMSEY	47	2	4	6	17	35	35	0	0	0	0	0	0
BOB ROUSE	58	0	6	6	5	48	49	0	0	0	0	0	0
CHRIS OSGOOD	50	1	2	3	0	4	1	0	0	0	0	0	0
JAMIE PUSHOR	5	0	1	1	2	17	6	0	0	0	0	0	0
STU GRIMSON	56	0	1	1	10-	128	19	0	0	0	0	0	0
ANDERS ERIKSSON	1	0	0	0	1	2	0	0	0	0	0	0	0
WES WALZ	2	0	0	0	0	0	2	0	0	0	0	0	0
KEVIN HODSON	4	0	0	0	0	0	0	0	0	0	0	0	0
MIKE VERNON	32	0	0	0	0	2	0	0	0	0	0	0	0

PLAYOFFS

PLAYER	GP	G	A	PTS	+/-	PIM	PP	SH	GW	OT	S
STEVE YZERMAN	18	8	12	20	1-	4	4	0	1	1	52
SERGEI FEDOROV	19	2	18	20	8	10	0	0	2	0	59
PAUL COFFEY	17	5	9	14	3-	30	3	2	1	0	49
NICKLAS LIDSTROM	19	5	9	14	2	10	1	0	0	0	50
IGOR LARIONOV	19	6	7	13	5	6	3	0	2	0	46
VYACHESLAV KOZLOV	19	5	7	12	3	10	2	0	1	0	38
VLAD. KONSTANTINOV	19	4	5	9	4	28	0	1	0	0	41
DINO CICCARELLI	17	6	2	8	6-	26	6	0	1	0	36
KRIS DRAPER	18	4	2	6	2	18	0	1	0	0	25
DOUG BROWN	13	3	3	6	0	4	0	1	0	0	18
DARREN MCCARTY	19	3	2	5	2-	20	0	0	1	0	30
KEITH PRIMEAU	17	1	4	5	1-	28	0	0	0	0	40
VIACHESLAV FETISOV	19	1	4	5	3	34	0	0	1	0	24
GREG JOHNSON	13	3	1	4	3-	8	0	0	0	0	11
BOB ERREY	14	0	4	4	1	8	0	0	0	0	21
MIKE RAMSEY	15	0	4	4	1	10	0	0	0	0	11
TIM TAYLOR	18	0	4	4	0	4	0	0	0	0	10
MARTIN LAPOINTE	11	1	2	3	2	12	0	0	0	0	15
MARC BERGEVIN	17	1	0	1	4-	14	1	0	0	0	14
BOB ROUSE	7	0	1	1	4	4	0	0	0	0	11
KIRK MALTBY	8	0	1	1	0	4	0	0	0	0	5
STU GRIMSON	2	0	0	0	0	0	0	0	0	0	0
ANDERS ERIKSSON	3	0	0	0	2	0	0	0	0	0	1
MIKE VERNON	4	0	0	0	0	2	0	0	0	0	0
CHRIS OSGOOD	15	0	0	0	0	4	0	0	0	0	0

GOALTENDER	GPI	MINS	AVG	W	L	T	EN	SO	GA	SA	SV %
CHRIS OSGOOD	15	936	2.12	8	7	0	2	2	33	322	.898
MIKE VERNON	4	243	2.72	2	2	0	0	1	1	81	.864
DET TOTALS	19	1182	2.34	10	9	0	2	4	6	405	.886

Edmonton Oilers

This is getting tiresome. The Oilers don't ever improve.

Potential. Potential. Potential. Blah, Blah, Blah.

Yes, they're young, but when are the young guys going to become old guys and do something? They never seem to get that far.

Whatever formula they're using, it's not working. So, it's time for Plan B, C, D, E, F or G. Or some combination of all of them.

Plan A - Get more Ex-Oilers

Get one of those guys and it's some kind of prize. St. Louis had eight former Oilers on their team last season. Mind you, they didn't win, but they were just one goal away from defeating Detroit and going to the conference finals. By the end of the year, they had Wayne Gretzky, Glenn Anderson, Craig MacTavish, Grant Fuhr, Charlie Huddy, Geoff Courtnall and Igor Kravchuk.

A lot of teams figure the ex-Oilers are winners, guys who know what it takes to win the Stanley Cup.

All seven of the top seven Edmonton all-time games played leaders were still playing in the NHL last season - but with other teams: Lowe, Messier, Anderson, Kurri, MacTavish, Gretzky and Huddy.

Plan B - Trade all Draft Picks

Instead of stocking up on them, as has become their habit, trade them. All of them, or at least the top couple. It's not like it's helping them, anyway. They're probably the worst drafting team in the league. Consider their top two draft picks since 1984:

1984 - Selmar Odelein (21st), Darryl Reaugh (42nd)

1985 - Scott Metcalfe (20th), Todd Karnelly (21st)

1986 - Kim Issel (21st), Jamie Nichols (42nd)

1987 - Peter Soberlak (21st), Brad Werenka (42nd)

1988 - Francois Leroux (19th), Petro Koivunen (39th)

1989 - Jason Soules (15th), Richard Borgo (36th)

1990 - Scott Allison (17th), Alexandre Legault (38th)

1991 - Tyler Wright (12th), Martin Rucinsky (20th)

1992 - Joe Hulbig (13th), Martin Reichel (37th)

1993 - Jason Arnott (7th), Nick Stajduhar (16th)

1994 - Jason Bonsignore (4th), Ryan Smyth (6th)

1995 - Steve Kelly (6th), Georges Laracque (31st)

Not exactly a list to make them proud. Most of the names you've never heard before. Of course, many of the early picks in the list were at the end of the first round because the Oilers were finishing first overall, but still, a sorry list just the same, and with the exception of Jason Arnott, and maybe Martin Rucinsky, none have made any kind of impact in the NHL.

Plan C - Move to Nashville

Now that the Oilers have a bit more money to play around with, announce the team is moving to Nashville. Free agents love the sun-belt teams and are easier to sign. Then, when they have a couple good ones on board, say they were just kidding.

Plan D - Get Slower Players

The Oilers looked like they were cornering the market on fast skaters. Speed kills, but apparently it isn't having any effect on opposing teams. Look at all the top scoring players. Not a lot of guys known for their speed.

Plan E - Change Jerseys

The Oilers will have new jerseys this year, but maybe they can have a third set too, which has become the rage in the NHL. Here's the kicker - make those jerseys look exactly like the Montreal Canadiens' and use them when Montreal visits. Since the fans cheer more for the Habs than the Oilers when they're in town, they should go over big.

Plan F - Dump the Potential

The atmosphere in Edmonton isn't conducive to developing younger players.

Part of the reason is that there aren't many older guys around to show the kids how to play. Hold on to the ones with the most potential, and dump off the rest for veterans. They'll be better for it.

If they don't want to do that, they should trade all the young potentials for draft picks, and then trade all the draft picks for somebody else's young potentials. That way they have a chance to work out better.

Plan G - Ease up on the Europeans

About half the Europeans in the league have passed through Edmonton at some time. They don't work out, yet Sather keeps bringing them in, and then trading them. Why not save everybody a lot of trouble, and don't get them in the first place. His days of doing wonders with the likes of Esa Tikkanen and Jari Kurri are over. Some of them, like Ciger, don't even want to play in the NHL. Great for team morale. Get rid of him and his like.

PLAN H - Trade for Brendan Shanahan

The Oilers put together a big offer for Ottawa's number one draft pick. They should be able to do something similar and get the power forward they need to make everyone else better. Shanahan has been rumored to be on the block, so go get him.

TEAM PREVIEW

GOAL: The Oilers started out with two of the best goalies in the league. Well, one in the league, and one playing in the IHL for nothing. And nobody was going anywhere until Sather was good and ready. For months, the deal was Joseph and whatever, for whatever, to Boston. Right team, wrong goaltender.

Ranford was sent to the Bruins for Boston's first round pick in the draft, Marius Czercawski and defenceman Sean Brown.

Joseph, who was leading the IHL in everything, came to the Oilers and played well, but perhaps his best was saved for the World Championships in Vienna, where he stood on his head, especially in a shootout that put Canada into the gold medal game.

Joaquin Gage started the season as the backup goalie, but Fred Brathwaite, who had the job the year before, came back into the fold. Brathwaite was a free agent, however, and the Oilers signed former NHLer Bob Essensa, who had spent the last two seasons in the minors.

Doesn't much matter, anyway, because Joseph will be playing almost every game.

DEFENCE: What you see is what you don't get. Whomever is on the Oiler defence at the start of the season, most of them won't be there for long.

Only Luke Richardson gets to stay, or has to stay, whatever the case may be. And he's probably the one guy most teams would want. He's a stay-at-homer who's known for his open-ice hits.

Bryan Marchment is another guy a lot of teams would like to have. He's well known for his hits, too, but his are considered less clean, and much lower.

The rest of the defence stinks. There's no nicer way to put, although there are some worse ways.

The Oilers need a quarterback from the defence, or at least an offensive threat. Boris Mironov and Jeff Norton are about as close as it gets, and neither is adequate, although Norton used to put up some good offensive numbers.

The Oilers may have a good one in prospect Sean Brown, obtained from Boston in the Ranford deal. He's big (6-3, 200), tough (262 PIM) and contributes offensively (18-40-58 with Sarnia in the OHL).

Jiri Slegr, Brett Hauer, Greg De Vries, Bryan Muir, and 1993 first rounder Nick Stadjuhar all got into games last year, so take your pick.

The best advice would be to tell your kids not to buy any Oiler jerseys with any of the above names on them. For more reasons than one.

FORWARD: The Oilers had a good first line, with Doug Weight between Ciger and Arnott. Weight is worth his weight in gold, which also means we've used up our quota in Weight puns. We'll have to weight for next year to use some more.

Weight was the team's first 100-point scorer since their glory days. During those glory days 100-point seasons were plentiful, which is why they've had more of them than any other team in the league.

100 Point Seasons by Team:

Edmonton	28	(1 last year)
Boston	23	
Los Angeles	23	
Pittsburgh	21	(3 last year)
NY Islanders	17	

GOALTENDER	GPI	MINS	AVG	W	L	T	EN	SO	GA	SA	SV %
FRED BRATHWAITE	7	293	2.46	0	2	0	1	0	12	140	.914
CURTIS JOSEPH	34	1936	3.44	15	16	2	4	0	111	971	.886
JOAQUIN GAGE	16	717	3.77	2	8	1	1	0	45	350	.871
BILL RANFORD	37	2015	3.81	13	18	5	2	1	128	1024	.875
EDM TOTALS	82	4978	3.66	30	44	8	8	1	304	2493	.878

Team		
Que-Col	18	(2 last year)
St. Louis	13	
Atl-Cgy	10	
Montreal	10	
Detroit	11	(1 last year)
Chicago	9	
Winnipeg	8	
NY Rangers	7	
Philadelphia	7	(1 last year)
Buffalo	6	
Hartford	5	
Min-Dal	4	
Toronto	4	
Vancouver	3	(1 last year)
Washington	2	
Anaheim	1	(1 last year)
Florida	0	
Ottawa	0	
San Jose	0	
Tampa Bay	0	
New Jersey	0	

Even with Weight's 104 points, the Oilers still scored the fewest goals in team history. How they're going to score more is going to be a problem, especially when you consider half the team had career seasons. Mind you, that's not so difficult because most have only been in the league a couple of years.

Jason Arnott should be able to put together a better season, but don't expect anything more out of Zdeno Ciger. He was a restricted free agent, and is only motivated to play in the NHL by money. Nothing else. He doesn't even like it here. Unless, as he says, he gets a contract worth staying for, he'll likely head back to Europe. See ya.

David Oliver suffered the same affliction as most of the Oiler forwards - inconsistency. The same with Mariusz Czerawksi, Todd Marchant, Mirolav Satan and Dean McAmmond. Coach Ron Low tried to motivate most of the above by having them sit out a game or two. Most of them probably thought they were being rewarded with a rest.

Ryan Smyth, Kelly Buchberger and Scott Thornton should round out the forwards, with nobody much making a scoring contribution. Jason Bonsignore could give it another go after having a poor start last season.

One of the characteristics of weak teams, or young teams, is that they have their toughest time in the third period. The Oilers fit the bill in that one.

Worst 3rd Period Goal Differentials:

	GF	GA	Diff
NY Islanders	56	115	-59
EDMONTON	60	99	-39
Dallas	67	102	-35

Look also at the Edmonton goals by period:

1st Period	92
2nd Period	84
3rd Period	60

As well, look at teams with the most games lost in the third. Those are games in which they started out the period either winning or tied, and ended up losing:

NY Islanders	16
Ottawa	14
Edmonton	13

All the evidence points to just what I told you - the Oilers were crummy in the third period. If games ended after just the first period, Edmonton would have a winning record of 32-31-8.

Why should they play so poorly in the third? A couple reasons to choose from: they were young and experienced; they lacked character to work hardest when it counted most; they didn't have the talent to compete when other teams turned it on.

SPECIAL TEAMS: A lousy power play and lousy penalty killing. No problem with Weight, of course, who carries his, and more. He was on the ice for 59 of the 72 power play goals Edmonton scored. His 46 power play points were seventh best in the league.

Arnott should be playing better with the man-advantage, and Oliver is the perfect garbage-goal getter, although he tailed off considerably last year.

They don't have a decent quarterback for the power play, in a defenceman that is. Weight played the point and is good at it, but obviously it's not doing wonders for them as a group. Norton and Mironov aren't the answer.

COACHING AND MANAGEMENT: Sather won't have any problem being the general manage for Team Canada in the World Cup Tournament. That's because he'll have a stacked team. He hasn't, however, been able to build a winner lately in Edmonton. But, what is lately anyway? They won the Stanley Cup seven years ago, which is a lot sooner than most teams.

Maybe now, with less financial restraints, he can get some better players. He never did become the Montreal Expos of the NHL, building winners with a low budget, and other problems.

Most of the time, though, when Sather talks, he makes a lot of sense. It's just the product on the ice that doesn't.

The Oilers put together an impressive ticket drive, topping the 13,000 mark for season tickets sales this year, and qualifying for almost 10 million in league subsidies. That should go a long way in easing the small market pain.

Coach Ron Low has done the job with what he has, but that isn't going to give him any job security. When the team stinks, again, eventually the pointed fingers will get around to him.

POWER PLAY	G	ATT	PCT	
Overall	72	452	15.9%	(T-20th NHL)
Home	34	229	14.8%	(24th NHL)
Road	38	223	17.0%	(11th NHL)

12 SHORT HANDED GOALS ALLOWED (T-14th NHL)

PENALTY KILLING	G	TSH	PCT	
Overall	80	417	80.8%	(18th NHL)
Home	34	204	83.3%	(13th NHL)
Road	46	213	78.4%	(T-21st NHL)

10 SHORT HANDED GOALS SCORED (T-17th NHL)

DRAFT

Round	Sel.	Player	Pos	Team
1	6	Boyd Devereaux	C	Kitchener (OHL)
1	19	Mathieu Descoteaux	D	Shawinigan (QMJHL)
2	32	Chris Hajt	D	Guelph (OHL)
3	59	Tom Poti	D	Cushing (US High School)
5	114	Brian Urich	RW	Notre Dame

6	141	Bryan Randall	C	Medicine Hat (WHL)
7	168	David Bernier	C	St. Hyacinthe (QMJHL)
8	195	Fernando Pisani	C	St. Albert (Tier II Jr.A)
9	221	John Hultberg	G G	Kingston (OHL)

Players might cringe when Edmonton calls their name at the draft table, not just because of their recent financial status, but rather because they rarely work out.

Devereaux is considered a character player, who excels at the defensive side of the game, and can play offence as well. He could be an exception to the Oiler drafting rule.

The second and third picks are curious because Hajt, taken 32nd, was projected in some quarters to be a higher pick than Descoteau, who was selected 19th. *The Hockey News* had Descoteaux slotted at 31st best, and Hajt at 14. Either way, the Oilers may have pulled off a coup.

PROGNOSIS: Not good. This team isn't going to make the playoffs. Maybe not next year either, or the year after, or ever. A widespread change in philosophy is needed before this club can rise out of the doldrums. Poor player evaluations mean they're doomed to repeat their failure.

There's almost no chance they can get lucky and squeeze into the post-season. A lot of the other teams have improved over the summer. They haven't. Each year they wait for their potential to develop. And when it doesn't, then they make some trades.

They need some more character players, more defencemen, more scoring, etc. Goaltending is okay though, and Curtis Joseph will develop a new respect for Bill Ranford.

PREDICTION:

Pacific Division: 6th

Western Conference: 12th

Overall: 24th

Team Rankings 1995-96

		Conference Rank	League Rank
Record	30-44-8	10	21
Home	15-21-5	12	23
Away	15-23-3	8	17
Versus Own Conference	19-30-7	11	22
Versus Other Conference	11-14-1	8	17
Team Plus\Minus	-56	12	22
Goals For	240	10	17
Goals Against	304	12	24
Average Shots For	29.9	9	17
Average Shots Against	30.4	7	13
Overtime	4-2-8	3	6
One Goal Games	11-13	9	20
Times outshooting opponent	40	6	13
Versus Teams Over .500	8-21-2	10	21
Versus Teams Under .500	22-23-6	11	20
First Half Record	13-22-6	10	21
Second Half Record	17-22-2	9	19

PLAYOFFS

- Did not make the playoffs.

ALL-TIME LEADERS

GOALS

Wayne Gretzky	583
Jari Kurri	474
Glenn Anderson	417

ASSISTS

Wayne Gretzky	1,086
Mark Messier	642
Jari Kurri	569

POINTS

Wayne Gretzky	1,669
Jari Kurri	1,043
Mark Messier	1,034

BEST INDIVIDUAL SEASONS

GOALS

Wayne Gretzky	1981-82	92
Wayne Gretzky	1983-84	87
Wayne Gretzky	1984-85	73

ASSISTS

Wayne Gretzky	1985-86	163
Wayne Gretzky	1984-85	135
Wayne Gretzky	1982-83	125

POINTS

Wayne Gretzky	1985-86	215
Wayne Gretzky	1981-82	212
Wayne Gretzky	1984-85	208

TEAM RECORD

Last 3 years

	GP	W	L	T	Pts	%
1995-96	82	30	34	8	68	.415
1994-95	48	17	27	4	38	.396
1993-94	84	25	45	14	60	.405

Best 3 regular seasons

1983-84	80	57	18	5	119	.744
1985-86	80	56	17	7	119	.744
1981-82	80	48	17	15	111	.694

Worst 3 regular seasons

1992-93	84	26	50	8	60	.357
1993-94	84	25	45	14	64	.381
1995-96	48	17	27	4	38	.396

Most Goals (min. 70 game schedule)

1983-84	446
1985-86	426
1982-83	424

Fewest Goals (min. 70 game schedule)

1995-95	240
1992-93	242
1993-94	263

Most Goals Against (min. 70 game schedule)

1992-93	337
1980-81	327
1979-80	322

Fewest Goals Against (min. 70 game schedule)

1990-91	272
1989-90	283
1986-87	284

STAT SECTION

Team Scoring Stats

	GP	G	A	PTS	+/-	PIM	SH	Power Play			Short Handed		
								G	A	P	G	A	P
DOUG WEIGHT	82	25	79	104	19-	95	204	9	37	46	0	0	0
ZDENO CIGER	78	31	39	70	15-	41	184	12	19	31	0	0	0
JASON ARNOTT	64	28	31	59	6-	87	244	8	8	16	0	0	0
MARIUSZ CZERKAWSKI	70	17	23	40	4-	18	142	3	6	9	0	0	0
DAVID OLIVER	80	20	19	39	22-	34	131	14	7	21	0	0	0
TODD MARCHANT	81	19	19	38	19-	66	221	2	1	3	3	2	5
MIROSLAV SATAN	62	18	17	35	0	22	113	6	5	11	0	0	0
BORIS MIRONOV	78	8	24	32	23-	101	158	7	10	17	0	0	0
JEFF NORTON	66	8	23	31	9	42	85	1	12	13	0	1	1
DEAN MCAMMOND	53	15	15	30	6	23	79	4	4	8	0	0	0
KELLY BUCHBERGER	82	11	14	25	20-	184	119	0	0	0	2	4	6
SCOTT THORNTON	77	9	9	18	25-	149	95	0	2	2	2	0	2
BRYAN MARCHMENT	78	3	15	18	7-	202	96	0	5	5	0	0	0
JIRI SLEGR	57	4	13	17	1-	74	91	0	5	5	1	0	1
DAVID ROBERTS	34	3	10	13	7-	18	47	1	2	3	0	0	0
RYAN SMYTH	48	2	9	11	10-	28	65	1	0	1	0	0	0
LUKE RICHARDSON	82	2	9	11	27-	108	61	0	0	0	0	2	2
KENT MANDERVILLE	37	3	5	8	5-	38	63	0	0	0	2	2	4
DONALD DUFRESNE	45	1	6	7	4-	20	21	0	0	0	0	0	0
BRETT HAUER	29	4	2	6	11-	30	53	2	1	3	0	0	0
LOUIE DEBRUSK	38	1	3	4	7-	96	17	0	0	0	0	0	0
RALPH INTRANUOVO	13	1	2	3	3-	4	19	0	1	1	0	0	0
GREG DE VRIES	13	1	1	2	2-	12	8	0	0	0	0	0	0
JASON BONSIGNORE	20	0	2	2	6-	4	13	0	0	0	0	0	0
TYLER WRIGHT	23	1	0	1	7-	33	18	0	0	0	0	0	0
CURTIS JOSEPH	34	0	1	1	0	4	1	0	0	0	0	0	0
NICK STAJDUHAR	2	0	0	0	2	4	1	0	0	0	0	0	0
BRYAN MUIR	5	0	0	0	4-	6	4	0	0	0	0	0	0
FRED BRATHWAITE	7	0	0	0	0	2	0	0	0	0	0	0	0
DENNIS BONVIE	8	0	0	0	3-	47	0	0	0	0	0	0	0
JOAQUIN GAGE	16	0	0	0	0	4	0	0	0	0	0	0	0

Los Angeles Kings

You can't accuse GM Sam McMaster of inactivity. In the chart below, it shows the Kings' opening night roster, and where those players were for the final game of the season.

Opening Night Lineup	Closing Night	Obtained in trade
Blake	Injured	
Conacher	Traded	Ferguson
Druce	Traded	4th round 1996 draft pick
Granato	Injured	
Gretzky	Traded	Johnson, Tardif, R.Vopat, 5th round pick 1996, 1st round pick 1997
Khristich	PLAYED	
Kurri	Traded	With Churla, Kurri and McSorley for Ferraro, LaFayette, Laperriere, Norstrom and 4th round pick 1997.
McSorley	Traded	
Todd	PLAYED	
Tocchet	Traded	Stevens
Lacroix	PLAYED	
Lang	PLAYED	
Sydor	Traded	With 1996 5th round pick for Churla and Zmolek.
Perreault	PLAYED	
O'Donnell	PLAYED	
Tsygurov	did not play	
Yachmenev	PLAYED	
Berg	did not play	
Dafoe	did not play	
Storr	did not play	

Only seven of the opening-nighters also played the final game. Of the traded players in the above chart, all of them, except Darryl Sydor, had seen their best days. GM Sam McMaster was trading over-the-hill types for potential.

That's not a bad move for a team as bad as the Kings were last season. When you have no chance of winning, you trade the veterans who aren't helping anyway, for players who can. And you trade them at the most opportune time - when other teams need them most.

The deals above aren't the only ones McMaster made during the season:

* Steven Finn from Tampa Bay for Michel Petit.

* John Slaney from Colorado for 1996 6th rounder

* Steve Larouche from NY Rangers for Chris Snell

* Jaroslav Modry from Ottawa and 1996 8th rounder for Kevin Brown
And it didn't stop when the season ended:

* Stephane Fiset from Colorado and 1998 first rounder, for Eric Lacroix and 1998 first rounder.

* Ed Olczyk signed as free agent.

So, with all those deals the Kings can expect to be in contention. Right? Wrong. Trading for quantity has its good points - e.g. more chances of one of them becoming very good. But, quantity doesn't mean quality.

The problem is the Kings still stink. While their lineup is sprinkled with some quality veterans, the only place the team could contend would be in the AHL or the IHL, which is where most of this lineup should be.

One way of seeing how far away they are from contention is to look at the best team - Colorado last year - and see how they compare. Only one player on the Kings, maybe two, could play for that team. They'd take Rob Blake, and maybe could use Ray Ferraro.

Eric Lacroix is somebody the Avalanche could use, however. And they got him during the summer in a deal for goaltender Stephane Fiset.

The problem with rebuilding is that if the materials aren't sound, you have to keep tearing it down and doing it over again. It wouldn't be a surprise if the Kings made a lot more trades this season.

Another team, on the other side of the country, is also rebuilding. The difference is the NY Islanders building parts are much stronger, so obviously have a much greater chance for success.

You want an idea of how the Kings' season might go. Take a look at the second half of last season after they made many of their trades.

Worst Second Half Records - 1995-96

Team	Record	Pts
Ottawa	10-27-4	24
NY Islanders	11-28-2	24
LOS ANGELES	8-24-9	25

Biggest Negative Differences - Between First and Second Half Records

	First Half	Second Half	Difference in Winning %
Florida	27-12-2 .683	14-19-8 .439	-.244
LOS ANGELES	16-16-9 .500	8-24-9 .305	-.195
NY Ranger	25-10-6 .683	16-17-8 .488	-.195
Toronto	20-14-7 .573	14-22-5 .402	-.171

Goals For and Against Comparison by Half

	1st Half	2nd Half	Difference
Average Goals/game	3.4	2.7	0.7 Decrease
Average Goals against/game	2.7	4.1	1.4 Increase

TEAM PREVIEW

GOAL: Life could be worse. Three good young goaltenders are on board.

The best thing about being a young goalie on this team is that you get lots of shots, which means more improvement. Below are the most shots allowed in each of the last two seasons.

Most Shots Against Per Game 1995-96

Buffalo	35.5
LOS ANGELES	35.4
Pittsburgh	34.6
Winnipeg	33.6
Hartford	33.6

Most Shots Against Per Game 1994-95

LOS ANGELES	34.8
Anaheim	33.0
Pittsburgh	32.9
Ottawa	32.5

Only Buffalo, last season, had more shots against per game. These numbers show how little the Kings have improved defensively, despite the hiring of Larry Robinson. There's nothing to suggest they'll get any better.

Kelly Hrudey had a good save percentage last year, but a mediocre goals against average of 3.26. If he maintained that same save percentage, say for a team like Detroit, let's see what his goals against average could have been.

The Red Wings allowed 24.1 shots per game, Hrudy faced 35.1 shots per 60 minutes. If Hrudey had faced 24.1 shots per 60 minutes, he would have had 834 shots in total, rather than 1,214. Keeping the same save percentage, he would have given up 78 goals, rather than 113, and had a goals against average of 2.25. That would have tied him for third in the league.

Hrudy is gone to free agency and San Jose, anyway, after eight seasons. He's 35-years-old, and doesn't fit the team's youth movement. He's a young 35, however, born 13 days before Wayne Gretzky, so he could have a good season with the Sharks.

Dafoe, almost a throw-in in the Khristich deal with Washington, was spectacular at times, especially early in the season when Hrudey was hurt. He will be battling it out with Jamie Storr for the backup role behind Stephane Fiset, who was obtained from Colorado.

For Fiset, it's a new beginning, and a chance to be number one. Playing behind Patrick Roy wasn't doing anything for him. His numbers aren't going to look great in Los Angeles, but he'll get lots of playing time...and lots of shots.

DEFENCE: If Larry Robinson wanted to lace them up again, he could probably make the team, and be one of the better defencemen.

That's how bad they are. There's a good

GOALTENDER	GPI	MINS	AVG	W	L	T	EN	SO	GA	SA	SV %
JAMIE STORR	5	262	2.75	3	1	0	0	0	12	147	.918
KELLY HRUDEY	36	2077	3.26	7	15	10	2	0	113	1214	.907
BYRON DAFOE	47	2666	3.87	14	24	8	3	1	172	1539	.888
L.A TOTALS	82	5025	3.61	24	40	18	5	1	302	2905	.896

egg or two in the bunch, but not many. Rob Blake is one of the better defencemen in the league, but is coming off knee surgery and two injury plagued campaigns. Last year he played just six games, and the year before just half the season.

The rest of them could be vying for the IHL all-star team. Most of them are sixth or seventh NHL defencemen, at least at the moment.

Aki-Petteri Berg might develop into something, although he didn't show much last season. He was the third pick in the 1994 draft. The Kings sent him down to the minors, where they might be wise to leave him for a while longer.

Philippe Boucher showed a little offensive flair last season, and could improve. Sean O'Donnell, and Steven Finn, the team's most valuable defenceman last year as voted by the media, give them some rare toughness on this outfit. Doug Zmolek plays a defensive game.

Others include Jaroslav Modry, John Slaney, Rob Cowie, Mattias Norstrom, and a bunch more minor-leaguers and castoffs.

Few of these guys are going to make life any easier for the Kings' netminders. Most wouldn't even be on the ice of a team with a decent defence. Washington's seventh through twelfth defenceman are better than the top six here.

FORWARD: Some teams have two number one lines; some teams have a number one line and a couple good enough for number two. The Kings have three third lines.

Yes, that's how bad it is. It doesn't get much worse, as a matter of fact.

Some of them have some decent numbers, though, which is exactly what happens when third liners get to play on the top line.

Ray Ferraro is the best of the bunch. He almost had 30 goals, although 25 of the 29 were with the Rangers.

Khristich and Yachmenev were on top and below Ferraro on the scoring list, but both of their low point totals were inflated by playing with Gretzky for most of the season. For Yachmenev, it will be something he'll be able to tell his grandchildren, playing with Gretzky. The small right-winger will have his problems scoring without him, however, so don't expect any improvement on his 53 point rookie season. He had problems at times even when Gretzky was around.

Yanic Perreault did have a decent season, scoring 25 goals, which is pretty good production for a player who seemed destined to be a career minor-leaguer.

Kevin Todd, who was the leading scorer in the AHL in 1990-91 while with the Devils organization, was selected by the media as the team's best defensive player. That's probably why Pittsburgh liked him when they signed him as a free agent.

Kevin Stevens, who was obtained for Rick Tocchet from Boston, looks like he may be finished as an NHL hockey player. He didn't score for the Bruins, and in 20 games for the Kings, had just three goals. Just a couple years ago, the 31-year-old was scoring 40 or 50 goals for the Penguins, so the possibility of a comeback still looms.

Ironically, Stevens was drafted originally by Los Angeles, but traded before he ever played a game. In that deal, the Kings got Anders Hakansson, who scored fewer goals in his career (52) than Stevens scored in his best season (55 with Pittsburgh in 1992-93). Another strange thing about this trade was that Stevens is only in the second year of a five-year contract. If he doesn't come around, Los Angeles will be stuck for the full amount, and chances are slim that anybody's going to trade for him. *And* he has a bad back, to boot.

The Kings signed free agent Ed Olczyk during the summer. He's a rather remarkable story in that he went from a washed-up press box attendant to a valuable sniper. In just 51 games for the Jets, he scored 27 goals, including 16 on the power play. He happened to fit in well with that team, but on the Kings there is no Keith Tkachuk, Teemu Selanne (before he was traded to Anaheim), Alexei Zhamnov or Craig Janney to give him the passes or for him to pass to.

In some bad news, Tony Granato had to undergo brain surgery last season. There was an abnormal cluster of blood vessels in the left temporal lobe of his brain. The surgery was pronounced a success, but his hockey future is in some doubt. The Kings obviously thought so, because they didn't offer him a contract, which made him a free agent.

Among the rest, Craig Johnson could come through and be a scorer; the same with Patrice Tardif; Robert Lang will have to do considerably better than six goals and 22 points; Ian Laperriere provides some toughness up front, almost all of it; and Nathan LaFayette was supposed to be a good one, but is running out of chances. The Kings signed Paul DiPietro during the summer, which is a perfect fit for this team - he was a big scorer in the IHL.

This is probably the worst forward unit in the league. There is some potential for it to move up to mediocrity, but not much.

SPECIAL TEAMS: The good news is that the Kings were right in the middle of the pack on the power play, something positive about a poor season. The bad news is that after Gretzky was traded, the power play operated at a 15.7% efficiency, which places it among the worst in the league. Interestly, the Kings

didn't fare all that poorly in the record department, with a mark of 6-9-3 once Gretzky left.

Los Angeles should have close to the worst power play this season. Getting Blake back should help on the point, so maybe they won't be last.

In some more good news, Los Angeles didn't allow the most shorthanded goals in the league. But, the 18 they allowed were still good enough for a team record.

Penalty killing was weak, too, with little prospects for improvement.

Special teams won't be special at all for the Kings this season. They have an opportunity to be the worst for both of them. Quite an achievement, if it happens.

POWER PLAY	G	ATT	PCT	
Overall	72	401	18.0%	(T-13th NHL)
Home	50	227	22.0%	(6th NHL)
Road	22	174	12.6%	(25th NHL)

18 SHORT HANDED GOALS ALLOWED (23rd NHL)

PENALTY KILLING	G	TSH	PCT	
Overall	72	381	81.1%	(16th NHL)
Home	38	194	80.4%	(21st NHL)
Road	34	187	81.8%	(9th NHL)

12 SHORT HANDED GOALS SCORED (T-9th NHL)

COACHING AND MANAGEMENT: If there was ever a coach that didn't suit the team, Larry Robinson is it. Many of the players on the Kings are pure offensive types, who don't play defence. In other words, it's nothing like the Cup winning New Jersey Devils of two years ago.

Robinson performed no miracles, or even half miracles. The team played lousy and if a defensive system was put into place, it was invisible. It could be that the players are just too bad for Robinson to perform those miracles. If he somehow can, this year, he can write his name on the Jack Adams Trophy as coach of the year.

GM Sam McMaster, dubbed McMaster the Disaster, after some earlier trades, had better at least show some improvement with this team if he wants to keep his job. Sure, it's a rebuilding year, but by the looks of things they'll still be rebuilding in the year 2000.

The probability of success in the building process is a direct result of management. In Florida, it worked right away; in Ottawa it didn't work at all when Randy Sexton was the GM, and wouldn't have no matter how many more years he tried.

This season will show whether McMaster has a clue, and whether his talent evaluation is sound. He's either going to come out looking like one of the best general managers in the game, or in a more likely scenario, one of the worst.

DRAFT

Round	Sel.	Player	Pos	
2	30	Josh Green	LW	Medicine Hat (WHL)
2	37	Marian Cisar	W	Slovakia
3	57	Greg Phillips	C	Saskatoon (WHL)
4	84	Mikael Simons	C	Sweden
4	96	Eric Belanger	C	Beauport (QMJHL)
5	120	Jesse Black	D	Niagara Falls (OHL)
5	123	Peter Hogan	D	Oshawa (OHL)
8	190	Stephen Valiquette	G	Sudbury (OHL)
8	193	Kai Nurminen	W	Finland
9	219	Sebastien Simard	LW	Drummondville (QMJHL)

The Kings didn't have a first round pick, traded away in the Khristich deal with Washington. Fortunately for McMaster, the pick didn't end up winning the lottery and being first overall. It was bad enough as it was, the fourth overall selection.

Josh Green was ranked number 15 by *The Hockey News*, so the Kings may have gotten a bonus. He's a big kid, who is coming off a bad junior year, which was hampered by shoulder surgery. His stock will rebound if he can put together a good season and start putting the puck in the net on a more consistent basis.

PROGNOSIS: The Kings will have some good stretches this year, just like many young teams. They might even win three in a row sometime if the schedule is just right.

But, they're not going to make the playoffs, and they could end up last in the Western Conference.

They have no impact player, not that Gretzky was doing all that much for them; they have no defence; they have little scoring, and even less that they can depend on; they don't have much size or muscle; they don't have many character players; they have a general manager who makes suspect trades; and they have a coach who was suppose to turn them into defensive wizards, who didn't.

On the positive side, they've got some good young goalies.

Add it all up, and this team is heavily in debt.

PREDICTION:

Pacific Division: 7th

Western Conference: 13th

Overall: 25th

Team Rankings 1995-96

		Conference Rank	League Rank
Record	24-40-18	12	23
Home	16-16-9	8	19
Away	8-24-9	12	23
Versus Own Conference	15-26-15	12	23
Versus Other Conference	9-14-3	10	20
Team Plus\Minus	-46	11	22
Goals For	256	6	11
Goals Against	302	12	24
Average Shots For	31.3	4	8
Average Shots Against	35.4	12	25
Overtime	3-2-18	7	12
One Goal Games	12-14	8	19
Times outshooting opponent	24	12	24
Versus Teams Over .500	11-16-4	6	14
Versus Teams Under .500	13-24-12	12	24
First Half Record	16-16-9	6	14
Second Half Record	8-24-9	13	26

PLAYOFFS

- Did not make the playoffs

ALL-TIME LEADERS

GOALS

Marcel Dionne	550
Dave Taylor	431
Luc Robitaille	392

ASSISTS

Marcel Dionne	757
Dave Taylor	638
Wayne Gretzky	619

POINTS

Marcel Dionne	1,307
Dave Taylor	1,069
Wayne Gretzky	858

BEST INDIVIDUAL SEASONS

GOALS

Bernie Nicholls	1988-89	70
Luc Robitaille	1992-93	63
Marcel Dionne	1978-79	59

ASSISTS

Wayne Gretzky	1990-91	122
Wayne Gretzky	1988-89	114
Wayne Gretzky	1989-90	102

POINTS

Wayne Gretzky	1988-89	168
Wayne Gretzky	1990-91	163
Bernie Nicholls	1988-89	150

TEAM RECORD

Last 3 years

	GP	W	L	T	Pts	%
1995-96	82	24	40	18	68	.415
1994-95	48	16	23	9	41	.427
1993-94	84	27	45	12	66	.393

Best 3 regular seasons

1974-75	80	47	17	21	105	.656
1990-91	80	46	24	10	102	.638
1980-81	80	43	24	13	99	.619

Worst 3 regular seasons

1969-70	76	14	52	10	38	.250
1971-72	78	20	49	9	49	.314
1985-86	80	23	49	8	54	.338

Most Goals (min. 70 game schedule)

1988-89	376
1990-91	340
1984-85	339

Fewest Goals (min. 70 game schedule)

1969-79	168
1968-69	185
1967-68	200

Most Goals Against (min. 70 game schedule)

1985-86	389
1983-84	376
1981-82	369

Fewest Goals Against (min. 70 game schedule)

1974-75	185
1967-68	224
1973-74	231

STAT SECTION

Team Scoring Stats

	GP	G	A	PTS	+/-	PIM	SH	Power Play			Short Handed		
								G	A	P	G	A	P
DIMITRI KHRISTICH	76	27	37	64	0	44	204	12	9	21	0	1	1
RAY FERRARO	76	29	31	60	0	92	178	9	10	19	0	0	0
VITALI YACHMENEV	80	19	34	53	3-	16	133	6	18	24	1	1	2
YANIC PERREAULT	78	25	24	49	11-	16	175	8	9	17	3	1	4
KEVIN TODD	74	16	27	43	6	38	132	0	3	3	2	0	2
KEVIN STEVENS	61	13	23	36	10-	71	170	6	5	11	0	0	0
TONY GRANATO	49	17	18	35	5-	46	156	5	4	9	0	1	1
ERIC LACROIX	72	16	16	32	11-	110	107	3	3	6	0	0	0
CRAIG JOHNSON	60	13	11	24	8-	36	97	4	0	4	0	0	0
PHILIPPE BOUCHER	53	7	16	23	26-	31	145	5	11	16	0	0	0
ROBERT LANG	68	6	16	22	15-	10	71	0	0	0	2	2	4
JAROSLAV MODRY	73	4	17	21	21-	44	106	1	4	5	0	0	0
JOHN SLANEY	38	6	14	20	7	14	75	3	5	8	1	2	3
IAN LAPERRIERE	71	6	11	17	11-	155	70	1	1	2	0	1	1
GARY SHUCHUK	33	4	10	14	3	12	22	0	0	0	0	0	0
VLADIMIR TSYPLAKOV	23	5	5	10	1	4	40	0	2	2	0	0	0
ROB COWIE	46	5	5	10	16-	32	86	2	2	4	0	0	0
DOUG ZMOLEK	58	2	5	7	5-	87	36	0	2	2	0	0	0
SEAN O'DONNELL	71	2	5	7	3	127	65	0	0	0	0	1	1
AKI BERG	51	0	7	7	13-	29	56	0	0	0	0	0	0
NATHAN LAFAYETTE	17	2	4	6	4-	8	28	1	0	1	0	0	0
DENIS TSYGUROV	18	1	5	6	0	22	21	1	1	2	0	0	0
PATRICE TARDIF	38	4	1	5	11-	49	50	1	0	1	0	0	0
BARRY POTOMSKI	33	3	2	5	7-	104	23	1	0	1	0	0	0
STEVEN FINN	66	3	2	5	12-	126	54	0	1	1	0	0	0
JAN VOPAT	11	1	4	5	3	4	13	0	3	3	0	0	0
MATTIAS NORSTROM	36	2	2	4	3-	40	34	0	1	1	0	0	0
ROB BLAKE	6	1	2	3	0	8	13	0	2	2	0	0	0
STEVE LAROUCHE	8	1	2	3	0	4	14	1	0	1	0	0	0
KEVIN BROWN	7	1	0	1	2-	4	9	0	0	0	0	0	0
TROY CROWDER	15	1	0	1	3-	42	11	0	0	0	0	0	0
ARTO BLOMSTEN	2	0	1	1	1	0	1	0	0	0	0	0	0
MATT JOHNSON	1	0	0	0	0	5	1	0	0	0	0	0	0
RUSLAN BATYRSHIN	2	0	0	0	0	6	0	0	0	0	0	0	0
DAN BYLSMA	4	0	0	0	0	0	6	0	0	0	0	0	0
JAMIE STORR	5	0	0	0	0	0	0	0	0	0	0	0	0
KELLY HRUDEY	36	0	0	0	0	4	0	0	0	0	0	0	0
BYRON DAFOE	47	0	0	0	0	6	0	0	0	0	0	0	0

Phoenix Coyotes

Phoenix might not be this year's Colorado, but they're likely to be more of a contender than they ever were in Winnipeg. Their legacy in Winnipeg will be one as losers.

17 Years in Winnipeg:

Record: 506-660-172

Home: 307-274-88

Road: 196-386-84

Seasons over .500: 5

Seasons under .500: 11

Seasons at .500: 1

Seasons in playoffs: 10

Seasons out of playoffs: 7

First round playoff losses: 9

Second round playoff losses: 1

Times advanced past second round: 0

First Team All-Stars: 1 - Teemu Selanne

Second Team All-Stars: 4 - Alexei Zhamnov, Keith Tkachuk, Phil Housley, Dale Hawerchuk.

Award Winners: Calder (Rookie) - Selanne, Hawerchuk; Jack Adams (Coach) - Bob Murdoch, Tom Watt.

No, there wasn't a heck of a lot for Winnipeg Jets fans to get excited about in their 17 years in the NHL. You'd have to go back to the WHA to find their glory days. That's when they had Bobby Hull, Anders Hedburg and Ulf Nilsson, and won three AVCO Cups.

So, the team will rise in Phoenix, and the first-year NHL fans in the southwest will probably get to enjoy one of the better seasons in franchise history.

They were a team on the rise, anyway, but a new home will help things move faster. It's not unusual for that to happen. Colorado, of course, is the ultimate example, winning in just their first season in their new home. The chart below shows all the teams that have moved.

Old Home	Final Season Record	New Home	Year	First Season Record	
Atlanta	35-32-13	Calgary	1980-81	39-27-14	
Quebec	30-13-5	Colorado	1995-96	47-25-10	Won Stanley Cup
Minnesota	36-38-10	Dallas	1993-94	42-29-13	
Kansas City	12-56-12	Colorado	1976-77	20-46-14	
Colorado	18-49-13	New Jersey	1982-83	17-49-14	

Every team did better in their first season in their new home, with the exception of the Colorado to New Jersey move, where the records were almost identical.

There are a lot of reasons for the improvements: newcomers to town want to impress their new fans; better attendance, which is why they moved from the last place; more enthusiasm from the fans, which again, probably wasn't high where they were moving from; more money in the new place, which again, is why they left their last place; often there is new management and new coaching, which is usually better at the beginning; happier players, once again because they probably didn't like the last place they were.

TEAM PREVIEW

GOAL: It has been a while since this team wasn't fussing around trying to find a dependable number one goalie. Not that they haven't had them on occasion, just that they were never satisfied. They're happy with Nikolai Khabibulin.

He wasn't up among the league leaders in goals against average, but he was in the top 10 in save percentage, tied with Patrick Roy. Khabibulin is only 23 years old, and is entering only his third season. This will be his second season as the undisputed number one netminder.

The Coyotes signed free agent Darcy Wakaluk, formerly with Dallas, to take care of the backup duties.

They also have a pretty good prospect in Scott Langkow, who played his first pro season last year in Springfield.

DEFENCE: The Coyotes could be very strong at this position - in a couple years. They have three great prospects in Oleg Tverdovsky, Deron Quint and Ian Doig.

But, they're three great prospects who have had their problems. Quint and Doig made the team last year, but couldn't stick around for all of it. Tverdovsky came over in the Selanne trade with Anaheim and is on everybody's list as a future all-star. Nobody doubts his talent, they're just waiting for the light to go on, and stay on.

The problem with having too many young defencemen at the same time is that it's the hardest position to learn. If they're learning by watching each other, then they've got lousy teachers. Sort of like teaching yourself to play golf. That's why the Coyotes signed Brad McCrimmon. He is 37-years-old, is far removed from his best years, and won't likely be in the lineup every night. But, he'll be like a playing defence coach. He can show through example, and by telling the younger players a thing or two about the game.

Another veteran free agent they signed was Jim Johnson, who was with Washington last season.

It's a funny thing about young players, though. They may have their problems and look like they're struggling, but 95 percent of the defencemen in the league started out the same way. There aren't many Ray Bourque's who make the all-star team in their first season.

If they're offensive types and they're used to controlling the play, all of a sudden they're in the NHL and they have to concentrate on their defence more. Defensive mistakes are going to cost them at this level, and it's going to be noticeable.

If they're defensive types, it's still not easy. They're not stopping kids anymore, they're stopping NHLers, almost all of which are better than the best they've faced before. With everything moving so much faster than they're used to, even something like handling the puck becomes something they have to think about, rather than just a natural part of their game.

It all takes time, so expect improvement from the youngsters, probably slow enough that it won't be noticable for a while.

Dave Manson is the type of defenceman every team in the league would like to have. He's tough, a little bit of a looney, plays well defensively and can contribute offensively.

Norm MacIver is a pretty good offensive, power play specialist type who gives good value from the offensive end. Plus, he's the type of player a lot of teams need during the season to give their power play a boost. Good trade value.

Teppo Numminen is coming off his best NHL season. He doesn't play a physical game but he plays the power play and was probably the Jets top defenceman last season.

FORWARD: When the Coyotes were the Jets they never seemed to get the right mix on their forward units. They either had too many youngsters, too many grinders, too many strictly offensive players, or too many Europeans.

One thing they've never had a problem with was too much talent. Things are changing.

They're packed solid down the middle, after the signing of free agent Cliff Ronning, and re-signing of Craig Janney. Then you've got Alexei Zhamnov, teenager Chad Kilger, and Mike Eastwood. That gives them two proven major league playmakers in Ronning and Janney; a 100 plus point and all-star possibility in Zhamnov; size and youth in Kilger; and checking, faceoff ability, tenacity and smarts in Eastwood. The only problem is that five doesn't go into four, so look for one or two to move to the wing where it's considerably weaker. Also a centreman is Dallas Drake, who set a career high with 19 goals, so that means even more juggling.

Ronning replaces Olczyk, who came back from the dead for a great season. He was a free agent, and signed with Los Angeles.

On the left side is Keith Tkachuk,

GOALTENDER	GPI	MINS	AVG	W	L	T	EN	SO	GA	SA	SV %
SCOTT LANGKOW	1	6	.00	0	0	0	0	0	0	2	1.000
N. KHABIBULIN	53	2914	3.13	26	20	3	4	2	152	1656	.908
DOMINIC ROUSSEL	7	285	3.37	2	2	0	0	0	16	134	.881
TIM CHEVELDAE	30	1695	3.93	8	18	3	5	0	111	948	.883
TOM DRAPER	1	34	5.29	0	0	0	0	0	3	14	.786
WPG TOTALS	82	4951	3.53	36	40	6	9	2	291	2763	.895

probably the best power forward in the game. He came on stronger as the season wore on. He had 18 goals before January 1, and 32 after. His 20 power play goals were second only to Mario Lemieux.

The Jets don't have much else in the way of scoring at left wing, which is why one of the centres will probably move there. They have Darrin Shannon, who is expected to get more goals than five, and they've got character grinders in Kris King and Jim McKenzie.

Mike Gartner is a new addition to the right side, and gives them some more scoring and speed. Even though the guy is ancient, 38-years-old in the first month of the season, he's still one of the fastest players in the NHL. He is invisible for varying stretches, but darned if he doesn't come up with over 30 goals by the end of the season. He led Toronto with 35 last season. Shane Doan should be better in his second season, and Craig Mills may get a chance to stick.

Igor Korolev opened up the season like gangbusters, but then faded badly. Ten of his 22 goals came in the first 11 games of the season, and 25 of his 51 points in the first 18.

There still isn't a lot of defence from this group, so they'll probably have to do what they did last year, which is try to score more than the other team, and hope they win 6-5 or 5-4. They were similar to Pittsburgh in that respect, except the Penguins have considerably more scoring power. The following chart shows the teams involved in the highest scoring games last season.

	GF/ Game	GA/ Game	Total
Pittsburgh	4.4	3.5	7.9
San Jose	3.1	4.4	7.5
WINNIPEG	3.4	3.5	6.9
Colorado	4.0	2.9	6.9

SPECIAL TEAMS: When you've got power forward Tkachuk on the power play, you've got one of the best in the league. Craig Janney is one of the best playmakers, and is made for the power play. Most of the defencemen on the team can play power play point, so that's good too - Numminen, MacIver, Tverdovsky, Manson, and Quint all have the ability to play there. Zhamnov gives the Coyotes one of the best power play forward units in the league.

The flip side is that their poor penalty killing nullifies their excellent power play. They allowed 88 goals, only five away from San Jose and the most in the league. In all, they allowed six more power play goals against than they scored themselves. There doesn't appear to be a lot of optimism for improvement in this area, but often a new coach will make something like that a priority. If they can cut down the power play goals against, it will equal a lot more wins.

POWER PLAY	G	ATT	PCT	
Overall	82	417	19.7%	(T-6th NHL)
Home	44	210	21.0%	(9th NHL)
Road	38	207	18.4%	(7th NHL)

12 SHORT HANDED GOALS ALLOWED (T-14th NHL)

PENALTY KILLING	G	TSH	PCT	
Overall	88	430	79.5%	(23rd NHL)
Home	38	199	80.9%	(T-19th NHL)
Road	50	231	78.4%	(T-21st NHL)

10 SHORT HANDED GOALS SCORED (T-17th NHL)

COACHING AND MANAGEMENT: There was an immediate impact on this team when they moved to Phoenix, both financially and environmentally. Winnipeg wasn't exactly first on the list of unrestricted free agents when deciding where they wanted to sign.

By the time the signing period started on July 1, they couldn't wait to get to Phoenix.

Ronning and Wakaluk were first, and they kept coming.

General Manager John Paddock, who always seemed to be on the verge of being fired, whether he deserved it or not, is secure now, and appears to be getting smarter and smarter. Funny what more money can do.

Terry Simpson was fired, although he didn't do a poor job, and Don Hay was hired away from Calgary, where he was an assistant with time remaining on his contract. But, the Coyotes really wanted Hay, even willing to give Calgary compensation.

Nobody knows how a new coach is going to handle things, but his resume is sound, he's had pressure positions before, and geez, the Coyotes really wanted him.

DRAFT

Round	Sel.	Player	Pos	
1	11	Dan Focht	D	Tri-City (WHL)
1	24	Daniel Brier	C	Drummondville (QMJHL)
3	62	Per-Anton Lundstrom	D	Sweden
5	119	Richard Lintner	D	Slovakia
6	139	Robert Esche	G	Detroit (OHL)
7	174	Trevor Letowski	D	Sarnia (OHL)
8	200	Nicholas Lent	RW	Omaha (USHL)
9	226	Marc-Etienne Hubert	C	Laval (QMJHL)

Focht moved steadily up the rankings all season, and moved up in leaps and bounds after the CHL Prospects game. He's 6-5, 226 pounds. In the skill testing, he came through with the second hardest shot, and won the puck agility drill. A big guy who is mobile

and can move the puck? A dream come true. His statistics haven't yet shown great offensive stats, but that may not be the point.

With their second round pick, the Coyotes went the opposite way. They took little Daniel Briere - 5-9, 160. He could turn out to be a bust, or he could turn out to be a major star. He led the Quebec junior league with 67-96-163, first in all three categories. Sometimes big junior scorers aren't great skaters, and flop at the NHL level, but that's not a problem with Briere.

PROGNOSIS: It's too bad for Winnipeg fans that they're going to miss out on an improving team. They've got lots of young up and comers, Tkachuk, scorers, a goalie who is showing signs of being a great one.

The Jets don't look to be major contenders just yet, but they are major playoff contenders and they're improving all the time.

They're predicted here for eighth in the conference, but they could easily move up and be one of the surprise teams of the year. At the very least they should provide some good, exciting hockey for their new fans in Phoenix.

PREDICTION:

Central Division: 5th

Western Conference: 8th

Overall: 15th

Team Rankings 1995-96

	Conference Rank	League Rank
Record	36-40-6	8	17
Home	22-16-3	5	13
Away	14-24-3	9	18

Versus Own Conference	25-26-5	7	16
Versus Other Conference	11-14-1	7	16
Team Plus\Minus	-10	7	16
Goals For	275	3	5
Goals Against	291	10	21
Average Shots For	29.3	10	18
Average Shots Against	33.6	12	23
Overtime	2-0-6	3	2
One Goal Games	13-11	5	8
Times outshooting opponent	27	11	22
Versus Teams Over .500	10-20-3	7	18
Versus Teams Under .500	26-20-3	7	16
First Half Record	18-20-3	8	16
Second Half Record	18-20-3	7	16

Results: Lost 4-2 to Detroit

Record: 2-4

Home: 1-2

Away: 1-2

Goals For: 10 (1.7 per game)

Goals Against: 20 (3.3 per game)

Overtime: 0-0

Power play: 0.0% (16th)

Penalty Killing: 78.4% (13th)

ALL-TIME LEADERS

GOALS

Dale Hawerchuk	379
Thomas Steen	259
Paul MacLean	248

ASSISTS

Dale Hawerchuk	550
Thomas Steen	543
Paul MacLean	270

POINTS

Dale Hawerchuk	929
Thomas Steen	802
Paul MacLean	518

BEST INDIVIDUAL SEASONS

GOALS

Teemu Selanne	1992-93	76
Dale Hawerchuk	1984-85	53
Keith Tkachuk	1995-96	50

ASSISTS

Phil Housley	1992-93	79
Dale Hawerchuk	1987-88	77
Dale Hawerchuk	1984-85	77

POINTS

Teemu Selanne	1992-93	132
Dale Hawerchuk	1984-85	130
Dale Hawerchuk	1987-88	121

TEAM RECORD

Last 3 years

	GP	W	L	T	Pts	%
1995-96	82	36	40	6	78	.476
1994-95	48	16	25	7	57	.594
1993-94	84	40	37	7	87	.518

Best 3 regular seasons

1984-85	80	43	27	10	96	.600
1986-87	80	40	32	8	88	.550
1989-90	80	37	32	11	85	.531

Worst 3 regular seasons

1980-81	80	9	57	14	32	.200
1979-89	80	20	49	11	51	.319
1993-94	84	24	51	9	57	.339

Most Goals (min. 70 game schedule)

1984-85	358
1983-84	340
1992-93	322

Fewest Goals (min. 70 game schedule)

1979-80	214
1993-94	245
1980-81	246

Most Goals Against (min. 70 game schedule)

1980-81	400
1983-84	374
1985-86	372

Fewest Goals Against (min. 70 game schedule)

1991-92	244
1986-87	271
1990-91	28

STAT SECTION

Team Scoring Stats

	GP	G	A	PTS	+/-	PIM	SH	Power Play			Short Handed		
								G	A	P	G	A	P
KEITH TKACHUK	76	50	48	98	11	156	249	20	21	42	2	1	3
CRAIG JANNEY	84	20	62	82	33-	26	91	7	28	35	0	0	0
ALEXEI ZHAMNOV	58	22	37	59	4-	65	199	5	23	28	0	0	0
TEPPO NUMMINEN	74	11	43	54	4-	22	165	6	22	28	0	1	1
NORM MACIVER	71	7	46	53	6	58	79	3	25	28	0	2	2
IGOR KOROLEV	73	22	29	51	1	42	165	8	7	15	0	0	0
ED OLCZYK	51	27	22	49	0	65	147	16	2	18	0	0	0
DALLAS DRAKE	69	19	20	39	7-	36	121	4	3	7	4	1	5
DAVE MANSON	82	7	23	30	8	205	189	3	6	9	0	0	0
OLEG TVERDOVSKY	82	7	23	30	7-	41	119	2	6	8	0	0	0
MIKE EASTWOOD	80	14	14	28	14-	20	94	2	1	3	0	0	0
MIKE STAPLETON	58	10	14	24	4-	37	91	3	0	3	1	0	1
DARRIN SHANNON	63	5	18	23	5-	28	74	0	1	1	0	0	0
KRIS KING	81	9	11	20	7-	151	89	0	0	0	1	2	3
DERON QUINT	51	5	13	18	2-	22	97	2	5	7	0	0	0
CHAD KILGER	74	7	10	17	4-	34	57	0	0	0	0	0	0
SHANE DOAN	74	7	10	17	9-	101	106	1	3	4	0	0	0
CRAIG MUNI	72	1	7	8	6-	106	41	0	0	0	0	0	0
JIM MCKENZIE	73	4	2	6	4-	202	28	0	0	0	0	0	0
JEFF FINLEY	65	1	5	6	2-	81	27	0	0	0	0	0	0
RANDY GILHEN	22	2	3	5	1	12	26	0	0	0	0	0	0
DENIS CHASSE	60	3	0	3	14-	125	31	1	0	1	0	0	0
IAIN FRASER	12	1	1	2	1	4	12	0	0	0	0	0	0
JASON DOIG	15	1	1	2	2-	28	7	0	0	0	0	0	0
CRAIG MILLS	4	0	2	2	0	0	0	0	0	0	0	0	0
BRENT THOMPSON	10	0	1	1	2-	21	7	0	0	0	0	0	0
DALLAS EAKINS	18	0	1	1	1-	34	6	0	0	0	0	0	0
TOM DRAPER	1	0	0	0	0	0	0	0	0	0	0	0	0
ROB MURRAY	1	0	0	0	1-	2	1	0	0	0	0	0	0
SCOTT LANGKOW	1	0	0	0	0	0	0	0	0	0	0	0	0
RAVIL GUSMANOV	4	0	0	0	3-	0	6	0	0	0	0	0	0
DOMINIC ROUSSEL	16	0	0	0	0	2	0	0	0	0	0	0	0
ED RONAN	17	0	0	0	3-	16	13	0	0	0	0	0	0
TIM CHEVELDAE	30	0	0	0	0	0	0	0	0	0	0	0	0
N. KHABIBULIN	53	0	0	0	0	12	0	0	0	0	0	0	0

PLAYOFFS

PLAYER	GP	G	A	PTS	+/-	PIM	PP	SH	GW	OT	S
DAVE MANSON	6	2	1	3	3	30	0	0	1	0	12
ALEXEI ZHAMNOV	6	2	1	3	0	8	0	0	0	0	11
CRAIG JANNEY	6	1	2	3	0	0	0	0	0	0	6
ED OLCZYK	6	1	2	3	0	6	0	0	0	0	15
KEITH TKACHUK	6	1	2	3	0	22	0	0	0	0	16
IGOR KOROLEV	6	0	3	3	2-	0	0	0	0	0	4
CHAD KILGER	4	1	0	1	0	0	0	0	1	0	2
NORM MACIVER	6	1	0	1	3	2	0	0	0	0	10
DARRIN SHANNON	6	1	0	1	0	6	0	0	0	0	2
KRIS KING	5	0	1	1	1	4	0	0	0	0	3
CRAIG MUNI	6	0	1	1	2-	2	0	0	0	0	1
MIKE EASTWOOD	6	0	1	1	1-	2	0	0	0	0	2
OLEG TVERDOVSKY	6	0	1	1	2-	0	0	0	0	0	8
JIM MCKENZIE	1	0	0	0	0	2	0	0	0	0	0
CRAIG MILLS	1	0	0	0	0	0	0	0	0	0	0
DALLAS DRAKE	3	0	0	0	2-	0	0	0	0	0	3
IAIN FRASER	4	0	0	0	0	0	0	0	0	0	0
JEFF FINLEY	6	0	0	0	4-	4	0	0	0	0	3
TEPPO NUMMINEN	6	0	0	0	3-	2	0	0	0	0	6
MIKE STAPLETON	6	0	0	0	1-	21	0	0	0	0	1
N. KHABIBULIN	6	0	0	0	0	0	0	0	0	0	0
SHANE DOAN	6	0	0	0	0	6	0	0	0	0	2

GOALTENDER	GPI	MINS	AVG	W	L	T	EN	SO	GA	SA	SV %
N. KHABIBULIN	6	359	3.18	2	4	0	1	0	19	214	.911
WPG TOTALS	6	360	3.33	2	4	0	1	0	20	215	.907

San Jose Sharks

I love to say I told you so, so I'll tell you so. I told you the Sharks would stink last year.

If you have last year's edition of *The Hockey Annual* don't bother looking back to find some of my other predictions. This one, however, was bang on.

This team was a joke, from top to bottom. A disaster, from top to bottom. Brutal, from top to bottom.

Most prognosticators in the pre-season had them pegged for seventh, eighth, ninth, or better, in the Western Conference. Something about an up-and-coming young team with great talent. I had them at 11th. They finished 13th out of 13. Even worse than I thought.

There's not much point going through all the numbers. Suffice to say they were last, or next to last, or close to last, in every category. There was one team with a worse record, Ottawa, but still some question about which team was worst.

The Sharks fooled people into thinking they were a good team because they pulled off a couple of playoff upsets. What they had was a hot goaltender, and a lousy team that played well for a spell.

They had no scoring; a weak, soft, defence; a team lacking in character; an arrogant attitude in management and coaching; and a misguided scouting system.

It should be pointed out, however, that all is not lost. Management was smart enough to realize how dumb they were, and they've taken major steps to correct themselves. They deserve a lot of credit for that; and their fans, which sold out the arena every single game, deserve it to.

The Sharks previously thought they were smarter than everyone else, but what happened was that they fooled themselves. They weren't the first club to try and build a team with Europeans. And they weren't the first team to fail.

Winnipeg tried it before when Mike Smith was the General Manager. Incidentally, Smith has let it be known he's tired of getting knocked by me in this and other publicatons. Fair enough. There ought to be a statute of limitations on criticism, and we're way past that.

It's not so much him, it's the concept that bothered me. It has nothing to do with disliking Europeans, or being xenophobic (fear of foreigners) as I've been accused. If the NHL is to be the best league in the world, it has to have the best players. That includes Europeans.

Some people think because there SHOULDN'T be a difference among different countries, that there actually isn't. It's better not to label and make stereotypes, and that's what we all should be teaching our children.

But, we're talking about hockey here, and I'm not saying European hockey players have smaller brains, or anything as ridiculous, I'm saying they've learned their hockey under a different system and play a different style, and think about the game differently.

You'd have to have your head buried in the sand not to notice which players are most often criticized for their lack of intensity, inferior checking skills, lack of heart, streakiness and lack of toughness. Criticized, by the way, publicly by their own coaches, management and players.

Of course, that's not to say it applies to all of them, but rather in general. I know, I know, it's not politically correct, but it's the truth. If you want to break it down further, there are differences between Russians, Swedes, Finns, and so on. There are differences between Canadians and Americans, as well.

You'd also have to have your head buried in the sand not to notice the skating, stickhandling and passing skills of Europeans. They are in general, better than Canadian and American trained players. And you know, it's okay to say that.

What some people don't understand is that the skills the Europeans possess in more abundant qualities than the Canadians doesn't automatically translate to winning hockey. The intensity, the checking skills, the heart, the toughest of Canadians doesn't automatically translate to winning hockey either, but as a whole they are better ingredients. Not so useful, of course, if it isn't combined with a lot of talent.

We're not even going to bring up the failure of the Red Wings' five-man Russian unit in the playoffs. They played great during the regular season, and any five-man unit can go into a slump.

The fact that Europeans "look" good on the ice doesn't make them good. Scouts, general managers and fans can be mesmerized by it, but you can't see what's inside a player when you're sitting in the stands. There are a zillion examples. One that comes to mind is Alexei Kudashov, who looked brilliant as a Maple Leaf. If you only saw the team play in practice, or in one game, you might consider him one of the best players on the team. Certainly, he was more "skilled" than the Leaf leaders at the time - Doug Gilmour and Wendel Clark. Kudashov played 25 games for Toronto and earned one measly point before being banished to the minors, and out of the organization.

His story is similar to many who have given teams high hopes, only to falter. Every Canadian kid playing hockey learns that they have to give it their all in order to be successful. They have to pay the price, sacrificing their bodies for the good of the team.

The ultimate compliment you can give a European is to say they play like a North American. Some, are the best of both worlds. Peter Forsberg comes to mind.

We also have to be fair about it. Europeans are leaving their homes, often to a completely strange existence, they're expected to play a style they've never used before, there are language problems, culture problems, etc. They have a lot to overcome.

Every team in the league has Europeans now. They're here to stay. What winning teams do, however, is understand their limitations and strengths, and build accordingly. Even European teams expect North American players to help the character quotient in their dressing rooms.

To build a team entirely of Europeans doesn't work. Twice it's been tried, twice it has failed miserably.

Nobody is going to try it again for a while, if ever. NHL team managements are smartening up. San Jose is one of them.

TEAM PREVIEW

GOAL: It was a quick transition for Arturs Irbe from hero to goat. Whatever the reasons for his dramatic drop in value, he's out of the picture in San Jose. The number one job went to Chris Terreri, who was close to a goal a game better than anyone else. He wasn't a miracle man, but he was the best.

Kelly Hrudey might have something to say about that number one job after being signed as a free agent. He's 35-years-old, but has been kept young by all the pucks aimed his way in Los Angeles.

Wade Flaherty is also still in the picture, although just barely. He's third on the list and will probably only play in case of injury.

Irbe received an offer sheet from Dallas, and it's unlikely the Sharks will match.

DEFENCE: When you have the worst defence in the league, and the softest, the position needs reconstructive surgery. The big softees on defence were ridiculously bad, and the Sharks have taken some big steps to get fewer sissy boys on the blueline.

In the off-season they obtained Todd Gill from Toronto for Jamie Baker. Gill is a character-type defenceman who plays for the team before himself. He's had a career-long

reputation for mental lapses and giveaways, and while he's relatively small, will play a lot bigger than most all of the previous San Jose defencemen. He'll stick up for his teammates in any situation, and will play whatever role the team requires of him.

The Sharks also took a risk in trading for Al Iafrate from Boston, for Jeff Odgers and a fifth round draft pick. The Wild Thing is a tremendous talent, but hasn't played in two years, recovering from various knee surgeries. It's probably worth a chance though, because if Iafrate plays without pain, he'll be the best defenceman on the team. He's big, plays tough, is great offensively, and one of the best in the league when he's on his game.

Marcus Ragnarsson had a good rookie season, effectively replacing Ozolinsh as the top offensive defenceman.

Doug Bodger, obtained from Buffalo last season, is still on board, as is Jayson More, Yves Racine, and Michal Sykora. Disappointments such as Mike Rathje and Vlastimil Kroupa, will have to show a lot to earn a spot on this team. Jim Kyte was an unrestricted free agent, although he could re-sign.

San Jose's defence gave up the most goals in the league, by a wide margin. They made good friends with most opposing forwards in the league, because they were so nice to them. It will be different this year. Opponents will no longer be able to waltz in untouched, and leave the same way.

GOALTENDER	GPI	MINS	AVG	W	L	T	EN	SO	GA	SA	SV %
CHRIS TERRERI	46	2516	3.70	13	29	1	10	0	155	1322	.883
ARTURS IRBE	22	1112	4.59	4	12	4	0	0	85	607	.860
WADE FLAHERTY	24	1137	4.85	3	12	1	0	0	92	689	.866
GEOFF SARJEANT	4	171	4.91	0	2	1	1	0	14	87	.839
S.J TOTALS	82	4959	4.32	20	55	7	11	0	357	2716	.869

FORWARD: There's some hope here, but not very much. The Sharks start with one of the best power winger snipers in the game, Owen Nolan. He's big, tough, and can pile up the goals if he has some linemates.

San Jose are counting on Bernie Nicholls, signed as a free agent, to be their number one centre, and take over the role of Craig Janney who was traded to Winnipeg last year. He's 35-years-old though, and is prone to lengthy goal-scoring slumps. He's still a good playermaker, however, and is good on the power play, which should help Nolan.

Jeff Friesen is the number two centre, or the number one left winger, or the number two left winger. This is Friesen's third year, which could be his breakout season. He's had 15 goals in each of his first two NHL seasons.

Darren Turcotte, obtained in the Janney deal, is the number three centre, or number two depending on where Friesen plays. Viktor Kozlov, who made the transition from wing to centre, could start to show this year why he was selected sixth overall in the 1993 draft. So far, he's shown he could be good, but that's it.

Most of the Sharks forwards can move around from position to position. On the left side, tentatively, could be Friesen, Kozlov, Ray Whitney, Chris Tancill, or prospects Ville Peltonen, Andrei Nazarov, or Alexei Yegorov. All of the first four names can also play centre, so who knows.

Tancill was a member on the almost-famous Dirt Bag Line. They played great for a while last year but won't get the same opportunity this year. Baker was traded to Toronto, and Odgers to Boston.

The right side isn't too bad, starting with Nolan. Add in late season scoring sensation, Jan Caloun, along with Ulf Dahlen and Shean Donovan.

Still a weak forward unit, but there are a lot of young players who could step up and make a major contribution.

SPECIAL TEAMS: The good thing about finishing last in penalty killing is that they can't get any worse. The fact that the Sharks no longer have Jamie Baker, and Kevin Miller, two of their best defensive forwards, means it will be up to somebody else to withstand the onslaught. With better defencemen on board, it could improve.

The Sharks were fairly proficient at scoring goals while shorthanded, with Baker's six shorthanded goals, a team record, tying for second in the league. That may have also been why other teams were scoring so often.

The power play was no prize, either, although Nolan is a specialist in that area, and had 16 goals with the man advantage. The problem is that nobody else had more than five. Nicholls is going to help out there, quite a bit. On the points they will have Ragnarsson, who had a good rookie season, and Iafrate if he's healthy, Bodger if he's not. Gill can help out there too, if needed.

POWER PLAY	G	ATT	PCT
Overall	62	385	16.1% (19th NHL)
Home	30	199	15.1% (22nd NHL)
Road	32	186	17.2% (10th NHL)

20 SHORT HANDED GOALS ALLOWED (T-24th NHL)

PENALTY KILLING	G	TSH	PCT
Overall	93	397	76.6% (26th NHL)
Home	45	191	76.4% (26th NHL)
Road	48	206	76.7% (25th NHL)

15 SHORT HANDED GOALS SCORED (T-5th NHL)

COACHING AND MANAGEMENT: The Sharks will have a new coach this season, and hopefully a new attitude. The job of Al Sims will be to do what the others couldn't, mainly instill a winning attitude and a disciplined system.

Kevin Constantine received a new three year million dollar contract at the start of last season. Not long after, he was fired when the team got off to a 3-18-4 record. Jim Wiley, who had been promoted as an assistant from IHL affiliate Kansas City, took over as interim coach. He didn't have much more luck, and even resorted to sitting out Nolan and Ray Sheppard for a game because he didn't like their attitude at practice.

Constantine kind of personified the Sharks organization; arrogant, self-assured, my-way-or-the-highway, attitude. Those attributes are only admirable when the team wins, and even not then sometimes. Nobody's likely to hire Constantine back in the NHL, especially with all the stories going around about his tyrannical nature.

So, what does Sims have that the others don't? We'll find out.

Management was a mess, and responsible for putting together this team. But, GM Dean Lombardi has shown they're also scrappers, and they're doing everything they can to turn it around. That means getting players with character, heart, and intensity.

They fired director of player personnel Chuck Grillo, who scouted all the dogs the team drafted. If you can believe it, the team didn't even have a full-time scout in Canada. That's why everybody was laughing at them when it was their turn to pick at the draft table — picking up obscure players that other teams didn't want anyway.

The Sharks tried to be innovative in their scouting, and you can't blame them for that. It was their inability to recognize winning hockey players over talented hockey players that got them into trouble.

The Sharks are not only rebuilding their team, they're rebuilding their organization, and it was sorely needed.

DRAFT

Round	Sel.	Player	Pos	
1	2	Andrei Zyuzin	D	Russia
1	21	Marco Sturm	C	Germany
3	55	Terry Friesen	G	Swift Current (WHL)
4	102	Matt Bradley	RW	Kingston (OHL)
6	137	Michel Larocque	G	Boston Univ.
7	164	Jake Deadmarsh	D	Kamloops (WHL)
8	191	Cory Cyrenne	C	Brandon (WHL)
9	217	David Thibeault	LW	Drummondville (QMJHL)

There's some doubt about whether Andrei Zyuzin will be playing in the NHL this year, but few doubts about his future. He was considered the best offensive defenceman in the draft, and was being compared to some of the better NHL types, including Ray Bourque and Brian Leetch.

Some things never change. The Sharks traded two second round picks to Chicago for their first rounder, 21st overall, and then selected a player who would probably be available anyway in the second round. Marco Sturm, the first German player ever selected in the first round, was ranked eighth among Europeans by Central Scouting, and was the second European chosen. *The Hockey News* had him at number 37. Sturm was considered one of the fastest skaters available in the draft.

PROGNOSIS: Bad news all around for the Sharks, at least this season. Clubs that go through a major overhaul of a team that was already weak, aren't likely to set any records.

Mind you, they could end up being the most improved team, even if it's only because they were so bad last year.

The playoffs are out of the question, but new coach Sims is going to have them playing disciplined, tough hockey.

They're not that far away as long as they stay on the right track.

PREDICTION:

Pacific Division: 5th

Western Conference: 11th

Overall: 22nd

Team Rankings 1995-96

		Conference Rank	League Rank
Record	20-55-7	13	25
Home	12-26-3	13	25
Away	8-29-4	13	25
Versus Own Conference	13-40-3	13	25
Versus Other Conference	7-15-4	12	26
Team Plus\Minus	-74	13	26
Goals For	252	7	13
Goals Against	357	13	26
Average Shots Fo	26.1	13	26
Average Shots Against	33.1	11	21
Overtime	1-1-7	8	13
One Goal Games	5-12	13	25
Times outshooting opponent	17	13	26
Versus Teams Over .500	7-22-3	12	24
Versus Teams Under .500	13-33-4	13	26
First Half Record	8-29-4	13	25
Second Half Record	12-26-3	12	23

PLAYOFFS

- Did not make the Playoffs

ALL-TIME LEADERS

GOALS

Pat Falloon	76
Ray Whitney	47
Johan Garpenlov	46

ASSISTS

Pat Falloon	86
Johan Garpenlov	85
Kelly Kisio	78

POINTS

Pat Falloon	162
Johan Garpenlov	132
Sandis Ozolinsh	116

BEST INDIVIDUAL SEASONS

GOALS

Sergei Makarov	1993-94	30
Owen Nolan (with SJ only)	1995-96	29
Sandis Ozolinsh	1993-94	26
Kelly Kisio	1992-93	26

ASSISTS

Kelly Kisio	1992-93	52
Johan Garpenlov	1992-93	44
Todd Elik	1993-94	41

POINTS

Kelly Kisio	1992-93	78
Sergei Makarov	1993-94	68
Todd Elik	1993-94	66
Johan Garpenlov	1992-93	66

TEAM RECORD

Last 3 years

	GP	W	L	T	Pts	%
1995-96	82	20	55	7	47	.287
1994-95	48	19	25	4	42	.438
1993-94	84	33	35	16	82	.488

Best 3 regular seasons

1993-94	84	33	35	16	82	.488
1994-95	48	19	25	4	42	.438
1995-96	82	20	55	7	47	.287

Worst 3 regular seasons

1992-93	84	11	71	2	24	.143
1991-92	80	17	58	5	39	.244
1995-96	82	20	55	7	47	.287

Most Goals (min. 70 game schedule)

1995-96	252
1993-94	252
1991-92	219

Fewest Goals (min. 70 game schedule)

1992-93	218
1991-92	219
1995-96	252
1993-94	252

Most Goals Against (min. 70 game schedule)

1992-93	414
1991-92	359
1995-96	357

Fewest Goals Against (min. 70 game schedule)

1993-94	265
1995-96	357
1991-92	359

STAT SECTION

Team Scoring Stats

	GP	G	A	PTS	+/-	PIM	SH	Power Play			Short Handed		
								G	A	P	G	A	P
OWEN NOLAN	81	33	36	69	33-	146	207	16	13	19	1	2	3
JEFF FRIESEN	79	15	31	46	19-	42	123	2	8	10	0	3	3
DARREN TURCOTTE	68	22	21	43	5	30	167	2	6	8	1	1	2
RAY WHITNEY	60	17	24	41	23-	16	106	4	8	12	2	1	3
MARCUS RAGNARSSON	71	8	31	39	24-	42	94	4	13	17	0	0	0
JAMIE BAKER	77	16	17	33	19-	79	117	2	0	2	6	1	7
ULF DAHLEN	59	16	12	28	21-	27	103	5	4	9	0	0	0
DOUG BODGER	73	4	24	28	24-	68	121	3	12	15	0	1	1
CHRIS TANCILL	45	7	16	23	12-	20	93	0	2	2	1	1	2
SHEAN DONOVAN	74	13	8	21	17-	39	73	0	0	0	1	0	1
MICHAL SYKORA	79	4	16	20	14-	54	80	1	0	1	0	0	0
YVES RACINE	57	1	19	20	10-	54	51	0	7	7	0	0	0
VIKTOR KOZLOV	62	6	13	19	15-	6	107	1	4	5	0	0	0
JEFF ODGERS	78	12	4	16	4-	192	84	0	0	0	0	0	0
ANDREI NAZAROV	42	7	7	14	15-	62	55	2	2	4	0	0	0
VILLE PELTONEN	31	2	11	13	7-	14	58	0	1	1	0	0	0
JAN CALOUN	11	8	3	11	4	0	20	2	0	2	0	0	0
DODY WOOD	32	3	6	9	0	138	33	0	0	0	1	0	1
JAY MORE	74	2	7	9	32-	147	67	0	0	0	0	0	0
VLASTIMIL KROUPA	27	1	7	8	17-	18	11	0	2	2	0	0	0
JIM KYTE	57	1	7	8	12-	146	32	0	0	0	0	0	0
MIKE RATHJE	27	0	7	7	16-	14	26	0	4	4	0	0	0
ALEXEI YEGOROV	9	3	2	5	5-	2	10	2	0	2	0	0	0
TOM PEDERSON	60	1	4	5	9-	40	59	1	0	1	0	1	1
CHRIS TERRERI	50	0	5	5	0	4	0	0	0	0	0	0	0
DAVE BROWN	37	3	1	4	4	46	8	0	0	0	0	0	0
SERGEI BAUTIN	1	0	0	0	1-	2	0	0	0	0	0	0	0
GEOFF SARJEANT	4	0	0	0	0	2	0	0	0	0	0	0	0
ARTURS IRBE	22	0	0	0	0	4	0	0	0	0	0	0	0
WADE FLAHERTY	24	0	0	0	0	0	0	0	0	0	0	0	0

St. Louis Blues

When Mike Keenan is running the show, he's the star. Bigger than Brett Hull, bigger than Grant Fuhr, bigger even than Wayne Gretzky.

The man has mystical power, no doubt about it, and more often than not his teams are winners. That's why he can make his own rules. Or perhaps his rules are more conducive to winning.

As a season goes on, virtually every player will be criticized publicly at some time or another. It appears the players respond to that, as his coaching history suggests. A player with something to prove is bound to play better than one who is not as highly motivated.

One of the more curious moves by Keenan last year was starting Grant Fuhr in every single game. After starting 79 in a row, however, Fuhr had to sit out the last two with an injury.

Why did Keenan do that? Ask him and chances are he'll tell us what he wants us to know. Here are some theories on why it really happened.

* Cujo Who?
Keenan knew the fans were upset at losing their favorite, Curtis Joseph. Even when Fuhr doesn't play very well, he has a way of making easy saves look like game-savers. Maybe he felt the fans would be taken by Fuhr.

* The Great Gretzkys
It was Wayne and Janet Gretzky, reportedly, especially Janet, who enthused about Fuhr and recommended him when they met up with Keenan at a chance meeting in New York. So, maybe Keenan wanted to make the Gretzkys feel like they had a stake in Fuhr and the Blues. That way getting Gretzky to play in St. Louis, after he became a free agent, would be easier.

* Fat and Skinny
With Grant Fuhr's penchant for overeating, this was a good way to keep him in shape. He had showed up to training camp 20 pounds overweight, and was sent home until he had slimmed down.

* Focus and Flash
Considering some of Fuhr's off-ice indulgences in the past, perhaps Keenan decided it wasn't worth taking any chances, so this was a way to ensure he kept focused on the job, and didn't let down, thinking he wasn't playing the next day anyway.

* **Confidence Game**

Most goalies need to feel confident to play at their best. Fuhr had a couple of bad seasons and was being written off as a has-been (exact hyphenated word used in last year's *The Hockey Annual*). If Keenan used Fuhr every game, Fuhr wouldn't be able to see another goalie playing better, so he couldn't lose his confidence.

* **Non-Confidence Game**

Maybe Keenan didn't have any confidence in his other goalies - Bruce Racine and Jon Casey - so with the lack of a competent backup, in his mind, he just stuck with his number one.

* **Good Old-Fashioned Inspiration**

There were a bunch of old-timers on the Blues. Maybe if they could see another old-timer playing every game, it wouldn't give them any excuses for being tired or not going all out, all the time.

* **Accidents Happen**

Maybe Keenan never planned on playing Fuhr all the time, it just sort of worked out that way. After he had played him for a lot of games in a row he saw little reason to change a good thing.

* **I'll Show You**

Keenan was widely criticized for taking a washed-up goaltender (see last year's *The Hockey Annual*) and figured he'd just show everyone how right he was. Or, along the same vein, he was scared to use somebody else because it might show that he made a mistake if someone else played better.

TEAM PREVIEW

GOAL: If Grant Fuhr hadn't been injured when Toronto's Nick Kypreos fell on him in the first round of the playoffs last year, there's no telling what the Blues might have done.

Fuhr was in his glory, in the postseason where he has a history of playing his best. And he was spectacular until getting injured.

During the regular season, Fuhr set NHL records in most games played by a goalie in one season with 79, and most consecutive games played with 76. Oddly enough, his previous minutes played record was beaten not by him, but by Martin Brodeur, who totalled 4,434, compared to 4,303 for Fuhr.

Bruce Racine backed up Fuhr for much of the season, but he never got a chance to start, although at the age of 29, he did make his NHL debut, coming in for relief 11 times.

The big surprise for the Blues was the play of Jon Casey in the playoffs. He spent most of the season in the minors, but played great when Fuhr was hurt, and earned himself another contract. He'll most likely get some playing time this year, with Keenan unlikely to duplicate his attempt at playing Fuhr in every single game.

For added insurance, the Blues signed free agent Jamie McLellan, formerly with the Islanders.

DEFENCE: Maybe Keenan knew what he was doing after all when it came to Chris Pronger. The much maligned second overall draft pick in 1993 has had a rough go of it since the start. He wasn't able to approach the level of play expected of him, not in his first two years with Hartford and not at the start of last season.

He wasn't Larry Robinson after all. Although, it did take Larry Robinson a number of years before he became Larry Robinson.

Pronger improved. He started using his size. He started to become an NHL defenceman. By the end of the year, he was the team's best defenceman on more than a few nights.

Al MacInnis played all 82 games, but he still registered his lowest point total in a full NHL season. Part of the reason was a weak power play. Another might be age. He will be 33-years-old at the start of this season. That's not as old as a 33-year-old forward, however. It's probably roughly equivalent to a 29-year-old forward. It takes longer to learn how to be a defenceman in the NHL, partly because there's so much more to know. They can remain useful longer because of it. And it doesn't appear his shot has gotten any slower.

Murray Baron is a big defenceman who gets very little attention. Even when they talked about which players were here before Keenan, he was sometimes left out when MacInnis and Hull's names were mentioned. He does his job solidly, was tougher this year, recording 190 penalty minutes, and he does so with little fanfare.

Igor Kravchuk is still with the team, another recruit of a player that Keenan had coached previously. He had an important overtime goal during the playoffs.

Christer Olsson played 26 games with the Blues last season, but was almost strictly a power play performer. That's a luxury not many teams can afford, and not the type of player at the top of Keenan's wish list, so he seems a likely throw-in for a future trade.

Keenan shored up with two defensive defencemen free agent signings - Trent Yawney from Calgary, and Marc Bergevin from Detroit.

FORWARD: So much for the Wayne Gretzky experiment.

Most players who score 102 points in a season earn a lot of praise. When Wayne Gretzky does it, he's just about washed up. Now that Gretzky is just an "average superstar" expectations should be lowered. But, it's difficult for people to revise their image of him. He's no longer the best player in the league, and he no longer can do everything at 35 that he could at 25.

In fact, the NHL's all-time greatest scorer, wasn't the savior the Blues hoped he'd be. Not that he was bad. But, the team didn't respond as expected, especially Brett Hull, who Keenan felt should go to town and score like never before.

* The Blues - Before and After Gretzky

	Before Gretzky	After Gretzky
Record	26-24-11	6-10-5
Goals for	166	53

GOALTENDER	GPI	MINS	AVG	W	L	T	EN	SO	GA	SA	SV %
GRANT FUHR	79	4365	2.87	30	28	16	1	3	209	2157	.903
BRUCE RACINE	11	230	3.13	0	3	0	0	0	12	101	.881
JON CASEY	9	395	3.80	2	3	0	0	0	25	180	.861
PAT JABLONSKI	1	8	7.50	0	0	0	0	0	1	5	.800
STL TOTALS	82	5003	2.97	32	34	16	1	3	248	2444	.899

Goals per game	2.7	2.5
Goals Against	176	72
Goals Against per game	2.9	3.4
Power Play %	16.0%	18.4%
Penalty Killing	84.0%	78.9%

Gretzky almost re-signed with the Blues, but didn't of course, choosing the New York Rangers. He was unhappy with the Blues' negotiating techniques and contract offer, and probably wasn't willing to endure another year with Keenan.

Hull is sort of in the same boat as Gretzky. In fact, much of last year's team was. Their best years were behind them. Forty-three goals on a team that didn't score much is not bad for mortals, but it's just half of the Hull's career high of 86.

Hull and Keenan have an ongoing feud in the newspapers that is hilarious. You get the feeling these guys never talk to each other in person, but just carry on a running conversation in the press. He said that? Well, this is the way it is. He said what? Yeah, sure, I'll tell you how it really is. And so on and so on. Funny.

Will Hull be traded? Not likely. Keenan may have learned a lesson from getting rid of other fan faves, such as Shanahan and Joseph.

Shayne Corson turned out to be a good acquisition. He plays it rough, tough, and is a power play sniper to augment Hull. Other forwards returning are Geoff Courtnall, Adam Creighton, Brian Noonan, Stephane Matteau, Mike Hudson, Peter Zezel, Rob Pearson, Tony Twist and Yuri Khmylev. Craig MacTavish and Steven Leach were un-signed and Glenn Anderson likely won't be invited back. Greg Gilbert, an all-time Keenan favorite, and Basil McRae, have a year remaining on their contracts but may no longer be part of the picture.

Jim Campbell was signed as a free agent and has a chance to stick, but the big-name free agent signing was Joe Murphy.

Murphy is coming off a poor season with Chicago, but could easily score in the 35 goal and 70 point range. He's a self proclaimed "big-game" player, which can be translated to an excuse for coasting through the regular season. We'll see how happy Keenan is with Murphy when he doesn't play so well in the "small games."

There's probably not a name in the above list that you could write in ink. Keenan isn't know for sitting still when a team needs help. They still need a scoring centre or two at this writing, so expect one before the start of the season.

SPECIAL TEAMS: One of the most curious things about Keenan is that he's known for spending little time working on the power play. The reason, we hear, is that teams can just figure out what you're doing if you have set power play tendencies, and can stop it, especially at playoff time.

But his teams aren't doing well on the power play and that hurts them during the regular season. If he expects the most out of his players every game then why not try for the most out of the power play. Eighteenth in the league is ridiculous with the talent they have.

Then again, on this team it should be simple. You put Hull on the perimeter so he can get open for the big shot; you put Corson in front of the net to cause havoc and pick up the garbage; and you use MacInnis as the focal point. The other guys on the ice just look to get the puck to MacInnis. When he gets it he can either drive one of his patented blasters, or look for Hull for another patented blaster.

Improve in this area and it will improve the Blues record. Keenan could do it if he wanted.

POWER PLAY	G	ATT	PCT
Overall	74	448	16.5% (18th NHL)
Home	36	221	16.3% (17th NHL)
Road	38	227	16.7% (T-14th NHL)

8 SHORT HANDED GOALS ALLOWED (6th NHL)

PENALTY KILLING	G	TSH	PCT
Overall	82	482	83.0% (T-9th NHL)
Home	38	24	84.5% (T-9th NHL)
Road	44	237	81.4% (12th NHL)

COACHING AND MANAGEMENT: What Keenan tried to do last season was put together a team of winners - guys who knew what it took because they had done it before. Twelve different players had won Stanley Cups, 33 of them in total.

Keenan took a lot of heat last season. A lot of people seem to take great joy in watching one of the best coaches in the game have his problems.

Here's some news for them. Keenan still is the best coach in the game, and he's got a history that proves it. What happened last year was that for the first time he had to build a team on a budget.

That seemed to cause him problems. Given a free hand, Keenan can almost guarantee a Stanley Cup contender. So, when he figures out the financial ins and outs, and he will, he will rise back up to the top.

Apart from that, Keenan has his own brand of motivation. That includes criticizing players in public, benchings and all kinds of other stuff.

Other stuff means offering to resign as coach if the players wanted. Why didn't they take him up on his offer? Everyone knows how much they hate him, right? The reason is that they want to win, and Keenan wins. And uh, maybe also because Keenan's the general manager.

There are winning players who have off-years, and there are winning coaches who have off-years.

Keenan is a winner. Just wait and see.

DRAFT

Round	Sel.	Player	Pos	Team
1	14	Marty Reasoner	C	Boston College
3	67	Gordie Dwyer	LW	Beauport (QMJHL)
4	95	Jonathon Zukiewski	C	Red Deer (WHL)
4	97	Andrei Petrakov	LW	Russia
6	159	Stephen Wagner	G	Olds (Atla. Tier II)
7	169	Daniel Corso	C	Victoriaville (QMJHL)
7	177	Reed Low	RW	Moose Jaw(WHL)
8	196	Andrei Podkonicky	C	Slovakia
8	203	Anthony Hutchins	C	Lawrence Academy (USHS)
9	229	Konstantine Shafranov	LW	Fort Wayne (IHL)

With the home town fans looking on, the Blues had their first first-round pick since 1989. Marty Reasoner is supposed to be a Craig Janney type player, which would make him a curious selection for Mike Keenan, who couldn't stand Janney's style of play.

Not that it matters much anyway. Most draft picks never make it as far as St. Louis. If they have any potential they're usually dealt for a veteran. Even two picks from the previous draft have already been shipped to other teams.

The second selection of the Blues, in the third round, appears to be more Keenan's style. The big winger racked up 358 penalty minutes in the Quebec Junior League. Even that total, however, wasn't near the league lead. Another player had 573 penalty minutes.

PROGNOSIS: Keenan advised everyone all year to just wait until the playoffs, and then they'd see what this team was really made of. They almost pulled it off, too, taking Detroit to seven games, and losing the seventh 1-0 in overtime. All with their backup goalie.

If they had won that game, and they had their chances, then who knows what would have happened afterwards.

You can't judge a Keenan-coached team very well before the start of the season because you know he'll make changes.

On paper, before the start of this season, you wouldn't rate them very high. They're old, there's not much depth, they have trouble scoring, and they don't have good prospects on the way up.

They play this game on ice, however, and in the general manager's office, and behind the bench.

This team will be a force, if not at first, then later in the season, and surely in the playoffs.

PREDICTION:

Central Division: 2nd

Western Conference: 4th

Overall: 10th

Team Rankings 1995-96

		Conference Rank	League Rank
Record	32-34-16	5	15
Home	15-17-9	9	20
Away	17-17-7	5	9

Versus Own Conference	23-23-10	6	15
Versus Other Conference	9-11-6	6	15
Team Plus\Minus	-21	9	19
Goals For	219	13	24
Goals Against	248	5	10
Average Shots For	31.0	5	9
Average Shots Against	29.8	5	11
Overtime	1-1-16	8	13
One Goal Games	11-8	2	4
Times outshooting opponent	41	5	11
Versus Teams Over .500	10-14-8	5	12
Versus Teams Under .500	22-20-8	9	18
First Half Record	18-18-5	4	12
Second Half Record	14-16-11	8	17

Results: Defeated Toronto 4-2

Lost to Detroit 4-3

Record: 7-6

Home: 5-1

Away: 2-5

Goals For: 37 (2.8 per game)

Goals Against: 37 (2.8 per game)

Overtime: 2-3

Power play: 15.9% (10th)

Penalty Killing: 80.0% (12th)

ALL-TIME LEADERS

GOALS

Brett Hull	458
Bernie Federko	352
Brian Sutter	303

ASSISTS

Bernie Federko	721
Brian Sutter	334
Brett Hull	324

POINTS

Bernie Federko	1,073
Brett Hull	782
Brian Sutter	636

BEST INDIVIDUAL SEASONS

GOALS

Brett Hull	1990-91	86
Brett Hull	1989-90	72
Brett Hull	1991-92	70

ASSISTS

Adam Oates	1990-91	90
Craig Janney	1992-93	82
Adam Oates	1989-90	79

POINTS

Brett Hull	1990-91	131
Adam Oates	1990-91	115
Brett Hull	1989-90	113

TEAM RECORD

Last 3 years

	GP	W	L	T	Pts	%
1995-96	82	32	34	16	80	.488
1994-95	48	28	15	5	61	.635
1993-94	84	40	33	11	91	.542

Best 3 regular seasons

1980-81	80	45	18	17	107	.669
1990-91	80	47	22	11	105	.656
1994-95	48	28	15	5	61	.635

Worst 3 regular seasons

1978-79	80	18	50	12	48	.300
1977-78	80	20	47	13	53	.331
1982-83	80	25	40	15	65	.406

Most Goals (min. 70 game schedule)

1980-81	352
1981-82	315
1990-91	310

Fewest Goals (min. 70 game schedule)

1967-68	177
1968-69	204
1973-74	206

Most Goals Against (min. 70 game schedule)

1981-82	349
1978-79	348
1982-83	316
1983-84	316

Fewest Goals Against (min. 70 game schedule)

1968-69	157
1969-70	179
1967-68	191

STAT SECTION

Team Scoring Stats

	GP	G	A	PTS	+/-	PIM	SH	Power Play			Short Handed		
								G	A	P	G	A	P
WAYNE GRETZKY	80	23	79	102	13-	34	195	6	41	47	1	0	1
BRETT HULL	70	43	40	83	4	30	327	16	17	33	5	1	6
AL MACINNIS	82	17	44	61	5	88	317	9	25	34	1	1	2
SHAYNE CORSON	77	18	28	46	3	192	150	13	9	22	0	1	1
GEOFF COURTNALL	69	24	16	40	9-	101	228	7	7	14	1	0	1
BRIAN NOONAN	81	13	22	35	2	84	131	3	5	8	1	1	2
YURI KHMYLEV	73	8	21	29	17-	40	136	5	5	10	1	2	3
STEPHEN LEACH	73	11	17	28	7-	108	157	1	2	3	0	0	0
STEPHANE MATTEAU	78	11	15	26	8-	87	109	4	4	8	0	0	0
CHRIS PRONGER	78	7	18	25	18-	110	138	3	8	11	1	0	1
IGOR KRAVCHUK	66	7	16	23	19-	34	173	3	10	13	0	0	0
ADAM CREIGHTON	61	11	10	21	0	78	98	2	4	6	0	0	0
PETER ZEZEL	57	8	13	21	2-	12	87	2	7	9	0	1	1
MIKE HUDSON	59	5	12	17	2	55	59	0	1	1	0	0	0
GLENN ANDERSON	32	6	8	14	11-	33	71	2	0	2	0	0	0
CRAIG MACTAVISH	68	5	9	14	9-	70	58	0	0	0	0	0	0
MURRAY BARON	82	2	9	11	3	190	86	0	0	0	0	0	0
ROB PEARSON	27	6	4	10	4	54	51	1	0	1	0	0	0
CHARLIE HUDDY	64	5	5	10	12-	65	70	2	0	2	0	0	0
CHRISTER OLSSON	26	2	8	10	6-	14	32	2	8	10	0	0	0
KEN SUTTON	38	0	8	8	13-	43	41	0	4	4	0	0	0
TONY TWIST	51	3	2	5	1-	100	12	0	0	0	0	0	0
ROMAN VOPAT	25	2	3	5	8-	48	33	1	0	1	0	0	0
JAY WELLS	76	0	3	3	8-	67	24	0	0	0	0	0	0
BASIL MCRAE	18	1	1	2	5-	40	5	0	0	0	0	0	0
PAUL BROTEN	17	0	1	1	1-	4	11	0	0	0	0	0	0
GREG GILBERT	17	0	1	1	1-	8	9	0	0	0	0	0	0
GRANT FUHR	79	0	1	1	0	8	0	0	0	0	0	0	0
ALEXANDER VASILEVSKI	1	0	0	0	1-	0	0	0	0	0	0	0	0
FRED KNIPSCHEER	1	0	0	0	0	2	2	0	0	0	0	0	0
JAMIE RIVERS	3	0	0	0	1-	2	5	0	0	0	0	0	0
JON CASEY	9	0	0	0	0	0	0	0	0	0	0	0	0
BRUCE RACINE	11	0	0	0	0	2	0	0	0	0	0	0	0

PLAYOFFS

PLAYER	GP	G	A	PTS	+/-	PIM	PP	SH	GW	OT	S
WAYNE GRETZKY	13	2	14	16	2	0	1	0	1	0	25
SHAYNE CORSON	13	8	6	14	1-	22	6	1	1	0	37
BRETT HULL	13	6	5	11	2	10	2	1	1	0	52
AL MACINNIS	13	3	4	7	2	20	1	0	0	0	48
IGOR KRAVCHUK	10	1	5	6	0	4	0	0	1	1	14
CHRIS PRONGER	13	1	5	6	0	16	0	0	0	0	20
BRIAN NOONAN	13	4	1	5	5-	10	0	0	0	0	21
STEPHEN LEACH	11	3	2	5	4	10	1	0	1	0	11
GLENN ANDERSON	11	1	4	5	5	6	0	0	1	1	20
PETER ZEZEL	10	3	0	3	4	2	0	1	0	0	17
GEOFF COURTNALL	13	0	3	3	2	14	0	0	0	0	26
YURI KHMYLEV	6	1	1	2	1	4	0	0	1	0	8
TONY TWIST	10	1	1	2	0	16	0	0	0	0	1
ADAM CREIGHTON	13	1	1	2	4-	8	0	0	0	0	18
STEPHANE MATTEAU	11	0	2	2	2-	8	0	0	0	0	13
JON CASEY	12	0	2	2	0	8	0	0	0	0	0
CRAIG MACTAVISH	13	0	2	2	0	6	0	0	0	0	11
MURRAY BARON	13	1	0	1	4	20	0	1	0	0	10
CHARLIE HUDDY	13	1	0	1	1	8	0	0	0	0	14
MIKE HUDSON	2	0	1	1	1	4	0	0	0	0	0
JAY WELLS	12	0	1	1	0	2	0	0	0	0	2
BRUCE RACINE	1	0	0	0	0	0	0	0	0	0	0
KEN SUTTON	1	0	0	0	0	0	0	0	0	0	1
GRANT FUHR	2	0	0	0	0	0	0	0	0	0	0
BASIL MCRAE	2	0	0	0	0	0	0	0	0	0	2
ROB PEARSON	2	0	0	0	1	14	0	0	0	0	2
CHRISTER OLSSON	3	0	0	0	1-	0	0	0	0	0	0

GOALTENDER	GPI	MINS	AVG	W	L	T	EN	SO	GA	SA	SV %
BRUCE RACINE	1	1	.00	0	0	0	0	0	0	0	.000
GRANT FUHR	2	69	.87	1	0	0	0	1	4	5	.978
JON CASEY	12	747	2.89	6	6	0	1	3	6	378	.905
STL TOTALS	13	818	2.71	7	6	0	1	3	7	423	.913

Toronto Maple Leafs

What a mess. Just when it looked like the Leafs couldn't get any worse, they did. And it's not getting better any time soon. This year, they won't make the playoffs, and just being competitive will be difficult.

Who's responsible for taking the Leafs down to the dregs of the NHL? Why, it's the same man who, not so long ago, brought them up from the dregs of the NHL.

Cliff Fletcher has run the gammut in Toronto, from well respected and admired, to something considerably less. To be sure, over the last year or so, it looked like Fletcher wasn't paying attention at times. He wasn't sitting up straight in class, and he was just staring out the window.

When he saw his report cards, he'd start raising his hand, and try to solve the problems.

Very little worked out for the team in the final analysis, but it wasn't completely Fletcher's fault. Although the Leafs were weak before the start of last year, at least according to the extremely insightful *The Hockey Annual,* they got off to a good start. At the halfway mark, they were 20-14-7. That was fourth best in the conference, and eighth best in the league. No problem there.

At that point, who could have predicted an 3-17-4 slide over the next two and a half months?

Once it started, there was no stopping it. Nothing worked, as Fletcher tried desperately to make some deals to help the team. Everything he touched turned to stone.

Let's at least try to be fair. Let's look at each major move a little closer. We'll just concentrate on last year, which means we'll forego one of the best deals of all-time, when Fletcher acquired Doug Gilmour in the famous trade with Calgary. It also means we'll omit one of the worst deals, when he traded Eric Fichaud to the Islanders for Benoit Hogue and a couple draft choices.

We'll start with last summer.

Problem: Lousy defence, before the start of last season.

Solution: A first round draft choice in 1996, a second round pick in 1997, and a fourth round pick in 1996, to Philadelphia for Dimitri Yushkevich and a second round pick in 1996.

Prognosis: Yushkevich wasn't even good enough to be one of the top six Philadelphia defencemen, and had injury problems, so getting a first rounder and more for him was like Christmas for Flyers' GM Bobby Clarke. Yushkevich was good enough to play in Toronto's top six, however, and was only 23-years old, so he gave the Leafs some much needed youth on defence.

Result: Yushkevich played great for about the first five games of the season, hitting everything in sight. Then, he became progressively worse, finally not even dressing for important games at the end of the season. The draft pick they gave up was 15th overall, and Yushkevich's reward was a new contract for big money.

Problem: An available Kirk Muller.

Solution: Three way deal in which Damian Rhodes and Ken Belanger went to the Islanders for Muller. The NYI sent Rhodes and Wade Redden to Ottawa for Bryan Berard and Martin Straka. Toronto received Don Beaupre from Ottawa.

Prognosis: Rhodes was a backup, Belanger a minor-league tough guy. In exchange, Toronto got a player considered to be a great leader, someone who wanted to play for the Leafs, and someone with a winning history. Looked like a good deal for Toronto.

Result: Rhodes starred for the Senators, Beaupre played terribly for Toronto, Muller didn't contribute near as much as hoped, and more importantly wasn't much of a factor in the playoffs.

Problem: Team in a horrendous slump.

Solution: Pat Burns was fired as coach and Nick Beverley moved downstairs to take over behind the bench.

Prognosis: The team needed a spark, and they couldn't do any worse with a new coach. Fletcher didn't have any choice.

Result: The Leafs were 9-6-2 under Beverley, good enough to make the playoffs.

Problem: Too much youth.

Solution: Trade it all. Kenny Jonsson, Darby Hendrickson, Sean Haggerty and Toronto's first round selection in 1997 to the Islanders for Wendel Clark, Mathieu Schneider and Denis Smith.

Prognosis: Although some would disagree, Schneider was a better defenceman at the time of the trade than Jonsson will ever be. Clark was also better than Henderickson and Haggerty will ever be. The first rounder, though, could be among the top couple in what is considered one of the best drafts in a long time. The move, however, was expected to help Toronto immediately.

Result: Schneider became Toronto's best defenceman, Clark had eight goals and 15 points in 13 games for the Leafs.

Problem: Lousy Defencemen.

Solution: Give them salaries far greater than their worth.

Prognosis: Good for Jamie Macoun and Dimitri Yushkevich, who received more money than they ever dreamed for playing so poorly.

Result: Bald spots on the heads of fans and media from scratching them so much.

Problem: High payroll because of inflated salaries handed out by Fletcher.

Solution: Give away Dave Andreychuk to New Jersey for some draft picks.

Prognosis: Andreychuk's best days were long gone, but with the Leafs struggling to make the playoffs, it might not have been the best time to dump him.

Result: Andreychuk had almost the same stats as Clark did for Toronto, 8-5-13 in 15 games, but didn't get the Devils into the playoffs.

Problem: Pitiful defence just before the trading deadline.
Solution: None.
Prognosis: No excuse, thinking the players they had on the blueline were good enough.
Result: They weren't.

Problem: Payroll too high, after the season.
Solution: Dump Mike Gartner and Dave Gagner.
Prognosis: They were getting on in years, but they don't have anybody to replace them.
Result: Higher ticket prices.

Problem: Lousy team and one of the worst defences in the league.
Solution: Sign some good free agents over the summer.
Prognosis: Toronto signed winger Scott Pearson, a player who couldn't crack the weak Buffalo lineup on a regular basis.
Result: Toronto is out of the running for the medals.

TEAM PREVIEW

GOAL: Felix Potvin has been doing the same thing for a couple years now, so he officially qualifies for a label: brilliant at times, terrible other times; concentration lapses lead to inconsistency; lets in bad goals too frequently.

Potvin hasn't risen to elite status among NHL goaltenders, as predicted. He could though, if he was at his best more often. Maybe he's one of those goalies who could benefit from more time off. Not because he gets tired physically, but to keep him prepared mentally for when he does play.

Interim coach, Nick Beverley, might have had something similar in mind when he declared that Don Beaupre, acquired from Ottawa, would be splitting the netminding chores. That plan was quickly scrapped, however, when Beaupre played like a stiff.

That meant a mediocre Potvin was still better than the backup, something that didn't happen when Damian Rhodes was around. Rhodes was an excellent backup who rarely disappointed when he got his chance. Too good, obviously, considering how well he played for the Senators.

The Leafs can't get by without a competent backup, so if Beaupre doesn't play better, look for changes.

DEFENCE: If they're not the worst defence in the league, they're pretty close. Mathieu Schneider is a good one. The rest aren't.

Dave Ellett, Larry Murphy and Jamie Macoun have long since seen their best days. Dimitri Yushkevich finished his best days the first week or so of last season. Matt Martin isn't getting much opportunity, and Rob Zettler is the designated press box sitter.

Murphy had a good offensive season.

GOALTENDER	GPI	MINS	AVG	W	L	T	EN	SO	GA	SA	SV %
DAMIAN RHODES	11	624	2.79	4	5	1	0	0	29	301	.904
FELIX POTVIN	69	4009	2.87	30	26	11	4	2	192	2135	.910
DON BEAUPRE	8	336	4.64	0	5	0	1	0	26	170	.847
TOR TOTALS	82	4989	3.03	34	36	12	5	2	252	2611	.903

Defensively, he was terrible. Maybe the Leafs knew what they were getting when they obtained him, but it took most by surprise. His defensive deficiencies are almost too great to compensate for the offence.

A good name for this group would be "The Pylon Defence" because that's how easily opposing forwards go around them. Any pressure in their own end and they'll happily hand the puck over.

Despite their veteran status, they also made bad decisions on when to join the play offensively. They probably gave up as many two-on-ones as any team in the league.

One defenceman who played with heart, and put the team first, was Todd Gill. Gill is now a Shark.

A positive note, besides the play of Schneider, was that Macoun was able to set a record. He played 82 games without scoring a goal, the most by any player in NHL history. Quite an accomplishment.

Zettler is probably in the record books too, if they had a record like this in the book. He is on a streak of 225 consecutive games without scoring a goal.

The Leafs could improve at this position by going out and getting four or five NHL defencemen. Failing that, they need a couple big guys, who play like big guys, and can keep up with the play.

FORWARD: We're starting to run out of ways to say how bad the Leafs are, so we'll just say the forward situation is...bad.

Doug Gilmour has had a great career, but he's no longer an impact player. Wendel Clark has had a great career, but he's no longer an impact player. Kirk Muller has had a great career, but he's no longer an impact player either. This is a recording....

The Leafs do have one impact forward -

Mats Sundin - who doesn't want to play like one. Still, he's the best of the bunch, and with the right linemates can score 100 points. The right linemates are not on the Leafs, however.

The above are the players expected to carry the scoring load for Toronto - pretty sad. They're pinning any additional hopes on two Europeans - Fredrik Modin and Sergei Berezin. Before any of those two have ever played an NHL game, they're pencilled in as members of the second line. Gee...better start preparing for a Stanley Cup parade.

The Leafs did acquire Jamie Baker over the summer, a useful defensive centre who does his best scoring when his team is shorthanded. Last year, he was tied for second in the league, behind Mario Lemieux, with six shorthanded markers.

Then, they've got Todd Warriner, who got a chance at playing regularly because they had nobody else; Brandon Convery, a player deemed a non-prospect as early as last season, but did well with seven points in 11 games for Toronto; Wayne Presley, a decent defensive forward; Mike Craig, a chronic underachiever; Mark Kolesar, a minor league fill-in; and free agent signee and former Leaf, Scott Pearson, who couldn't even cut it as a Buffalo Sabre.

Mike Gartner, who led the team in goals last season, was dumped to Phoenix because of his salary and age; Dave Gagner was handed over to Calgary for the same reason.

So, is there anything positive we can say? Uhhh...ummm...ahhhh....

Nope.

Hold on, not so fast. Sit back down.

The Leafs were one of the top shooting teams in the league last season:

Most Shots Per Game - 1995-96

Boston	34.6
Toronto	32.6
NY Rangers	32.6
Detroit	32.3
Pittsburgh	32.3

So, what do you think about that? Some nice company in that list.

The problem there is that Toronto was 17th in shots against. Normally, a weak team with a lot of shots, means they were playing catchup in the third period, and had to press on offence. Not so in Toronto's case, however, because they had more shots in the first and second periods than they did in the third. Toronto's team shooting percentage was one of the worst in the league, so maybe that had something to do with it.

There is one other hope. If Modin and Berezin both set rookie scoring records the Leafs might make the playoffs.

SPECIAL TEAMS: The Leafs power play was very good at times last season. Too bad they don't have their top power play scorers anymore. Gartner had 15 power play goals and Andreychuk had 12. Doug Gilmour was next, with just 10.

Clark should be scoring more power play goals, however, and so should Sundin. They do have an excellent point duo, with Murphy and Schneider, so it shouldn't be too big a problem area.

While shorthanded, the Leafs could score a lot of goals. Sundin and Baker were second in the league with six last year, Gilmour can score when down a man, and it's Presley's specialty.

POWER PLAY	G	ATT	PCT	
Overall	83	438	18.9%	(9th NHL)
Home	47	220	21.4%	(8th NHL)
Road	36	218	16.5%	(16th NHL)

9 SHORT HANDED GOALS ALLOWED (T-7th NHL)

PENALTY KILLING	G	TSH	PCT	
Overall	70	403	82.6%	(T-11th NHL)
Home	28	185	84.9%	(8th NHL)
Road	42	218	80.7%	(17th NHL)

11 SHORT HANDED GOALS SCORED (T-12th NHL)

COACHING AND MANAGEMENT: In the end, the coaching job of the Leafs went to the guy who wanted it most, not the guy the Leafs wanted most.

All the top coaching prospects were rumored to be going to the Leafs, and as they dropped off one by one, Mike Murphy was the one who was left. Tom Renney, Marc Crawford, Terry Crisp, were some of the serious candidates presumably ahead of Murphy.

Not a great show of support for Murphy to know he wasn't one of the top three choices, but he doesn't seem to care, he's just happy to get the job. Fletcher tried to repair the damage by saying Murphy was the man they wanted all along. Yeah, right.

Coaches like a challenge, but what the coaching candidates saw in Toronto might have been just a bit too much. That probably scared them off, knowing there was little they could do with that bunch.

Cliff Fletcher is coming off his worst year. But, at least he tried. That's not the problem with him.

He pays out exhorbitant salaries to undeserving players and then pronounces that because the payroll is too high they have to dump off players and raise ticket prices. Then, during the summer, he gives a huge contract to Yushkevich, a player who wouldn't be playing for most NHL teams.

While free agents were being signed during the summer, Fletcher says he can't understand what other teams are doing, throwing the salary structure out of whack by playing those guys too much.

Ridiculous.

DRAFT

Round	Sel.	Player	Pos	
2	36	Mark Posmyk	D	Czech. Rep.
2	50	Francis Larivee	G	Laval (QMJHL)
3	66	Mike Lankshear	D	Guelph (OHL)
3	68	Konstantin Kalmikov	LW	Detroit (Colonial)
4	86	Jason Sessa	RW	Lake Superior State
4	103	Vladimir Antipov	W	Russia
5	110	Peter Cava	C	Sault Ste. Marie (OHL)
5	111	Brandon Sugden	D	London (OHL)
6	140	Dimitriy Yakushin	D	Pembroke (COJHL)
6	148	Chris Bogas	D	Michigan Univ.
6	151	Lucio Demartinis	LW	Shawinigan (QMJHL)
7	178	Reggie Berg	C	Minnesota U.
8	204	Tomas Kaberle	D	Czech Rep.
9	230	Jared Hope	C	Spokane (WHL)

Lots of quantity, if not quality. Toronto squandered their first round draft pick when they obtained Dimitri Yushkevich. Their 1997 first round pick is gone as well, in a deal with the New York Islanders.

Cliff Fletcher said after the draft that it could be their best ever. That's not saying much, but maybe he thinks all the middle rounders should have been drafted in the first round. That would make the Leafs smarter than 25 other teams. Little chance of that when it comes to drafting.

Thirty-five other selections went by before Toronto got their first treasure, 6-5, 209, defenceman Marek Posmyk from the Czech Republic. He was predicted as a possible first rounder, but some teams weren't impressed with his attitude. Francis Larivee, chosen second by the team is a goalie short on style but big on toughness. He's a scrapper in the Ron Hextall mold, compiling 125 minutes in the QMJHL last season.

With the Toronto farm system so weak, a lot of these players should get the chance to show their stuff that maybe wouldn't normally.

PROGNOSIS: The Leafs are not going to make the playoffs. They're old; weak at every position; have no depth; have no legitimate prospects; have regulars who shouldn't be playing in the NHL; they can't score; and they can't stop other teams from scoring.

Did we leave anything out?

Yes, they can't get the players they need to improve because all the bargaining chips are gone, and they don't want to spend money on free agents.

Meanwhile, virtually every other team in the conference has done things to improve during the summer. The Leafs have done nothing.

PREDICTION:
Central Division: 7th
Western Conference: 10th
Overall: 20th

Team Rankings 1995-96

		Conference Rank	League Rank
Record	34-36-12	4	13
Home	19-15-7	6	16
Away	15-21-5	7	16
Versus Own Conference	27-21-8	3	9
Versus Other Conference	7-15-4	11	24
Team Plus\Minus	-18	8	18
Goals For	247	8	14
Goals Against	252	7	14
Average Shots For	32.6	1	2
Average Shots Against	31.8	9	17
Overtime	4-2-12	5	7
One Goal Games	13-14	6	17
Times outshooting opponent	41	4	10
Versus Teams Over .500	7-22-4	10	22
Versus Teams Under .500	27-14-8	4	11
First Half Record	20-14-7	4	8
Second Half Record	14-22-5	11	22

PLAYOFFS

Results: Lost 4-2 to St. Louis
Record: 2-4
Home: 2-1
Away: 0-3
Goals For: 15 (2.5 per game)

Goals Against: 21 (3.5 per game)
Overtime: 2-1
Power play: 25.0% (2nd)
Penalty Killing: 85.3% (6th)

ALL-TIME LEADERS

GOALS

Darryl Sittler	389
Dave Keon	365
Ron Ellis	332

ASSISTS

Borje Salming	620
Darryl Sittler	527
Dave Keon	493

POINTS

Darryl Sittler	916
Dave Keon	858
Borje Salming	768

BEST INDIVIDUAL SEASONS

GOALS

Rick Vaive	1981-82	54
Dave Andreychuk	1993-94	53
Rick Vaive	1983-84	52

ASSISTS

Doug Gilmour	1992-93	95
Doug Gilmour	1993-94	84
Darryl Sittler	1977-78	72

POINTS

Doug Gilmour	1992-93	127
Darryl Sittler	1977-78	117
Doug Gilmour	1993-94	111

TEAM RECORD

Last 3 years

	GP	W	L	T	Pts	%
1995-96	82	34	36	12	80	.488
1994-95	48	21	19	8	50	.521
1993-94	84	43	29	12	98	.583

Best 3 regular seasons

1950-51	70	41	16	13	95	.679
1934-35	48	30	14	4	64	.667
1940-41	48	28	14	6	62	.646

Worst 3 regular seasons

1918-19	18	5	13	0	10	.278
1984-85	80	20	52	8	48	.300
1987-88	80	21	49	10	52	.325

Most Goals (min. 70 game schedule)

1989-90	337
1980-81	322
1985-86	311

Fewest Goals (min. 70 game schedule)

1954-55	147
1953-54	152
1955-56	153

Most Goals Against (min. 70 game schedule)

1983-84	387
1985-86	386
1981-82	380

Fewest Goals Against (min. 70 game schedule)

1953-54	131
1954-55	135
1950-51	130

STAT SECTION

Team Scoring Stats

	GP	G	A	PTS	+/-	PIM	SH	Power Play			Short Handed		
								G	A	P	G	A	P
MATS SUNDIN	76	33	50	83	8	46	301	7	23	30	6	0	6
DOUG GILMOUR	81	32	40	72	5-	77	180	10	19	29	2	2	4
LARRY MURPHY	82	12	49	61	2-	34	182	8	31	39	0	0	0
WENDEL CLARK	71	32	26	58	5-	76	237	8	10	18	0	0	0
MIKE GARTNER	82	35	19	54	5	52	275	15	6	21	0	0	0
MATHIEU SCHNEIDER	78	13	41	54	20-	103	191	7	33	40	0	0	0
DAVE GAGNER	73	21	28	49	19-	103	215	7	11	18	0	2	2
KIRK MULLER	51	13	19	32	13-	57	102	7	4	11	0	1	1
TODD GILL	74	7	18	25	15-	116	109	1	3	4	0	2	2
DAVE ELLETT	80	3	19	22	10-	59	153	1	6	7	1	1	2
MIKE CRAIG	70	8	12	20	8-	42	108	1	0	1	0	0	0
TODD WARRINER	57	7	8	15	11-	26	79	1	0	1	0	0	0
WAYNE PRESLEY	80	6	8	14	3	85	113	1	1	2	1	0	1
TIE DOMI	72	7	6	13	3-	297	61	0	0	0	0	0	0
DIMITRI YUSHKEVICH	69	1	10	11	14-	54	96	1	2	3	0	1	1
NICK KYPREOS	61	4	5	9	1	107	49	0	0	0	0	0	0
PETER WHITE	27	5	3	8	14-	0	34	1	1	2	0	0	0
PAUL DIPIETRO	20	4	4	8	3-	4	23	1	1	2	0	0	0
JAMIE MACOUN	82	0	8	8	2	87	74	0	0	0	0	1	1
BRANDON CONVERY	11	5	2	7	7-	4	16	3	0	3	0	0	0
MARK KOLESAR	21	2	2	4	0	14	10	0	0	0	0	0	0
ZDENEK NEDVED	7	1	1	2	1-	6	7	0	1	1	0	0	0
DON BEAUPRE	41	0	2	2	0	31	0	0	0	0	0	0	0
KELLY FAIRCHILD	1	0	1	1	1	2	1	0	0	0	0	0	0
ROB ZETTLER	29	0	1	1	1-	48	11	0	0	0	0	0	0
DAVID HARLOCK	1	0	0	0	0	0	0	0	0	0	0	0	0
SEAN HAGGERTY	1	0	0	0	0	0	0	0	0	0	0	0	0
JAMIE HEWARD	5	0	0	0	1-	0	8	0	0	0	0	0	0
MATT MARTIN	13	0	0	0	1-	14	3	0	0	0	0	0	0
FELIX POTVIN	69	0	0	0	0	4	0	0	0	0	0	0	0

PLAYOFFS

PLAYER	GP	G	A	PTS	+/-	PIM	PP	SH	GW	OT	S
DOUG GILMOUR	6	1	7	8	4-	12	1	0	0	0	15
MIKE GARTNER	6	4	1	5	5-	4	2	0	1	1	18
KIRK MULLER	6	3	2	5	1-	0	2	0	0	0	12
MATS SUNDIN	6	3	1	4	8-	4	2	0	1	1	23
WENDEL CLARK	6	2	2	4	6-	2	1	0	0	0	17
MATHIEU SCHNEIDER	6	0	4	4	7-	8	0	0	0	0	13
TODD WARRINER	6	1	1	2	0	2	0	0	0	0	13
TIE DOMI	6	0	2	2	0	4	0	0	0	0	4
DAVE GAGNER	6	0	2	2	5-	6	0	0	0	0	8
JAMIE MACOUN	6	0	2	2	3	8	0	0	0	0	10
LARRY MURPHY	6	0	2	2	8-	4	0	0	0	0	16
MARK KOLESAR	3	1	0	1	1	2	0	1	0	0	2
DON BEAUPRE	2	0	0	0	0	0	0	0	0	0	0
ROB ZETTLER	2	0	0	0	0	0	0	0	0	0	1
DIMITRI YUSHKEVICH	4	0	0	0	1	0	0	0	0	0	3
NICK KYPREOS	5	0	0	0	0	4	0	0	0	0	5
WAYNE PRESLEY	5	0	0	0	0	2	0	0	0	0	4
BRANDON CONVERY	5	0	0	0	0	2	0	0	0	0	4
MIKE CRAIG	6	0	0	0	0	18	0	0	0	0	7
DAVE ELLETT	6	0	0	0	5-	4	0	0	0	0	16
TODD GILL	6	0	0	0	2-	24	0	0	0	0	9
FELIX POTVIN	6	0	0	0	0	2	0	0	0	0	0

Vancouver Canucks

How about just writing it off. Just forgetting last season ever happened. Why not? It's over and done with and nothing went according to plan anyway. Bure was injured for most of the season so it wasn't as if the A team was out there. Fifty goals and a hundred points from Bure would have made a huge impact on their season, don't you think?

It wasn't all bad. Alexander Mogilny came through in a big way, and there's probably some other positive stuff, too, if we look hard enough.

Instead, let's look at Vancouver from a statistical angle. They've been a weird team in the numbers game in recent years for some reason, and last year was no exception.

* The Canucks scored 278 goals and gave up 278 goals. They had a total of 2,472 shots on net, and gave up 2,743.

* They were sixth on the road in power play percentage, and 25th at home.

* When the Canucks outshot their opponents, they had a 13-16-8 record; when they were outshot they were 17-17-6.

* The Canucks were one of two teams to have a better road record than home record (St. Louis was the other). The winning road record was their fourth season in a row (not counting the labor-shortened season) when they were .500 or better on the road, the only four times they've accomplished that. It was the second best home record in team history, and the fourth worst road record.

* At one time last season, Vancouver was 16-10-8 away from home, second best in the league behind Detroit. Then they lost five in a row on the road and were outscored 24-6.

* Vancouver was 32-14-7 when they scored at least three goals. When they didn't get three goals, they were 0-21-8. They were the only team in the league not to get a win when scoring less than three goals.

* Trevor Linden has scored exactly 33 goals now three different times. He's also scored 30, 31, and 32.

* Cliff Ronning has earned exactly 42 penalty minutes in three of the last five years.

* Markus Naslund scored 15-29-44 in the first half of the season; 7-4-11 in the second half.

* Bret Hedican had three goals in his first 200 NHL games, an average of one goal every 67 games. Then he scored five goals over a seven-game span last year. He added just one more late in the season. To summarize: five career goals in one seven-game period; four goals in his other 230 career games.

* Alexander Mogilny had 55 goals on the season, the same as the total number scored by Jyrki Lumme, Esa Tikkanen and Mike Sillinger. However, Mogilny had just 10 on the power play, while the three others had a total of 23.

* Roman Oksuita scored 16 goals for Vancouver in 56 games before being traded to Anaheim. Ten of those goals came in one 10-game span.

* Russ Courtnall, who not long ago, would never even see the ice when his team had a penalty, led the league in shorthanded points with 9.

* Courtnall scored two goals in the first two games of the season, and then just once in the next 20 games. He had other goal-less droughts of nine games, and two of eight games, but still managed 26 on the season. He scored 7 goals in the first half of the season, and 17 in the second half.

* Guaranteed win night? Almost certain after the Canucks tied. In games following a draw Vancouver had a 12-1-2 record.

* Esa Tikkanen was acquired from New Jersey for a second round draft choice. The Devils had acquired him from St. Louis a couple weeks before, for a third round draft pick. So, the Devils actually traded a third round pick for a second round pick. Nice deal if you can get it.

* When they were good, they were very good. Half of Vancouver's wins came by at least three goals. Only Colorado and Chicago had significantly higher percentages of their games won by that margin.

TEAM PREVIEW

GOAL: There's a new kid in town, and Kirk McLean doesn't want to hear it. Corey Hirsch started out last season as planned, getting spot duty to relieve the number one man. But, then McLean got hurt and Hirsch was impressive, starting and finishing 19 games in a row. He had a winning record over that span and allowed two or fewer goals in eight of the games, a rare accomplishment on the offensive minded team.

When McLean came back, they pretty much split the chores, with McLean getting 14 starts, and Hirsch nine.

But, then in the playoffs, it was all Hirsch. McLean got the initial call in game one, and lasted 20 minutes and 53 seconds, allowing three goals. Hirsch played the rest of the six game series.

McLean is still fairly young for a goaltender, at 30, so he's not ready for the pasture. What the Canucks will probably do is split the goaltending chores a little more evenly during the regular season, or make Hirsch number one and shop McLean around. There would be a lot of interest in McLean, especially as the season goes on and teams become dissatisfied with their goaltending situation. And trading McLean would also reduce a hefty payroll.

Goaltending is usually a coach's preference. Some like to split the duties, others like to go with one and spot the other, and others like to go with the hot hand. More and more, however, teams are sticking with just one guy.

Down on the farm, Mike Fountain continues his strong minor league play. Perhaps, he's earned a shot at the NHL in a backup role.

DEFENCE: This is a problem area for the Canucks because they have too many pussycats back there. Because their forwards aren't all that adept at the defensive side of the game, more defensive-oriented defencemen would be a more prudent plan of non-attack.

With forechecking back in vogue last season because of the crackdown on obstruction fouls, a mobile defence seemed like a good idea. Maybe, but for the same reason, size and toughness for those battles in the corner would also help. Jrkyi Lumme took over the main offensive role after the Canucks tired of Jeff Brown and traded him. Lumme responded with 17 goals, the most of his career, and 54 points, one short of his career high.

That's all the offence they need from the blueline. They have plenty of scoring power up front.

Actually, they do have a lot of size on defence, with 6-2, 200 being about their average. But, toughness? Forget it.

Lumme isn't going to scare anyone physically, which is okay if he's going to handle the offensive duties. He had 50 penalty minutes. Then you've got players like Frantisek Kucera, with 20 PIM; Leif Rohlin with 32; and Adrian Aucoin with 34. These are not scary defencemen, no matter how tall they are.

That's not to say they should run around and take stupid penalties so they can look tougher statistically, but aggressive, physical defencemen are going to get penalties as a matter of course.

The only noted toughness came from Dana Murzyn, and rookie Dean Malkoc, who had 136 PIM in 41 games. Also on defence is speedster Bret Hedican and veteran Dave Babych, who still contributes at age 35. Jassen Cullimore was on board too, but rarely played last year. He's another big guy at 6-5, 225.

The number one prospect for the Canucks is Mattias Ohlund, who was selected 13th overall in the 1994 draft. He's projected as a star, but if you had a dollar for every Swede who was supposed to be an impact player, and wasn't, you could buy the Phoenix Coyotes and move them to Winnipeg.

Ohlund could be the exception, however, because he was named the top defenceman at the World Junior Championships last year. In other words, he didn't just look good playing against other Swedes, which is

GOALTENDER	GPI	MINS	AVG	W	L	T	EN	SO	GA	SA	SV %
COREY HIRSCH	41	2338	2.93	17	14	6	4	1	114	1173	.903
KIRK MCLEAN	45	2645	3.54	15	21	9	4	2	156	1292	.879
AN TOTALS	82	5003	3.33	32	35	15	8	3	278	2473	.888

where a lot of teams make their mistake.

But, once again, he fits the Canuck mold: big, doesn't play physical, skates well, more offensive-minded than defensive-minded. He can stay probably, but lots of the others have to go.

They do have a behemoth in their system: 6-7, 238 Chris McAllister, who was 0-2-2 in 68 games with 142 PIM in Syracuse.

Unless the Canucks make some big-time changes at this position, they will continue to have one of the worst defences in the league. Maybe a good name for them would be, The Friendly Giant Defence.

FORWARD: The Canucks always seem to be looking for a centre. Not just any centre, but a big-scoring impact guy. Trevor Linden does the job there and more, but he could do the same thing playing wing, and there's always this impression that the converted winger is just filling at centre until they get someone else.

Vancouver were rumored to be chasing Joe Nieuwendyk, Pat LaFontaine, and Kirk Muller at various times last season, so obviously they would like to strengthen that position. Unhealthy Mike Ridley is about the only one left there. Jesse Belanger, Josef Beranek and Cliff Ronning were all free agents. Ronning signed with Phoenix the first day that free agent signings were allowed.

There are others who can play there on their current roster, but it's likely they're going to have to go outside the organization.

Rumors during the summer suggested the Canucks were after free agent Wayne Gretzky, and reports say they almost had him. Gretzky, of course, signed with the Rangers.

The Canucks had seven 20-goal scorers last season, so there's scoring balance, and Bure and Mogilny could give them two 50-goal scorers. Mogilny and Bure didn't work out too well on the same line, however, before Bure got hurt. Maybe too much of a good thing. Besides, Mogilny had to switch to left wing and he's more comfortable on the right side. They did try it again and it worked better after the initial failure, so we'll have to see. Having them both on the same line could reduce one or the other's efficiency. Or it could be a major bonanza.

The Canucks can put out two good scoring lines, mixing and matching Bure, Mogilny, Trevor Linden, Martin Gelinas, Mike Ridley, Esa Tikkanen, Mike Sillinger and Markus Naslund. A couple health risks there though, such as Tikkanen and Ridley.

The fourth line is the home of the tough guys, and they have a couple good ones in Gino Odjick and Scott Walker.

The downside to the Canucks' offence is that many of the forwards don't spend much time helping out in their own end. Mogilny, for one, felt when he was in Buffalo that it took too much away from his offence.

SPECIAL TEAMS: The Canucks had a lousy power play, and it shouldn't have been. For some reason Mogilny just didn't score much with the man-advantage, so the Canucks had to have a sniper by committee. Bure, however, is a big-time power play man, so that should improve things this year.

The Canucks traded power play quarterback Jeff Brown to the Hartford Whalers, disatisfied with his play, and his criticism of coaching and management. Lumme took over that role, so it's not a big problem area. And there are lots of defencemen aboard who can play on the power play.

When the Canucks are killing a penalty, opposing clubs better watch out. They set a team record with 18 shorthanded goals, tied for second in the league with Pittsburgh, three behind Colorado. Courtnall tied with Mario Lemieux for the lead league with nine shorthanded points. Mogilny wasn't far behind with seven points, and Gelinas contributed four goals.

Power Play	G	ATT	PCT	
Overall	69	411	16.8%	(17th NHL)
Home	30	204	14.7%	(25th NHL)
Road	39	207	18.8%	(6th NHL)

13 SHORT HANDED GOALS ALLOWED (T-19th NHL)

Penalty Killing	G	TSH	PCT	
Overall	78	418	81.3%	(15th NHL)
Home	37	195	81.0%	(18th NHL)
Road	41	223	81.6%	(10th NHL)

18 SHORT HANDED GOALS SCORED (T-2nd NHL)

COACHING AND MANAGEMENT: For a while it looked like Rick Ley was never going to be fired. He even was fired once on television, four months before it happened. With the whole city screaming for his head, Pat Quinn finally dropped the axe on his pal, and took over behind the bench. He wasn't able to perform miracles, however, and in the off-season they may have found a gem in Tom Renney. Mind you, all new coaches are gems when they're hired, or they wouldn't be hired.

Tom Renney has done an outstanding job with Canada's Olympic and National team, getting results where little was expected. He was also pursued by Toronto and Phoenix before choosing to stay in his home province.

An NHL team with selfish, greedy players is a lot different than coaching a bunch of hungry, young, patriotic players playing for their country, not their next contract. It remains to be seen how he will handle the egos of the NHL superstars.

If we're to believe Ley, then this is a group of selfish players who are not very smart.

Pat Quinn is a good NHL GM who has stockpiled a lot of talent on this team. He's never been able to get the centre he wants and while he recognizes the need for toughness, he's been unable to get it on the defence.

DRAFT

Round	Sel.	Player	Pos	Team
1	12	Josh Holden	C	Regina (WHL)
3	75	Zenith Komarniski	D	Tri-City (WHL)
4	93	Jonas Soling	W	Sweden
5	121	Tyler Prosofsky	C	Kelowna (WHL)
6	147	Nolan McDonald	G	Vermont (NCAA)
7	175	Clint Cabana	D	Medicine Hat (WHL)
8	201	Jeff Scissons	F	Vernon (BCJHL)
9	227	Lubomir Valc	C	Slovakia

The Canucks feel fortunate that Holden lasted as long as he did. He was ranked fourth by Central Scouting, and fourth by *The Hockey News.* He's not the big centre the Canucks are always looking for, at 5-11, 167, but he's a big-time scorer, getting 57-55-112 for Regina. Holden holds one of the stranger stats of the year. He had 105 penalty minutes last season, but had eight 10-minute misconducts.

PROGNOSIS: The Canucks are going to be better than last year, just based on Bure's return alone. They should be one of the top scoring teams in the league, but since most of their scorers don't check, they're going to give up a lot of goals unless they improve on defence.

New coach Tom Renney might be the difference in this team. He's done a great job wherever he's been before. He's an early candidate for best new coach, and if he can do the job, the Canucks might be this year's turnaround team.

PREDICTION:

Pacific Division: 2nd

Western Conference: 3rd

Overall: 7th

Team Rankings 1995-96

		Conference Rank	League Rank
Record	32-35-15	7	16
Home1	5-19-7	10	22
Away	17-16-8	4	6
Versus Own Conference	23-22-11	5	14
Versus Other Conference	9-13-4	9	18
Team Plus\Minus	+9	5	10
Goals For	278	4	7
Goals Against	278	8	18
Average Shots For	30.1	6	13
Average Shots Against	30.1	6	13
Overtime	1-4-15	12	20
One Goal Games	8-10	10	21
Times outshooting opponent	37	7	15
Versus Teams Over .500	7-17-6	8	19
Versus Teams Under .500	25-18-9	5	14
First Half Record	14-16-11	10	18
Second Half Record	18-19-4	6	15

PLAYOFFS

Results: Lost to Colorado 4-2

Record: 2-4

Home: 1-2

Away: 1-2

Goals For: 17 (2.8 per game)

Goals Against: 24 (4.0 per game)

Overtime: 0-1

Power play: 17.9% (7th)

Penalty Killing: 77.8% (14th)

ALL-TIME LEADERS

GOALS

Stan Smyl	262
Tony Tanti	250
Trevor Linden	231

ASSISTS

Stan Smyl	411
Thomas Gradin	353
Dennis Kearns	290

POINTS

Stan Smyl	673
Thomas Gradin	550
Trevor Linden	508

BEST INDIVIDUAL SEASONS

GOALS

Pavel Bure	1993-94	60
Pavel Bure	1992-93	60
Alexander Mogilny	1995-96	55

ASSISTS

Andre Boudrias	1974-75	62
Andre Boudrias	1973-74	59
Thomas Gradin	1983-84	57

POINTS

Pavel Bure	1992-93	110
Alexander Mogilny	1995-96	107
Pavel Bure	1993-94	107

TEAM RECORD

Last 3 years

	GP	W	L	T	Pts	%
1995-96	82	32	35	15	79	.482
1994-95	48	18	18	12	48	.500
1993-94	84	41	40	3	84	.506

Best 3 regular seasons

1992-93	84	46	29	9	101	.601
1991-92	80	42	27	12	96	.600
1974-75	80	38	32	10	86	.538

Worst 3 regular seasons

1971-72	78	20	50	8	48	.308
1972-73	78	22	47	9	53	.340
1977-78	80	27	43	17	57	.359

Most Goals (min. 70 game schedule)

1992-93	346
1983-84	306
1982-83	303

Fewest Goals (min. 70 game schedule)

1971-72	203
1978-79	217
1973-74	224

Most Goals Against (min. 70 game schedule)

1984-85	401
1972-73	339
1985-86	333

Fewest Goals Against (min. 70 game schedule)

1991-92	250
1988-89	253
1974-75	254

STAT SECTION

Team Scoring Stats

	GP	G	A	PTS	+/-	PIM	SH	Power Play			Short Handed		
								G	A	P	G	A	P
ALEXANDER MOGILNY	79	55	52	107	14	16	292	10	19	29	5	2	7
TREVOR LINDEN	82	33	47	80	6	42	202	12	18	30	1	3	4
CLIFF RONNING	79	22	45	67	16	42	187	5	10	15	0	0	0
RUSS COURTNALL	81	26	39	65	25	40	205	6	4	10	4	5	9
MARTIN GELINAS	81	30	26	56	8	59	181	3	4	7	4	1	5
MARKUS NASLUND	76	22	33	55	20	42	144	4	4	8	0	0	0
JYRKI LUMME	80	17	37	54	9-	50	192	8	17	25	0	2	2
ESA TIKKANEN	58	14	30	44	1	36	95	8	14	22	1	0	1
JESSE BELANGER	72	20	21	41	5-	14	151	8	13	21	0	0	0
MIKE SILLINGER	74	14	24	38	18-	38	159	7	9	16	1	0	1
BRET HEDICAN	77	6	23	29	8	83	113	1	7	8	0	4	4
DAVE BABYCH	53	3	21	24	5-	38	69	3	6	9	0	1	1
LEIF ROHLIN	56	6	16	22	0	32	72	1	7	8	0	0	0
MIKE RIDLEY	37	6	15	21	3-	29	32	2	3	5	0	0	0
JOSEF BERANEK	61	6	14	20	11-	60	131	0	1	1	0	0	0
JIM DOWD	66	5	15	20	9-	23	76	0	0	0	0	2	2
ADRIAN AUCOIN	49	4	14	18	8	34	85	2	6	8	0	0	0
PAVEL BURE	15	6	7	13	2-	8	78	1	4	5	1	0	1
SCOTT WALKER	63	4	8	12	7-	137	45	0	0	0	1	1	2
DANA MURZYN	69	2	10	12	9	130	68	0	0	0	0	2	2
FRANTISEK KUCERA	54	3	6	9	2	20	77	0	2	2	0	1	1
GINO ODJICK	55	3	4	7	16-	181	59	0	0	0	0	0	0
JIM SANDLAK	33	4	2	6	3-	6	44	0	0	0	1	0	1
BRIAN LONEY	12	2	3	5	2	6	19	0	0	0	0	0	0
JOEY KOCUR	45	1	3	4	7-	68	20	0	0	0	0	0	0
TIM HUNTER	60	2	0	2	8-	122	26	0	0	0	0	0	0
JASSEN CULLIMORE	27	1	1	2	4	21	12	0	0	0	0	0	0
DEAN MALKOC	41	0	2	2	10-	136	8	0	0	0	0	0	0
COREY HIRSCH	41	0	2	2	0	2	0	0	0	0	0	0	0
KIRK MCLEAN	45	0	2	2	0	6	0	0	0	0	0	0	0
LARRY COURVILLE	3	1	0	1	1	0	2	0	0	0	0	0	0
LONNY BOHONOS	3	0	1	1	1	0	3	0	0	0	0	0	0

PLAYOFFS

PLAYER	GP	G	A	PTS	+/-	PIM	PP	SH	GW	OT	S
ALEXANDER MOGILNY	6	1	8	9	1-	8	0	0	0	0	18
TREVOR LINDEN	6	4	4	8	1-	6	2	0	0	0	14
ESA TIKKANEN	6	3	2	5	3-	2	2	0	0	0	13
GINO ODJICK	6	3	1	4	2	6	0	0	2	0	6
RUSS COURTNALL	6	1	3	4	4-	2	0	0	0	0	8
JYRKI LUMME	6	1	3	4	1-	2	1	0	0	0	13
JOSEF BERANEK	3	2	1	3	0	0	0	0	0	0	7
MARKUS NASLUND	6	1	2	3	2-	8	1	0	0	0	16
MARTIN GELINAS	6	1	1	2	1-	12	1	0	0	0	8
JESSE BELANGER	3	0	2	2	0	2	0	0	0	0	3
CLIFF RONNING	6	0	2	2	0	6	0	0	0	0	12
FRANTISEK KUCERA	6	0	1	1	3-	0	0	0	0	0	6
BRET HEDICAN	6	0	1	1	2-	10	0	0	0	0	2
JOEY KOCUR	1	0	0	0	0	0	0	0	0	0	0
KIRK MCLEAN	1	0	0	0	0	0	0	0	0	0	0
JIM DOWD	1	0	0	0	1-	0	0	0	0	0	0
YEVGENY NAMESTNIKOV	1	0	0	0	0	0	0	0	0	0	1
MIKE RIDLEY	5	0	0	0	3-	2	0	0	0	0	3
JIM SANDLAK	5	0	0	0	2	2	0	0	0	0	5
LEIF ROHLIN	5	0	0	0	1-	0	0	0	0	0	7
DANA MURZYN	6	0	0	0	0	25	0	0	0	0	2
MIKE SILLINGER	6	0	0	0	5-	2	0	0	0	0	5
COREY HIRSCH	6	0	0	0	0	2	0	0	0	0	0
ADRIAN AUCOIN	6	0	0	0	5-	2	0	0	0	0	7

Townsend's Ultimate Pool Picks

Like who knew? Last year, in *The Hockey Annual* pool section, I told you Mario Lemieux would finish 44th in scoring. He would have too, if he hadn't stayed healthy and scored so darned many points.

One wrong out of 300 isn't bad.

This year, I've changed the pool format. Instead of 300 names, there are how ever many are predicted to score at least 40 points. There aren't any pools picking 300 players anyway.

Not all the players are going to score at their predicted range, of course. We can't forecast injuries, and certain other things. We're assuming regulars will play 82 games, with a few exceptions, such as Mario Lemieux.

With each of the players, their games and points from last year are included, along with their age, and a comment. The comment will point out pertinent information about that player that should help with your draft selections.

Many different factors are considered when compiling the ratings. Some of them are outlined below, along with other information you need to know to be successful in your hockey pool.

AGE

It's been proven (by me, actually) that most players have their best NHL season between the ages of 24 and 28. Those are the peak years, but recently more older players are coming up with good seasons. There are a couple reasons.

Money, of course, is a factor. Huge contracts and potential free agency are an incentive for players not to rest on their laurels. Unrestricted free agency kicks in at 31-years-old.

Free agency means veteran players can go to a team situation that better suits their talents, which in turn means their chances of success are greater. Given a choice, free agents will pick a club looking for a first line left winger, than a team looking for a third-liner, even if the money is the same.

A lot of teams are considering veterans a more attractive part of their game plan. They like the experience they provide, the winning history they might have, the patience they bring, the attitude they carry over from a previous era, and the ability to provide on-ice tutoring for younger players.

Another factor to consider is that if a player is a playmaker, as opposed to a goal scorer, then age is not as important. Older guys sometimes have more patience and smarts to get the puck to the people who can put it into the net.

As well, defencemen often become more valuable with age, probably because it's such a difficult position to learn. A 32-year-old defenceman is not the same as a forward of the same age.

Ages are provided in the chart later in the chapter. Even though older players have been playing better, it's still wise to consider the peak ages for point production. You would expect a career season out of 25-year-old before a player who is 32.

Below are the ages of the top 10 scorers from last season, as of October 1 of last year. Most fit within the time frame of peak years.

Mario Lemieux	Pit	29
Jaromir Jagr	Pit	23
Joe Sakic	Col	26
Ron Francis	Pit	32
Peter Forsberg	Col	22
Eric Lindros	Phi	22
Paul Kariya	Ana	21
Teemu Selanne	Wpg/Ana	25
Alexander Mogilny	Van	26
Sergei Fedorov	Det	25

DEPTH CHART

So much depends on the role expected of a player and how the coach utilizes him. Put anyone in the league on the Pittsburgh power play and watch their scoring stats soar.

Teams normally have one top scoring line, a secondary scoring second line, a checking third line, and a fourth line for enforcers and extras.

A player's point totals are a direct result of where they fit in that scheme, as well as which other players are slotted with them. Of course, lines don't stay together very much anymore, so a player can move around a lot.

In some cases, it's actually better, for a player's point potential, to have worse players on his team. That way, he won't be replaced on the power play or top line, and it be that more responsibility means enhanced performance. Brian Bradley is probably a good example of that on Tampa Bay. If he hadn't had the good fortune to show his stuff in Tampa Bay, it would have been unlikely he would have somewhere else.

Sometimes, though, we can be fooled. Last year, rookie Dave Roche started out on Mario Lemieux's line in Pittsburgh. Smart poolsters may have snapped him up early, but he didn't last there long, and it would have been a wasted pick.

EMERGING PLAYERS

Many of the players who end up being scoring stars in the NHL, start showing that ability in their third or fourth season. Look for players who were big junior scorers or high draft selections. If they haven't produced much in their first two seasons, but still played a lot, they have definite breakout possibilities.

POWER PLAY

When selecting defencemen, especially, the power play is the most important consideration. If they're one of the top two on the power play point their value is high; if not, forget it. Most offensive defencemen are labelled, so we know who they are, and there aren't many surprises. Much of their expected point production, therefore, depends on their team. Kevin Hatcher, for example, traded from Dallas to Pittsburgh, gets a big lift because of the rest of that power play unit.

In each team's section in the book, scoring stats include their power play points. Those will give you an idea of who was playing with the man-advantage last year. The more of those players you can get, the better.

TRADED PLAYERS

Players can get stale, so going to a new team with new things to prove almost always gives them a lift.

If your pool has a provision for changing players during the year, look closely at those who have been traded during the season. They've got new motivation, and they get it immediately. But, be careful. Often traded players who show a big rise in point production, revert to form the following season.

EUROPEANS

They're often unpredictable with their scoring. One year they're up, the next year they're down, and then the next year they're back up again. Without going into all the reasons here, just keep that in mind when selecting your players.

Europeans are also more likely to make a bigger immediate splash when they enter the league, part of the reason being that they're usually a couple years older.

Sometimes, too, they can make teams in training camp, and take us by surprise because we've never heard of them. Keep an eye on training camp developments.

PRE-SEASON

Your best bet is to almost completely ignore the exhibition schedule. Year after year it proves to have nothing to do with what happens during the regular season.

The only benefit you might get is that it will help determine new players. Even if they're playing a lot, it's no guarantee they're going to make the big club, however, because the team might just want to get a better look at them.

PREPARATION

There's no substitute for preparation, unless you have dumb luck. Do your homework.

One thing you can do is look at players who missed a lot of time last year because of injury. Other poolsters might miss them because they're not as high on the scoring lists. Highlight them, and that in itself could be your draft key to victory. The trick is to also pick the players others have rated highly, and save your sleepers for later rounds.

100 POINT POTENTIAL

Player	Team	Age	GP	Pts	Comment
Lemieux,M	Pit	30	70	161	Injury situation only concern
Jagr	Pit	24	82	149	Most points in NHL last two seasons
Lindros	Phi	23	73	115	Could be first overall if Lemieux injured
Kariya	Ana	22	82	108	100 point man for next 10 years
Bure, P	Van	25	15	13	Big return from injury season
Selanne	Ana	26	79	108	Dynamic duo with Kariya
Forsberg	Col	23	82	116	Was 5th in scoring in 1st full NHL season
Sakic	Col	27	82	120	Post Stanley Cup letdown may mean fewer points
Gretzky	NYR	35	80	102	Playing with his buddy Messier now
Mogilny	Van	27	79	107	Finally gets to play with Bure in lineup
Fleury	Cgy	28	80	96	Will have help this year with Reichel back
Fedorov	Det	26	78	107	Few are more consistently good
Tkachuk	Pho	24	76	98	Ready to hit 100-point mark for first time
Turgeon	Mtl	27	80	96	Great linemates; can't lose
Zhamnov	Pho	26	58	59	Is capable of 100 points on this team
Oates	Bos	34	70	92	Great playmaker but running out of linemates
Bondra	Wsh	28	67	80	More pp points and less injuries = 100 points
Francis	Pit	33	77	119	Hasn't started showing age yet

80-99 POINT POTENTIAL

Player	Team	Age	GP	Pts	Comment
Messier	NYR	35	74	99	Renewed determination with buddy Gretzky
Modano	Dal	25	36	81	Will be revitalized with improved team
LeClair	Phi	27	82	97	Can't go wrong with Lindros at centre
LaFontaine	Buf	31	76	91	Would get more points on good team
Damphousse	Mtl	28	80	94	Has had four seasons in the 90-point range
Roenick	Chi	26	66	67	Will rebound from two mediocre seasons
Recchi	Mtl	27	82	78	Was off-season for him; will move back up
Reichel	Cgy	25	-	-	Returns from Germany - 93 points NHL high
Palffy	NYI	24	81	87	NHL's most improved player last year
Shanahan	Hfd	27	74	78	Came on big after slow start and injuries
Hull,B	StL	32	70	83	Is slowing down, but not too much yet
Weight	Edm	25	82	104	Should drop some after career season
Brind'Amour	Phi	26	82	87	Overshadowed, but always gets his points
Yzerman	Det	31	80	95	No more career years but still up there
Bourque	Bos	35	82	82	Ageless wonder, but has to slow down sometime
Verbeek	Dal	32	69	82	Sniper for power play - makes others better
Renberg	Phi	24	51	43	Good sleeper pick, coming off injury
Linden	Van	26	82	80	Should benefit from Bure's return
Leetch	NYR	28	82	85	Top scoring defenceman in league last season
Yashin	Ott	22	46	39	Pure scorer, despite off-ice troubles
Nedved	Pit	25	80	99	Great year, but can be inconsistent

60-79 POINT POTENTIAL

Nieuwendyk	Dal	30	52	32	Will put good numbers back on the board
Housley	Wsh	32	81	68	Few better defencemen on power play
Murphy,J	StL	28	70	51	Should play hard every game, for Keenan
Arnott	Edm	21	64	59	Will improve off troubled season
Sundin	Tor	25	87	83	Tough call - potential for more, but iffy
Juneau	Wsh	28	80	64	Off year for him - can score much higher
Bradley	TB	31	75	79	Has led TB in scoring four years in a row
Kamensky	Col	30	81	85	Can't lose with Sakic or Forsberg as centre
Zubov	Dal	26	64	66	Offence only - but one of best at that
Nolan	SJ	25	81	69	One of best power forwards in the game
Janney	Pho	28	84	82	Playmaker with good scorers to pass to
Kozlov	Det	24	82	73	Guaranteed in the 70's
Pivonka	Wsh	28	73	81	81 points was career high
Sandstrom	Pit	32	58	70	One of league's most injury-prone
Audette	Buf	27	23	25	Good sleeper pick; coming off injury
MacInnis	StL	33	82	61	Coming off worst career season; so tough call
Amonte	Chi	26	81	63	No competition for top RW, with Murphy gone
Robitaille	NYR	29	77	69	Faded badly; could rebound
Coffey	Det	35	76	74	Can't keep it up forever
Green	NYI	25	69	69	One of league's most improved last year
Graves	NYR	28	82	58	Should do better after sub-par season
Gilmour	Tor	33	81	72	Glory days are history
Kovalev	NYR	23	81	58	Might finally emerge, with Gretzky on board
Lemieux,C	Col	31	79	71	Has history of up and down regular seasons
Thomas	NJ	33	81	61	Getting up in age; but one of best on NJ
Chelios	Chi	34	81	71	Norris Trophy winner never ages
Primeau	Det	24	74	52	Should score more than last year
Tocchet	Bos	32	71	60	Too many injuries; getting too old
Sanderson	Hfd	24	81	65	Has the potential to score much more
Ozolinsh	Col	24	73	54	PP pointman for great power play
Ronning	Pho	31	79	67	Over from Vancouver - has new life
Dawe	Buf	23	67	50	Still improving
Perreault	LA	25	78	49	Pure scorer keeps getting better
Friesen	SJ	20	79	46	Third year - breakout time
Brown,J	Hfd	30	76	55	One of top offensive defensemen in league
Gratton	TB	21	82	38	Breakout season
Suter	Chi	32	82	67	41 PP points - 3rd among defencemen
Rucinsky	Mtl	25	78	75	Had excellent scoring streak; hard to repeat
Courtnall,R	Van	31	81	65	Slowed down some to mid-range scorer
Clark	Tor	29	71	58	History of injury problems
Smolinski	Pit	24	81	64	Has probably reached point peak with this team
Nikolishin	Hfd	23	61	51	Playmaker improving steadily

Iginla	Cgy	19	-	-	Rookie-of-the-year candidate
Daze	Chi	21	80	53	Watch out for sophomore jinx
Hamrlik	TB	22	82	65	Best young offensive defenceman in league

40-59 POINT POTENTIAL

Hatcher,K	Plt	30	74	41	Takes over on PP point from Zubov
Nicholls	SJ	35	59	60	Age not as important for playmakers
O'Neill	Hfd	20	65	27	Possible breakout season, but might be early
Bonk	Ott	20	76	35	This could be his year
Lumme	Van	28	80	54	Top man for Canucks power play point
Bertuzzi	NYI	21	76	39	Second-year player just getting started
Khristich	LA	27	76	64	No Gretzky this year
Guerin	NJ	25	80	53	Could be his breakout season
Murphy,L	Tor	35	82	61	Age is showing
Berard	NYI	19	-	-	Defenceman is possible rookie-of-the-year
Gagner	Cgy	31	73	49	Look for good comeback season
Cassels	Hfd	27	81	63	Has career high of 85 points
Ciger	Edm	26	78	70	Might decide to play in Europe this season
Konowalchuk	Wsh	24	70	45	Could be breakout year
Lidstrom	Det	26	81	67	Half of great pp point, with Coffey
Koivu	Mtl	21	82	45	Getting used to NHL style
Burridge	Buf	30	74	58	Could play with LaFontaine and Audette
Muller	Tor	30	51	32	Can do better than last year couple of years
Young	Col	29	81	60	Dependable scoring range;rarely misses a game
MacLean	NJ	31	76	48	Often follows poor seasons with great ones
Hogue	Dal	29	78	64	Inconsistent scorer
Schneider	Tor	27	78	54	Last year's points were a career high
Whitney	SJ	24	60	51	Misses a lot of games, but points improving
Duchesne	Ott	31	62	36	Only offensive defenceman on Ottawa
Oliver	Edm	25	80	39	Good pp performer, but inconsistent
Plante	Buf	25	76	56	Good comeback season after sophomore jinx
Emerson	Hfd	29	81	58	Coming off lowest point season; could improve
Alfredsson	Ott	23	82	61	Last year's rookie-of-the-year
Johnson,G	Det	25	60	40	All he needs is full-time work
Deadmarsh	Col	21	78	48	Will keep getting better
Blake	LA	26	6	3	Offensive defenceman coming off injury
Turcotte	SJ	28	68	43	Averages 62 points per 82 career games
Hawerchuk	Phi	33	82	61	Scoring is fading quickly with age
King,D	NYI	29	61	32	Has a chance to return to form
Titov	Cgy	30	82	67	Should move down to second line
Stumpel	Bos	24	76	54	Second line centre - nobody to pass to
Ferraro	LA	32	76	60	Erratic career season totals; age now a factor
Andreychuk	NJ	33	76	57	Fading, but still has power play value

Kovalenko	Mtl	26	77	56	Could move down depth chart in Montreal
Ricci	Col	24	62	27	Big rebounding possibility - 78 is career high
Harvey	Dal	21	69	29	Possible breakout season
Selivanov	TB	25	79	52	Was top goal-scorer for TB
Kron	Hfd	29	77	50	Season point totals have been erratic
Gartner	Pho	36	82	54	Will still be scoring 30 goals when he's 50
Falloon	Phi	24	71	51	May have found his way in Philly
Quinn	Pit	31	63	45	Has changed teams 10 teams over career
Cullen	TB	32	76	50	Getting older, but dependable so far for TB
Gelinas	Van	26	81	56	Coming off career high - could go down a bit
Peake	Wsh	23	62	36	Among league leaders in injuries
Stevens,K	LA	31	61	36	Can't be as bad as last year
McInnis	NYI	25	74	46	Could be on NYI's top line
Bure,V	Mtl	22	77	42	Surprise season; will be tough to repeat
Rucchin	Ana	25	64	44	Could play with Selanne and Kariya
Numminen	Pho	27	74	54	Points might go down if Tverdovsky's goes up
Klima	TB	31	67	52	Has settled into 50-point range
Malakhov	Mtl	28	61	28	Will rebound - with Montreal or not
Galley	Buf	33	78	54	Had 35 power play points
Richer	NJ	30	73	32	Has rebounded from poor seasons before
Ragnarsson	SJ	25	71	39	Pointman on power play
Corson	StL	30	77	46	between 47 and 54 points last 5 full seasons
Larionov	Det	35	73	73	Had great season, but look for huge drop
Karpov	Ana	25	37	17	Time to step up and show potential
Donato	Bos	27	82	49	Very rarely misses a game
McEachern	Ott	27	82	53	Comes over from Boston
Niedermayer	NJ	23	79	33	Might step up big offensively
Zhitnik	Buf	23	80	35	Should be scoring more than he has
Johnson, C	LA	24	60	24	Has opportunity now to show his stuff
Savage	Mtl	25	75	33	Showed something; has to show it more often
Jones	Wsh	27	68	41	Not great scorer, but dependable
Nylander	Cgy	23	73	55	Better scorers on board - should move down
Drake	Pho	27	69	39	Career high is 44 points
Ciccarelli	Det	36	64	43	Risky pick at age, but could be worth it
Miller,Kev	Chi	31	81	53	Between 44 and 53 points each season of career
Rolston	NJ	23	58	24	Ready to step up for bigger role
Daigle	Ott	21	50	17	He just has to get better
Tikkanen	Van	31	58	44	Injuries a problem
Desjardins	Phi	27	80	47	Gets to play point on Philly power play
Andersson	NYI	25	48	26	Good rookie season start
Craven	Chi	32	66	47	Age plus injuries equals risky business
Marchant	Edm	23	81	38	Breakout possibility, but unlikely
Oksuita	Ana	26	70	51	Undependable but could be PP sniper

Olczyk	LA	30	51	49	Not the same linemates he had in Winnipeg
Pronger	StL	21	78	25	Improvement has been slow, but getting there
Tverdovsky	Pho	20	82	30	Could be his year to break out offensively
Elik	Bos	30	59	46	Scored plenty when with Oates
Adams	Dal	33	66	43	Won't be counted on as much for scoring
May	Duf	24	79	44	Seems to have settled into his scoring range
Czerkawski	Edm	24	70	40	Mystery pick - chance of points going way up
MacIver	Pho	32	71	53	Power play specialist
Courtnall	StL	34	69	40	Age could be too big a factor
Todd	Pit	26	74	43	Handles defensive duties, but can score too
Olausson	Ana	30	56	24	Injury prone but could get pp point
Holzinger	Buf	23	58	20	Poor rookie season; but could break out
Yachmenev	LA	21	80	53	Won't put up same points without Gretzky
Sykora	NJ	19	63	42	Needs to improve consistency, but still young
Satan	Edm	21	62	35	Talented, but far from sure thing
Kozlov	SJ	21	62	19	Could be breakout year
Naslund	Van	23	76	55	Dropped to almost nothing in second half

TOWNSEND'S STAT GRAB BAG

EASTERN CONFERENCE

Northeast Division

	GP	W	L	T	GF	GA	PTS	PCTG
PITTSBURGH	82	49	29	4	362	284	102	.622
BOSTON	82	40	31	11	282	269	91	.555
MONTREAL	82	40	32	10	265	248	90	.549
HARTFORD	82	34	39	9	237	259	77	.470
BUFFALO	82	33	42	7	247	262	73	.445
OTTAWA	82	18	59	5	191	291	41	.250

Atlantic Division

	GP	W	L	T	GF	GA	PTS	PCTG
PHILADELPHIA	82	45	24	13	282	208	103	.628
NY RANGERS	82	41	27	14	272	237	96	.585
FLORIDA	82	41	31	10	254	234	92	.561
WASHINGTON	82	39	32	11	234	204	89	.543
TAMPA BAY	82	38	32	12	238	248	88	.537
NEW JERSEY	82	37	33	12	215	202	86	.524
NY ISLANDERS	82	22	50	10	229	315	54	.329

WESTERN CONFERENCE

Central Division

	GP	W	L	T	GF	GA	PTS	PCTG
DETROIT	82	62	13	7	325	181	131	.799
CHICAGO	82	40	28	14	273	220	94	.573

	GP	W	L	T	GF	GA	PTS	PCTG
TORONTO	82	34	36	12	247	252	80	.488
ST LOUIS	82	32	34	16	219	248	80	.488
WINNIPEG	82	36	40	6	275	291	78	.476
DALLAS	82	26	42	14	227	280	66	.402

Pacific Division

	GP	W	L	T	GF	GA	PTS	PCTG
COLORADO	82	47	25	10	326	240	104	.634
CALGARY	82	34	37	11	241	240	79	.482
VANCOUVER	82	32	35	15	278	278	79	.482
ANAHEIM	82	35	39	8	234	247	78	.476
EDMONTON	82	30	44	8	240	304	68	.415
LOS ANGELES	82	24	40	18	256	302	66	.402
SAN JOSE	82	20	55	7	252	357	47	.287

TEAM STANDINGS BY CONFERENCE

Eastern Conference

	GP	W	L	T	GF	GA	PTS	PCTG
PHILADELPHIA	82	45	24	13	282	208	103	.628
PITTSBURGH	82	49	29	4	362	284	102	.622
NY RANGERS	82	41	27	14	272	237	96	.585
FLORIDA	82	41	31	10	254	234	92	.561
BOSTON	82	40	31	11	282	269	91	.555
MONTREAL	82	40	32	10	265	248	90	.549
WASHINGTON	82	39	32	11	234	204	89	.543
TAMPA BAY	82	38	32	12	238	248	88	.537
NEW JERSEY	82	37	33	12	215	202	86	.524
HARTFORD	82	34	39	9	237	259	77	.470
BUFFALO	82	33	42	7	247	262	73	.445
NY ISLANDERS	82	22	50	10	229	315	54	.329
OTTAWA	82	18	59	5	191	291	41	.250

Western Conference

	GP	W	L	T	GF	GA	PTS	PCTG
DETROIT	82	62	13	7	325	181	131	.799
COLORADO	82	47	25	10	326	240	104	.634

CHICAGO	82	40	28	14	273	220	94	.573
TORONTO	82	34	36	12	247	252	80	.488
ST LOUIS	82	32	34	16	219	248	80	.488
CALGARY	82	34	37	11	241	240	79	.482
VANCOUVER	82	32	35	15	278	278	79	.482
WINNIPEG	82	36	40	6	275	291	78	.476
ANAHEIM	82	35	39	8	234	247	78	.476
EDMONTON	82	30	44	8	240	304	68	.415
DALLAS	82	26	42	14	227	280	66	.402
LOS ANGELES	82	24	40	18	256	302	66	.402
SAN JOSE	82	20	55	7	252	357	47	.287

OVERALL STANDINGS

	GP	W	L	T	GF	GA	PTS	PCTG
DETROIT	82	62	13	7	325	181	131	.799
COLORADO	82	47	25	10	326	240	104	.634
PHILADELPHIA	82	45	24	13	282	208	103	.628
PITTSBURGH	82	49	29	4	362	284	102	.622
NY RANGERS	82	41	27	14	272	237	96	.585
CHICAGO	82	40	28	14	273	220	94	.573
FLORIDA	82	41	31	10	254	234	92	.561
BOSTON	82	40	31	11	282	269	91	.555
MONTREAL	82	40	32	10	265	248	90	.549
WASHINGTON	82	39	32	11	234	204	89	.543
TAMPA BAY	82	38	32	12	238	248	88	.537
NEW JERSEY	82	37	33	12	215	202	86	.524
TORONTO	82	34	36	12	247	252	80	.488
ST LOUIS	82	32	34	16	219	248	80	.488
CALGARY	82	34	37	11	241	240	79	.482
VANCOUVER	82	32	35	15	278	278	79	.482
WINNIPEG	82	36	40	6	275	291	78	.476
ANAHEIM	82	35	39	8	234	247	78	.476
HARTFORD	82	34	39	9	237	259	77	.470
BUFFALO	82	33	42	7	247	262	73	.445
EDMONTON	82	30	44	8	240	304	68	.415
DALLAS	82	26	42	14	227	280	66	.402
LOS ANGELES	82	24	40	18	256	302	66	.402
NY ISLANDERS	82	22	50	10	229	315	54	.329
SAN JOSE	82	20	55	7	252	357	47	.287
OTTAWA	82	18	59	5	191	291	41	.250

TEAMS' HOME-AND-ROAD RECORD BY CONFERENCE

HOME
Eastern Conference

	GP	W	L	T	GF	GA	PTS	PCTG
PITTSBURGH	41	32	9	0	215	136	64	.780
PHILADELPHIA	41	27	9	5	143	83	59	.720
FLORIDA	41	25	12	4	137	97	54	.659
NY RANGERS	41	22	10	9	150	122	53	.646
MONTREAL	41	23	12	6	139	122	52	.634
BOSTON	41	22	14	5	147	138	49	.598
TAMPA BAY	41	22	14	5	138	121	49	.598
HARTFORD	41	22	15	4	134	120	48	.585
WASHINGTON	41	21	15	5	124	97	47	.573
NEW JERSEY	41	22	17	2	120	94	46	.561
BUFFALO	41	19	17	5	125	111	43	.524
NY ISLANDERS	41	14	21	6	114	146	34	.415
OTTAWA	41	8	28	5	91	133	21	.256
CONFERENCE TOTAL	533	279	193	61	1,777	1,520	619	.581

Western Conference

	GP	W	L	T	GF	GA	PTS	PCTG
DETROIT	41	36	3	2	172	80	74	.902
COLORADO	41	24	10	7	171	115	55	.671
CHICAGO	41	22	13	6	139	108	50	.610
ANAHEIM	41	22	15	4	132	111	48	.585
WINNIPEG	41	22	16	3	147	139	47	.573
TORONTO	41	19	15	7	129	116	45	.549
CALGARY	41	18	18	5	114	103	41	.500
LOS ANGELES	41	16	16	9	144	144	41	.500
ST LOUIS	41	15	17	9	101	120	39	.476
VANCOUVER	41	15	19	7	146	142	37	.451
DALLAS	41	14	18	9	116	132	37	.451
EDMONTON	41	15	21	5	118	143	35	.427
SAN JOSE	41	12	26	3	139	183	27	.329
CONFERENCE TOTAL	533	250	207	76	1,768	1,636	576	.540
HOME TOTAL	1,066	529	400	137	3,545	3,156	1,195	.561

ROAD
Eastern Conference

	GP	W	L	T	GF	GA	PTS	PCTG
PHILADELPHIA	41	18	15	8	139	125	44	.537
NY RANGERS	41	19	17	5	122	115	43	.524
BOSTON	41	18	17	6	135	131	42	.512
WASHINGTON	41	18	17	6	110	107	42	.512
NEW JERSEY	41	15	16	10	95	108	40	.488
TAMPA BAY	41	16	18	7	100	127	39	.476
MONTREAL	41	17	20	4	126	126	38	.463
PITTSBURGH	41	17	20	4	147	148	38	.463
FLORIDA	41	16	19	6	117	137	38	.463
BUFFALO	41	14	25	2	122	151	30	.366
HARTFORD	41	12	24	5	103	139	29	.354
OTTAWA	41	10	31	0	100	158	20	.244
NY ISLANDERS	41	8	29	4	115	169	20	.244
CONFERENCE TOTAL	533	198	268	67	1,531	1,741	463	.434

Western Conference

	GP	W	L	T	GF	GA	PTS	PCTG
DETROIT	41	26	10	5	153	101	57	.695
COLORADO	41	23	15	3	155	125	49	.598
CHICAGO	41	18	15	8	134	112	44	.537
VANCOUVER	41	17	16	8	132	136	42	.512
ST LOUIS	41	17	17	7	118	128	41	.500
CALGARY	41	16	19	6	127	137	38	.463
TORONTO	41	15	21	5	118	136	35	.427
EDMONTON	41	15	23	3	122	161	33	.402
WINNIPEG	41	14	24	3	128	152	31	.378
ANAHEIM	41	13	24	4	102	136	30	.366
DALLAS	41	12	24	5	111	148	29	.354
LOS ANGELES	41	8	24	9	112	158	25	.305
SAN JOSE	41	8	29	4	113	174	20	.244
CONFERENCE TOTAL	533	202	261	70	1,625	1,804	474	.445
ROAD TOTAL	1,066	400	529	137	3,156	3,545	937	.439

TEAMS' INTER-CONFERENCE RECORD

AGAINST OWN CONFERENCE
Eastern Conference

	GP	W	L	T	GF	GA	PTS	PCTG
PITTSBURGH	56	34	19	3	240	189	71	.634
PHILADELPHIA	56	30	19	7	185	146	67	.598
BOSTON	56	29	20	7	188	177	65	.580
NEW JERSEY	56	28	20	8	155	133	64	.571
NY RANGERS	56	27	19	10	187	160	64	.571
FLORIDA	56	29	22	5	164	153	63	.563
WASHINGTON	56	26	23	7	152	133	59	.527
MONTREAL	56	26	23	7	171	168	59	.527
TAMPA BAY	56	25	23	8	155	170	58	.518
BUFFALO	56	24	27	5	178	182	53	.473
HARTFORD	56	19	29	8	143	176	46	.411
NY ISLANDERS	56	14	34	8	157	206	36	.321
OTTAWA	56	10	43	3	126	208	23	.205
CONFERENCE TOTAL	728	321	321	86	2,201	22,01	728	.500

Western Conference

	GP	W	L	T	GF	GA	PTS	PCTG
DETROIT	56	43	6	7	236	125	93	.830
COLORADO	56	34	17	5	229	164	73	.652
TORONTO	56	27	21	8	179	166	62	.554
CHICAGO	56	25	19	12	174	149	62	.554
VANCOUVER	56	23	22	11	189	190	57	.509
ST LOUIS	56	23	23	10	147	159	56	.500
WINNIPEG	56	25	26	5	189	196	55	.491
CALGARY	56	22	26	8	166	171	52	.464
DALLAS	56	21	26	9	157	183	51	.455
ANAHEIM	56	22	30	4	153	174	48	.429
EDMONTON	56	19	30	7	169	211	45	.402
LOS ANGELES	56	15	26	15	180	208	45	.402
SAN JOSE	56	13	40	3	165	237	29	.259
CONFERENCE TOTAL	728	312	312	104	2,333	2,333	728	.500

VS. OWN
CONFERENCE   1,456 633   633   190   4,534   4,534   1,456 .500

AGAINST OTHER CONFERENCE
Eastern Conference

	GP	W	L	T	GF	GA	PTS	PCTG
PHILADELPHIA	26	15	5	6	97	62	36	.692
NY RANGERS	26	14	8	4	85	77	32	.615
PITTSBURGH	26	15	10	1	122	95	31	.596
HARTFORD	26	15	10	1	94	83	31	.596
MONTREAL	26	14	9	3	94	80	31	.596
WASHINGTON	26	13	9	4	82	71	30	.577
TAMPA BAY	26	13	9	4	83	78	30	.577
FLORIDA	26	12	9	5	90	81	29	.558
BOSTON	26	11	11	4	94	92	26	.500
NEW JERSEY	26	9	13	4	60	69	22	.423
BUFFALO	26	9	15	2	69	80	20	.385
OTTAWA	26	8	16	2	65	83	18	.346
NY ISLANDERS	26	8	16	2	72	109	18	.346

CONFERENCE
TOTAL   338   156   140   42   1,107   1,060   354   .524

Western Conference

	GP	W	L	T	GF	GA	PTS	PCTG
DETROIT	26	19	7	0	89	56	38	.731
COLORADO	26	13	8	5	97	76	31	.596
CHICAGO	26	15	9	2	99	71	32	.615
ANAHEIM	26	13	9	4	81	73	30	.577
CALGARY	26	12	11	3	75	69	27	.519
ST LOUIS	26	9	11	6	72	89	24	.462
WINNIPEG	26	11	14	1	86	95	23	.442
EDMONTON	26	11	14	1	71	93	23	.442
VANCOUVER	26	9	13	4	89	88	22	.423
LOS ANGELES	26	9	14	3	76	94	21	.404
TORONTO	26	7	15	4	68	86	18	.346
SAN JOSE	26	7	15	4	87	120	18	.346
DALLAS	26	5	16	5	70	97	15	.288

CONFERENCE
TOTAL   338   140   156   42   1,060   1,107   322   .476

VS. OTHER
CONFERENCE   676   296   296   84   2,167   2,167   676   .500

TEAMS' POWER PLAY RECORD

(ADV) TOTAL ADVANTAGES (PPGF) POWER-PLAY GOALS FOR
(PCTG) ARRIVED BY DIVIDING NUMBER OF POWER-PLAY GOALS BY TOTAL ADVANTAGES

	HOME					ROAD					OVER ALL				
	TEAM	GP	ADV	PPGF	PCTG	TEAM	GP	ADV	PPGF	PCTG	TEAM	GP	ADV	PPGF	PCTG
1	PIT	41	206	57	27.7	PIT	41	214	52	24.3	PIT	82	420	109	26.0
2	PHI	41	212	51	24.1	COL	41	192	42	21.9	COL	82	404	86	21.3
3	DET	41	212	51	24.1	NYI	41	192	37	19.3	DET	82	455	97	21.3
4	NYR	41	208	50	24.0	CHI	41	181	35	19.3	T.B	82	400	83	20.8
5	T.B	41	213	50	23.5	DET	41	243	46	18.9	NYR	82	429	85	19.8
6	L.A	41	227	50	22.0	VAN	41	207	39	18.8	PHI	82	417	82	19.7
7	MTL	41	195	42	21.5	WPG	41	207	38	18.4	WPG	82	417	82	19.7
8	TOR	41	220	47	21.4	CGY	41	188	34	18.1	MTL	82	405	77	19.0
9	WPG	41	210	44	21.0	T.B	41	187	33	17.6	TOR	82	438	83	18.9
10	COL	41	212	44	20.8	S.J	41	186	32	17.2	NYI	82	372	70	18.8
11	BOS	41	196	40	20.4	EDM	41	223	38	17.0	BOS	82	363	68	18.7
12	HFD	41	207	42	20.3	FLA	41	214	36	16.8	CGY	82	386	71	18.4
13	CGY	41	198	37	18.7	BOS	41	167	28	16.8	HFD	82	372	67	18.0
14	NYI	41	180	33	18.3	STL	41	227	38	16.7	L.A	82	401	72	18.0
15	FLA	41	254	45	17.7	MTL	41	210	35	16.7	CHI	82	356	63	17.7
16	DAL	41	226	38	16.8	TOR	41	218	36	16.5	FLA	82	468	81	17.3
17	STL	41	221	36	16.3	NYR	41	221	35	15.8	VAN	82	411	69	16.8
18	BUF	41	253	41	16.2	BUF	41	224	35	15.6	STL	82	448	74	16.5
19	CHI	41	175	28	16.0	WSH	41	207	32	15.5	S.J	82	385	62	16.1
20	WSH	41	196	31	15.8	HFD	41	165	25	15.2	BUF	82	477	76	15.9
21	N.J	41	192	30	15.6	PHI	41	205	31	15.1	EDM	82	452	72	15.9
22	S.J	41	199	30	15.1	N.J	41	176	25	14.2	WSH	82	403	63	15.6
23	ANA	41	221	33	14.9	DAL	41	217	29	13.4	DAL	82	443	67	15.1
24	EDM	41	229	34	14.8	ANA	41	205	27	13.2	N.J	82	368	55	14.9
25	VAN	41	204	30	14.7	L.A	41	174	22	12.6	ANA	82	426	60	14.1
26	OTT	41	216	29	13.4	OTT	41	214	24	11.2	OTT	82	430	53	12.3
		1,066	5,482	1,043	19.0		1,066	5,264	884	16.8		1,066	10,746	1,927	17.9

TEAMS' PENALTY KILLING RECORD

(TSH) TOTAL TIMES SHORT-HANDED (PPGA) POWER-PLAY GOALS AGAINST
(PCTG) ARRIVED BY DIVIDING -TIMES SHORT MINUS POWER-PLAY GOALS AGAINST- BY TIMES SHORT

	HOME TEAM	GP	TSH	PPGA	PCTG	ROAD TEAM	GP	TSH	PPGA	PCTG	OVER ALL TEAM	GP	TSH	PPGA	PCTG
1	DET	41	169	14	91.7	DET	41	206	30	85.4	DET	82	375	44	88.3
2	N.J	41	152	17	88.8	T.B	41	222	33	85.1	PHI	82	437	62	85.8
3	CHI	41	222	26	88.3	PHI	41	227	34	85.0	CHI	82	447	65	85.5
4	PHI	41	210	28	86.7	MTL	41	192	30	84.4	N.J	82	319	49	84.6
5	COL	41	216	29	86.6	BUF	41	222	37	83.3	T.B	82	439	68	84.5
6	FLA	41	185	27	85.4	WSH	41	197	33	83.2	BUF	82	461	74	83.9
7	PIT	41	240	36	85.0	CHI	41	225	39	82.7	COL	82	439	71	83.8
8	TOR	41	185	28	84.9	NYR	41	256	45	82.4	PIT	82	467	78	83.3
9	STL	41	245	38	84.5	L.A	41	187	34	81.8	FLA	82	370	63	83.0
10	BUF	41	239	37	84.5	VAN	41	223	41	81.6	STL	82	482	82	83.0
11	ANA	41	201	32	84.1	PIT	41	227	42	81.5	TOR	82	403	70	82.6
12	T.B	41	217	35	83.9	STL	41	237	44	81.4	WSH	82	385	67	82.6
13	EDM	41	204	34	83.3	COL	41	223	42	81.2	MTL	82	382	68	82.2
14	WSH	41	188	34	81.9	DAL	41	201	38	81.1	NYR	82	495	89	82.0
15	CGY	41	188	34	81.9	BOS	41	162	31	80.9	VAN	82	418	78	81.3
16	HFD	41	213	39	81.7	N.J	41	167	32	80.8	L.A	82	381	72	81.1
17	NYR	41	239	44	81.6	TOR	41	218	42	80.7	ANA	82	423	81	80.9
18	VAN	41	195	37	81.0	FLA	41	185	36	80.5	EDM	82	417	80	80.8
19	OTT	41	199	38	80.9	HFD	41	216	44	79.6	HFD	82	429	83	80.7
20	WPG	41	199	38	80.9	CGY	41	214	46	78.5	BOS	82	341	67	80.4
21	L.A	41	194	38	80.4	EDM	41	213	46	78.4	DAL	82	418	82	80.4
22	MTL	41	190	38	80.0	WPG	41	231	50	78.4	CGY	82	402	80	80.1
23	BOS	41	179	36	79.9	ANA	41	222	49	77.9	WPG	82	430	88	79.5
24	DAL	41	217	44	79.7	NYI	41	227	52	77.1	NYI	82	414	90	78.3
25	NYI	41	187	38	79.7	S.J	41	206	48	76.7	OTT	82	375	83	77.9
26	S.J	41	191	45	76.4	OTT	41	176	45	74.4	S.J	82	397	93	76.6
		1,066	5,264	884	83.2		1,066	5,482	1,043	81.0		1,066	10,746	1,927	82.1

SHORT HAND GOALS FOR

	HOME TEAM	GP	SHGF	ROAD TEAM	GP	SHGF	OVER ALL TEAM	GP	SHGF
1	PIT	41	13	BOS	41	10	COL	82	21
2	COL	41	12	COL	41	9	PIT	82	18
3	DET	41	11	MTL	41	9	VAN	82	18
4	S.J	41	10	FLA	41	8	DET	82	17
5	VAN	41	10	VAN	41	8	MTL	82	15
6	CHI	41	10	NYI	41	7	S.J	82	15
7	L.A	41	9	STL	41	7	BOS	82	13
8	N.J	41	7	CGY	41	7	CHI	82	13
9	WSH	41	7	EDM	41	7	PHI	82	12
10	PHI	41	7	DET	41	6	WSH	82	12
11	ANA	41	7	TOR	41	6	L.A	82	12
12	MTL	41	6	BUF	41	5	TOR	82	11
13	WPG	41	5	PHI	41	5	N.J	82	11
14	TOR	41	5	PIT	41	5	FLA	82	11
15	BUF	41	5	WPG	41	5	STL	82	11
16	STL	41	4	WSH	41	5	CGY	82	11
17	DAL	41	4	HFD	41	5	BUF	82	10
18	NYR	41	4	S.J	41	5	WPG	82	10
19	CGY	41	4	DAL	41	4	EDM	82	10
20	BOS	41	3	N.J	41	4	ANA	82	10
21	HFD	41	3	CHI	41	3	NYI	82	8
22	OTT	41	3	ANA	41	3	HFD	82	8
23	T.B	41	3	OTT	41	3	DAL	82	8
24	FLA	41	3	T.B	41	3	NYR	82	6
25	EDM	41	3	L.A	41	3	OTT	82	6
26	NYI	41	1	NYR	41	2	T.B	82	6
		1,066	159		1,066	144		1,066	303

SHORT HAND GOALS AGAINST

	HOME TEAM	GP	SHGA	ROAD TEAM	GP	SHGA	OVER ALL TEAM	GP	SHGA
1	PHI	41	1	TOR	41	3	ANA	82	5
2	ANA	41	1	STL	41	3	BOS	82	7
3	BOS	41	2	HFD	41	3	PHI	82	7
4	DET	41	2	NYR	41	4	WSH	82	7

5	MTL	41	3	CHI	41	4	CHI	82	7
6	WSH	41	3	ANA	41	4	STL	82	8
7	FLA	41	3	PIT	41	4	DET	82	9
8	CHI	41	3	WSH	41	4	HFD	82	9
9	N.J	41	4	CGY	41	5	TOR	82	9
10	WPG	41	4	BOS	41	5	N.J	82	9
11	CGY	41	4	N.J	41	5	CGY	82	9
12	EDM	41	5	PHI	41	6	NYR	82	11
13	STL	41	5	VAN	41	6	MTL	82	11
14	BUF	41	5	DET	41	7	PIT	82	12
15	HFD	41	6	BUF	41	7	BUF	82	12
16	T.B	41	6	EDM	41	7	FLA	82	12
17	TOR	41	6	OTT	41	7	WPG	82	12
18	OTT	41	7	T.B	41	7	EDM	82	12
19	VAN	41	7	L.A	41	7	T.B	82	13
20	NYR	41	7	NYI	41	8	VAN	82	13
21	NYI	41	7	DAL	41	8	OTT	82	14
22	PIT	41	8	WPG	41	8	NYI	82	15
23	COL	41	11	MTL	41	8	L.A	82	18
24	S.J	41	11	FLA	41	9	DAL	82	20
25	L.A	41	11	S.J	41	9	S.J	82	20
26	DAL	41	12	COL	41	11	COL	82	22
		1,066	144		1,066	159		1,066	303

TEAM STREAKS

MOST CONSECUTIVE WINS

GM	TEAM	FROM	TO
9	DETROIT	DEC. 12	DEC. 31
9	DETROIT	MAR. 3	MAR. 22
8	COLORADO	OCT. 18	NOV. 5
8	PHILADELPHIA	NOV. 16	DEC. 3
8	PITTSBURGH	NOV. 25	DEC. 9
7	DETROIT	NOV. 2	NOV. 22
7	FLORIDA	NOV. 2	NOV. 14
7	PHILADELPHIA	MAR. 23	APR. 4

MOST CONSECUTIVE UNDEFEATED

GM	TEAM	W	T	FROM	TO
13	DETROIT	12	1	MAR. 3	MAR. 31
10	COLORADO	9	1	OCT. 18	NOV. 11
10	NY RANGERS	7	3	NOV. 27	DEC. 13
10	DETROIT	9	1	DEC. 12	JAN. 3
10	DETROIT	9	1	JAN. 10	FEB. 6
10	NEW JERSEY	7	3	FEB. 23	MAR. 15

MOST CONSECUTIVE HOME WINS

GM	TEAM	FROM	TO
12	DETROIT	NOV. 4	DEC. 31
12	DETROIT	JAN. 12	FEB. 29
9	DETROIT	MAR. 12	APR. 12 #
8	PITTSBURGH	JAN. 22	MAR. 7
8	MONTREAL	FEB. 12	MAR. 20
7	PHILADELPHIA	NOV. 16	DEC. 7

MOST CONSECUTIVE HOME UNDEFEATED

GM	TEAM	W	T	FROM	TO
24	NY RANGERS	18	6	OCT. 24	FEB. 15
14	DETROIT	13	1	NOV. 4	JAN. 6
12	DETROIT	12	0	JAN. 12	FEB. 29
10	COLORADO	8	2	OCT. 6	NOV. 22
9	COLORADO	4	5	JAN. 4	FEB. 7
9	ANAHEIM	8	1	MAR. 8	APR. 14
9	DETROIT	9	0	MAR. 12	APR. 12

MOST CONSECUTIVE ROAD WINS

GM	TEAM	FROM	TO
7	DETROIT	FEB. 18	MAR. 20
5	COLORADO	OCT. 25	NOV. 11
5	DETROIT	DEC. 12	DEC. 29
5	CHICAGO	JAN. 31	FEB. 8
5	HARTFORD	JAN. 31	FEB. 11
5	BOSTON	MAR. 10	MAR. 31

MOST CONSECUTIVE ROAD UNDEFEATED

GM	TEAM	W	T	FROM	TO
8	CHICAGO	6	2	JAN. 9	FEB. 8
8	DETROIT	7	1	FEB. 18	MAR. 24
8	BOSTON	7	1	MAR. 10	APR. 7
7	ST LOUIS	5	2	JAN. 31	MAR. 3
6	PITTSBURGH	4	2	OCT. 20	NOV. 10
6	CHICAGO	2	4	NOV. 24	DEC. 6
6	NEW JERSEY	4	2	FEB. 24	MAR. 10

TEAMS' OVERTIME RECORDS

	HOME						ROAD						OVERALL					
	GP	W	L	T	PTS	PCTG	GP	W	L	T	PTS	PCTG	GP	W	L	T	PTS	PCTG
N.J	4	2	0	2	6	.750	15	5	0	10	20	.667	19	7	0	12	26	.684
ANA	9	3	2	4	10	.556	7	3	0	4	10	.714	16	6	2	8	20	.625
WPG	5	2	0	3	7	.700	3	0	0	3	3	.500	8	2	0	6	10	.625
WSH	9	3	1	5	11	.611	7	1	0	6	8	.571	16	4	1	11	19	.594
DET	2	0	0	2	2	.500	9	3	1	5	11	.611	11	3	1	7	13	.591
EDM	8	2	1	5	9	.563	6	2	1	3	7	.583	14	4	2	8	16	.571
TOR	10	1	2	7	9	.450	8	3	0	5	11	.688	18	4	2	12	20	.556
PIT	4	2	2	0	4	.500	5	1	0	4	6	.600	9	3	2	4	10	.556
DAL	9	0	0	9	9	.500	6	1	0	5	7	.583	15	1	0	14	16	.533
NYR	10	1	0	9	11	.550	7	1	1	5	7	.500	17	2	1	14	18	.529
PHI	8	2	1	5	9	.563	12	2	2	8	12	.500	20	4	3	13	21	.525
L.A	11	1	1	9	11	.500	12	2	1	9	13	.542	23	3	2	18	24	.522
T.B	9	1	3	5	7	.389	9	2	0	7	11	.611	18	3	3	12	18	.500
STL	10	0	1	9	9	.450	8	1	0	7	9	.563	18	1	1	16	18	.500
S.J	4	0	1	3	3	.375	5	1	0	4	6	.600	9	1	1	7	9	.500
CGY	9	2	2	5	9	.500	7	0	1	6	6	.429	16	2	3	11	15	.469
COL	9	0	2	7	7	.389	6	2	1	3	7	.583	15	2	3	10	14	.467
MTL	9	1	2	6	8	.444	6	1	1	4	6	.500	15	2	3	10	14	.467
HFD	6	1	1	4	6	.500	8	1	2	5	7	.438	14	2	3	9	13	.464
VAN	9	0	2	7	7	.389	11	1	2	8	10	.455	20	1	4	15	17	.425
CHI	7	0	1	6	6	.429	12	1	3	8	10	.417	19	1	4	14	16	.421
NYI	9	1	2	6	8	.444	8	1	3	4	6	.375	17	2	5	10	14	.412
BOS	8	0	3	5	5	.313	11	2	3	6	10	.455	19	2	6	11	15	.395
FLA	7	0	3	4	4	.286	6	0	0	6	6	.500	13	0	3	10	10	.385
BUF	8	1	2	5	7	.438	7	1	4	2	4	.286	15	2	6	7	11	.367
OTT	8	0	3	5	5	.313	0	0	0	0	0	.000	8	0	3	5	5	.313
TOT	201	26	38	137	189	.470	201	38	26	137	213	.530	201	64	64	137	402	1.00

INDIVIDUAL SCORING LEADERS

PLAYER	TEAM	GP	G	A	PTS	+/-	PIM	PP	SH	GW	GT	S	PCTG
MARIO LEMIEUX	PITTSBURGH	70	69	92	161	10	54	31	8	8	0	338	20.4
JAROMIR JAGR	PITTSBURGH	82	62	87	149	31	96	20	1	12	1	403	15.4
JOE SAKIC	COLORADO	82	51	69	120	14	44	17	6	7	1	339	15.0
RON FRANCIS	PITTSBURGH	77	27	92	119	25	56	12	1	4	0	158	17.1
PETER FORSBERG	COLORADO	82	30	86	116	26	47	7	3	3	0	217	13.8
ERIC LINDROS	PHILADELPHIA	73	47	68	115	26	163	15	0	4	0	294	16.0
PAUL KARIYA	ANAHEIM	82	50	58	108	9	20	20	3	9	0	349	14.3
TEEMU SELANNE	WPG-ANA	79	40	68	108	5	22	9	1	5	0	267	15.0
A. MOGILNY	VANCOUVER	79	55	52	107	14	16	10	5	6	3	292	18.8
SERGEI FEDOROV	DETROIT	78	39	68	107	49	48	11	3	11	1	306	12.7
DOUG WEIGHT	EDMONTON	82	25	79	104	19-	95	9	0	2	1	204	12.3
WAYNE GRETZKY	L.A-STL	80	23	79	102	13-	34	6	1	3	1	195	11.8
MARK MESSIER	NY RANGERS	74	47	52	99	29	122	14	1	5	1	241	19.5
PETR NEDVED	PITTSBURGH	80	45	54	99	37	68	8	1	5	1	204	22.1
KEITH TKACHUK	WINNIPEG	76	50	48	98	11	156	20	2	6	0	249	20.1
JOHN LECLAIR	PHILADELPHIA	82	51	46	97	21	64	19	0	10	2	270	18.9
THEOREN FLEURY	CALGARY	80	46	50	96	17	112	17	5	4	0	353	13.0
PIERRE TURGEON	MONTREAL	80	38	58	96	19	44	17	1	6	2	297	12.8
STEVE YZERMAN	DETROIT	80	36	59	95	29	64	16	2	8	0	220	16.4
V. DAMPHOUSSE	MONTREAL	80	38	56	94	5	158	11	4	3	0	254	15.0
ADAM OATES	BOSTON	70	25	67	92	16	18	7	1	2	0	183	13.7
PAT LAFONTAINE	BUFFALO	76	40	51	91	8-	36	15	3	7	1	224	17.9
ZIGMUND PALFFY	NY ISLANDERS	81	43	44	87	17-	56	17	1	6	0	257	16.7
R. BRIND'AMOUR	PHILADELPHIA	82	26	61	87	20	110	4	4	5	4	213	12.2
V. KAMENSKY	COLORADO	81	38	47	85	14	85	18	1	5	0	220	17.3
BRIAN LEETCH	NY RANGERS	82	15	70	85	12	30	7	0	3	0	276	5.4

DEFENCEMEN SCORING LEADERS

PLAYER	TEAM	GP	G	A	PTS	+/-	PIM	PP	SH	GW	GT	S	PCTG
BRIAN LEETCH	NY RANGERS	82	15	70	85	12	30	7	0	3	0	276	5.4
RAY BOURQUE	BOSTON	82	20	62	82	31	58	9	2	2	1	390	5.1
PAUL COFFEY	DETROIT	76	14	60	74	19	90	3	1	3	0	234	6.0
CHRIS CHELIOS	CHICAGO	81	14	58	72	25	140	7	0	3	0	219	6.4
PHIL HOUSLEY	CGY-N.J	81	17	51	68	6-	30	6	0	1	0	205	8.3
GARY SUTER	CHICAGO	82	20	47	67	3	80	12	2	4	0	242	8.3
N LIDSTROM	DETROIT	81	17	50	67	29	20	8	1	1	1	211	8.1
SERGEI ZUBOV	PITTSBURGH	64	11	55	66	28	22	3	2	1	0	141	7.8
ROMAN HAMRLIK	TAMPA BAY	82	16	49	65	24-	103	12	0	2	3	281	5.7

AL MACINNIS	ST LOUIS	82	17	44	61	5	88	9	1	1	1	317	5.4
LARRY MURPHY	TORONTO	82	12	49	61	2-	34	8	0	1	2	182	6.6

INDIVIDUAL ROOKIE SCORING LEADERS

PLAYER	TEAM	GP	G	A	PTS	+/-	PIM	PP	SH	GW	GT	S	PCTG
D ALFREDSSON	OTTAWA	82	26	35	61	18-	28	8	2	3	1	212	12.3
ERIC DAZE	CHICAGO	80	30	23	53	16	18	2	0	2	0	167	18.0
V. YACHMENEV	LOS ANGELES	80	19	34	53	3-	16	6	1	2	0	133	14.3
SAKU KOIVU	MONTREAL	82	20	25	45	7-	40	8	3	2	1	136	14.7
VALERI BURE	MONTREAL	77	22	20	42	10	28	5	0	1	2	143	15.4
PETR SYKORA	NEW JERSEY	63	18	24	42	7	32	8	0	3	0	128	14.1
TODD BERTUZZI	NY ISLANDERS	76	18	21	39	14-	83	4	0	2	0	127	14.2
M. RAGNARSSON	SAN JOSE	71	8	31	39	24-	42	4	0	0	0	94	8.5
MIROSLAV SATAN	EDMONTON	62	18	17	35	0	22	6	0	4	0	113	15.9
CORY STILLMAN	CALGARY	74	16	19	35	5-	41	4	1	3	0	132	12.1
G. MARSHALL	DALLAS	70	9	19	28	0	111	0	0	0	1	62	14.5
JERE LEHTINEN	DALLAS	57	6	22	28	5	16	0	0	1	0	109	5.5
STEPHANE YELLE	COLORADO	71	13	14	27	15	30	0	2	1	0	93	14.0
RADEK DVORAK	FLORIDA	77	13	14	27	5	20	0	0	4	0	126	10.3
JEFF O'NEILL	HARTFORD	65	8	19	27	3-	40	1	0	1	0	65	12.3
N. ANDERSSON	NY ISLANDERS	47	14	12	26	3-	12	3	2	1	0	89	15.7
CRAIG JOHNSON	STL-L.A	60	13	11	24	8-	36	4	0	0	0	97	13.4
BRYAN MCCABE	NY ISLANDERS	82	7	16	23	24-	156	3	0	1	0	130	5.4
SHEAN DONOVAN	SAN JOSE	74	13	8	21	17-	39	0	1	2	0	73	17.8
ED JOVANOVSKI	FLORIDA	70	10	11	21	3-	137	2	0	2	0	116	8.6
N. SUNDSTROM	NY RANGERS	82	9	12	21	2	14	1	1	2	0	90	10.0
B. HOLZINGER	BUFFALO	58	10	10	20	21-	37	5	0	1	0	71	14.1
VIKTOR KOZLOV	SAN JOSE	62	6	13	19	15-	6	1	0	0	0	107	5.6
DERON QUINT	WINNIPEG	51	5	13	18	2-	22	2	0	0	0	97	5.2
ADRIAN AUCOIN	VANCOUVER	49	4	14	18	8	34	2	0	0	0	85	4.7
STEFAN USTORF	WASHINGTON	48	7	10	17	8	14	0	0	1	0	39	17.9

INDIVIDUAL LEADERS

GOAL SCORING   ASSISTS

NAME	TEAM	GP	G	NAME	TEAM	GP	A
MARIO LEMIEUX	PITTSBURGH	70	69	MARIO LEMIEUX	PITTSBURGH	70	92
JAROMIR JAGR	PITTSBURGH	82	62	RON FRANCIS	PITTSBURGH	77	92
A. MOGILNY	VANCOUVER	79	55	JAROMIR JAGR	PITTSBURGH	82	87

PETER BONDRA	WASHINGTON	67	52	PETER FORSBERG	COLORADO	82	86
JOHN LECLAIR	PHILADELPHIA	82	51	WAYNE GRETZKY	L.A-STL	80	79
JOE SAKIC	COLORADO	82	51	DOUG WEIGHT	EDMONTON	82	79
KEITH TKACHUK	WINNIPEG	76	50	BRIAN LEETCH	NY RANGERS	82	70
PAUL KARIYA	ANAHEIM	82	50	JOE SAKIC	COLORADO	82	69
ERIC LINDROS	PHILADELPHIA	73	47	ERIC LINDROS	PHILADELPHIA	73	68
MARK MESSIER	NY RANGERS	74	47	SERGEI FEDOROV	DETROIT	78	68
THEOREN FLEURY	CALGARY	80	46	TEEMU SELANNE	WPG-ANA	79	68
PETR NEDVED	PITTSBURGH	80	45	ADAM OATES	BOSTON	70	67
B. SHANAHAN	HARTFORD	74	44	MICHAL PIVONKA	WASHINGTON	73	65
BRETT HULL	ST LOUIS	70	43	RAY BOURQUE	BOSTON	82	62
ZIGMUND PALFFY	NY ISLANDERS	81	43	CRAIG JANNEY	S.J-WPG	84	62
PAT VERBEEK	NY RANGERS	69	41	ROD BRIND'AMOUR	PHILADELPHIA	82	61
PAT LAFONTAINE	BUFFALO	76	40	PAUL COFFEY	DETROIT	76	60
TEEMU SELANNE	WPG-ANA	79	40	STEVE YZERMAN	DETROIT	80	59

POWER PLAY GOALS

NAME	TEAM	GP	PP
MARIO LEMIEUX	PITTSBURGH	70	31
KEITH TKACHUK	WINNIPEG	76	20
JAROMIR JAGR	PITTSBURGH	82	20
PAUL KARIYA	ANAHEIM	82	20
SCOTT MELLANBY	FLORIDA	79	19
JOHN LECLAIR	PHILADELPHIA	82	19
VALERI KAMENSKY	COLORADO	81	18
TOMAS SANDSTROM	PITTSBURGH	58	17
PAT VERBEEK	NY RANGERS	69	17
B. SHANAHAN	HARTFORD	74	17
THEOREN FLEURY	CALGARY	80	17
PIERRE TURGEON	MONTREAL	80	17
ZIGMUND PALFFY	NY ISLANDERS	81	17
JOE SAKIC	COLORADO	82	17
ED OLCZYK	WINNIPEG	51	16
BRETT HULL	ST LOUIS	70	16
STEVE YZERMAN	DETROIT	80	16
OWEN NOLAN	COL-S.J	81	16

SHORT HAND GOALS

NAME	TEAM	GP	SH
MARIO LEMIEUX	PITTSBURGH	70	8
DAVE REID	BOSTON	63	6
MATS SUNDIN	TORONTO	76	6
JAMIE BAKER	SAN JOSE	77	6
TOM FITZGERALD	FLORIDA	82	6
JOE SAKIC	COLORADO	82	6
BRETT HULL	ST LOUIS	70	5
A. MOGILNY	VANCOUVER	79	5
THEOREN FLEURY	CALGARY	80	5
JEREMY ROENICK	CHICAGO	66	4
PETER BONDRA	WASHINGTON	67	4
DALLAS DRAKE	WINNIPEG	69	4
STEPHANE RICHER	NEW JERSEY	73	4
MIKE MODANO	DALLAS	78	4
SHJON PODEIN	PHILADELPHIA	79	4
V. DAMPHOUSSE	MONTREAL	80	4
RUSS COURTNALL	VANCOUVER	81	4
MARTIN GELINAS	VANCOUVER	81	4
TONY AMONTE	CHICAGO	81	4
ROD BRIND'AMOUR	PHILADELPHIA	82	4

POWER PLAY ASSISTS

NAME	TEAM	GP	PPA
MARIO LEMIEUX	PITTSBURGH	70	48
RON FRANCIS	PITTSBURGH	77	42
WAYNE GRETZKY	L.A-STL	80	41
TEEMU SELANNE	WPG-ANA	79	39
BRIAN LEETCH	NY RANGERS	82	37
DOUG WEIGHT	EDMONTON	82	37
MATHIEU SCHNEIDER	NYI-TOR	78	33
JOE SAKIC	COLORADO	82	33
BRIAN BRADLEY	TAMPA BAY	75	32
PETER FORSBERG	COLORADO	82	32
JAROMIR JAGR	PITTSBURGH	82	31
LARRY MURPHY	TORONTO	82	31
PAUL COFFEY	DETROIT	76	30
ROMAN HAMRLIK	TAMPA BAY	82	30
SERGEI ZUBOV	PITTSBURGH	64	29
PHIL HOUSLEY	CGY-N.J	81	29
NICKLAS LIDSTROM	DETROIT	81	29
RAY BOURQUE	BOSTON	82	29
GARY SUTER	CHICAGO	82	29

SHORT HAND ASSISTS

NAME	TEAM	GP	SHA
CHRIS CHELIOS	CHICAGO	81	6
STEVE YZERMAN	DETROIT	80	5
RUSS COURTNALL	VANCOUVER	81	5
BRET HEDICAN	VANCOUVER	77	4
NICKLAS LIDSTROM	DETROIT	81	4
KELLY BUCHBERGER	EDMONTON	82	4
PETER FORSBERG	COLORADO	82	4
GERMAN TITOV	CALGARY	82	4

POWER PLAY POINTS

NAME	TEAM	GP	PPP
MARIO LEMIEUX	PITTSBURGH	70	79
RON FRANCIS	PITTSBURGH	77	54
JAROMIR JAGR	PITTSBURGH	82	51
JOE SAKIC	COLORADO	82	50
TEEMU SELANNE	WPG-ANA	79	48
WAYNE GRETZKY	L.A-STL	80	47
DOUG WEIGHT	EDMONTON	82	46
BRIAN LEETCH	NY RANGERS	82	44
ROMAN HAMRLIK	TAMPA BAY	82	42
BRIAN BRADLEY	TAMPA BAY	75	41
KEITH TKACHUK	WINNIPEG	76	41
GARY SUTER	CHICAGO	82	41
PAUL KARIYA	ANAHEIM	82	41
MATHIEU SCHNEIDER	NYI-TOR	78	40
ERIC LINDROS	PHILADELPHIA	73	39
PAT LAFONTAINE	BUFFALO	76	39

SHORT HAND POINTS

NAME	TEAM	GP	SHP
MARIO LEMIEUX	PITTSBURGH	70	9
RUSS COURTNALL	VANCOUVER	81	9
JOE SAKIC	COLORADO	82	8
DAVE REID	BOSTON	63	7
JEREMY ROENICK	CHICAGO	66	7
JAMIE BAKER	SAN JOSE	77	7
A. MOGILNY	VANCOUVER	79	7
STEVE YZERMAN	DETROIT	80	7
PETER FORSBERG	COLORADO	82	7
BRETT HULL	ST LOUIS	70	6
BILL LINDSAY	FLORIDA	73	6
MATS SUNDIN	TORONTO	76	6
THEOREN FLEURY	CALGARY	80	6
CHRIS CHELIOS	CHICAGO	81	6
KELLY BUCHBERGER	EDMONTON	82	6
ROD BRIND'AMOUR	PHILADELPHIA	82	6

ZIGMUND PALFFY	NY ISLANDERS	81	39	TOM FITZGERALD	FLORIDA	82	6
LARRY MURPHY	TORONTO	82	39	PAUL KARIYA	ANAHEIM	82	6
PETER FORSBERG	COLORADO	82	39	GERMAN TITOV	CALGARY	82	6

GAME WINNING GOALS   GAME TYING GOALS

NAME	TEAM	GP	GW	NAME	TEAM	GP	GT
JAROMIR JAGR	PITTSBURGH	82	12	R BRIND'AMOUR	PHILADELPHIA	82	4
SERGEI FEDOROV	DETROIT	78	11	PETER BONDRA	WASHINGTON	67	3
CLAUDE LEMIEUX	COLORADO	79	10	A. MOGILNY	VANCOUVER	79	3
JOHN LECLAIR	PHILADELPHIA	82	10	ROMAN HAMRLIK	TAMPA BAY	82	3
PAUL KARIYA	ANAHEIM	82	9				
MARIO LEMIEUX	PITTSBURGH	70	8				
STEVE YZERMAN	DETROIT	80	8				
MURRAY CRAVEN	CHICAGO	66	7				
PETER BONDRA	WASHINGTON	67	7				
RAY SHEPPARD	DET-S.J-FLA	70	7				
KEITH PRIMEAU	DETROIT	74	7				
PAT LAFONTAINE	BUFFALO	76	7				
MATS SUNDIN	TORONTO	76	7				
YANIC PERREAULT	LOS ANGELES	78	7				
GEOFF SANDERSON	HARTFORD	81	7				
ALEXEI KOVALEV	NY RANGERS	81	7				
JOHAN GARPENLOV	FLORIDA	82	7				
JOE SAKIC	COLORADO	82	7				
V. KOZLOV	DETROIT	82	7				

SHOTS

NAME	TEAM	GP	S
JAROMIR JAGR	PITTSBURGH	82	403
RAY BOURQUE	BOSTON	82	390
THEOREN FLEURY	CALGARY	80	353
PAUL KARIYA	ANAHEIM	82	349
JOE SAKIC	COLORADO	82	339
MARIO LEMIEUX	PITTSBURGH	70	338
BRETT HULL	ST LOUIS	70	327
PETER BONDRA	WASHINGTON	67	322
MIKE MODANO	DALLAS	78	320
AL MACINNIS	ST LOUIS	82	317
CLAUDE LEMIEUX	COLORADO	79	315

GEOFF SANDERSON	HARTFORD	81	314
SERGEI FEDOROV	DETROIT	78	306
MATS SUNDIN	TORONTO	76	301
PIERRE TURGEON	MONTREAL	80	297
ERIC LINDROS	PHILADELPHIA	73	294
ALEXANDER MOGILNY	VANCOUVER	79	292
ROMAN HAMRLIK	TAMPA BAY	82	281
BRENDAN SHANAHAN	HARTFORD	74	280
BRIAN LEETCH	NY RANGERS	82	276

SHOOTING PERCENTAGE (MIN 82 SHOTS)

NAME	TEAM	GP	G	S	PCTG
GARY ROBERTS	CALGARY	35	22	84	26.2
PETR NEDVED	PITTSBURGH	80	45	204	22.1
CRAIG JANNEY	S.J-WPG	84	20	91	22.0
ANDREI KOVALENKO	COL-MTL	77	28	131	21.4
MURRAY CRAVEN	CHICAGO	66	18	86	20.9
GREG JOHNSON	DETROIT	60	18	87	20.7
DINO CICCARELLI	DETROIT	64	22	107	20.6
MARIO LEMIEUX	PITTSBURGH	70	69	338	20.4
KEITH TKACHUK	WINNIPEG	76	50	249	20.1
BOB PROBERT	CHICAGO	78	19	97	19.6
MARK MESSIER	NY RANGERS	74	47	241	19.5
IGOR LARIONOV	S.J-DET	73	22	113	19.5
ROMAN OKSIUTA	VAN-ANA	70	23	119	19.3
JASON DAWE	BUFFALO	67	25	130	19.2
BERNIE NICHOLLS	CHICAGO	59	19	100	19.0

PENALTY MINUTES

NAME	TEAM	GP	PIM
MATTHEW BARNABY	BUFFALO	73	335
ENRICO CICCONE	T.B-CHI	66	306
TIE DOMI	TORONTO	72	297
BRAD MAY	BUFFALO	79	295
ROB RAY	BUFFALO	71	287
TODD EWEN	ANAHEIM	53	285
DENNIS VIAL	OTTAWA	64	276
DAVE KARPA	ANAHEIM	72	270
SCOTT DANIELS	HARTFORD	53	254

CHRIS SIMON	COLORADO	64	250
BOB PROBERT	CHICAGO	78	237
PAUL LAUS	FLORIDA	78	236
SHANE CHURLA	DAL-L.A-NYR	55	231
KELLY CHASE	HARTFORD	55	230
LYLE ODELEIN	MONTREAL	79	230
DONALD BRASHEAR	MONTREAL	67	223
JEFF BEUKEBOOM	NY RANGERS	82	220
DAVE MANSON	WINNIPEG	82	205
SHAWN ANTOSKI	PHILADELPHIA	64	204

PLUS/MINUS

NAME	TEAM	GP	+/-
VLAD. KONSTANTINOV	DETROIT	81	60
SERGEI FEDOROV	DETROIT	78	49
VIACHESLAV FETISOV	DETROIT	69	37
PETR NEDVED	PITTSBURGH	80	37
VYACHESLAV KOZLOV	DETROIT	82	33
CURTIS LESCHYSHYN	COLORADO	77	32
IGOR LARIONOV	S.J-DET	73	31
RAY BOURQUE	BOSTON	82	31
JAROMIR JAGR	PITTSBURGH	82	31
KEITH CARNEY	CHICAGO	82	31
BOB ERREY	DETROIT	71	30
ALEXEI GUSAROV	COLORADO	65	29
PAT VERBEEK	NY RANGERS	69	29
MARK MESSIER	NY RANGERS	74	29
STEVE YZERMAN	DETROIT	80	29
NICKLAS LIDSTROM	DETROIT	81	29
SERGEI ZUBOV	PITTSBURGH	64	28
PETR SVOBODA	PHILADELPHIA	73	28
ADAM FOOTE	COLORADO	73	27

CONSECUTIVE SCORING STREAKS

GOALS SCORED IN MOST CONSECUTIVE GAMES

GM	PLAYER	TEAM	FROM	TO	G
7	ZIGMUND PALFFY	NY ISLANDERS	Feb 29	Mar 16	11
7	ALEXANDER MOGILNY	VANCOUVER	Jan 27	Feb 09	7

6	THEOREN FLEURY	CALGARY	Jan 14	Jan 30	9
6	JOHN LECLAIR	PHILADELPHIA	Mar 23	Apr 02	9
6	PETR NEDVED	PITTSBURGH	Jan 03	Jan 13	7
6	MATS SUNDIN	TORONTO	Jan 05	Jan 17	6

ASSISTS AWARDED IN MOST CONSECUTIVE GAMES

GM	PLAYER	TEAM	FROM	TO	A
10	RON FRANCIS	PITTSBURGH	Mar 05	Mar 26	19
10	MARIO LEMIEUX	PITTSBURGH	Dec 01	Dec 22	17
10	BENOIT HOGUE	TOR-DAL	Feb 11	Mar 05	12
10	VINCENT DAMPHOUSSE	MONTREAL	Feb 07	Feb 28	12
9	TEEMU SELANNE	WINNIPEG	Dec 29	Jan 16	12
9	CHRIS CHELIOS	CHICAGO	Nov 11	Nov 28	11
9	BRIAN LEETCH	NY RANGERS	Jan 03	Jan 31	9
8	ERIC LINDROS	PHILADELPHIA	Mar 17	Mar 31	18
8	WAYNE GRETZKY	LOS ANGELES	Nov 02	Nov 16	14
8	WAYNE GRETZKY	LOS ANGELES	Jan 03	Jan 16	14
8	NORM MACIVER	PITTSBURGH	Nov 01	Nov 17	13
8	MARK RECCHI	MONTREAL	Oct 21	Nov 04	13
8	BRIAN LEETCH	NY RANGERS	Nov 29	Dec 11	9

POINTS GAINED IN MOST CONSECUTIVE GAMES

GM	PLAYER	TEAM	FROM	TO	G	A	PTS
16	MARIO LEMIEUX	PITTSBURGH	Nov 18	Dec 22	13	23	36
16	STEVE YZERMAN	DETROIT	Feb 10	Mar 12	10	16	26
15	TEEMU SELANNE	WINNIPEG	Dec 28	Feb 01	5	18	23
15	CHRIS CHELIOS	CHICAGO	Oct 26	Nov 28	4	16	20
12	JAROMIR JAGR	PITTSBURGH	Nov 17	Dec 09	10	16	26
12	RON FRANCIS	PITTSBURGH	Mar 05	Mar 30	2	20	22
12	ERIC LINDROS	PHILADELPHIA	Oct 07	Nov 02	11	11	22
11	JAROMIR JAGR	PITTSBURGH	Feb 16	Mar 09	10	17	27
11	JAROMIR JAGR	PITTSBURGH	Oct 14	Nov 11	12	13	25
11	JOHN LECLAIR	PHILADELPHIA	Mar 16	Apr 04	15	8	23
11	ALEXANDER MOGILNY	VANCOUVER	Nov 03	Nov 23	9	8	17
11	STEVE THOMAS	NEW JERSEY	Jan 03	Jan 30	8	9	17
11	BENOIT HOGUE	TOR-DAL	Feb 10	Mar 05	3	12	15
11	MIROSLAV SATAN	EDMONTON	Feb 28	Mar 23	6	9	15
10	PAT VERBEEK	NY RANGERS	Dec 30	Jan 27	10	8	18
10	VINCENT DAMPHOUSSE	MONTREAL	Feb 07	Feb 28	5	12	17

10	SERGEI FEDOROV	DETROIT	Nov 02	Nov 28	6	10	16
10	BRETT HULL	ST LOUIS	Jan 31	Feb 18	6	9	15
10	ALEXANDER MOGILNY	VANCOUVER	Jan 22	Feb 09	9	6	15
10	LUC ROBITAILLE	NY RANGERS	Oct 16	Nov 03	5	9	14
10	SERGEI FEDOROV	DETROIT	Feb 10	Feb 29	5	8	13

GOALTENDING LEADERS (MIN. 25 GPI)

GOALS AGAINST AVERAGE

GOALTENDER	TEAM	GPI	MINS	GA	AVG
RON HEXTALL	PHILADELPHIA	53	3102	112	2.17
CHRIS OSGOOD	DETROIT	50	2933	106	2.17
JIM CAREY	WASHINGTON	71	4069	153	2.26
MIKE VERNON	DETROIT	32	1855	70	2.26
MARTIN BRODEUR	NEW JERSEY	77	4434	173	2.34
JEFF HACKETT	CHICAGO	35	2000	80	2.40
DAREN PUPPA	TAMPA BAY	57	3189	131	2.46
J. VANBIESBROUCK	FLORIDA	57	3178	142	2.68
MIKE RICHTER	NY RANGERS	41	2396	107	2.68
ED BELFOUR	CHICAGO	50	2956	135	2.74
DAMIAN RHODES	TOR-OTT	47	2747	127	2.77
PATRICK ROY	MTL-COL	61	3565	165	2.78
TREVOR KIDD	CALGARY	47	2570	119	2.78
DOMINIK HASEK	BUFFALO	59	3417	161	2.83
GUY HEBERT	ANAHEIM	59	3326	157	2.83
JOCELYN THIBAULT	COL-MTL	50	2893	138	2.86
GRANT FUHR	ST LOUIS	79	4365	209	2.87
FELIX POTVIN	TORONTO	69	4009	192	2.87
GARTH SNOW	PHILADELPHIA	26	1437	69	2.88
GLENN HEALY	NY RANGERS	44	2564	124	2.90

WINS

GOALTENDER	TEAM	GPI	MINS	W	L	T
CHRIS OSGOOD	DETROIT	50	2933	39	6	5
JIM CAREY	WASHINGTON	71	4069	35	24	9
PATRICK ROY	MTL-COL	61	3565	34	24	2
BILL RANFORD	EDM-BOS	77	4322	34	30	9
MARTIN BRODEUR	NEW JERSEY	77	4434	34	30	12
RON HEXTALL	PHILADELPHIA	53	3102	31	13	7

FELIX POTVIN	TORONTO	69	4009	30	26	11
GRANT FUHR	ST LOUIS	79	4365	30	28	16
TOM BARRASSO	PITTSBURGH	49	2799	29	16	2
DAREN PUPPA	TAMPA BAY	57	3189	29	16	9
GUY HEBERT	ANAHEIM	59	3326	28	23	5
SEAN BURKE	HARTFORD	66	3669	28	28	6
JOCELYN THIBAULT	COL-MTL	50	2893	26	17	5
N. KHABIBULIN	WINNIPEG	53	2914	26	20	3
J. VANBIESBROUCK	FLORIDA	57	3178	26	20	7

SAVE PERCENTAGE

GOALTENDER	TEAM	GPI	MINS	GA	SAS	PCTG	W	L	T
DOMINIK HASEK	BUFFALO	59	3417	161	2011	.920	22	30	6
DAREN PUPPA	TAMPA BAY	57	3189	131	1605	.918	29	16	9
JEFF HACKETT	CHICAGO	35	2000	80	948	.915	18	11	4
GUY HEBERT	ANAHEIM	59	3326	157	1820	.914	28	23	5
RON HEXTALL	PHILADELPHIA	53	3102	112	1292	.913	31	13	7
MIKE RICHTER	NY RANGERS	41	2396	107	1221	.912	24	13	3
MARTIN BRODEUR	NEW JERSEY	77	4434	173	1954	.911	34	30	12
CHRIS OSGOOD	DETROIT	50	2933	106	1190	.911	39	6	5
FELIX POTVIN	TORONTO	69	4009	192	2135	.910	30	26	11
PATRICK ROY	MTL-COL	61	3565	165	1797	.908	34	24	2
N. KHABIBULIN	WINNIPEG	53	2914	152	1656	.908	26	20	3
JOCELYN THIBAULT	COL-MTL	50	2893	138	1480	.907	26	17	5
KELLY HRUDEY	LOS ANGELES	36	2077	113	1214	.907	7	15	10
JIM CAREY	WASHINGTON	71	4069	153	1631	.906	35	24	9
SEAN BURKE	HARTFORD	66	3669	190	2034	.906	28	28	6
DAMIAN RHODES	TOR-OTT	47	2747	127	1342	.905	14	27	5
KEN WREGGET	PITTSBURGH	37	2132	115	1205	.904	20	13	2
GRANT FUHR	ST LOUIS	79	4365	209	2157	.903	30	28	16
J. VANBIESBROUCK	FLORIDA	57	3178	142	1473	.903	26	20	7
MIKE VERNON	DETROIT	32	1855	70	723	.903	21	7	2

SHUTOUTS

GOALTENDER	TEAM	GPI	MINS	SO	W	L	T
JIM CAREY	WASHINGTON	71	4069	9	35	24	9
MARTIN BRODEUR	NEW JERSEY	77	4434	6	34	30	12
CHRIS OSGOOD	DETROIT	50	2933	5	39	6	5
DAREN PUPPA	TAMPA BAY	57	3189	5	29	16	9

JEFF HACKETT	CHICAGO	35	2000	4	18	11	4
RON HEXTALL	PHILADELPHIA	53	3102	4	31	13	7
GUY HEBERT	ANAHEIM	59	3326	4	28	23	5
SEAN BURKE	HARTFORD	66	3669	4	28	28	6